The Great African Island: Chapters On Madagascar: A Popular Account Of Recent Researches In The Physical Geography, Geology, And Exploration Of The Country, And Its Natural History And Botany ...

James Sibree

ROFIA PALM (*Sagus ruffia*) AND TRAVELLER'S TREE (*Urania speciosa*).

THE GREAT AFRICAN ISLAND.

CHAPTERS ON MADAGASCAR.

A POPULAR ACCOUNT OF RECENT RESEARCHES IN THE
PHYSICAL GEOGRAPHY, GEOLOGY, AND EXPLORATION OF THE COUNTRY,
AND ITS NATURAL HISTORY AND BOTANY;
AND IN THE ORIGIN AND DIVISIONS, CUSTOMS AND LANGUAGE,
SUPERSTITIONS, FOLK-LORE, AND RELIGIOUS BELIEFS
AND PRACTICES OF THE DIFFERENT TRIBES.

TOGETHER WITH

ILLUSTRATIONS OF SCRIPTURE AND EARLY CHURCH HISTORY
FROM NATIVE STATISTS AND MISSIONARY EXPERIENCE.

BY THE

Rev. JAMES SIBREE, Jun., F.R.G.S.
OF THE LONDON MISSIONARY SOCIETY;
AUTHOR OF "MADAGASCAR AND ITS PEOPLE," ETC.

WITH PHYSICAL AND ETHNOGRAPHICAL SKETCH-MAPS
AND FOUR ILLUSTRATIONS.

LONDON:
TRÜBNER & CO., LUDGATE HILL.
1880.

PREFACE.

————◆————

ALTHOUGH many books have been written about Madagascar
during the last twenty years, the majority of these have had
reference chiefly to the religious history of the country, and
to the political and social changes which have followed upon
the acceptance of Christianity by the Government and people
of the central provinces.   And while much has been written
about the Hovas, in the interior of Madagascar, little is still
known about the numerous tribes inhabiting other portions
of the island.   In writing the following pages my object
has been to supply information of a more general character
than is given in most previous works; and especially to
arrange in a systematic form numerous interesting facts
which have only recently come to light.   During the last
nine or ten years many journeys have been made in previously
little known, or entirely unknown, parts of Madagascar, so
that our knowledge of the various tribes inhabiting the island
is greatly increased; and every year continual accessions are
being made to our information as to the physical geography
and geology of the country, its luxuriant flora, its remarkable
and exceptional fauna, and as to the origin and divisions,
language and customs, superstitions and folk-lore, and religious beliefs and practices of the Malagasy.

For several years past I have been noting down facts of

interest on these various subjects; and it will be seen that I have also made extensive use of the volumes of a yearly periodical, printed and published in Madagascar, called *The Antanànarìvo Annual.* This was commenced four years ago at my suggestion, and was designed to be a repository of information on all the points just mentioned with regard to the country and people; and as I edited the first three numbers, and their circulation has been almost entirely confined to Madagascar itself, and to those in England who are immediately connected with the island, I have not hesitated to quote largely from it, as well as from other pamphlets and notes of journeys, also published at Antanànarìvo, and consequently almost unknown here in England.

It was intended, in the original prospectus of this book, to have added another chapter, giving specimens of the folk-tales and legendary lore of the Malagasy, and of native songs and proverbs, fairy and nursery tales, and traditional history; but this part of the work has had to be relinquished partly owing to the exigencies of space,—for more than one chapter would be required to treat of all these points satisfactorily,—and partly also from the pressure of other work arising from my immediate departure from England; indeed the last sheets of the book have been corrected within a few hours of sailing.

I have to acknowledge, with many thanks, the courtesy of Messrs. Macmillan & Co. and of Mr. Alfred Russel Wallace, in allowing a woodcut from Mr. Wallace's valuable work on *The Geographical Distribution of Animals* to be used as an illustration for this book. It will be seen that I have derived much help from that work in treating of the animal life of Madagascar.

I have also to express my thanks to H. W. Bates, Esq., Assistant Secretary of the Royal Geographical Society, and to the Council of that Society, for their readily-accorded permission to use the physical sketch-map of Madagascar from their *Proceedings.* I must also add that this map has been slightly altered from the original sketch I supplied, and in one or two points is not perfectly correct, particularly in the cross-section.

Three or four of the chapters of the book have already appeared as separate papers in the Proceedings and Transactions of various societies, the Royal Geographical Society, The Anthropological Institute, The Folk-lore Society, as well as in *Nature.*

Remembering with gratitude the kindly reception given to my former work, *Madagascar and its People* (R. T. S., 1870), I trust that much of the information given in this second book will not be without interest to many in this and in other countries.

J. S. J.

Forest Hill, *November* 1879.

LIST OF ILLUSTRATIONS.

———◆———

CONTENTS.

CHAPTER I.

NAMES, DISCOVERY, EARLY ACCOUNTS, AND MAPS OF MADAGASCAR.

CHAPTER II.

THE PHYSICAL GEOGRAPHY AND GEOLOGY OF MADAGASCAR.

CHAPTER III.

THE ANIMAL LIFE OF MADAGASCAR.

CHAPTER IV.

NOTES ON THE VEGETABLE PRODUCTIONS OF MADAGASCAR.

CHAPTER V.

ORIGIN AND DIVISIONS OF THE MALAGASY PEOPLE.

CHAPTER VI.

CHARACTERISTICS OF THE DIFFERENT TRIBES INHABITING MADAGASCAR IN ANCIENT AND MODERN TIMES.

CHAPTER VII.

CURIOSITIES OF THE MALAGASY LANGUAGE: WITH NOTES UPON THE "HISTORY," "POETRY," AND "MORALITY" EMBODIED IN NATIVE WORDS.

CHAPTER VIII.

CURIOSITIES OF MALAGASY NAMES: PERSONAL, TRIBAL, AND GEOGRAPHICAL.

CHAPTER IX.

CURIOUS AND NOTEWORTHY CUSTOMS AMONG THE DIFFERENT TRIBES.

CHAPTER X.

CURIOUS AND NOTEWORTHY CUSTOMS AMONG THE DIFFERENT TRIBES
—*(continued).*

CHAPTER XI.

CURIOUS AND NOTEWORTHY CUSTOMS AMONG THE MALAGASY TRIBES
—*(concluded).*

CHAPTER XII.

CHAPTER XIII.

NOTES UPON MALAGASY ART IN DECORATION AND MANUFACTURE.

CHAPTER XIV.

MALAGASY FOLK-LORE AND POPULAR SUPERSTITIONS.

CHAPTER XV.

MALAGASY IDOLATRY AND RELIGIOUS BELIEFS AND OBSERVANCES.

CHAPTER XVI.

NEW LIGHT ON OLD TEXTS: ILLUSTRATIONS OF SCRIPTURE FROM MALAGASY CUSTOMS.

CHAPTER XVII.

MALAGASY CHURCH LIFE, AS ILLUSTRATIVE OF THE HISTORY OF THE APOSTOLIC AND EARLY CHURCHES.

CHAPTER XVIII.

THE

GREAT AFRICAN ISLAND.

—•—

CHAPTER I.

NAMES, DISCOVERY, EARLY ACCOUNTS, AND MAPS OF MADAGASCAR.

THE NAMES BY WHICH THE COUNTRY WAS KNOWN TO THE ANCIENTS AND TO
MEDIÆVAL WRITERS—ITS DISCOVERY BY EUROPEANS—ACCOUNTS GIVEN OF
IT BY EARLY VOYAGERS, AND FIRST REFERENCES TO IT IN ENGLISH
LITERATURE, TOGETHER WITH NOTICES OF THE MAPS OF THE ISLAND,
ANCIENT AND MODERN, AND OUR KNOWLEDGE OF ITS GEOGRAPHY AT
THE PRESENT TIME.

ALTHOUGH only seen by Europeans within the last 380 years,
the great African island of Madagascar has been known to
the Arabs for many centuries, probably for at least a thousand
years past; and also, but perhaps not for so long a time, to
the Indian traders of Cutch and Bombay.* The former,
indeed, have left ineffaceable traces of their influence in the
words they introduced into the Malagasy language, principally in the names of the days and months, and in those
connected with divination and astrology, and also in the
various superstitions they engrafted upon the original religious
belief and charm-worship of the inhabitants.†

But even before the Arabian intercourse, it seems probable
that the Phœnician traders, in some of those long voyages
made by the "ships of Tarshish" (1 Kings x. 22), touched
at Madagascar, or at least obtained information about the
island. For it is mentioned by some of the classical writers
under various names: thus, Ptolemy in his *Tabulæ* appears

* See Sir Bartle Frere's despatches in Blue-book on the East African Slave
Trade.
† See Rev. L. Dahle in the *Antananarivo Annual*, No. ii. pp. 75–91.

to refer to it under the name of *Menuthias ;* * and Pliny writes about an island which, in the opinion of many authors, could hardly be any other than Madagascar, under the name of *Cerné.*† And it has been supposed to be obscurely indicated in the book *De Mundo* ascribed to Aristotle, under the name of *Phanbalon.* Some other names are also given in early writers; thus, in a quaint old book published in 1609 by Hieronymus Megiserus, entitled *Beschreibung der Mechtigen und Weitberhümbten Insul Madagascar* (Altenbourg in Meissen), it is stated that Arrian calls it *Menutheseas*, Stephanus Byzantinus *Menuthis*, and Diodorus Siculus *Iamboli.* Tharetus is also quoted as saying that it was called *Pacras* on account of the many tortoises found there; afterwards *Albargra*, then *Manutia-Alphil*, and then *Magadascar*, a corruption of the name of Magadoxo, on the mainland of Africa, whose king is said to have invaded the island. Finally, this word was changed to Madagascar. So runs the account, some of the particulars of which are probably not very reliable, although they may possess a basis of fact.‡

Madagascar is mentioned by several of the Arabian writers, being known to them also by various names, as *Serandah* and *Chebona ;* and by the geographers Edrisi and Abulfeda (twelfth and thirteenth centuries), under the strangely different titles of *Phelon* (or Phenbalon), *Quambalon* (or Chambalon), *Zaledz* (also variously spelt), and *Gezirat al-Komr* or " Island of the Moon."

---

* "Huic de processo promontorio hodie Mozambique adjacet ab æstivo ortu insula nomine Menuthias; cujus positio 85 Austral 12.0" (lib. 4, cap. 9).

† "Contra Sinum Persicum Cerne, nominetur insula adversa Æthiopiæ, cujus neque magnitudo, neque intervallum a continente constat, Æthiopiæ tantum populos habere traditur" (lib. vi. cap. 31). The bishop appointed to Madagascar four years ago has adopted this name Cerné as that of his see on his official seal.

‡ Since writing the above, I have referred to the original texts of some of the classical authors mentioned by the old German writer, as well as to his own book; and also to a learned French author, Gossellin, who, in his work entitled *Récherches sur la Géographie Systématique et Positive des Anciens* (4 vols. Paris, 1813), disputes the opinion of earlier writers that Madagascar was mentioned by classical authors under the names of Cerné and Menuthias (see tom. i. pp. 80, 191-193). With regard to the former of these names, I think his opinion is correct, but I am not so sure about the second. Gossellin maintains that Menuthias was the name of a very small island in the estuary of one of the great rivers on the East African coast.

The country was first made known to (modern) European nations by the celebrated Venetian traveller Marco Polo, in the thirteenth century. He, however, did not himself visit the island, but heard various accounts of it during his travels in Asia, under the name of *Magaster* or *Madeigascar*. A chapter of his book of travels (33, B. iii. Yule's ed. pp. 345-354) is devoted to a description of it; but much of what he relates is evidently confused with accounts of Zanzibar and countries on the mainland of Africa, as he says that ivory is one of the chief productions, and that elephants, giraffes, and other animals (which never existed in the island), were numerous. His well-known account of the *rukh* or gigantic bird, long thought to be entirely fabulous, has during the last few years been discovered to have a basis of fact in the existence of the now-extinct *Æpyornis*, a struthious bird allied to the New Zealand Moa, and which produced the largest of all known eggs.

It was not until the commencement of the sixteenth century that Europeans set foot upon the great island. Towards the end of the previous century the adventurous Portuguese navigators Bartholomew Diaz and Vasco de Gama reached the southernmost portions of Africa and rounded the Cape of Good Hope, thus discovering the sea route to India and the farther East. On the Mozambique coast they found numbers of Arabs trading with India and well acquainted with Madagascar. But in 1505 King Manoel of Portugal sent out a great expedition of twenty-two ships to the Indies, under the command of Don Francisco de Almeida, the first viceroy, with orders to build fortresses at Sofala and Quiloa for the protection of the Portuguese commerce in Africa. Juan de Nova, whose name is preserved in that of a small island in the Mozambique Channel, sailed in this expedition. Almeida sent back in the beginning of the following year eight ships loaded with spices to Portugal, under the command of Fernando Soares. On their way they discovered, on the 1st of February 1506, the east coast of Madagascar.* From this

---

* See *The Life of Prince Henry of Portugal, surnamed "The Navigator,"* Major's ed., London, 1868, p. 415.

it appears clear that Soares, and not Almeida, as commonly said in histories, was the real discoverer of the island.

"In that same year João Gomez d'Abreu discovered the west coast of Madagascar on the 10th of August, St. Lawrence's Day, from which circumstance [following the usual custom of the early Spanish and Portuguese navigators] the island received the name of San Lorenço [which it retained for more than a hundred years]. He gave the name of Bahia Formosa, apparently the bay between Point Barrow and Point Croker" [S.W. coast]. The famous navigator Tristan da Cunha, who was sent out to India in the same year, also heard of the island through one of his captains, Rodrigo Pereira Coutinho. This officer had been obliged to take refuge in one of the southern ports of Madagascar from a storm which scattered Da Cunha's squadron off the Cape of Good Hope. Hearing glowing accounts of the newly-found country from his subordinate, Da Cunha visited various parts of the same coast, making with his own hand a chart of what he discovered, and was accordingly, though of course mistakenly, celebrated in song by his countryman Camöens in the *Lusiad* (c. x. s. 39) as the discoverer of Madagascar :—

"Green Madagascar's flowery dale shall swell
His echoed fame, till ocean's southmost bound
O'er isles and shores unknown his fame resound." *

He reached the northern end of the island on Christmas Day, and accordingly gave it the name of Cape Natal—a name which, however, it has not retained, but has been for long known as Cape Amber or Ambro.

The ship of Gomez d'Abreu doubled the northern cape, and running along the east coast, reached the mouth of the river Màtitànana in the south-east, where he landed. In a letter dated Mozambique, 8th February 1507, to King Manoel from the celebrated Alfonso d'Albuquerque, who was with

---

* Mickle's translation of the *Lusiad*. See Lyons M'Leod's *Madagascar and its People*, p. 6. The original Portuguese runs thus—

"Pelo CUNHA tambem, que nunca extinto
Será seu nome em todo o mar que lava
As Ilhas do Austro, e praias, que se chamam
De saõ LOURENÇO, e em todo o Sul se affam."

Da Cunha's expedition, he speaks of the discovery of the island; so that within a short time several of the most intrepid Portuguese navigators discovered various portions of the Madagascar coast while on their voyages to or from the far East; in fact, they seem to have almost, if not quite, circumnavigated the island.

During the early times of the French intercourse with Madagascar (reign of Henri IV.), they called it by the name of *Ile Dauphiné*, but this appellation was never accepted by other nations.

A few words may here be said about the name by which the island has been known for the last two hundred years.

There is much reason to believe that *Madagascar* is not a native name, but one given to the country by foreigners, and has only in modern times been accepted by the inhabitants. The spelling of the word in its present form is opposed to the laws of the native orthography, which do not allow the joining of two such consonants as *s* and *c* (*c*, moreover, is not used), and all native words end in a vowel. *Nòsin-dàmbo*, or "Isle of Wild Hogs," was a name occasionally given to it; but when the Malagasy speak of the whole of the island, they usually call it *Izao rehétra izao*, "This all," or *Izao tontòlo izao*, "This whole," thinking, like many insular people, that their own country was the most important part of the world, and that the Arabs and other foreigners who visited their northwest coast came from some insignificant islands across the sea. Another term, somewhat poetical in form, and occasionally used by the people, is *Ny anìvon' ny rìaka, i.e.*, "The (land) in the midst of the moving waters," a term which might be used of any island, but is only applied to Madagascar itself, *nòsy* being the word employed to denote the small islands off the mainland. This term was engraved on the huge silver coffin of the first Radàma, who was there called *Tòmpon' ny anìvon' ny rìaka*, "Lord of the island," as above described. The form of the word,* like the name

---

* By Copland and other writers the island is called *Madecassa*, which, by substituting *k* for *c*, would be a correct enough native word. In many books the people are called *Madecasse*, but the origin of these forms of the name is obscure.

of the inhabitants of the country, Màlagàsy (also probably not a native name), seems to indicate an African origin, so that possibly there may be some foundation of truth in the accounts given by the German writer already quoted from. *Ma*, it is well known, is a frequent prefix to words indicating tribal names on the African continent, as Makololo, Matabele, &c.

The early accounts given of Madagascar by voyagers and other writers are full of glowing and extravagant praises of its fertility and natural wealth. But in all this, of course, it formed no exception to other newly-found countries, for the imagination of the people of the sixteenth and seventeenth centuries invested with a halo of beauty and mystery all the strange new lands which were being yearly discovered by the bold seamen of Portugal and Spain, and of England and Holland. The luxuriance of the tropical vegetation of the New World and the far Eastern Archipelago, and the undoubted wealth in precious metals of some of those regions, made every fresh addition to their geography a possible El Dorado, with gold and gems waiting to be collected in every stream, and precious spices to be gathered from every tree. Even the title-pages of some of the early books upon Madagascar are eloquent panegyrics upon the resources and wealth of the island; while their quaint descriptions, as well as the strong religious feelings so many of them evince, make them by no means uninteresting reading.

Although the Portuguese discovered the island, they made no lengthened occupation of any part of it. Probably they found that their extensive possessions in South America and Africa and the Malay Archipelago demanded all their strength to occupy; and accordingly their colony was soon abandoned. For a few years towards the close of the sixteenth century (1595–98), the Dutch had some little intercourse with Madagascar, but were not much impressed in its favour; for they lost through sickness so many of their number that an island where they landed was called " The Dutchmen's Graveyard." A book written by Johan Hugen von Lindschot (1628) describes these voyages, and it is evident that they paid some considerable attention to the country, for two of the very earliest books upon Madagascar were published at

Amsterdam in 1603, both of them giving vocabularies of Malagasy words (see chapter on the language).

As the Portuguese discovered Madagascar, probably the earliest descriptions of the country are to be found in Portuguese books, notably in the *Commentarios do grande Afonso D'Alboquerque* (Lisbon, 1576, fol.), but this book contains little of interest beyond the mere fact of the discovery of the island.

Next in date come the two Dutch linguistic works already mentioned, and then the little German work of Hieronymus Megiserus, from which quotations have been made as to the early names of the island. The title-page of this book promises to give us—

A Genuine, Thorough, and Ample,
as well as
Historical and Chronographical Description
of the
Exceedingly Rich, Powerful, and Famous
ISLAND OF MADAGASCAR,
called also
St. LAWRENCE;
Together with an Account
of all its Qualities, Peculiarities, Inhabitants, Animals, Fruits and Vegetables.
Also
A History of what has happened there
before and since its Discovery.

The title-page, like those of other books we shall have occasion to mention, leads one therefore to expect much valuable information; but except some curious particulars about the names given to the island at that period, there is little of value about either country or people, while some of the same mistakes are made as to the productions as are found in Marco Polo's account. At the end is added " A Dictionary and Dialogues of the Madagascar Language, collected with special industry from the Portuguese, Italian, and Latin Histories and Geographies; " and this portion, more than half of the whole book, has considerable interest, the greater part of the words being easily recognisable. It has a small map, and seven or eight engravings of the people, and of the animal and vegetable productions.

The earliest English book upon Madagascar of which I have any knowledge is by one Walter Hamond, surgeon, and published in 1640, entitled "A Paradox: Proving the Inhabitants of the Island called Madagascar, or St. Lawrence (in Things temporal), to be the happiest People in the World." * This work may be almost regarded as a satire upon the extravagance and luxury of the times, for its general purport is to show that the inhabitants of Madagascar, in their poverty and ignorance, are much better off than civilised peoples, being not much troubled with clothing or ornaments, or with the fatigues of commerce, navigation, and civilisation, the varieties of food and drink, and the evils arising from the use of gunpowder and the arms of European nations. All this is argued out in a comically serious style. Possibly a diligent search in the larger libraries would discover earlier books, or at least pamphlets or tracts on Madagascar; and doubtless there are many notices of the country to be found in the narratives of the early English voyagers.

The same author published three years later (1643) another book, whose title-page may be given in full, as it is curious from its quaintness, and as showing the great expectations formed of the island. It is as follows:—

MADAGASCAR,

The Richest
and most
Frvitefvll Island
In the World.
Wherein
the Temperature of the Clymate, the
Nature of the Inhabitants, the Commodities of
the Countrie, and the facility and benefit of a Plantation by our People there, are compendiously
and truely described.

---

* Reprinted in the *Harleian Miscellany, a Collection of Scarce, Curious, and Entertaining Pamphlets and Tracts, as well in Manuscript as in Print.* London, 1808.

𝕯𝖊𝖉𝖎𝖈𝖆𝖙𝖊𝖉

To the Honourable IOHN BOND,

Governour of the Island, whose proceeding is Authorized for
this Expedition, both by the King and Parliament.

—

By WALTER HAMOND.

—

London:

Printed for Nicholas Bourne, *and are to bee sold at his
Shop, at the South Entrance of the Royall Exchange.*
1643. [4to.]

The promise of the title-page (as in the case of the German book already described) is hardly borne out by the book itself, which does not contain much of value, except some information about the author's experiences with the people, chiefly those about St. Augustine's Bay on the south-west coast. He seems to have been greatly impressed by the honesty and good faith of the inhabitants; again and again is this mentioned in such words as "in all our trayding with them we never sustained so much as the losse of one bead." He even says, "they retaine the first incorrupt innocence of man," and are "a people approaching in some degree neere Adam, naked without guilt, and innocent, not by a forc't vertue, but by ignorance of evill, and the creatures as innocent and serviceable to man as they were before his transgression." (How wofully, according to all accounts, must they have depreciated since then!) We find, however, in the book, that among these innocent people wars were going on between them and the neighbouring tribes, as there still are, and probably always have been. There is a notice of some of the valuable trees of the country, ebony, tamarind, and others, and of a remarkable tree he calls the "flesh-tree," probably a dragon-tree, yielding a sanguine-coloured sap. The book contains an urgent appeal to the writer's countrymen to "go in and possess the land," which "doth here by me friendly and lovingly invite our nation to take some compassion of her nakednesse, her poverty, and her simplicity, both corporall and spirituall, and doth earnestly and affectionately even beg of us to redeeme her out of her miserable thraldome under the tyranny of Satan [curiously inconsistent this with the preceding eulogy of the people], to be united with us into the fellowship of the sons of God by our union in Christ Jesus." Who this Hon. John Bond, "Governour and Captaine-Generall of Madagascar," was, I have been unable to discover, or to find what claim he had to such large powers in the great island.

In the same decade of the seventeenth century other books on Madagascar were also published, the next in date being one with an extremely long title, which is also perhaps worth quoting nearly in full, not only for its quaint language but as affording additional evidence of the sanguine expectations formed respecting the island. It runs thus :—

A BREIFE
DISCOVERY or DESCRIPTION
Of the most Famous Island of
MADAGASCAR or ST. LAWRENCE
in Asia neere unto East India.

With relation of the Healthfulness, Pleasure, Fertility, and Wealth of that Country, comparable if not transcending all the Easterne parts of the World, a very Earthly Paradise ; a most fitting and desirable place to settle an English Colony and Plantation there, rather than in any other parte of the knowne World.

Also the condition of the Natives, there inhabiting, their Affability, Habit, Weapons, and Manner of living, the plenty and cheapnesse of Food, Flesh, Fish, and Fowle, Oringes and Lemonds, Amber-Greece, Gold, Tortle-Shels, and Drugs, and many other Commodities fit for trade and commerce, to be had and gotten there at cheaper Rates than in India or elsewhere.

Also trading from Port to Port all India and Asia over, and the great profit gained thereby ;

The chiefest place in the World to inrich men by Trade, to and from India, Persia, Moco, Achine, China, and other rich Easterne Kingdoms. It being the fittest place for a Magazine or Store-house of Trade between Europe and Asia, farre exceeding all other Plantations in America or elsewhere.

Also the excellent meanes and accommodation to fit the planters there, with all things needfull and superfluous for back and belly (out of India neere adjacent, at one fourth part of the price, and cheaper then it will cost in England ; yea, Fat Bullocks, Sheep, Goats, Swine, Poultry, Rice, (and Wheat and Barley reasonable, &c.) exceeding cheap, for the value of 12 pence or one shilling English will purchase or buy of the Natives as much as 5, 6, 7 pounds or more in England, in this famous Island at their first arrivall, which no other country hath afforded.

———

By RICHARD BOOTHBY, Merchant.

LONDON : *Printed by E. G. for* JOHN HARDESTY *at the Signe of the Black-Spread Eagle in Duck Lane,* 1646.

It seems from the preface to Boothby's work, which is a small octavo of seventy-two pages, that two years previous to the publication of this book there had been a project to found an English plantation in Madagascar, Prince Rupert having been named at the Privy Council board as Viceroy for King Charles I., from whom he was to have had twelve men-of-war and thirty merchantmen to form the colony. The Governor and Committee of the East India Company were also ordered to give all possible assistance to the enterprise. Rupert, however, going away to the Continent, the Earl of Arundel, Earl Marshal of England, was appointed; and it appears that that nobleman had also written a book on the subject, urging the desirability of forming a magazine or victualling station on the island. However, the calling of the parliament immediately preceding the Long Parliament, and the political troubles which soon ensued, put a stop to this projected English colony in Madagascar. It is stated in Boothby's book that the island had been previously visited by other distinguished Englishmen, viz., the ambassadors from Charles I. to the King of Persia, who landed there on their way to the East.

The appointment of Prince Rupert called forth another book upon the island, but this time in the shape of a poem, by Sir William Davenant, entitled "Madagascar, with other Poems, by W. Davenant, Knight" (London, 1648). This production occupies only twenty-one pages of print, and gives no information whatever about Madagascar itself, being simply a complimentary effusion, "written to the most illustrious Prince Rupert." Following the strange conceits common to the literary productions of the time, such as are seen in Beaumont and Fletcher, Donne, Herbert, and other writers, the poem is in the form of a dream, in which the country where the Prince was going is described in an inflated style, with extravagant laudation of Rupert, so that even the sun is described as being absorbed in contemplating what the Prince is supposed to have conquered :—

> . . . " The good old planet's business is
> Of late only to visit what is his ; "

while as to the government of the Prince,

> " Chronologers pronounce his style
> The first true monarch of the golden isle ;
> An isle so seated for predominance,
> Where naval strength its power can so advance."

The supposed riches of the country are next described, the colonists employing themselves

> " In virgin mines, where shining gold they spy,
> Some root up coral trees, where mermaids lie
> Sighing beneath those precious boughs, and die."

Some from " old oysters " rifle pearls,

> " Whose ponderous size sinks weaker divers ;
> Their weight would yoke a tender lady's neck."

Some

> " Search the rocks till each have found
> A saphyr, ruby, and a diamond."

The poem is a poor enough production in itself, but has a certain interest as showing the extravagant notions then entertained about the wealth of distant countries. But it nevertheless met with great commendation from the poet's contemporaries, Endymion Porter saying that it was a

> . . . " Poem in so sweet a style
> As never yet was lauded in this isle."

Another of the poet's friends, Sir John Suckling, Comptroller of the Household to King Charles I., wrote a sonnet entitled, " To my friend Will Davenant, on his Poem of Madagascar," which is perhaps amusing enough to be quoted in full, especially as he concludes by a sly hit at his friend for having nothing but words to show in proof of the enormous wealth he describes :—

> " What mighty princes poets are ! Those things
> The great ones stick at, and our very kings
> Lay down, they venture on ; and with great ease
> Discover, conquer, what and where they please.
> Some phlegmatic sea-captain would have staid
> For money now, or victuals ; not have weigh'd
> Anchor without 'em : Thou (Will) dost not stay
> So much as for a wind, but go'st away,
> Land'st, view'st the country ; fight'st, put'st all to rout
> Before another could be setting out ;
> And now the news in town is, ' Davenant's come
> From Madagascar, fraught with laurel, home ;'
> And welcome (Will) for the first time, but prithee,
> In thy next voyage, bring the gold with thee."

The fifth decade of the seventeenth century was thus, it appears, most prolific in works upon the great African island.

Towards the end of the century an account was written (but not published until some years later) of the adventures and extreme hardships suffered by an English sailor upon a small island off the western coast of Madagascar.   This was entitled—

"A Relation of Three Years' Sufferings of Robert Everard upon the Island of Assada, near Madagascar, in a Voyage to India, in the year 1686, and of his Wonderful Preservation and Deliverance and arrival at London, Anno 1693." *

This account, which occupies twenty-three pages of small folio print, contains several interesting particulars of the customs of the people, amongst which is the statement that on one occasion twenty children were circumcised by the *women*.   The writer had evidently a hard time during his three years' residence ; for, although he made shot for the king, because he could not also find gun-flints he was turned out of doors and left to shift for himself.   He obtained food in the shape of fruit and roots, shell-fish and turtles, but he had to lodge under a tree only, for two years and nine months, although on one occasion, he says, it rained continuously for *three months.*   As he was quite naked, he kept a fire burning

* Pages 259–282 in vol. vi. of *A Collection of Voyages and Travels, some now first printed from the Original Manuscripts, &c.* London, Churchill, 1732.

for warmth, not being allowed to enter the houses. Eventually he became (no wonder) very ill, and at his request was bought by an Arab, and at last taken to India, where he obtained his liberty. This island of " Assada " is probably one of those numerous ones off the north-west coast of Madagascar.

The last of these early books which can be here noticed is that by Robert Drury, an English lad, who, at the commencement of the last century, went as a passenger to the East on board an Indiaman named the *Degrave*. On their homeward voyage the vessel was wrecked on the south-west coast of Madagascar, and owing to imprudent conduct and collisions with the natives, the whole of the ship's company and passengers were eventually killed, with the exception of Drury and another lad, whose lives were spared. He thus became a slave, and remained as such in the island for fifteen years (1702–17), meeting with varied experience and many hardships, and occasionally being harshly treated, and narrowly escaping being killed. At last, however, he obtained his liberty, and returned to England, afterwards writing the book describing his adventures, or possibly had it written from his dictation. Drury being comparatively uneducated, the narrative is in a most artless style, with an evident impress of truth, and, from its undoubted genuineness, is a very valuable record of the customs of some of the Malagasy tribes at that period, and throws important light upon many questions connected with their customs, superstitions, and beliefs. He describes their ancient and patriarchal system of worship in connection with the *ódy*, or household gods; and we see the political state of that part of the island, really unaltered to the present time, in which the different tribes are constantly engaged in warfare, making raids on each others' cattle, and capturing slaves. There is added to the book a pretty full vocabulary, which is one of the most valuable portions of it, the great majority of the words being easily recognisable as identical with those in the Hova dialect, and thus giving another proof of the substantial unity of the language over portions of the island far distant from one another. Curiously enough, he gives a decidedly " Cockney " pronunciation and spelling to his list of Malagasy words; *héna* (meat) he calls "henar;" *vòla*, money, "voler;" and *àndro*, day, "hawndro;" &c.

From the year 1651, when a work describing a voyage to Madagascar by one François Cauche, of Rouen, was issued, a considerable number of books upon Madagascar have been published in the French language. A list of between thirty and forty of these is given by M. Barbié du Bocage in a book entitled, *Madagascar: Possession française depuis* 1642, the title of which work explains the interest taken in the island by the French. But it is quite an unfounded assumption to call Madagascar a French possession, and is warranted neither by conquest or treaty, or by any other claim or right; and although it is quite true that the French have for two centuries past been attempting to gain power in the country, their colonies, or rather, military posts, have never been permanent, nor have they been able to maintain their hold upon any portion of the mainland. They have, however, seized the small island of St. Marie's, off the eastern coast, and they have also possession of the island of Nòsibé, on the northwest coast. This latter was ceded to them in 1840 by the Sàkalàva inhabitants of that portion of Madagascar.

Turning now to the Maps of Madagascar, and our present knowledge of the geography of the island, it may be affirmed that a considerable portion of the country is still a *terra incognita* to us; and notwithstanding all that has been done of late years to increase our knowledge of it, there are extensive regions still unknown and unexplored. Among them may be mentioned the greater part of the triangle formed by the northern portion of the island, from Antsihànaka to Cape Amber at the apex of the triangle; almost all the Sàkalàva country on the western seaboard; large portions of the eastern side, from the central plateaux to the sea; and, lastly, an extensive district to the south of the Bétsiléo province, from the Bàra country to the southern Cape of St. Mary.

The earliest map of Madagascar which I have discovered is one in the British Museum, and is an extremely curious specimen of chartography. The outline of the island there given is so different from the reality, that it would hardly be recognised but for the name, "S. Lorenzo," which is marked upon it. The towns shown on the map, six in number, are true medieval strongholds, with walls and gates, and crowded with spires and towers, one of them boasting of a grand cathedral!—while they are all on such a scale that they would be disproportionately large even if the island were only two or three miles wide. Similarly gigantic ships, with banks of oars, are depicted along the coast, and strange sea-monsters are here and there seen emerging from the waves around the island. From its very incorrect outline I am strongly inclined to think that it is of considerably earlier date than that given in the catalogue, viz., 1570 * (Venice), the more so as another map, also Venetian, and dated three years earlier (1567), is far more correct in outline, and the principal capes, bays, and rivers can be recognised, and are tolerably accurate, as far as regards the coast-line.

Another very curious old map, to a small scale, is given in the quaint German work of Megiser's already referred to. But I find that it is taken from an earlier book, a neat little atlas of maps, with descriptions of the different countries, entitled *Thresor de Chartes*, and dated 1602.

A glance at several of the numerous maps of Madagascar that have been published since these dates would lead one to suppose that what is stated above as to the incompleteness of our knowledge of the country was all a mistake. On many of these we find the so-called provinces defined with a minuteness resembling that of the divisions of the counties on an Ordnance map of England; the rivers, with their tributaries, are all unhesitatingly laid down, and mountain chains of singular regularity and wall-like straightness cross the country in all directions. Far from imitating the ingenuous confessions of ignorance shown on some maps, where—

> "Geographers on pathless downs
> Put elephants instead of towns,"

many of these early maps of Madagascar are, strange to say,

---

* I am confirmed in this opinion by a further reference to the catalogue, in which a note of interrogation is affixed both to the date and the place of publishing.

the most minute and exact in their fulness of detail; and knowing how little certainly was then ascertained as to the interior of the island, we look at them with a feeling of wonder as to whence their information could have been derived.

One of the most curious of these early maps is that prefixed to an English edition of the Abbé Rochon's book entitled, *A Voyage to Madagascar and the East Indies* (London, 1793). According to this map, no part of the island would appear to have been unknown to the map-maker; the rivers with their tributaries have a picturesque symmetry resembling that of stately trees, and the mountains a regular cone-like outline only possessed by mountains seen on a map. But on examining this map more minutely to find out well-known places in the interior, we are puzzled to find that neither the central and most important province of Imérina, nor the capital city, Antanànarivo, are shown; and it is the same with the important province of Bétsiléo and its chief towns; while some other places are strangely transposed. Clearly this map owes more of its filling-in to a lively imagination than to any exploration of the country, notwithstanding the somewhat ambiguous assurance in its title that it is "from the original design, drawn on the spot;" but what and where "the spot" was, is not specified.*

Again, take a very pretentious-looking map published by Arrowsmith, and purporting to be "*Madagascar, from Original Drawings, Sketches, and Oral Information,* by J. A. Lloyd, F.R.S., &c., &c., Surveyor-General of the Mauritius." The last edition I have seen is dated 1850. In a journey to the south-east part of Madagascar in 1876 I consulted this on many occasions, but found that not the slightest reliance was to be placed upon it. But subsequently meeting with a pamphlet read by Colonel Lloyd before the Royal Geographical Society upon Madagascar (10th December 1849), I discovered a clue to the reason for all this; for at page 22, in a few remarks upon the map accompanying his paper (a

* Since writing the above, I find that Rochon's map is little more than a copy of that given in Flacourt's *Histoire de la Grande Isle de Madagascar*, published in 1661, a hundred and thirty years before Rochon's book.

B

reduced copy of the above-mentioned map), Colonel Lloyd makes this ingenuous admission: "For the detail of the interior I cannot claim the slightest pretensions to correctness. It is only an attempt to form approximately some foundation for future inquiries and more correct and extensive research." And yet this map, confessedly so problematical, appears to have been the source of most subsequent maps of the island as given in English books or published separately.

The coast-line of Madagascar, with a narrow strip of country bordering the sea, was accurately surveyed by Captain W. F. W. Owen, R.N., of H.M.S. *Leven* and *Barracouta*, about forty-seven years ago. This survey was published by the Admiralty, and Captain Owen described his experiences in a book entitled *Narrative of Voyages to Explore the Shores of Africa, Arabia, and Madagascar, &c.* (London, 1833).

With regard to the later French maps of Madagascar, they also appear to have been chiefly constructed from verbal information, with an occasional itinerary of a priest, or naturalist, or trader; for the interior detail of most of them prior to 1870 seems little more reliable than that given in the English maps. (The island has been crossed in various directions by a good many travellers, as shown in a valuable list of routes compiled by M. Grandidier, and given in a paper published in the *Bulletin de la Société de Géographie* [Avril 1872, pp. 408–411]; but very few of these travellers have left any accurate observations or scientific surveys of the line of country they traversed.) How some of these French maps have been constructed is amusingly described by M. Grandidier in a paper upon the island before the Paris Geographical Society. Speaking of a book by a M. Leguevel de Lacombe, entitled *Voyage à Madagascar*, he says: "This writer relates that he has at different periods traversed the island from north to south, from east to west; he gives the most precise details of his journeys. M. de Lacombe has told me, and I am myself well assured of it, with his book in my hand, that he has never left the east coast! It is from his imagination that he has drawn the accounts, to which geographers have attached so much importance that the maps of Madagascar have to the present day been constructed upon the topographical data taken from his work." *

To a French traveller, however, we owe the most accurate general map of the island yet produced. M. Alfred Grandidier, who explored the country from 1865 to 1870, published in 1871 a sketch-map (*Esquisse d'un Carte de l'Ile de Madagascar*). It is somewhat roughly lithographed, and was merely intended to illustrate the brief summary of his travels and explorations read before the Paris Geographical Society; but from the prospectus of his magnificent work on the island and its natural history, botany, ethnology, &c., now in process of publication in twenty-eight quarto volumes, a much more complete map may be expected. Meanwhile, this preliminary map has already done much to clear away some traditional mistakes, and to establish two or three facts of great interest in the physical geography of the country, namely, the existence in the island of two strongly contrasted regions: the elevated granitic district, and the low maritime plains region to the west and south, of Secondary and Tertiary formation; † and also the existence of a belt of forest surrounding the whole island. On this map most of the Hova military stations and the more important places in the interior are laid down; and having had opportunities of testing its accuracy in more than one direction, I feel confident that it is by far the most trustworthy map of the island yet published. Indeed, no previous traveller has been so thoroughly prepared by scientific knowledge and with full appliances to make an accurate survey of the country; and as many hundreds of principal points were fixed astronomically, a reliable basis has been formed for future work. It must, however, be remembered that M. Grandidier has not traversed the island in every direction, and, as already remarked, extensive portions of it have still to be explored,

---

* *Bulletin de la Société de Géographie*, Aout 1871, p. 82.

† M. Grandidier says: "Je vais maintenant tâcher de tracer en quelques mots la physionomie générale que présente Madagascar. Cette île comprend deux parties bien distinctes : la partie nord et est qui est toute montagneuses, et la partie sud et ouest qui est rélativement plate."—*Bull. de la Soc. de Géog.*, Aout 1871, p 100.

so that there is still much to be added to this map of the
French traveller and savant.

Far surpassing everything else previously attempted as a
delineation of *the interior* must be mentioned the map of *The
Central Provinces of Madagascar*, by the Rev. Dr. Mullens,*
published, together with his book entitled *Twelve Months in
Madagascar*, in 1875. Stretching over five degrees of latitude, from the Antsihànaka province in the north to Imàhazòny in Southern Bétsiléo, it depicts on a scale of twelve
miles to the inch the physical features of the central portion
of the island and the sites of the chief towns and most important villages. The late Mr. James Cameron had previously
fixed astronomically some of the chief points in Imérina, and
measured a base-line from which the triangulation was constructed, so that a reliable foundation for the map was provided, and the series of angles was extended right down into
the Bétsiléo province. This map is a great gain to our knowledge of the interior, and is full of detail; it is, however, im-
perfect in many directions, and plenty of room is still left for
additions and improvements.

Since Dr. Mullens's visit several important contributions
have been made towards a fuller geographical knowledge of
various portions of the island not previously mapped. Among
these are sketch-maps illustrating journeys, made chiefly by
members of the London Missionary Society and the Friends'
Mission Association, into the Sàkalàva country, the Bàra
province in the south, to the Southern Tanàla or forest tribes,
and the south-east coast, the north-east coast, and northern
central portions of the island, and to the north-west and
extreme north.† The results of these journeys are embodied
in a map prepared by Mr. W. Johnson of the Friends'
Mission, and lithographed at their press in Antanànarìvo, the
work being done by native lads. The same gentleman has

---

* Since the above was written, I deeply regret to add that Dr. Mullens's
name must now be prefixed by the word "late." He died at Mpwapwa on July
10, 1879, having nobly volunteered to head a party to relieve the Central
African Mission of the London Missionary Society. Had his life been spared,
he would doubtless have done something in Africa, as in Madagascar, to add to
our geographical knowledge of the country he traversed.

† See *Proc. Roy. Geog. Soc.*, January 17, 1877.

also published a very minute and complete map of the south-western portions of the central province.

In the year 1877 a journey was made by Rev. J. Richardson from the Bétsiléo province to St. Augustine's Bay on the south-west coast, across new ground, and thus much light has been thrown upon the northern portion of that extensive tract of Southern Madagascar, which is still largely an unknown region.

The results of all these recent additions to our knowledge of the geography of Madagascar have been embodied in a very fine general map prepared by Dr. Mullens and published in May last. This is the largest map of the island yet constructed, being on the same scale as those of the central provinces and Southern Madagascar. These are included in it without much alteration, but three or four other routes are also laid down, Grandidier's sketch-map forming the authority for other parts of the country.

There is still, however, much to be done in all directions before we can be said to have a tolerably complete general map of the island, while of course there is ample room for hundreds of more detailed maps of special portions of the country. An island nearly a thousand miles long and three hundred and fifty at its greatest breadth gives "ample space and verge" for map-making. Still, so far, every journey lately made appears to confirm the general truth of M. Grandidier's sketch-map as to the broad outlines of the elevated mountainous and granitic region in the northern and eastern central portion of the island; but we still need much information as to the contour of this in various directions, and the steps by which it rises from the plains on all sides.

From the usually brilliantly clear and pure atmosphere, and the large number of prominent and lofty hills all over the central regions of the island, Madagascar offers especial facilities for map-making, as some well-known points can almost always be seen, from which to get good bearings. What is most wanted is that a few more of these be exactly fixed by astronomical observations.

CHAPTER II.

THE PHYSICAL GEOGRAPHY AND GEOLOGY OF MADAGASCAR.

ELEVATED GRANITIC REGION—SCENERY—RIVERS AND LAKES—LOWER REGION
AND MARITIME PLAINS—MOUNTAINS—BELT OF FOREST—VOLCANIC DIS-
TURBANCES—GEOLOGY OF THE CHIEF DIVISIONS—SECONDARY FOSSILS—
RECENTLY EXTINCT FAUNA—LIGNITE FORMATION—CORAL REEFS—METALS
AND MINERALS—FERTILITY OF SOIL.

ALTHOUGH Madagascar is known to be the third largest island
in the world, its actual size and extent is not very generally
understood. And it is easy to see how misconception on this
point arises, for in maps the island is usually seen only in
connection with Africa, and that continent is of such immense
extent that it dwarfs by comparison with itself everything in
its near neighbourhood; so that the really large island shel-
tering under its south-eastern side appears but an incon-
siderable appendage to its vast neighbour. If, however, we
take a good-sized map of Madagascar, and put by its side
the outline, to the same scale, of another country with whose
dimensions we are familiar—such, for instance, as England—
we begin to realise how important an island it is as regards
size, being nearly 1000 miles long* by about 250 in average
breadth, and reaching to 350 miles at its widest part. It
has, therefore, an area of about 230,000 square miles, so that
it is nearly four times as large as England and Wales.

During the last ten years much light has been thrown
upon the physical geography of Madagascar, principally
through the researches of M. Alfred Grandidier, and the
numerous exploratory journeys made in various parts of the
country by missionaries and others. Until a very recent
period there was no reliable map of the island, and the
physical geography was completely misunderstood. But it is

* More exactly, 975 miles.

now quite clear that, instead of a "central mountain chain," as described in most histories and gazetteers, there is *an elevated mountainous region*, which, however, does not occupy the centre of the island, but is more to the east and north, leaving a considerable extent of country to the west, and all beyond the twenty-third parallel of south latitude, at a much lower level above the sea. Broadly speaking, therefore, Madagascar consists of two great divisions, viz.—(1) An elevated interior region raised some 3000 to 5000 feet above the sea-level, and (2) a comparatively level country surrounding it, and not much exceeding 400 or 500 feet of elevation, but most extensive on the west and south.

The elevated region is largely composed of Primary and crystalline rocks. Lines of hills traverse it in all directions, but they do not rise to a very great height; the highest points in the island, the peaks of the Ankàratra group of hills, being a little under 9000 feet above the sea-level. A very large extent of this portion of Madagascar is covered with bright red clay, through which the granite and basaltic rocks protrude. But there are also extensive rice plains, especially in the neighbourhood of the capital cities of the two chief provinces, where there is a rich black alluvial soil; and it can hardly be doubted that some at least of these plains, from their perfect level; out of which the red clay hills rise like islands, have formerly been the beds of extensive lakes, subsequently drained, possibly by slight changes in the level through subterranean action.

A good deal of this portion of Madagascar is bare and somewhat dreary-looking country. The long rolling moor-like hills are only covered with a coarse grass, which becomes very brown and dry towards the end of the seven months' rainless season; but the hollows and river valleys are often filled with a luxuriant tropical vegetation, and, wherever there is population, with the bright green of the rice-fields. There is, nevertheless, an element of grandeur in the landscape, from the great extent of country visible from many points in the clear pure atmosphere, which renders very distant objects wonderfully sharp and distinct. And many portions of the central region possess still greater claims to admiration from the picturesque mountain scenery. In the Southern Bétsiléo country the grand and varied forms of the mountains filled me with an exultant kind of delight. To the south was a crowd of mountain-tops, peak beyond peak, with the greatest variety of outline: one had the appearance of a colossal trun- cated spire; another had a jagged saw-like ridge; another was a pyramid with successive steps; and another an enor- mous dome. Their summits were never long free from clouds, and many of the peaks must be at least 3000 feet above the plain.

Sections taken by the aneroid across this elevated region from east to west, at the latitude of the capital, show that it has a depression in the centre, the edges on either side being considerably higher than the country between them. At some points this height of 4000 or 5000 feet is gained by a series of steps from the maritime plains, each range of hills rising higher and higher; while at other points it descends almost at one steep slope for nearly 3000 feet. The watershed is not near the centre of the island, but is much more towards the eastern side. Through the eastern wall many of the rivers cut their way by magnificent gorges, amidst dense forest, finding their way to the sea by a suc- cession of rapids and cataracts, and occasionally by stupen- dous falls, as in the case of the Màtitànana, which descends at one plunge 500 or 600 feet. Some of the western rivers also are said to form grand waterfalls, particularly that of the Manìa, whose sound is reported to be heard at a distance of two days' journey, *i.e.*, from forty to fifty miles.

The largest river in Madagascar is probably the Bétsibòka, which, with its affluent the Ikiopa, is the great drain of the central province of Imérina, and falls into the Bay of Bem- batòka. It is about 300 miles long. Many other rivers of considerable size flow to the west, the Manìa and Matsìatra being almost as large as the Bétsibòka, but few are navigable for vessels of large size. The Bétsibòka could be ascended by steamers of light draught for about ninety miles from its mouth, and perhaps also several others of those which fall into the Mozambique Channel. The eastern rivers are almost all blocked at their outlets by a sandy bar thrown up by the ever-restless surf driven by the strong south-east trade winds.

This contest between the fresh and the salt water has given rise to one of the most curious geographical features of the east coast, namely, the long chain of lagoons which stretch for several hundred miles along the shore. Many of these look like a river following the coast-line, but often they spread out into extensive sheets of water and form large lakes. So short is the distance between the detached links, that by cutting about thirty miles of canal to connect them, a continuous waterway could be formed for 260 miles along the eastern coast, a circumstance which will no doubt at some future day be taken advantage of for commercial purposes, as it would be a most valuable means of communication between distant portions of this side of the island.

Except these lagoons, there are few lakes in Madagascar, although, as already noticed, there were probably some very extensive ones in a recent geological period. Of one of the largest of these, the lake Alaôtra in the Sihànaka province is the relic; this sheet of water is about twenty-five miles long, and from four to five miles wide, spreading out at the northern end into a hammer-head shape. The next in size is Itàsy in Imérina, which is about eight miles long; and there is another of some extent in the south-western part of the island.

The lower region of Madagascar consists of extensive plains only a few hundred feet above the sea-level, but there are at least three prominent chains of hills traversing it from north to south, one of which appears nearly continuous in a very straight line for above 600 miles. The eastern side of the island is, for the greater part of its extent, without any bay or indentation; indeed, for 500 miles, from Foule Pointe to Fort Dauphin, the coast forms almost a straight line. North of the first-named of these two places there is a deep inlet forming the Bay of Antongil, and protected by the mountainous peninsula of Maròa. Close to the northern point of the island is one of the finest harbours in the world, that of Diego Suarez or British Sound; and the north-western side is deeply indented with large bays, into which

some of the chief rivers fall. All this part of the coast is
bold and mountainous; and some of the finest scenery in
Madagascar is to be found here, as the northern extremity
of the volcanic region forms several very grand mountains,
particularly the one called Amber or Ambòhitra. This is said
to be about 6000 feet high, and, from its isolated position in
the low country surrounding it, is a remarkably majestic hill
as seen from every direction, as well as from far out to sea.[*]
It has three summits, and its sides are clothed with impenetrable woods.

South-west of this mountain is a remarkable rock fortress
of the tribe inhabiting this part of the country, who are
called Antankàrana, that is, "the people of the rocks." It is
an enormous lofty and precipitous rock, having an elevation of nearly 1000 feet, and covering an area of about
eight square miles. Its sides are so precipitous that they
cannot be climbed unless artificial means are used, and it is
thickly wooded wherever trees can possibly grow. The only
entrance into the interior of the rock, which is full of caves,
is by means of a subterranean passage, a portion of which is
extremely narrow, allowing only a single person to pass along
it at a time, and has on each side of it deep water.

The other principal group of mountains in Madagascar is
the great mass of elevated peaks called Ankàratra, in the
central province. This has hardly the grand appearance of
Mount Amber (although it considerably exceeds the latter in
absolute height), since it rises from the elevated region of
Imérina, which is at the capital about 4000 feet above the
sea-level. Ankàratra is, nevertheless, a noble group of hills,
and is the most conspicuous feature of the landscape over
a considerable portion of the central regions of the island.
There are five or six principal peaks, and these are in two
ranges, lying in the form of a cross. They vary from 8000
to 9000 feet in height, the most lofty one, a peak called
Tsiàfajàvona ("that which the mists cannot climb"), being
8950 feet above the sea-level, and so is the highest point
in the whole country.

* According to a French engineer's estimate, it considerably exceeds the
above-given altitude, being—so he says—2700 metres high.

Another interesting physical feature of Madagascar, which has only been made clear very recently, is the existence of an almost continuous belt of virgin forest all round the island, and generally following the coast-line. This forest divides into two belts on the eastern side of the country, leaving a long narrow valley about 250 miles long between the two lines. The uppermost of these clothes the slopes which form the edge of the upper plateau of the island. North of this valley the two lines unite, and here is the widest portion of the forest, it being about forty miles across. The average breadth is from fifteen to twenty miles. On the north-west side the two lines overlap each other nearly 100 miles, leaving an opening about seventy miles wide. The total length of this forest must be about 2300 miles, and much of this is yet unexplored, so that there is doubtless still much of interest in botanical science awaiting research. Besides the forest belt, a good deal of the country to the west and south is well wooded.

A third fact of interest in the physical geography of Madagascar is the extensive evidence of recent volcanic action throughout a great part of the country. It has been known for several years that there were signs of this on the northwest coast, and that in the island of Nòsibé and the adjacent mainland there are numerous extinct craters and much igneous rock. A few years ago the Rev. T. Campbell, of the Church Missionary Society, pointed out evident traces of volcanic agency in the district near the Ankàratra hills. He says : " It seemed as if the whole place were once a great smeltery, from the enormous number of clinkers lying about. There were altogether five mountains, all near to each other, which have been active volcanoes at some remote period ; each has one of its sides melted down, and the inside hollowed out. The flow of lava looks as if it had been some immense reservoir bursting its banks, and the water dashing and foaming through, bearing everything away with it, or covering the plain beneath."

In a journey I took to the lake Itàsy in 1866, I was struck with the number of truncated cones in the hills surrounding the lake. But extensive journeys made more recently in various directions have revealed the existence of a very widespread and powerful subterranean action throughout a great part of the island, probably extending almost unbroken from the south-east to the north-west and extreme north. There seems reason to believe that this volcanic belt is part of a line which has its eastern extremity in the island of Réunion, where there is a volcano still showing occasional signs of activity; while the other (north-western) extremity passes through the Comoro group (the islands of which consist of grand masses of lofty volcanic mountains), and terminates in the island of Great Comoro, where also, as in Réunion, is a still active volcano. It would seem as if the subterranean forces had expended their energy in the intermediate space, for there is no active volcano in Madagascar, while at each end of the line their presence is still occasionally felt. There are, however, signs of not altogether extinct forces in the slight earthquake-shocks which are felt almost every year, and in the hot springs of various kinds which occur in many parts of the country.

A large number of extinct volcanoes are found west of Lake Itàsy. These are thus described by Dr. Mullens: "When we ascended the lofty hill overhanging the western end of the lake, crater after crater met our astonished gaze. Some were of enormous size, some were small; some were cones, others were hollow, or were horseshoe in shape, and had long ridges of lava running out from the open side. There were forty craters in all, of which we were sure; we think there were others beyond to the north." "Fifty miles farther south we came on the volcanoes again. We climbed a lofty rounded hill called Ivòko, and then found that we were on the crater wall. The inner hollow was a quarter of a mile wide, the height of the wall above the level country outside was 1000 feet. Two lava streams went out towards the south and west; three small craters were at the foot, and others, large and conspicuous, were around us on every side. Close by, another huge crater, Iatsìfitra, had its opening towards the north, and the lava that had issued from it was fresh, black, and sharp, as if broken yesterday. But stranger still, at its eastern side was a plain a mile square, covered with heaps of lava like stone cottages, fortresses, ruined palaces. I counted thirty greater piles and noted numberless smaller ones; it was clear that at one time the entire plain had been on fire, that a hundred jets of fire and flame and molten lava had spouted from its surface. The heaps were now old and moss-grown, but we were informed of a vague tradition among the people that their ancestors had seen these flames bursting forth. Altogether, in that important journey, we saw and counted a hundred extinct craters, extending over an arc of ninety miles, not reckoning the central mass of Ankàratra, round one side of which that arc bends."[*]

In a journey to the south-east of Madagascar I discovered traces of volcanic action in many places, in some parts shown in the deposits of rolled pebbles of lava, and in others in the streams of lava rock running into the sea and forming reefs which are being gradually broken up by the surf. And in the very opposite part of the island, on the extreme northwest coast, opposite the Minnow group of islets, Bishop Kestell-Cornish observes: "This coast is the most distinctly volcanic that I have seen in Madagascar; at one point the lava must have run down to be quenched in the sea, and it looked as if this had taken place only last year." [†]

In the Antsihànaka province also the same plutonic agency is distinctly visible. A great part of this region consists of an immense marshy plain, about thirty-five miles long by fifteen wide, with the lake Alaòtra at its north-east corner and surrounded by hills; and it has evidently been the seat of some powerful subterranean force by which this depression was caused. This is clear from the fact that the lines of hills which are seen on both sides of the Antsihànaka plain do not run in the same direction as the main valley or depression of the country, but cut it at an angle of about 45°; so that while the general direction of the valley is N.N.E. and S.S.W., the lines of hills on either side have a bearing of N.N.W. and S.S.E. Many of the ridges seem to be broken off more or less abruptly by the level ground for several miles, and then are continued on the other side of the plain. It was impossible to avoid the conclusion that by some great convulsion

[*] *Proc. Roy. Geog. Soc.*, January 25, 1875.
[†] *Antanànarìvo Annual*, No. iii. p. 22.

a vast rent and depression had been made across the lines of hills in a diagonal direction; while the water-worn and wasted remains of some few of these towards the south, forming a line of low detached hills, suggested that probably the action of water, either as an arm of the sea or a great river, had completed what was commenced by more violent agencies. The evidence of former volcanic action in the presence of extinct craters and lava streams to the west, north, and north-east of the plain, gives considerable support to this supposition.

About a hundred miles north of the Antsihånaka province there seem to be further traces of volcanic action. The Rev. J. A. Houlder thus describes a remarkable valley called Måndritsåra, which, until he saw it in 1876, was unknown to Europeans even by name, and not marked upon any map: " It is a great basin, or rather a mighty elongated pit, sunk deep down among the surrounding heights. It is about thirty miles long, and nearly 2000 feet below the level of the country east and west of it. Dante would have imagined it, not a 'circle' certainly, but a remnant of some region of the horrible pit itself, which for a wise and gracious purpose had been gently touched by the cooling breath of heaven. There had evidently been a great commotion going on there in the ages gone by, for all the long valley was dotted with rounded hills, giving it the look of boiling water or bubbling pitch, which by some strange process had suddenly become congealed."

It will therefore be seen that igneous agency has been a powerful factor in shaping the physical geography of many portions of Madagascar, and that in few places could that agency have been present on a grander scale than in the great volcanic region of which Madagascar is the centre, and the Comoro and Mascarene groups the extreme points in either direction.

An attempt has been made in the accompanying sketch-map to show the prominent features in the physical geography of the island already noted. Probably closer examination would show that the detached groups of extinct craters are all connected by intermediate links, so as to form a continuous

line of igneous disturbance from the extreme northern point
of Madagascar to at least as far south as the twenty-third
parallel; and from the appearance of a line of hills seen at a
distance south of this latitude, I am strongly inclined to
believe that there has been subterranean agency at work even
beyond the upper granitic plateaux, but no examination has yet
been made of this southernmost region.

With regard to the geology of Madagascar, but little is at
present known with any exactness, for no competent geolo-
gist has yet made a systematic examination of the country.
There are, however, a few facts of a general character which
have been noted by various observers, and these may be here
collected together as a slight contribution to a knowledge of
this subject, pending a more complete and scientific treatment
of it.

As already mentioned, the elevated region which forms so
large a part of the central, northern, and eastern portions of
the island is largely composed of Primary and igneous rocks.
Granite, gneiss, and basalt are present almost all through
this high region, and generally form the loftiest points in the
country. In a single hill there is often a considerable variety
of rock both in colour and texture—granite of various shades
of grey, red, and rose-colour, with the constituent parts both
fine and coarse. Veins of quartz, running both through these
and the clays by which they are overlaid, are often met with,
and very fine specimens of rock-crystal are frequently found.
A hard, whitish, and durable stone, which has some resemblance to the Yorkshire stone called Bramley Fall, is used
in Antanànarìvo for public buildings, as well as for the
native tombs.

The lower hills, as well as the high moors, are usually composed of a bright red clay, but below the surface this often
seems to pass into a light pink or white earth, resembling
kaolin or china clay. This frequent change of colour would
lead one to infer that atmospheric influences had something
to do with the difference between the surface clay and that
exposed in the numerous precipitous clefts which the rains
excavate on the hillsides. In many places the material
found amongst the rock seems exactly like granite in its con-

Antananarivo is roofed with this native slate. According to some accounts, greywacke or whinstone, silex, and chert, with chalcedony, are also met with in the southern highlands.

From certain of the facts above given, as well as from other considerations, it appears highly probable that this extensive elevated region of Madagascar is very ancient land, and has probably remained for many ages above the waters of the Indian Ocean; otherwise some trace of marine deposits would surely be found in portions of this great extent of country. I may, however, here note the fact that there are in some places such rounded boulder-like masses of blue basalt rock, sometimes on the surface, and sometimes partially embedded in the soil, that did these occur in the temperate region one would certainly ascribe them to glacial action; but the point requires fuller investigation, and possibly some other solution may be given to the rather puzzling inquiry suggested. But in travelling to the north-west coast, as we got near the sea-level on the banks of the Bétsibòka, we met with rounded boulders composed of rock which certainly does not exist *in situ* anywhere near the spot where these boulders occur, but has come from far away in the interior.

With regard to the lower region of Madagascar—the extensive plains to the west and south of the island, as well as the narrower extent of country on the east coast—we have a little more definite information as to the geology of some portions of it. This division of the country is at a much less elevation above the sea, being only as many *hundreds* of feet above it as the granitic region is *thousands* of feet. Here we find not only deposits of the later Tertiary epochs, containing fossils of animals but recently extinct, but also fossils of the Secondary age. This fact was first pointed out by M. Grandidier, who, in speaking of the south and west portions of the country, says: "*Nerinea* and other characteristic fossils of the Jurassic formation which I have there collected prove the existence of Secondary strata which cover a vast extent of this island" (*Bull. de la Soc. de Géog.,* Août 1871, p. 88). In a later number of the same publication (Avril 1872) he also speaks of an extensive "terrain nummulitique parfaitement charactérisé par des *Neritina schmideliana,* et pétri de foraminifères appartenant aux genres *Alveolina, Orbitoïdes, Triloculina,*" &c. This is confirmed by the fossils discovered in the south-west of Madagascar, in the upper part of the valley of the St. Augustine River, by the Rev. J. Richardson in 1877. These occur in vast numbers, and from a drawing he gives of them appear to belong to the Neocomian formation, and are species of the genera *Ammonites, Terebratula, Nerinea* or *Turritella, Einoceramus,* and *Rhynconella,* together with an *Echinoderm.*

It is evident, also, that there are deposits of a much later date than the above, for in the south-west of Madagascar M. Grandidier discovered the fossil remains of a hippopotamus (a pachyderm not now found living in the island), of gigantic tortoises (which are now only found in the little island of Aldebra to the north of Madagascar), and of the probably very recently-extinct struthious bird, the *Æpyornis maximus,* whose egg ($12\frac{1}{4}$ in. × $9\frac{1}{4}$ in.) so far exceeds that of any other known bird. It seems highly probable, therefore, that a systematic examination of these less elevated portions of Madagascar would reveal the existence of much that is interesting and valuable both in palæontology and geology, and so light would be thrown upon many problems connected with the anomalous animal life of the country and of neighbouring islands in the Indian Ocean. It is evident that these maritime plains were under water during portions at least of the Secondary period, at which epoch the high granitic region alone formed the island of Madagascar, then a country probably only a third of its present extent.[*]

Dr. Auguste Vinson speaks of seeing yellow sandstone on the eastern coast, and he also describes the plain between the two eastern lines of forest as being composed of beds of sedimentary formations, " rich in fossil remains." Unfortunately he gives no particulars as to these alleged extinct organisms, so we are still in the dark as to the geological age of these formations. In sailing down the river Bétsibòka to the north-west coast, I noticed at one point that for a considerable distance the river bank was formed by layers of yellowish sandstone closely resembling a wall of masonry. Some of the courses appeared much weathered, while others had a smooth face, as if of much harder material.

[*] This is confirmed by what is said in a "Notice sur une Exploration Géologique de Madagascar, par M. Ed. Guillemin," in *Annales des Mines,* 6me série, t. x., 1806, pp. 277-319, who speaks of fragments of basalt being found far from the sea, at the foot of the mountains and many metres above the sea-level, with sea-shells, apparently of a recent date, attached.

From the account given by an intelligent native of some rocks in the western part of Madagascar, and a little to the south of the centre, a conglomerate seems to be found there, for he describes hard rocks of great size as being filled as thickly as possible with rolled pebbles of all dimensions and shapes. He also mentions that near the sea he found a hard black stone which rang like iron when struck. This occurred in large, flat masses, scattered over the plain, and was full of shells in good preservation. But here, again, no specimens were brought for examination.

A little more information as to the geology of Madagascar is found in papers contributed to scientific periodicals in England and France several years ago. The earliest of these is by the late Dr. Buckland, who, in a "Notice on the Geological Structure of a Part of the Island of Madagascar" * (Port Louquez, near the northern extremity), describes a sandstone without fossils, which he compares to the New Red Sandstone, and in which are intercalated trap rocks similar to those of Antrim in Ireland.

As to the north-west side of Madagascar, in the *Annales des Mines* (1854, 5me série, t. vi. pp. 570–576) there is an account of the discovery of beds of lignite, both in the island of Nòsibé and at two points on the neighbouring coast. In the opinion of the officers who made the exploration, the beds of this combustible are more ancient than the Tertiary formation. It is contained in layers of sandstone and clay schists, is fibrous and shining, and burns readily with a long and white flame, leaving little ash. If beds of this lignite should be discovered in greater thickness, it would therefore be valuable both as steam coal and for use in the industrial arts.

In the same French publication of a little later date (5me série, t. viii., 1856) there is an "Essai sur la Géologie de Nòsibé," in which the soil of that island is described as consisting of three different groups of strata: (1) Granitic rock, gneiss, mica schist, slaty schist, and plastic clay; (2) red and yellow sandstones, traversed by veins of gneiss and quartz; while (3) is essentially volcanic, consisting of basaltic and trap lavas, overlaid in some places by beds of sandy material,

* *Trans. Geol. Soc.*, London, vol. v. p. 478.

tuffs, and volcanic *rappilis.* This essay is accompanied by a complete geological map of Nòsibé.

Since the date of this last paper some further attention has been paid to this part of the country, in connection with the French company promoted by M. Lambert (see *Annales des Mines*, 6me série, t. x. pp. 277–319), but hardly anything more has been done towards a scientific examination of other portions of Madagascar, except a notice of the peninsula enclosing Antongil Bay on the north-east coast (*Bull. de la Soc. de Géog.*, Sept. et Oct. 1867), although probably M. Grandidier will have some fuller information in his great work now in progress.

It may be here observed that a (barrier?) reef of coral extends from 200 to 300 miles along the south-east coast of Madagascar, varying in its distance from the land from a quarter of a mile to three or four miles; while fringing reefs surround the northern end of the island, extending for 250 miles along its western side, and for 400 miles down its eastern side, and are also found on the south-west coast. Mr. Darwin gives in his work on "The Structure and Distribution of Coral Reefs" (pp. 104, 105) some facts showing the wonderfully rapid growth of various species of coral on the east coast of Madagascar. The northern extremity of the country is said by Captain Owen to be formed of madreporitic rock.

With regard to minerals, Madagascar is tolerably rich in some of the most useful metals. Iron is found in great abundance in Imérina, sometimes almost in a pure state. In some of the hills it is so plentiful that it is difficult to get a bearing with a compass from the deflection caused by the iron in the ground. Copper and silver have also been discovered, and from the geological structure of the country it is highly probable that gold would also be found in some of the ravines of the granitic highlands; but as it is at present a serious offence against the native laws to search for the precious metals, hardly anything has been done in this direction. Rock-salt is found near the coast, and nitre is also met with. Iron pyrites, from which sulphur is extracted, is also found in abundance; and in the northern part of the island antimony seems to be plentiful; and oxide of manganese has been found about fifty miles south of the capital. A substance resembling plumbago exists in great abundance, and is used by the Malagasy to colour and glaze some of the articles of pottery. A considerable variety of ochres and coloured earths are met with, and are used not only for colouring the native houses, but also in dyeing some of the woven cloths made by the people.

In conclusion, it may be remarked that there is a vast extent of country on the coast plains where the soil is most fertile, but which is only thinly peopled, or has no population at all. Many parts of the island which separate the territory of one tribe from another are well watered and wooded, and seem to invite occupation. Madagascar could well sustain a population from ten to twenty times its present amount, for hardly any portion of it is rainless or desert, except a small section of the extreme south-western coast. Surrounded by the ocean, it enjoys an abundant rainfall, so that the droughts which constantly afflict large portions of Southern Africa never occur in Madagascar, while its insular position gives it a more equable climate, freer from extremes of temperature, than is enjoyed in most tropical countries.

CHAPTER III.

THE ANIMAL LIFE OF MADAGASCAR.

PECULIAR AND SPECIALISED CHARACTER OF THE FAUNA—ONE OF THE MOST
REMARKABLE GEOLOGICAL REGIONS—LEMURS—AYE-AYE—INSECTIVORA—
CARNIVORA— UNGULATA — FOSSIL HIPPOPOTAMUS — RODENTIA — REMOTE
AFFINITIES OF THE AVI-FAUNA— RAPTORES — WATER-BIRDS—PERCHING
BIRDS—CARDINAL-BIRD—SUN-BIRDS—ÆPYORNIS AND ITS ENORMOUS EGG—
REPTILES—SCARCITY OF VENOMOUS SERPENTS—LIZARDS—GIGANTIC TOR-
TOISES—CROCODILES—FISHES—INSECTS— BUTTERFLIES—BEETLES—WASPS
—FIREFLIES—MANTIS—ANTS— LOCUSTS—MOSQUITOES — SPIDERS — SCOR-
PIONS AND CENTIPEDES—AN ARMOUR-PLATED CREATURE—MINUTE AND
AQUATIC FAUNA—ORIGIN AND MEANING OF THE SPECIALISED FAUNA OF
MADAGASCAR—OPINIONS OF EMINENT NATURALISTS.

As already pointed out in the preceding chapter, a large
extent of country in Madagascar is covered with forest, a
broad belt of which surrounds the island in an almost unbroken line; while there is in addition to this a considerable
tract of country, less densely wooded, occupying much of the
western and southern plains. Here, then, there appears to
be a congenial habitat for a vast number of living creatures
—birds, reptiles, and arboreal mammals—in the thousands
of square miles of woods, which cover not only a great
portion of the warmer coast region, but also the slopes of the
elevated interior plateaux.

From these physical conditions of the country, it might
therefore be supposed that Madagascar, situated as it is almost
entirely within the tropics, would be profusely filled with
animal life. But it is not so, at least not nearly to such an
extent as one would expect; and a stranger crossing the
forest for the first time is always struck with the general
stillness of the woods and the apparent scarcity of birds
seen on the route. The fauna of the country does, it is true,
contain some most interesting and exceptional forms of life,

but it is almost as remarkable for what is omitted in it as for what it contains. Not only so, but from the position of the island with regard to Africa—being separated from it by a sea only 230 miles wide at its narrowest part, a distance further reduced by a bank of soundings to only 160 miles—one would also suppose that the fauna of the island would largely resemble that of the continent. But it is remarkably different: whole families of the larger mammalia are entirely absent; there are no representatives of the larger felines, no lions, leopards, or hyænas; and none of the ungulate order, except a single species of river-hog, sole relative of the hippopotamus, rhinoceros, and buffalo; and there is no zebra, quagga, or giraffe, or any of the numerous families of ante-lope which scour the African plains. There is no elephant browsing in the wooded regions of Madagascar, and, stranger still, there are no apes or monkeys living in its trees. The few horses and asses found in the island are of recent intro-duction by Europeans; even the humped cattle, which exist in immense herds, are probably not indigenous, but have been brought at a somewhat remote period from Africa; and the hairy fat-tailed sheep and the few goats found in Madagas-car are also of foreign introduction.

But for all that, the sub-region speaking zoologically—of which Madagascar is the largest and most important por-tion—is pronounced by every zoologist who has studied it to be one of the most remarkable districts on the globe, bearing, says Mr. Alfred Wallace, "a similar relation to Africa as the Antilles to tropical America, or New Zealand to Australia, but possessing a much richer fauna than either of these, and in some respects a more remarkable one even than New Zealand." The Madagascar fauna is very deficient in the number of the orders and families of mammalia, but some of these, especially the Lemuridæ among the Primates, the Viverridæ among the Carnivora, and the Centetidæ among the Insectivora, are well represented in genera and species.

I will notice the mammalia in the order now generally followed by zoologists in classifying this great division of the vertebrate animals; premising, however, that in the following pages no pretension is made to exact or minute scientific knowledge or research. I have, however, taken a great interest in what has been done by others in investigating the fauna of Madagascar. I have kept my eyes open during long journeys made in different parts of the country; and I have been at some pains to study the papers contributed by naturalists to our scientific journals upon the fauna of the country. While, therefore, of little value to the scientific student, the following *resumé* of what is known as to the animal life of Madagascar may not be without interest to the general reader.

Lemuridæ.—The Primates are represented in Madagascar only by a portion of the eight families into which this order of mammals is divided; the anthropoid and other apes, the baboons and the numerous families of monkeys, being altogether absent. But their place is taken by a much more attractive and beautiful division of quadrumana, the Lemuridæ, which are found in great variety of form and colour all through the encircling ring of forest. In travelling from the coast to the elevated plateaux of the interior, one is sure to frequently hear their loud wailing cries, which sometimes make the woods resound for some minutes together, and have a most startling effect when heard for the first time. For a moment one supposes that there is a company of people not far distant in deep distress; but after discovering the source of the sounds, I always found a curious pleasure in listening to the long-drawn-out melancholy cries, which are doubtless rather signs of the little creatures' enjoyment of their forest life than any expression of pain or fear. The lemurs have all the agility of monkeys, but with none of their comic half-human expression, the head being more like that of a dog or a fox, with sharp muzzle and large expressive eyes; the fur is thick and soft, and the tail often long and bushy. There is a good deal of variety in size and colour among the lemurs and the allied genera, the largest species (*Indris*) being equal to a good-sized monkey, from three to four feet long, while the smallest (*Lepilemur*) is no larger than a rat or a small squirrel. One species, found abundantly in a spur of forest crossing the centre of the island, is entirely of a glossy black; others are of various shades of brown and of warm dark red; others are a silvery white; one species has a curious development of hair round the face, giving it the apppearance of having a pair of very bushy white whiskers; while another has a thick bushy tail banded with black and white, which, when the creature is in repose, is usually coiled, like a comforter, round its neck. Lemurs are gentle and affectionate animals and easily tamed, and are frequently kept as pets in Madagascar, being secured by a long cord to a post of the verandah. Their agility is marvellous, for they leap to considerable distances from branch to branch; so that a wood frequented by a company of them is all alive with their rapid movements, and resounds with their cries as they dart from tree to tree..

The true lemurs are mostly fruit-eaters, but they are said occasionally to feed also on the smaller animals found in the woods: lizards, small birds, and insects. Most of them are diurnal in their habits, but there are some species which are chiefly nocturnal.

One species, at least, of lemur, the Ring-tailed variety (*L. catta*), does not live in the forests, but among the rocks, where it is impossible to follow them. Mr. G. A. Shaw describes their hands as having long, smooth, level, and leather-like palms, so that the animal can find a firm footing on wet slippery rocks; while the thumbs on the hinder hands are very much smaller in proportion than those of the forest lemurs, who depend upon their grasping power for their means of progression. These lemurs are, therefore, an exception to the general habits of the Lemuridæ in that they are not arboreal. Their chief winter food consists of the fruit of the prickly-pear; and they are said not to drink water. They defend themselves with great spirit if attacked. Another species, the Broad-nosed lemur (*Hapalemur simus*), is said to subsist on the young shoots of the bamboo and upon grass. One of the smallest species, the Brown-mouse lemur (*Chirogaleus milii*), hibernates, making for itself a nest of leaves or dry grass in hollow trees for its winter sleep. It is an exceedingly pretty animal, brown in colour, but white below, with large and brilliant eyes, and legs nearly equal in length, so that it does not leap, like the majority of the lemurs. The most diminutive of all these active little animals is the Dwarf lemur (*Microcebus Smithii*); this lives on the tops of the highest trees, making a nest very much like that of a bird. Its food consists of fruit and insects, and probably also honey. It is exceedingly pugnacious. For these particulars I am indebted to Mr. Shaw's "Notes on Four Species of Lemurs, specimens of which were brought alive to England in 1878." (*Proc. Zool. Soc.*, February 4, 1879.)

Madagascar may be called the head-quarters of the Lemuridæ; and of the four sub-families into which the family is divided (embracing the true lemurs, the typical animals of Professor St. George Mivart's sub-order Lemuroidæa), two —by far the largest—belong exclusively to the island, and contain six genera and thirty-four species; but there are two other sub-families of allied forms which are found in other countries. One of these (Nycticebidæ) comprises some small short-tailed animals, called slow lemurs, found in India and China, Borneo and Java; another similar animal, the loris, inhabits South-East India and Ceylon; another, the potto, is found in West Africa, at Sierra Leone; and another, the angwantibo, is also found in West Africa, at Old Calabar. The meaning of the extraordinary fact that animals so nearly allied to the lemur are found in such remote regions both east and west of Madagascar, we shall discuss further on in connection with the other strange anomalies in geographical distribution, which are shown both by the relations of other mammals found in the island, and also by many of the birds, reptiles, and insects. There is a fourth sub-family of Lemuridæ, the galagos, not however so nearly allied to the true lemurs as those just mentioned, which is found all over the central portions of the African continent, from Senegal and Fernando Po to Zanzibar and Natal.

M. Grandidier has pointed out with regard to several genera of the lemurs, that they have embryological features which render them very distinct from the other quadrumana, the placenta being altogether different from the discoid form common to other members of the order. This fact, together with a number of other anatomical differences, induces him to think that they require to be placed in a

AYE-AYE (*Cheiromys Madagascariensis*).

distinct order from the rest of the quadrumanous animals.
M. Grandidier also thinks that the number of species of
lemur is much less than has been supposed, many specimens
formerly reckoned as distinct species being only local varieties
(*Bull. Soc. Géog.*, Avril 1872, p. 373).

But there is another quadrumanous animal allied to the
Lemurs, and classed as one of the three families in Professor
Mivart's sub-order Lemuroidæa, which is one of the most
remarkable forms of mammalia to be found in any part of
the world. This is the Aye-aye, or *Cheiromys Madagascariensis.* This animal is the sole representative of the
family with which it is classed, and is peculiar to Madagascar. From the few specimens available for examination,
it is only lately that it has been thoroughly known to
naturalists. It was at first supposed to belong to the
Rodentia, with which it was classed both by Cuvier and
Buffon, but it is now determined to be "an exceedingly
specialised form of the lemuroid type." Its organisation
presents perhaps one of the most interesting examples of
typical forms modified to serve special ends that animal
structure can furnish us with. Its food consists of a wood-
boring larva, which tunnels beneath the bark of certain
hard-wooded trees. To obtain these, the animal is furnished
with most powerful chisel-shaped teeth, with which it cuts
away the outer bark. As, however, the caterpillar retreats to
the end of its hole, one of the fingers of the Aye-aye's fore-
hands is slightly lengthened, but considerably diminished in
thickness, and is furnished with a hook-like claw. Thus
provided, the finger is used as a probe, inserted in the tunnel,
and the dainty morsel drawn from its hiding-place. There
are also other modifications, all tending to the more perfect
accomplishment of the purposes it fulfils in nature; the eyes
being very large to see by night; the ears expanded widely,
and of most delicate membrane, to catch the faint sound of
the caterpillar at work; and the thumbs of the hinder feet, or
rather hands, being largely developed to enable the animal to
take a firm hold of the tree when at work. It has also been
observed that this claw-like middle finger is used as a scoop
when the creature drinks; being bent so as to separate it

from the other fingers, it is carried so rapidly from the water to the mouth, passing sideways through the lips, that the liquid seems to pass in a continual stream. The natives of Madagascar have a superstitious dread of the animal, believing that the person who kills an Aye-aye will certainly die within a year. This fear, added to the nocturnal habits of the creature, has made it difficult to obtain specimens.

The Bats may be dismissed in a word or two. The six known species all belong to families which are widely extended over the world; and they have no special peculiarity of appearance or habit which marks them from the familiar forms found in every tropical country.

Insectivora.—Coming, however, to the next order of mammalia, the Insectivora, we find them represented in Madagascar by two families, one of which, the shrews, is well known and widely spread, and contains but a single species; but the other family, that of the Centetidæ, is, with the exception of one genus, peculiar to the island. It contains five genera in Madagascar, and nine species. These are all small animals, allied to our European hedgehogs, some of them having a covering of strong spines, while in others it consists rather of firm prickly hairs, which however do not cover the whole of the body. They are used as food, having very much the taste of pork, and are called *tràndraka* or tenrec. They are found in the woods, and especially in the low scattered brushwood and fern-overgrown land in the vicinity of the forests, from which the trees have been removed. During our usual yearly holiday at our sanatorium on the outskirts of the inner line of forest, we frequently met with three or four varieties of these harmless creatures while rambling in the outskirts of the woods. Our dog often chased them, but she generally came back with her mouth and nostrils stuck as full of prickles as a pincushion is of pins. Some of the species are prettily banded transversely with alternate shades of dark and light brown, or brown and yellow. One day a female tenrec was brought to us for sale, with eight or nine tiny young ones only a few days old. These were yellow and brown in colour, their hair being still soft; they were about the size of a large egg, and a most amusing family of · creatures they looked. The various genera of these Centetidæ do not roll themselves into a ball like the hedgehogs, but place the head between the fore-paws, and their spines and prickly hairs probably serve them equally well as a protection from their enemies.

Small as the insectivorous animals of Madagascar are, they are remarkable from the fact that " in no equally con-fined area are they represented by so many peculiar types as in Madagascar." But it is still more remarkable that the only other known genus of Centetidæ is found in the West India Islands. The animal representing this genus, the Solenodon, is more slender in form than the Madagascar Centetidæ, and more active in its habits. It has a long rat-like tail, and a tapering snout, like that of a shrew. One species is found in Cuba, and the other in Hayti, and they are among the very few mammals which are known to be indigenous to the West India Islands. "Although," says Mr. Wallace, " presenting many points of difference in detail, the essential characters of this curious animal are, according to Professors Peters and Mivart, identical with the rest of the Centetidæ. We have thus a most remarkable and well-established case of discontinuous distribution, two portions of the same family being now separated from each other by an extensive continent, as well as by a deep ocean." *

Carnivora.—The carnivorous animals of Madagascar are small compared with those of Africa. They belong chiefly to the Viverridæ or Civets, a family now chiefly found in Africa and South-east Asia, but which, during the Miocene period, also flourished in Europe. The typical animal of this family, called by the natives *fòsa* (which is also its generic name), is a long-bodied animal, with short legs and long bushy tail, and with longitudinal stripes of dark-brown spots on a ground of light-greyish brown. It is between two and three feet long, and very destructive to birds and small quadrupeds. There are only two species of it yet known.

The true viverra has not yet been found in Madagascar, but it inhabits the Comoro Islands, which are doubtless part of the ancient land of which Madagascar is the most considerable

* Wallace, *The Geographical Distribution of Animals,* vol. ii. p. 188.

remaining portion. As will be seen from drawings, it is a handsome creature, beautifully banded with lines of spots on a light-brown ground, which shades into black on the back and the neck.

Another carnivorous animal is an ichneumon (*Eupleres goudotii*), which is a bulkier animal than the fosa, but with small head and fine muzzle; it is about two feet long, and has long claws. The smaller species of carnivora (of two genera, *galidia* and *galidictis*) are called *vontsira*, and somewhat resemble the weasels and ferrets of Europe, but they are not so long and slender in body. They are also much less ferocious, and are not exclusively flesh-feeders. They are all striped longitudinally with shades of grey and brown.

The only other family in this order consists of a single genus and species named *Cryptoprocta* (*ferox*). It is a plantigrade animal, and is the largest of the Madagascar carnivora being about three feet long, with tail of equal, or slightly greater, length. It is like a small leopard in shape, but with thick warm-brown fur of a uniform colour. It is "peculiar to Madagascar, and was formerly classed among the Viverridæ, but is now considered by Professor Flower to constitute a distinct family between the cats and the civets." * A very fine specimen of this animal may be seen in the British Museum, as well as examples of most of the other carnivora. It appears to be chiefly found in the western portion of the island, where it is known under the names of *pintsàla* or *kintsàla*. It is greatly dreaded by the people for its ferocity and destructiveness; and, from its mode of attack, appears to be like an immense weasel, but preying upon the largest animals, wild hogs, and even buffaloes.

A wild cat is very plentiful in many parts of the island. This is a handsomely striped animal, and very destructive to domestic fowls; but, in the opinion of most naturalists, it is not to be included in the indigenous fauna of Madagascar. I am, however, inclined to think that this is a mistake.

Ungulata.—As already remarked, the very large and important order of hoofed animals is all but entirely absent from Madagascar. There is, however, a single species of

* Wallace, *op. cit.*, vol. ii. p. 194.

potamochœrus or river-hog, closely allied to an African species. It is described by a French writer as an ugly animal, with high withers, low back, and little hair. It has an enormous tubercle, supported by a bony prominence in the jaw, which renders the face of the animal extremely disagreeable. The specimen in the British Museum hardly bears out this not very flattering portrait; but I fancy it is a young one, in which the adult ugliness above described has not been developed. I have never seen this hog in Madagascar, but have frequently met with its tracks in the forest, where it digs up the ground in search of roots, and often does much damage to plantations situated near the woods. The presence in Madagascar of this single peculiar species of river-hog, with so near a relative in Africa, may, in the opinion of Mr. Wallace, " be perhaps explained by the unusual swimming powers of swine, and the semi-aquatic habits of this genus leading to an immigration at a later period than in the case of the other mammalia." *

But although the larger pachydermata are now absent from Madagascar, it is an interesting fact that they have not all of them been so in former times; for M. Grandidier has discovered the bones of a small species of hippopotamus (*H. lemerlii*) in the south-west provinces in a sub-fossil state, indicating that this quadruped was an inhabitant of the island at a not very remote period. A large proportion of the maritime plains of Madagascar has extensive reaches of river and lagoon, which would seem to be just the sort of country best suited to the habits of the hippopotamus; so that it is difficult to account for the fact of its having become extinct. But this is only one of those numerous yet unsolved problems with which the subject of the geographical distribution of animals abounds.

Rodentia.—The only remaining order of mammalia found in Madagascar is that of the Rodentia, represented by three genera, each with a single species of *Muridœ*, about which there is nothing of special interest to remark. Although poor in genera and species, however, this family is very rich indeed in individuals; for the whole inhabited parts of the

* Wallace, *op. cit.,* vol. i. p. 273.

country swarm with rats and mice; and every traveller has
stories to relate of his adventures with these creatures. "A
night with the rats" is one of the never-failing Madagascar
"traveller's tales."

Birds.—We now turn to the birds, in which the island is
much richer than in mammals, although here, again, there
are none of the largest forms, and many of the most brilliantly
coloured and striking tropical genera are absent. There is
no living representative of the Struthidæ, either ostrich, cassowary, or emu; neither are there any of the trogons, golden-
pheasants, or birds-of-paradise of the Eastern hemisphere, or
the toucans or humming-birds of the Western. But there is
a large variety of the order Passeres, or perching birds, and
many of these, although of moderate size, are beautifully
coloured; and many of them, in common with birds of other
orders—the Raptores, the Waders, and the Gallinæ—are of
remarkable forms. No fewer than 88 genera and 111 species
of land-birds are already known, and the number is being
added to every year. But "the number of peculiar genera
in Madagascar constitutes one of the main features of its
ornithology, and many of these are so isolated that it is very
difficult to classify them, and they remain to this day a puzzle
to ornithologists." * Of the 111 known species, 50 belong
to 33 genera which are peculiar to the island, and 56 to
peculiar species, the genera of which are found also in Africa
and South-eastern Asia; and thus, says Mr. Wallace, "there
is an amount of specialty hardly to be found in the birds of
any other part of the globe. Out of 111 land-birds in
Madagascar, only 12 are identical with species inhabiting the
adjacent continents, and most of these belong to powerful-
winged or wide-ranging forms." What is most astonishing
is that many of the birds are much more nearly allied to
South Asian or Malayan forms than to those of Africa, while
many are of such doubtful affinities that it is yet quite unde-
cided what family they belong to, several requiring a distinct
family to be formed for their reception; and the nearest
affinities of others are found in South America, and even in
the Pacific Islands. So many perfectly isolated forms are

* Wallace, *op. cit.*, vol. i. p. 274.

certainly nowhere else to be found.   The explanation of this may be deferred for a little to consider it on the widest available data.

Raptores.—The rapacious birds are well represented in Madagascar by a number of species of hawks, kites, and falcons, but there is only one known eagle (*Halietes vociferoides*), while the owls are also numerous.   These latter are considered by the Malagasy as birds of evil omen, and are consequently persecuted by the natives.   On the other hand, one of the hawks (the *vòromahéry, i.e.*, "strong bird") has been adopted as a sort of crest or national emblem by the Hova Government.   It gives a name to the tribe inhabiting the capital and its neighbourhood, and an immense figure of the bird crowns the lofty high-pitched roof of the two chief royal palaces in Antanànarìvo.   In the neighbourhood of the ancient capital of Imérina I have occasionally seen flocks of several hundred hawks hovering in the air at an immense height, and have wondered how such numbers could obtain food.

In the same place the crows are equally numerous and almost as bold.   The Madagascar crow is not quite so much like an undertaker in appearance as is his English relative. He is as large as a raven, and has a more clerical air about him, having a white tie or collar round his neck, and a white breast that may easily be imagined to be a very large pair of bands.   He is probably nearly related to *Corvus capella*, the " chaplain crow."

Water-Birds.—Many parts of Madagascar are exceedingly attractive to sportsmen from the variety of species and great numbers of the water-birds—wild ducks, divers, teal, muscovy ducks, waterhens, sandpipers, herons, storks, and ibis—found in the marshes, lakes, and rivers.   One of the finest countries that a sportsman could desire is the province of Antsihànaka, which is situated at the northern termination of the long narrow valley between the two eastern lines of forest.   It consists of an almost perfectly flat plain, about thirty-five miles long by fifteen broad, the greater part of which is marsh, and at the north-east corner deepens into an extensive lake. As the villages are few, and are mostly situated at the foot of the rising grounds surrounding these marshes, it may be easily supposed that the whole district is a favourite resort of waterfowl.   During a tour of a fortnight round this marshy country, in 1874, I was greatly struck with the abundance and variety of bird-life found there.   One day especially, on a wet and drizzly morning, long lines of wild ducks and other waterfowl flew over our heads and seemed to fill the air, while the marshes and shallow expanses of water swarmed with divers, teal, and black geese.   Very similar in its abundance of bird-life is the lake of Itàsy, some forty miles to the west of the capital, upon which I once spent a long day in a canoe shooting waterfowl, herons, and divers. And from what I have seen in other parts of the island, especially on the banks of the principal rivers on the eastern coast of Madagascar, as well as from accounts given by other travellers in the northern part, the whole island seems to abound in this class of birds.   A pretty little diving duck (*Nettopus auritus*), a large brown duck with exquisite blending of brown, fawn, and slate-coloured plumage, and a duck-like widgeon with a rose-coloured beak, afford good sport.   The purple or Sultana waterhen is a very beautiful bird, with its bluish-purple body, red patch on the head, and coral feet adorned with a tuft of white feathers.   A species of Jacana, a bird of the waterhen family, is found in Madagascar. Mounted on long legs, it has also very long feet, with which it walks upon the broad flat leaves of water-lilies and other plants in search of its food.   One of the strangest-looking birds is a grebe (*Podiceps polzelni*), in which the massive legs and immense broad-webbed feet seem curiously disproportioned to the size of the body.   Species of snipe are plentiful, but they have a different flight from the European bird: one is known as the painted snipe (*Rhynchæa capensis*) from its beautiful markings.   Guinea-fowl are tolerably abundant, and also three species of quail, one (*Margaroperdix striata*) a little smaller than the English partridge, and the smallest no bigger than a sparrow, with a flight like that of a landrail.

There are several species of heron.   "The sacred ibis of Egypt is found in large flocks, as well as the green variety of Europe.   The crested ibis is peculiar to the country; it is

a bright red, with yellow beak and claws; a green head, from
which the long plume of white and green feathers lies back."
The white egret, called by the people *vòrompòtsy*, a small bird
of pure white, with long legs, neck, and beak, is very common
on the coast and in the marshes of the interior. On the
coast large flocks may be seen following the herds of cattle
for the sake of the ticks and flies, being often perched on
the backs or necks of the oxen. When living at Ambòhimànga, we used to be interested every evening during the
cold seasons in watching the arrival of a large flock of these
birds, about four hundred in number. During the day they
were feeding in the marshes a few miles south, but at sunset
they came altogether and settled for a few minutes in a wide
open space of ground about a quarter of a mile distant in
front of our house. Having apparently rested from their
flight, the leader rose, then the whole flock, and flew steadily
round to the north-west side of the lofty hill on which
Ambòhimànga is built, where they roosted in the trees on the
lee side, sheltered from the cold south-east trade-wind. In
summer they seemed to remain day and night in their feed-
ing-grounds.

Perching Birds.—In the forests a slaty-black parrot and
also a dark-green species (*Coracopsis obscura* and *nigra*) are
often seen. The former is very intelligent and easily taught
to talk. In the more open country, in the warmer parts of
the island, flocks of small bright-green parroquets are
frequently met with. They are about the size, and not
much unlike, the love-birds so common in cages in England.
The family of the cuckoos is well represented in Madagascar;
the most conspicuous is a large bird of dark blue, with a long
tail (*Coua cærulea?*); it has a slow, heavy flight, and is
frequently seen in the woods. Another bird (*Dicrurus Wal-
deni*) is of a blackish glossy green, with extremely long tail,
bifurcated at the extremity.

Some of the smaller birds found plentifully in the open
moory hills of the interior are interesting examples of the
"survival of the fittest" by protective resemblance to the
surrounding vegetation. As there is no rain for six or seven
months during the dry season, the grass, as may be readily

supposed, becomes dull-greenish grey or brown in colour for the last three or four months. Now the smaller birds so exactly resemble the dry grass in colour that I have frequently been startled to see a bird start up from a spot only a few yards in front of me, upon which I had had my eyes fixed for some seconds and had not detected the slightest sign of a living creature. There is, however, a small bird about the size of a lark which is extremely conspicuous during the warm season from its livery of brilliant scarlet. In a grove of mango-trees close to our house at Antanànarìvo, these little cardinal-birds were very plentiful during the breeding season, darting from tree to tree like living flames, often engaged in fierce conflict with each other for the favour of the females. These latter are quite a contrast to the males, being clad in as sober a suit of brown as an English sparrow. I have occasionally seen the male birds in flocks of from thirty to forty together in the rice-fields. The male bird is in the habit of choosing the very tip of the highest branch of the trees, where he sits for a few seconds, but speedily darts off. There are several species found in Madagascar and the Mascarene Islands, some having scarlet only on the breast. The typical bird of the genus (called *fòdy* by the natives) is entirely scarlet except the wings; but the colour becomes much less brilliant after the breeding season is over. The bird belongs to the family of the Ploceidæ or weaver-finches.

There are few streams or sheets of water in Madagascar where one will not see species of a bird not quite so conspicuous as the scarlet *fòdy*, but as large and quite as beautiful—the kingfisher. The most conspicuous species in the interior is a bird with most lovely purplish-blue body and wings, with yellow breast and scarlet throat (*Alcedo vintsoides*). Its food appears to be chiefly aquatic insects, and not fish.

In some accounts of the natural history of Madagascar it is said that humming-birds have been discovered there. But this is no doubt a mistake, as the Trochilidæ are believed to be confined to the New World. There are, however, several species of Nectarinidæ, or sun-birds, as they are commonly called, but more correctly, sugar-birds; and these, although not very nearly allied to the humming-birds, are sufficiently like them in general appearance to deceive any but a practised naturalist. They have the same brilliant metallic hues, one of them being very beautiful, "with its bright-green body shaded with violet, the large feathers of the wings brown edged with green, a violet band on the breast, succeeded by one of brown and yellow beneath."

But I must not dwell longer on the avi-fauna of the island. There are numbers of beautifully-coloured birds which are shown in exquisitely tinted lithography in the work of Messrs. Pollen and Van Dam, Dutch naturalists, and in M. Grandidier's magnificent work, of which only four volumes of the promised twenty-eight are yet published. It must suffice here to say, in brief, that, in addition to the birds already noticed, the thrushes, warblers, bulbuls, orioles, cuckoo and other shrikes, fly-catchers, hoopoes, pigeons, goat-suckers, flower-peckers, weaver-finches, wagtails, rollers, bee-eaters, pittas, swallows, and swifts are all represented among the Passeres and Picariæ, inhabiting chiefly the woods; and that grouse, partridges, quails, peafowl, snipes and curlew, herons and bitterns, flamingoes, storks, and spoonbills are all among the birds inhabiting the open country, and living in the water and by the seashore.

But, as already remarked, the ornithology of Madagascar is more remarkable for the specialty of many of its forms, and for the remote affinities of several of the birds, than for the beauty or strangeness of appearance of many individual members of the avi-fauna; and it is also most curious that several families which are peculiar to Africa and well re-presented there are entirely absent from Madagascar.

The Æpyornis maximus.—Before, however, referring to the inferences which have been drawn from the anomalous fauna of Madagascar, there is one other bird which must be mentioned, not indeed one of its present inhabitants, but so recently extinct that it cannot be overlooked in considering the animal life of the country and its neighbouring islands. Of course I refer to that gigantic struthious bird the *Æpyornis*, which, if not the largest of all *birds*, certainly laid the largest of known *eggs*. It is only within the last thirty years that a few of the eggs have been discovered in the southern portions of the island. These have the capacity or contents of six or seven ostrich eggs, or of one hundred and forty-eight eggs of the common fowl. At first nothing but some fragments of bone were discovered together with the eggs, and many were the speculations of naturalists as to the size and nature of the bird laying such an egg. One learned professor supposed it to be that of a gigantic penguin; another, that of an enormous bird of prey, surpassing the condor in size, and representing the *roc* of Arabian romance, and the *rukh* of Marco Polo's description. Professor Owen, however, with M. St. Hilaire, refers the egg to a three-toed species of terrestrial or struthious bird, allied to the *Dinornis* of New Zealand, and probably somewhat less in height and size. About ten years ago, M. Grandidier discovered leg-bones and some vertebræ of the bird, from which it seems clear that the *Æpyornis* was about the height of an ostrich, but more robust and massive in the legs and feet. Since then, remains of two other and smaller species have been discovered: one the height of a cassowary, and the other that of a bustard; so that it appears probable that Madagascar was formerly tenanted by as numerous and varied a family of *rukhs* as New Zealand was of *moas*. A diagram will show more clearly than any description the size of the egg as compared with those of other well-known birds. The larger axis of the egg is $12\frac{1}{4}$ inches, the shorter $9\frac{3}{8}$ inches. Mr. Wallace says, but I do not know on what authority, that "there is reason to believe that the *Æpyornis* may have lived less than two hundred years ago;" unless indeed he considers that Marco Polo's account may be granted as founded on fact, when he writes: "The people of Madagascar report that at certain seasons of the year an extraordinary kind of bird, which they call a 'rukh,' makes its appearance *from the southern region.*" It seems quite possible that the bird was living at that time; while in the earlier ages the immense egg may easily have given rise to the Arabian stories of a bird of such gigantic size that it could carry an elephant in its talons, and had wings stretching over thirty paces, together with other equally marvellous details. Apart from its scientific interest, therefore, this enormous Eastern egg has another interest, as showing that some of the medi-æval stories, long thought to be wholly mythical, had an actual basis of fact. Colonel Yule, in his beautiful edition of Marco Polo's travels, has suggested that the enormous quill feathers of the *rukh*, said to have been brought from Madagascar, were really leaf-stalks of the traveller's-tree (see vol. ii. p. 354); but it is much more likely that they were the immensely long mid-ribs of the leaves of the *rofia* palm. These are from twenty to thirty feet long, and are not at all unlike an enormous quill stripped of the feathery portion.

It will be unnecessary to say much upon the remaining classes of vertebrata, or upon the other divisions of animal life found in Madagascar, not only because, with two or three notable exceptions, they are less remarkable than the mammals and birds, but also because several groups are yet imperfectly known and their affinities still undetermined.

Reptilia.—With regard to the Reptiles, " these present some very curious features, comparatively few of the African groups being represented, while there are a considerable number of Eastern, and even of American, forms." * In the desert-snakes, tree - snakes, and whip - snakes there are peculiar genera, and the pythons or boas are also represented by a genus peculiar to the island. But the most remarkable fact in connection with this order of reptiles, so deadly in all the great continents, is that, with two or three exceptions, the serpents of Madagascar are harmless. No venomous snake is known in the interior of the island or in the upper forests, and it is not quite certain that the larger species found in the warmer southern and western plains and on the coast generally are deadly, although some are undoubtedly venomous. In the open country and forests of the upper plateau the snakes are all small and innocuous. A pretty kind of water-snake may be often seen in the forest streams and pools, swimming over the surface with its head gracefully held up out of the water. One of my missionary brethren, the Rev.

* Wallace, *op. cit.*

J. A. Houlder, met with some examples of the larger species on a journey to the north-east coast in 1876. One of these which he shot is called *akòma*, and although about nine feet long, and as thick round the middle as the calf of a man's leg, he calls a medium-sized specimen. "On each side of its body was a long, yellow, black, and reddish chain on a brownish ground, and near the extremity of the tail were two abortive claws like the anal hooks of the boa." Some of these serpents are brilliantly green in colour, this being doubtless a protective resemblance to the surrounding vegetation. This *akòma* "is nocturnal in its habits, and appears to be more often on the ground and in the water than in the trees." Another serpent, which seems undoubtedly a species of boa, is described as living in the Sàkalàva country. "Hanging from the branches of trees, it pounces suddenly on its victim, and, enveloping it in its folds, speedily squeezes it to death. It is even said to kill oxen and occasionally man. Some of the natives say that it strikes with a spur in its tail, then sucks the blood which flows from the wound thus made."

The Lizards are no less remarkable than the snakes from their Oriental and American, and, in some cases, Australian relationships. But, as in the case of the Ophidia, the species of Lacertidæ found in the interior of Madagascar are all small; they are delicately striped and spotted, and are most rapid in their movements. Several species of beautifully-marked chameleons are found in the open country of the interior, and others, larger, and of bright-green and golden tints, in the upper forest of the eastern side of the island. In passing through the woods a day or two after a destructive cyclone in February 1876, which had prostrated thousands of great trees, we found a number of new forms of lizards, chameleons, and tree-frogs among the upper branches of those which had fallen across the paths. Had a naturalist been then in the interior, he would have found a harvest of arboreal reptiles usually inaccessible from living at a height above the ground; while a botanist would have had an unusually good opportunity of examining flowers and fruits which are generally elevated one hundred feet or more overhead, in the struggle for light and air amongst the dense vegetation of the forest. The tree-frogs are very numerous in the southern interior provinces, and with their webbed feet cling by scores to the verandahs of houses, as well as to the trees, looking like a small patch of bright-green jelly.

The other groups are of less interest. There are several species of tortoises allied to African genera; one (*Pyxis*), the geometric or box-tortoise, having the carapace divided into large hexagons beautifully marked. These may be seen basking in the sun on small spits of sand rising just above the surface of the rivers. In a very recent geological era Madagascar was also the home of at least two very large species of tortoise (*Testudo abrupta* and *Emys gigantea*), the remains of which have been found by M. Grandidier in the south of the island. These are probably extinct on the mainland of Madagascar, but they seem to have inhabited the Mascarene group of Mauritius, Bourbon, and Rodriguez up to the arrival of man in these islands. But having been recklessly destroyed, they now survive only in the small and uninhabited Aldebra islands, near the Seychelles group. There is a fine specimen of this gigantic tortoise in the British Museum, and two living examples in the Regent's Park Gardens. The male tortoise, which is much the larger of the two, is 5 feet 5 inches in length, and 5 feet 9 inches in breadth—broader, in fact, than it is long. It weighs about eight hundred pounds, and is believed to be able to carry a ton weight on its back. It is now seventy years old, but is still young, and likely to grow to a much greater size. From its geometric-shaped plates it seems to be allied to the small living geometric tortoise of Madagascar, and probably still more closely to the elephantine tortoise of the Seychelles and Comoro Islands.

The smaller amphibia are not very well known; but the crocodiles are familiar to every traveller in the island. These unpleasant-looking reptiles swarm in every river and lake, and even in many small pools. During a journey down the Bétsibòka river we saw as many as a hundred in a day, a dozen together being often seen basking in the sun on a sandbank; while other travellers have seen as many as a thousand in as short a space of time. They are mostly yellowish-green in colour, but some are slaty, and others spotted with black. The back is serrated like a coarse pit-saw, and the head seems small in proportion to the body. They are often attended by a small bird which feeds upon the crocodile's parasites, and in return is said to warn it of any danger. They are regarded with a superstitious dread by many of the Malagasy tribes, and are so dangerous in some parts of the island that at every village on the banks of the rivers a space is carefully fenced off with strong stakes, so that the women and girls can draw water without the risk of being seized by the jaws or swept off by the tail of these disgusting-looking creatures. This I saw all along the banks of the Màtitànana, one of the largest rivers of the south-east coast. Amongst the tribes dwelling on either side of this same river, there used to be, and perhaps still is, practised a kind of ordeal for those who are suspected of certain crimes, in which the crocodile has an important part to play. (See chapter on Folk-lore and Popular Superstitions.) Cattle are frequently carried off by crocodiles when a herd of them ford or swim across a river, and one of my friends told me that in the Mangòro he saw an ox suddenly disappear, and in less than half an hour he noticed an empty skin floating on the water a little lower down the stream, having been completely divested of what it covered. I was somewhat inclined to think he was drawing on *his* imagination or *my* credulity; but he assured me it was a simple statement of fact. The eggs of the crocodile are collected and sold for food in the markets, but I never brought myself to test the merits of these delicacies. They are about the size of a turkey's egg, with a very thick and rough white shell.

Fishes.—The fresh-water fish of Madagascar are not yet well known; and in the interior provinces of elevated land they are few in species, and, except of small fish, there are not many edible varieties. Large quantities of brilliantly-coloured fish, much resembling the gold and silver fish of our ornamental ponds, are, however, found in the rice-fields, and sold in the markets for food, but are only eaten by the poorer people. The eels are of large size and great thickness;

they are plentiful, and are excellent in quality. Although
fish is somewhat scarce in the waters of the interior, the
beautiful drawings in Pollen and Van Dam's work on the
Madagascar fauna show that in the north-western rivers of
the island there is a considerable variety of bright-coloured
and grotesquely-shaped fish. These are striped with wavy
bands of bright blue from the head to the tail, these bands
looking as if they were painted over the ground-colour of the
fish, which is golden-red or brown. As soon as the fresh-
water fish have been carefully collected all over the island,
they will doubtless furnish some important facts, throwing
light upon the derivation of the fauna.

Insects.—The insects of Madagascar present much that is
remarkable as regards their relationship, and a great deal that
is interesting and beautiful in the shape and colouring of the
various orders.

Many parts of the island are rich in butterflies, some of
the finest being found in the bare interior plateaux, amongst
them the magnificent diurnal moth, *Urania riphœus.* This
was frequently brought to me, and is certainly one of the
most beautiful of lepidopterous insects; its gorgeous wings of
green and gold, ending in several tails like a papilio, are edged
with a delicate fringe of purest white feathery scales. It is
also one of the most interesting of the Madagascar lepidoptera,
from the fact that all the other species of the genus inhabit
tropical America and the West India Islands. In a journey
to the south-east of Madagascar, in 1876, I was greatly struck
with the numbers of individuals and variety of species of
butterfly seen on the banks of the Màtitànana; and in coming
up the eastern forest on the Tamatave route, I have seen some
of the streams covered with a cloud of green and black and
blue and black butterflies. Some of the nocturnal moths are
very large, the wings spreading over six or seven inches, and
with lovely shading and spots of brown and fawn colour.
There seems, however, to be only one genus peculiar to
Madagascar, and this belongs to the family of Satyridæ.
There are two species of caterpillar from which silk is obtained; from one of these the silk is of so strong a quality,
although not brilliant, that it is asserted that pieces of it,

when exhumed from the graves, where they have been for
centuries enveloping the dead, have lost none of their firmness.
There is a caterpillar found in the interior which is so large
and brightly coloured that the bushes on which it feeds are
quite conspicuous from some distance.   It is from five to
six inches long, in a gorgeous livery of yellow, black, and
scarlet.

The Coleoptera are more remarkable than the Lepidoptera for their widely-spread affinities, and they have been
better collected.   The tiger-beetles, stag-beetles, carnivorous
beetles, and also the Cerambycidæ and Lamiidæ, are all well
represented, and the rosechafers have twenty genera peculiar
to Madagascar, while the metallic beetles have one genus
(*Polybothris*) containing a large number of peculiar species;
and the longicorn beetles are numerous and interesting, containing no less than twenty-four genera peculiar to the island.
Most of these insects are found in the lower and warmer
portions of the country, so that only a few of them are met
with in the upper forest, although there are many species even
there of great beauty and interest.   A small beetle of most
vivid colouring of metallic green, blue, and scarlet is extremely plentiful, and may be caught by scores on a particular
kind of bush; and many beautiful Buprestidæ and carnivorous
beetles may also be obtained in the forest-clearings.   But the
beetle which most interested me was one with a long, tapir-
like proboscis—a large weevil, I believe.   This creature is
about one and a half inches long, black in colour, with tufts
of yellow hairs.   Examining with a hand lens one at work on
the bark of young trees, I observed that the long proboscis
was toothed at the extremity, and was used to detach the
fibres of the wood; these were cut across, seized by the
minute pincers, and then drawn up, a day's work of the insect producing a considerable hole in the tree, the object being
apparently either to feed on the flowing sap, or to prepare a
nest for the eggs.   Insects allied to our English ladybirds,
but larger, are very common; one of these has a transparent,
glass-like covering, more like the carapace of a minute tortoise than the wing-cover of a beetle, and this is ornamented
with gold spots, just like burnished gilding.

One of the mason-wasps found in the central province builds a pocket-like nest of clay. These are often constructed within dwelling-houses, the busy little worker coming in with a loud hum, bearing a pellet of clay in its jaws; this is deposited on the edge of the work already finished, the wasp getting inside the little chamber and finishing it off smoothly with her antennæ and fore-limbs, the loud triumphant note changing to a lower one of apparent satisfaction during the process of working. These nests are about two inches deep, and wide enough to admit a little finger, and I frequently found several of them securely fixed to the underside of the unceiled rafters of my study. I believe they are filled with insects as food for the young of the wasp.

In the warmer parts of Madagascar the nights are lighted up by numbers of fireflies. On the south-east coast I was once lost in the woods for some time during a dark evening, and was extremely interested with the numbers of minute lamps which danced through the air and amongst the trees. So brightly did a particular one shine out now and then, that we were several times deceived by them, and felt sure that we saw the lights of a village a few hundred yards ahead of us. The light of these insects is of a greenish hue; it is not continuous, but is quenched every second or two; as in some lighthouses, the interval of darkness is a little longer than the time when the light is visible. When caught and held in the hand, the insect gives a continuous glow, and not the series of flashes seen when it is flying.

In some other orders of insects there are most interesting forms. A mantis, closely allied to those of Africa and America, goes through his seemingly devotional, but really bloodthirsty, attitudes; folding his saw-like arms, as if in prayer, but in reality to strike an unwary insect. This creature is called by the natives *famàkilòha, i.e.,* "headsman," literally "head-breaker." It has a peculiarly weird, "uncanny" look, from the large green head turning round on the neck, and staring at one in a way no other insect seems able to do.

Over many portions of the central provinces great numbers of ant-hills occur. These are conical mounds of a yard or

so high, and are made by a white or yellowish ant called
vìtsikàmbo.   If a piece of one of these mounds is broken off,
the ants are seen in a state of great excitement, running in
and out of the circular galleries which traverse their city in
every direction.   There are vast numbers in one nest, and
they have a queen, who is nearly an inch long, while the
workers are about three-eighths of an inch in length.   A
serpent is said to live in many of these ant-hills.

Several insects found in the upper plateaux have a marvellous resemblance, in their long bodies, legs, and wings, to the
green stalks and blades of grass, while others are equally like
the dry brown grass of the rainless months.

There are many species of locust in Madagascar, one kind
being a very large brilliantly-coloured insect; the body is
green, yellow, and blue, and the under-wings a bright crimson,
making it a very conspicuous object when flying.   But it has
such an unpleasant odour when handled that the Malagasy
have a proverb, "*Valalan' amboa : ny tompony aza tsy tia azy,*"
i.e., "The dog-locust: even its owner dislikes it."   It may be
remarked in passing that the native language is exceedingly
rich in proverbs; and a very interesting paper might be
written on those proverbs which refer to animals, as illustrating not only native habits of thought and observation, but
giving also many particulars as to the living creatures inhabiting the country.   Some of the smaller species of locust
are used for food by the people.   Divested of wings and
limbs, they are dried, and exposed for sale in great heaps in
the markets.   They are generally fried in fat, and are not
unpleasant in taste; I must confess, however, to getting this
information at secondhand.   Although locusts occasionally
appear in vast numbers in Madagascar, they do not often cause
much destruction to the vegetation.   They are sometimes
seen filling the air as thick as snowflakes, to which they bear
no slight resemblance when the sun catches the glittering
surface of the wings.   In the year 1869 an immense cloud
of these insects passed over the capital, darkening the air,
and being an hour or more in their passage above the city.

Among the Hemipterous insects there is none more conspicuous by its noise than a species of cicada called *joréry.*

This little creature is only about an inch long, but by the friction of the wings on a pair of minute roughened tubes, it produces a shrill stridulous sound which causes the woods to resound with the vibration, and when very near to it seems to make the ears tingle.

There is another insect common to every part of the tropics, and to many temperate countries also, which is far too numerous in Madagascar—I mean the mosquito. In the interior we are comparatively free from this minute plague in the cold season, but in many parts of the warmer maritime plains it is a terrible pest all the year round, and is said to often cause the death of young animals left exposed to its attacks. This I can well believe from what I have seen in several places—*seen*, but also *heard*, and unmistakably *felt*. But in travelling to the north-west coast we fell in with another insect pest in addition to the mosquito. This was a stinging fly called *alòy*. It is about a third the size of a house-fly, but with the wings less divergent. It attacks with a sharp prick, sometimes drawing blood. The flies are found in swarms along a belt of beautifully-wooded country with clear streams of bright sparkling water. They fly by day, but retire as soon as the sun sets, when their place is taken by the mosquitoes, who roam by night; so that the unfortunate traveller has little respite either by night or day.

Many of the spiders of Madagascar are very large and brilliantly coloured. The legs of some of the largest spread over a circle of six or seven inches in diameter. They spin immense geometric webs, which span the beds of considerable streams or wide paths; and these are anchored to the surrounding vegetation by such strong silken cords that it requires an effort to break them. Some years ago I spent a long afternoon on a hill to the south of the capital with two friends, catching spiders. We obtained a great number, including from thirty to forty different species; some of these were like small crabs rather than spiders. Only recently, however, did I meet with one of the venomous spiders of the island. This insect is about the size of a small marble, almost perfectly globular in shape, of a shining glossy black, and with black legs, but it has a small red spot on the abdomen. Its bite is said by the natives to be fatal, and it probably is so unless speedy measures are taken to cauterise the wound. Dr. Vinson, a French naturalist, ascertained that this spider is closely allied to the malignant *Latrodectus* of Elba and Corsica, whose bite is believed to be mortal, and also to another species found in Martinique, which is equally dangerous. He proposed for it the name of *Latrodectus mena-vody*. One of the crab-like spiders just alluded to is also said to be deadly in its bite; it probably requires a new genus to be formed for its reception.

While speaking of venomous creatures, it may be observed that small scorpions are not uncommon in the warmer parts of Madagascar, and that centipedes are numerous. These latter have an unpleasant habit of getting into any small hole or crevice in the woodwork of houses, often choosing the hollows for the bolts of shutters and windows. One morning, just before getting up, I was startled to see a large centipede six or seven inches long crawling over the mats of our bedroom. Their bite is extremely painful, resembling—so I have been told—the touch of a red-hot iron, but it is not dangerous if some simple remedies are applied.

Besides the venomous centipedes there are in the forest great numbers of a perfectly harmless millipede, a series of shining black rings, eight or nine inches long, with an infinity of legs, which move like successive waves. And the mention of this ringed creature brings me to notice another of the Annulosa which is frequent in the forests. This animal is called by the natives *Tainkìntana*, lit., "star-droppings," and is completely covered with a wonderfully beautiful coat of mail, each segment folding upon the other, and finished at the head by a helmet, and at the tail by another rounded and hollow plate. These are so shaped that when the creature is alarmed it rolls itself into a ball, every plate fitting into the other, and forming an almost perfect sphere, from which no force, save that of tearing it asunder, can induce it to uncoil. There are two, if not more, species; one, about six inches long and one and a half inches wide, is of a beautifully grained bronze, like Russia leather; the other is about half that size, and is of a japanned black. But both present

... is said by the natives ...

... Now, a branch ... ... allied to the national *Z*... ... whose bite is believed to be most ... ... ies found in Martinique, which is ... ... It proposed for it the name of *for. latus* ... ... needle-like spines just alluded to ... said to ... ly in its life ... probably repels a ... ... to its reception.

W... ... ... poisonous centipedes it may be desc... ... ... not uncommon in the warmer parts ... Ma... ... ... centipedes are numerous. The... ... ... habit of getting into any sm... ... ... woodwork of houses, often closing the ... ... of shutters and windows. One m... ... ... getting up, I was startled to see a larg... ... seven inch... ... long crawl... over the ... ... extremely painful, resembling ... ... touch of a red-hot iron, but m... ... ... are small.

... ... centipedes th... are n... the ... ... dly harm... ... ... entire inch ... long, ... than an or... ... ... he series. And the larg... ... ... present in this forest. This ... ... I was a ... really beautiful ... ... upon the other ... ... and a ... ... for a p... Those ... ... when the creat... ... roll itself into a ball every year ... ... from an almost perfect... ... from wh... ... of seeing it a ... ... induc... ... ... species; ... ... about st... ... ... half ... long, ... of a ... ... fles-h-c... ... ... ; the other is ab... ... of a japanned black. But both ...

beautiful examples of protective armour, and of exquisite contrivance and creative skill.

Not only the woods of Madagascar, but the waters also are full of interest from their abundant animal life. Crossing the river Mananjàra one day, I noticed that, at a point where the river was wide and with a powerful current, the stones in the stream were thickly covered with a graceful plant, which in the water looked like a fern, from one to two feet long, but with very thick and fleshy stem and fronds. On examining one of these, I found it to be the home of a variety of minute animals: some of them caterpillars, which were burrowing into the stalk; others, small green creatures like caddis-worms, but with a transparent shell; others, minute leeches; others, again, a tiny lump of clear jelly with a double nucleus; others, like a fresh-water hydra; with several other kinds, all finding house and provision on one frond in the rushing waters.

Origin and Meaning of the Specialised Fauna of Madagascar.—We may now inquire the meaning of the strangely exceptional character of the Madagascar fauna. What are we to infer from the remarkable deficiencies in the mammals and in some families of birds, as compared with the African fauna, from the presence of such groups as the Lemuridæ and Centetidæ, hardly represented in other countries, and those countries far-distant ones? What is the key to the existence of such isolated and specialised forms as the Aye-aye, the Æpyornis, and several others of the birds? And why are so many of the living creatures of the island allied, not to African forms, but rather to those of Southern Asia or Malaya? Answers to these questions have been given by two or three naturalists; amongst others, by Dr. Philip L. Sclater, who, in an article in the *Quarterly Journal of Science* (April 1864), says the following deductions may perhaps be arrived at from what we have before us:—

" 1. Madagascar has never been connected with Africa, *as it at present exists.* This would seem probable from the absence of certain all-pervading Ethiopian types in Madagascar, such as antelope, hippopotamus, felis, &c. But, on the other hand, the presence of lemurs in Africa renders it certain

F

that Africa, as it at present exists, contains land that once formed part of Madagascar.

"2. Madagascar and the Mascarene Islands (which are universally acknowledged to belong to the same category) must have remained for a long epoch separated from every other part of the globe, in order to have acquired the many peculiarities now exhibited in their mammal fauna—*e.g.*, lemur, chiromys, eupleres, centetes, &c.—to be elaborated by the gradual modification of pre-existing forms.

"3. Some land-connection must have existed in former ages between Madagascar and India, whereon the original stock—whence the present Lemuridæ of Africa, Madagascar, and India are descended—flourished."

He concludes by saying that "the anomalies of the mammal fauna of Madagascar can be best explained by supposing that anterior to the existence of Africa in its present shape a large continent occupied parts of the Atlantic and Indian Oceans, stretching out towards (what is now) America to the west, and to India and its islands on the east; that this continent was broken up into islands, of which some have become amalgamated with the present continent of Africa, and some, possibly, with what is now Asia; and that in Madagascar and the Mascarene Islands we have existing relics of this great continent, for which, as the original focus of the *stirps lemurum*, I should propose the name Lemuria!"

Dr. Hartlaub, who has described minutely the birds of Madagascar, lays great stress upon their Indian affinities, as if these were equal in number and value to the African relationships; an extreme view, which is apparently not borne out by the facts of the case.

The most careful study of the subject is, however, to be found in Mr. Alfred Wallace's recent work on *The Geographical Distribution of Animals*, to which I have already repeatedly referred, and to which I am greatly indebted for exact and minute information with regard to the classification of the animals of Madagascar.

I can only indicate in a very few words the main points which I think are established by this valuable work. Mr. Wallace agrees to a great extent with Dr. Sclater in deeming it probable that in the Tertiary period the Indian Ocean was occupied in part by a continent or archipelago, of which we have relics in Madagascar and the Mascarene Islands, the Seychelles, Amirante, and Chagos groups, and, nearer to India, the Maldive and Laccadive groups, all of which have encircling reefs, a fact which has not been much noticed, but which, from Mr. Darwin's researches on the subject of the formation of coral, indicates that these islands are *still sinking land.* But he also contends that both Madagascar and the Mascarene and Comoro Islands must have been connected with Africa in some Tertiary geological epoch, probably while the Sahara was still a shallow sea-bottom, and before the incursion of the numerous ungulate animals and the larger felines from the Asiatic continent. A bank of soundings now existing in the Mozambique Channel reduces the width of that strait from 230 miles, its present narrowest width, to 160 miles, clearly indicating a former closer connection between the island and the continent. The Mascarene Islands probably represent the portion of land which was separated earliest, before *any* carnivora had reached the country. The lemuride type of animals evidently existed in Africa at that period, but has since become almost extinct, excepting the Galagos, a family of the Lemuridæ which are not very nearly allied to the lemuride forms now found in Madagascar, These latter, probably from long isolation, have become modified into many exceptional and peculiar species, especially as they have been free from the attacks of all large carnivora. The small insectivora are probably relics of a much more extensive fauna of that order of mammals, which was greatly developed in the early Tertiary epochs. To the fact of the long isolation of Southern Africa from the Oriental region and fauna is probably also due the development of the struthious or ostrich type of birds in the southern continents of South Africa, South America, and Australia, as well as of birds of other families also incapable of flight. Free from the incursions of destructive felines, the dodo and other birds flourished in Mauritius and Rodriguez, and the huge Æpyornis in Madagascar, while the gigantic tortoises, now only left in Aldebra, an uninhabited island, were also free to develop in size and numbers, isolated from any enemy. The nearest allied gigantic tortoises, those of the Galapagos, are no doubt survivals in the same manner, on the opposite side of the southern hemisphere, of a group which probably, from the evidence of fossil remains, once had a wide range over the whole globe. The existence in widely-separated countries of species nearly allied to Madagascar animals, such as the *solenodon* amongst the Centetidæ in the West India Islands, species of the *urania* amongst the Lepidoptera found also in the West Indies and in Madagascar, and the South American, and even Pacific, relations of some of the birds, may be explained, not on the hypothesis of any former closer connection between these now far-separated lands, but by supposing that each are survivals of once widely-extended groups, which have become exterminated through various causes in the intermediate regions.

It will be seen from the particulars already given that Madagascar is a country which presents a most interesting field for a naturalist. I only wish that some one with competent scientific knowledge, as well as literary and artistic ability, would describe its fauna and flora in such a delightful way as Mr. Bates has done that of the Amazons, Mr. Wallace that of the Malay Archipelago, and Mr. Belt that of Nicaragua. The materials for such a work are abundant; and volumes quite as interesting as those just named might easily be written upon the natural history and botany of the great African island.

CHAPTER IV.

NOTES ON THE VEGETABLE PRODUCTIONS OF MADAGASCAR.

FOREST SCENERY—VALUABLE WOODS—COAST VEGETATION—PANDANUS—TAN-GÉNA POISON-TREE—PALMS—BARK CLOTH—BAMBOOS : THEIR APPLICA-TIONS—BAOBAB—MOSSES, CREEPERS, AND LIANAS—FERNS — BEAUTIFUL-LEAVED PLANTS—PITCHER PLANTS—VEGETATION OF THE INTERIOR—SPINY AND PRICKLY PLANTS—GRASSES—REEDS AND RUSHES—VEGETABLE FOODS —RICE AND ITS CULTURE—ROOTS—ARUMS—COFFEE—SUGAR—SPICES—FRUITS—BANANAS—TRAVELLER'S TREE—MEDICINAL PLANTS—GOURDS—TOBACCO—HEMP AND COTTON—DYES—LICHENS—FLOWERING PLANTS AND TREES—ORCHIDS—GUMS—INDIA-RUBBER—LACE-LEAF PLANT.

IN the preceding chapter on the animal life of Madagascar, it was premised that the writer made no pretensions to exact scientific knowledge of zoology. So also the present notes upon the vegetable productions of the island must be pre-faced by saying that I know still less of scientific botany, being but imperfectly acquainted even with much of the nomenclature of the science. All I can here attempt is to describe in a very familiar and unsystematic way some of those more prominent features in the flora of Madagascar which would strike any intelligent traveller in passing through the country; to note how largely the vegetable productions of the island are connected with the civilisation and handi-crafts of the inhabitants; and to say something about a few of those remarkable trees and plants which are acknowledged by botanists to be among the most curious and interesting of nature's productions.

The main features of the physical geography of Madagascar will be remembered by those who have read the first chapters of this book, viz., the interior highlands of granitic rocks and red clay, the secondary coast plains, and the almost unbroken ring of forest surrounding the island. As already pointed out, these geographical features have necessarily a very great influence upon the distribution of animal life; while in considering the botany, it is of course obvious that they do not merely *influence* this latter, but that the Madagascar flora to a large extent *consists* of this circling girdle of woods. Besides, however, this forest region, which extends for so many hundreds of miles round the island, a considerable portion of the lower southern and western plains is also covered with a less dense vegetation; and as the forest is found at all elevations, from the level of the sea up to 6000 feet of altitude, there is a great variety of temperature, and consequently of vegetable products, from those which are strictly tropical to those characteristic of the temperate zones. The elevated plateaux of the interior are generally destitute of trees, but in the sheltered river-valleys a luxuriant tropical flora is often found.

Forest Scenery.—Some of the most picturesque scenery in the island, and perhaps, of its kind, hardly to be surpassed in any other part of the world, is to be found on the eastern coast. This being the windward side of Madagascar, receives the greatest amount of rainfall: the vapour-laden south-eastern trades being condensed into rain by the steep forest-covered slopes of the hills, which rise line after line from the coast up to the level of the interior table-land. These hills are scored into deep gorges by many of the rivers, and through these they find their way to the sea by a succession of rapids and cataracts. Such are the valleys of the Mangòro, the Mànanjàra, the Màtitànana, and many others; and in these there are endless combinations of luxuriant and dense vegetation with rocks and waterfalls, presenting a thousand scenes in which a landscape-painter might find an exhaustless field for his pencil.

The most frequented routes from the coast to the capital necessarily pass through this girdle of woods, and four or five days is usually spent in traversing the double line cf forest. Here, although few trees of great size or bulk. have been left in the immediate neighbourhood of the rough paths which form the only roads through the country, one is always impressed with the luxuriance of the vegetation. There is a vigorous struggle for light and air as each tree strives to overtop its neighbour and reach the upper region above the crowd of its competitors. Amongst this throng of vegetable life are seen numbers of palms, the feathery crowns often overtopping the other trees. Most of the exogenous trees are of hard-wooded species, allied to mahogany, satin-wood, teak, and ebony. A great variety of beautifully-veined and durable woods, suitable for all kinds of building and of cabinet-work, are found in the Madagascar forests, and are already used to a considerable extent for furniture and the parquetrie floors of the houses of the upper classes in the capital city and its neighbourhood. Of these woods a kind called *vòambòana* is the most plentiful, and has a great variety of colour and veining. Another wood, the *varòngy (Calophyllum inophyllum)* is largely used for rafters and joists, and for the native canoes. The height of some of these forest trees may be imagined from the fact that the three central posts of the chief royal palace at Antanànarìvo are each formed of a single trunk, and are 120 feet high above the ground, besides a considerable depth below.

In the south-eastern forests a large proportion of the trees are of considerable girth, owing to their being buttressed round the trunk with aerial roots, which seem to ascend with the growth of the tree to give the additional support required by the increasing height. The hollows between these buttresses form a number of small chambers large enough to enclose several people. In these woods the growth of the trees is so dense that it is difficult to get a palanquin through in many places, and there is a deep gloom below even at mid-day.

It may be here remarked that a Hova house of the old style and of the better class is entirely constructed of vegetable materials. So also are the dwellings of the people in almost every other part of the island; they are so made that no metal whatever is needed; all fastenings are either of wood or of tough fibrous plants, which tie the whole firmly together.

Coast Vegetation.—For several hundred miles along the eastern coast of Madagascar there runs a chain of lagoons into which the rivers flow, leaving an irregular strip of land between them and the sea. This level belt is covered with the richest greensward, and dotted over with masses of shrubs and clumps of trees. On one side are the ever-restless waves of the Indian Ocean, and on the other the broad reaches of the lagoon, bordered by dense vegetation, and the blue line of the distant mountains of the interior in the background.

Amongst the trees of this eastern coast are several species of pandanus, which form a very marked feature in the flora of the shores of Madagascar, both on this and on the western side of the island. The most common kind, one with a branching head and aerial roots rising high above the ground, occurs in dense masses all along the eastern coast. Its long tough leaves with serrated prickly edges serve many useful purposes. They are made into bags for the transport of sugar from Mauritius; they are used to protect all kinds of goods in their transit from the coast to the interior, making a perfectly watertight covering for the most perishable articles; and amongst the tribes of the south-east they are the only plates and dishes used by the poorer people, fresh leaves being procured without any trouble for every meal. The fruit of this pandanus is a hard yellow cone, with a number of hexagonal facets, something like a pine-apple in shape, but quite woody in texture. Another species of pandanus (*P. obeliscus*?) has a lofty pyramidal outline, not unlike a low poplar or a larch, but with a tuft of sword-shaped leaves at the head, and frequently from forty to fifty feet high. The stem is as straight as that of a fir, and the branches, which grow in spiral lines round the trunk, are horizontal, with feathery tips of ribbon-shaped leaves.

A very common tree along this coast is the *vŏavŏntaka*, a tree belonging to the *Strychnos* family of plants. It grows to the size of a small apple-tree, and bears a fruit resembling in size and shape a cricket-ball, and yellow in colour when ripe. On breaking the hard shell, which is about a fifth of an inch in thickness, a soft yellowish-grey pulp is seen, containing a number of black seeds. This pulp has a pleasant acid flavour, very refreshing when travelling on a sultry day.

A prominent feature in the vegetation of this coast is presented by numbers of dense but low and spreading box-like trees, which cover a large extent of ground. Two species of

Barringtonia are also found on this seaboard, and also certain kinds of *Hibiscus*, from the bark of which twine and cordage are manufactured, and the *Aleurites* or candle-nut also occurs. (See *Proc. Linn. Soc., Bot.*, vol. vii. May 13, 1863.)

While passing through the woods bordering the sea, one frequently comes across the celebrated *tangèna*, the tree producing a poisonous nut which was long used in Madagascar as an ordeal for the detection of certain crimes. The tangèna is about the size of a cherry-tree, and with its glossy green leaves, somewhat resembling those of a horse-chestnut in shape, would be a handsome addition to our ornamental shrubs, could it be acclimatised in England. But the tree was valued because of the power supposed to be inherent in the fruit, in which a kind of divine influence was believed to be embodied. The customs connected with this poison ordeal will, moreover, be more appropriately described in the chapter on Folk-lore and Popular Superstitions.

Another tree which frequently occurs along the eastern coast is the *filao* (*Casuarina equisetifolia*) or beef-wood tree. It is a tall graceful tree, with fine wire-like leaves, resembling the fir. Its wood, however, is quite distinct from that of the fir, and it belongs to another botanical order, that of the Amentaceæ. It is indigenous to Madagascar, but it is also found in the Malayo-Polynesian and Australian regions. It is never, I believe, found far from the sea.

Palms and Bamboos.—The sago-palm is rather common on the maritime plains, but sago is not used for food by the people. Among the palms, both on the eastern and western sides of the island, the fan-palm (*Borassus flabelliformis?*) is found very plentifully. Surely among the thousand of beautiful objects in this beautiful world these graceful palms, with their spreading crowns of enormous fans, are not the least worthy of admiration. They are not met with in considerable numbers on the east coast, but are more plentiful in the warmer plains of the western side of Madagascar. In sailing down the river Bétsibòka we passed for several hours along groves of these palms. As we swept down the stream with the rapid current, the tall trunks seemed to pass by us as in a panorama, rising from the water's edge like columnar shafts, and with the lovely crown of green fans in sharp contrast against the deep blue of the sky. These large leaves are used for roofing on the north-west coast, and make a very impervious thatch, beautifully neat in appearance from the under side.

Many still undescribed species of palm are found in the eastern woods. I was much interested in the southern parts of the island to see to what a height some palms attain in the universal striving for light and air amongst the other trees. The *anìvona* palm (I believe allied to, if not a species of, *areca*) often grows side by side with the traveller's tree, both soaring up to eighty, ninety, and even a hundred feet in height. The former has its trunk banded with narrow lines of green and brown. The bark is one of the toughest known vegetable substances, and is used not only in building houses, but also in making the remarkable native boats used along the south-east coast (see Chapter ix.) Numbers of the delicate and graceful bamboo-palm are to be seen in the upper forests ; the stem of this palm is only the size of a fine bamboo, about one and a half inch in diameter.

That most useful of palms, the cocoa-nut, is found sparingly both on the eastern and western coasts of Madagascar. It is said by some writers not to be indigenous, but to have been introduced accidentally some 200 years ago through some nuts having been washed ashore. From what I have seen, however, I am strongly inclined to doubt this, as I very much question whether any natural causes could have spread the nut over a large extent of the island in such a space of time ; and, until a very recent period, there has not been sufficient intercourse between the different tribes to render it probable that it has spread by being planted. The native name (*vòanìo*) is identical with that given to the cocoa-nut by many of the Polynesian islanders.

Before leaving the palms, there is another of this graceful family of trees which must be described, not only for its beauty and abundance, but also for the numerous uses to which it is applied. This is the rofia palm (*Sagus ruffia*). It is not found on the coast, but on ascending from the plains to the height of a few hundred feet above the level of the

sea, it is found in profusion in every valley, until one reaches
the upper plateaux of the interior, where it also grows, but
more sparingly, in sheltered positions. The rofia has a
trunk of from thirty to fifty feet in height, and at the head
divides into seven or eight immensely long leaves. The
midrib of these leaves is a very strong but extremely light
and straight pole, being at the base about the size of the
calf of a man's leg, and tapering to half those dimensions at
the extremity. These poles are often twenty feet or more in
length, and the leaves proper consist of a great number of fine
and long pinnate leaflets, set at right angles to the midrib,
from eighteen inches to two feet long, and about one and a
half inch broad. From the way in which the leaf-stalks break
off, leaving an irregular patch attached to the trunk, this latter
has a rough appearance, very different from the smooth
circular shaft of most of the palms. From the extreme
strength and lightness of the midribs of the rofia leaves they
are used for a variety of purposes. They form the framework of the roof of the houses on the eastern coast, and are
also used for rafters and joists. They are most useful for
ladders, being so very light and easily carried, and they are
also fixed to ladies' palanquins as carrying-poles. But the
fine pinnate leaves are yet more serviceable to the people.
From the inner fibre the women weave a variety of strong
cloths; the majority of these are coarse, for the use of the
slaves and the lower class of the people; but a very fine and
beautiful fabric, mixed with cotton, and of a light straw
colour, is also manufactured to be worn by the more wealthy
classes. The coarser cloths, under the name of *rabànnas*,
form an important article of export from the eastern ports.

During a journey made in 1876 in the south-eastern
provinces of Madagascar, I was much interested to find that
the people of that part of the island make a kind of cloth
from the inner bark of certain trees. This cloth is reddish
brown in colour and of no great strength; it is made by the
women, who beat it out with a mallet, the head of which is
lined and grooved in a particular way. Almost every one
wears a girdle of this coarse cloth, by which the sack of rush
matting which forms their only clothing is kept in its place.

Among the larger trees on the south-east coast one called *atàfa* is prominent by its peculiar manner of growth and its colour. In many specimens the branches strike directly at right angles from the trunk, and then spread away horizontally for a considerable distance. The leaves are from eight to ten inches long, and are spatula-shaped; a large proportion of them are always ruddy brown or scarlet in colour.

As in almost every tropical country the bamboo is one of the most beautiful and useful of plants, so it also is in Madagascar. On many parts of the eastern coast, at the foot of the forest-covered ranges of hills, the bamboo forms the most striking feature in the vegetation. Extensive tracts of country are almost covered with the long graceful stems, curving over the paths like enormous whips. The thickly-set pinnate leaves are of the brightest green, forming a delightful contrast to the darker colour of the woods on the higher slopes. One of the strangest as well as most beautiful sights that can meet the eye is when passing through a thicket of these bamboos. All around rise the smooth, shining, and many-jointed stems, like the slenderest shafts, while the dense leafage overhead makes a green twilight below. Another species of bamboo has a climbing habit, and covers the sturdier trees with a dense mantle of green drapery. In this species "the cane is almost as small as a quill, with a circle of fine small leaves around the joints, which are not more than five or six inches apart. These long slender canes hang pendent from the branches of the trees, or stretch in graceful curves from tree to tree along the sides of the road." [*]

The economic uses of the bamboo are numerous in Madagascar, although not so extensive as in many Asiatic countries. It is universally employed for the small rafters of houses, and the larger stems form the usual *bao* or carrying-pole, by which every kind of merchandise and produce is conveyed on the shoulders of the bearers from one part of the country to the other. A piece of bamboo forms a very popular musical instrument; portions of the strong outer fibre are detached and strained over bows of hard wood to form the strings.

[*] Ellis: *Three Visits to Madagascar*, p. 321.

These are played by the fingers, and from this apparently rude instrument a very pleasing music can be obtained, resembling the tones of a guitar. Many of the people are very skilful in performing upon it. On the eastern coast, long pieces of bamboo form the only waterpots of the people. The soil is not suitable for making earthen vessels, and accordingly in every house half-a-dozen bamboos stand in one corner, from which the water for domestic use is obtained. All but one of the diaphragms at the joints are broken through, and the upper end is stopped by a handful of grass. In many parts of the interior and on the eastern coast, long pieces of the finer bamboo are used by the boys as blow-guns, with which they kill small birds and animals, in the same way as is customary among the Indians of the Brazils. Pieces of a fine kind of bamboo called *vòlotàra* are used by the people as a snuff-box. These are fitted with a stopper, and beautifully polished, and are sometimes ornamented with designs burnt in on the smooth shining surface. Fifes and flutes are also made of bamboo, so that it is useful both for wind and string instruments.

On some of the rivers of the south-eastern coast there are no canoes, but a kind of raft made of bamboo, and called a *zàhitra*, is the only means of crossing them. And of all the rude and primitive contrivances ever invented for water-carriage, commend me to a *zàhitra;* at any rate, to the first of which I had experience when crossing the Màtitànana. This one consisted of about thirty or forty pieces of bamboo, from ten to twelve feet long, lashed together at the head by bands of some tough creeper, and spreading out like a fan at the stern, these bamboos constantly slipping out of their places and needing trimming at every trip across the river. When loaded, the *zàhitra* was from a third to a half under water, and although my companion and I crossed safely, he took an involuntary foot-bath, and I a sitz-bath, during our voyage across. But subsequently the whole concern came to pieces, and several of our bearers had to swim ashore from the scattered bamboos composing the crazy craft.

In the interior and on the western coast a small species of prickly bamboo called *bàraràta* is very plentiful. The leaves being pointed with sharp needle-like prickles, it is no pleasant task for the bare-legged bearers to pass through a thicket of these canes. They grow profusely along the banks of the Ikiòpa and Bétsibòka rivers, the long, feathery, grey heads of flower giving a distinct character to the scenery of this part of the country. Divested of their prickly leaves, these small bamboos are very largely used for building purposes.

One of the most common and striking plants seen along the rivers of the eastern coast is the *via*, a gigantic arum (*A. costatum* or *A. colocasia*), growing in dense masses along the bank in the water. On the shores of the river Màtità-nana I found this arum seven or eight feet high, and it has been seen as high as ten or twelve feet. It has thick fleshy stems and leaf-stalks, and lily-like leaves two or three feet long. The fruit and root are edible when cooked.

On the western side of Madagascar the baobab tree (*Adansonia*) is somewhat plentiful. It is called *bontòna*, and also *mòfom-bàrika*, or "monkey's bread," from its small fruit being eaten by the lemurs. This tree is immediately distinguished from others by its enormous bulk of trunk and small spread of branches, which are bare of foliage during several months of the year, and also by its shining dark-brown bark. It is frequently seen from twenty to thirty feet in diameter.

On the same side of Madagascar, the tamarind tree is one of the finest and most plentiful of the many beautiful trees found in that wooded region. It attains a great size on the banks of the chief rivers. During a canoe voyage down the Ikiòpa we encamped one day under the shadow of a magnificent tamarind tree, one of a grove of these trees. The branches, which swept the ground, covered a circle of nearly 100 feet; but the foliage was very thin, as it consisted of minute mimosa-like leaves, millions of which strewed the ground, as well as hundreds of the dried fruits. These consist of a long pod, containing several shining black seeds, imbedded in a reddish-brown acid pulp.

Mosses, Lianas, and Ferns.—In travelling through the forests on the eastern side of Madagascar, I was struck with the venerable aspect given to the trees in many places by the masses of fine whitish-grey moss (or lichen, I am not sure which) hanging from its branches in long thread-like filaments. This grey moss or lichen occurs chiefly in the upper and colder portions of the woods. In a spur of forest which crosses the road from Imérina to Bétsiléo, at a height of nearly 6000 feet above the sea, almost every tree bears long festoons of this venerable-looking appendage hanging from its branches. I believe it is allied to, if not identical with, *Rocella fuciformis* of Eastern Africa.

A more usual feature of tropical woods is the way in which, in the Madagascar forests, the trees are bound together in all directions by countless creepers and lianas, which cross and intertwine in an inextricable tangle, like the disordered cordage of a hundred ships. Some of these stretch from the topmost boughs to the ground like the backstays of a lofty ship's mast, and others cross at every conceivable angle. These lianas form without any preparation a very strong tough cordage, and in carrying goods from the coast to the interior they are largely used for securing all kinds of packages. Great quantities of the fibrous bark of certain trees (especially that of *Astrapœa cannabina*, which has long oval leaves and white pendent flowers) are brought up to the capital every year by the woodmen, and are there manufactured at the Government workshops into rough-looking but strong ropes.

In the dim twilight of the Madagascar woods, the ground is generally covered with a dense undergrowth of shrubs and young trees, the latter shooting up wherever an opening appears in the leafy canopy overhead. A great variety of ferns are found in every damp hollow or shady bank; great masses of hart's-tongue or stag's-horn fern are seen in every crevice in the tree trunks or fork of the branches; and tree-ferns spread their graceful fronds wherever there is any moisture. Large collections of ferns have been made by some of the English ladies, and these have been described in the *Journal of the Linnæan Society* by Mr. J. G. Baker, F.L.S., of the Kew Herbarium. Many of these are new and peculiar to the country. Mr. Baker says, in reference to one of these collections, that it "contains altogether 112 species, of which 28 prove to be novelties. That such should be the case in an

order where the diffusion of the species is so wide as in the
ferns is calculated to raise our expectation of what we may
expect when the flowering plants of the same region are
gathered; and it is interesting to notice that some of the
species, such as *Asplenium trichomanes, Nephrodium filix-
mas*, and *Aspidium aculateum*, are thoroughly temperate
types. The development of lamina in the species known
elsewhere, and the strong tendency shown by many of them
to become viviparous, indicates a damp humid climate, with
localities excellently suited for the development of fern-
growth." * The genera *Asplenium* and *Pteris* are largely
represented, and *Ophioglossum* and *Adiantum* are also found,
but more sparingly. Dr. Charles Meller describes a pendent
ribbon-like fern (*Ophioglossum pendulum*) hanging from a part of
the fork of a tree on the east coast, with its roots fixed in a mass
of earth and leaves collected in the hollow. Each ribbon fell
to a distance of from three to five feet, then bifurcated, send-
ing down a spore-case, some of the bands of which measured
twelve feet long. Fine specimens of the Mascarene gold
and silver ferns (*Gymnogramme argenta* and *G. aurea*) are
found in the outskirts of the Madagascar woods; and also
several Lycopodiums, one of which (*L. complanatum*), although
widely spread, was not known before either in Continental
Africa or any of the islands of the Mascarene archipelago.
Some of the finest ferns are found in the deep and damp
fosses which surround the old towns in the central provinces.
Although the tree-ferns are fine and plentiful in every place
where there is shade and moisture, they hardly attain the
size of the New Zealand species, of which there is such a
grand specimen to be seen in the tropical department of the
Crystal Palace.

On my first journey through the eastern forests of Madagascar, I found several species of those plants with variegated-
coloured leaves, which have since become so popular in
England in our drawing-rooms and hothouses. Some of
these are veined with gold and resemble the *Echites*, though
not so shrubby. They were to be seen along the roadsides,
but I doubt not that researches in the denser recesses of the

* *Linn. Soc. Jour., Bot.,* xv. p. 422; xvi. pp. 197–206.

forests would reveal many others new to science. Of this class of plants Dr. Meller also says : " In the shady and moist parts of the woods I found several plants with variegated leaves—a *Coleus* with bright pink markings along the mid-rib and veins, and a *Sonerila* with silvery intra-marginal markings ; another with white spots in a row, another with pink dotting and lines. There were four herbs in these woods with beautiful leaves of variegated tints."

Species of the pitcher-plant (*Nepenthes*) are said to be found in southern portions of the island ; and a story is related of a naval officer who was saved, if not actually from death by thirst, at least from extreme exhaustion, by finding a number of the natural vessels filled with water.

Vegetation of the Interior Upland Region.—But I must not linger longer in these attractive woods, with their delightful recollections, but proceed to say something about the vegetation of the upper portions of Madagascar.

These extensive plateaux of elevated land are very bare of wood, except in the sheltered hollows and valleys of the rivers ; but the hills on which many of the ancient towns are built are often crowned with a number of old trees, which show out conspicuous amongst the red clay hills and the bare granite and basalt-capped mountains of Imérina. The most beautiful and picturesque of these old towns is the former capital, Ambòhimànga. This old city is about twelve miles north of the present capital ; it is on a triangular hill, some 400 feet high, and covered with wood from base to summit, so that from time immemorial " the woods of Ambòhimànga, bending down in their growth," have been celebrated in the songs of the native poets.

The trees which crown the ancient towns are chiefly *aviàvy*, a species of *Ficus*. They have much the shape and appearance of elms ; they shed their leaves in the cold season, and bear a small insipid fig. A finer tree than the *aviàvy* is the *amòntana*, a magnificent tree with wide-spread gnarled branches like an oak, but with large glossy leaves like those of the India-rubber tree now so common in English houses, to which tree it is closely allied. Numbers of the villages are marked out by a couple or more of these fine trees, which

F

stand out conspicuous above the houses and are visible far over the plains. Perhaps the finest specimen in Imérina is to be found at the ancient town of Ambòhidratrìmo, where it rises like a great dome of foliage above the other trees, and has a trunk about eighteen feet in girth. The *amòntana* is remarkable for its vitality, a dry and apparently lifeless stick of the tree rapidly taking root if stuck in the ground.

Perhaps the most conspicuous tree now to be seen in and around the capital is the Cape lilac, which was introduced by missionaries from the Cape of Good Hope about fifty years ago. Of this tree the Rev. R. Baron says: " I believe it to be the *Melia Azederach*, and not a lilac. Its strong scent is similar to that of the lilacs, and hence, probably, it has been supposed to be one of them. All its parts contain bitter and purgative properties." It has been extensively planted in Imérina, and grows very rapidly.

Growing among these hard-wooded trees is often found the tall straight stem of the *amìana* (*Urtica furialis*), a tree bearing a large velvety leaf which stings like a nettle when touched. The leaf, although so unpleasant to one of the senses, is beautiful in outline, being deeply cut and indented, and would in an artist's hand serve admirably for decorative purposes. The largest leaves are found on the youngest and lowest trees, one specimen I found measuring about thirty inches each way. The wood is soft and spongy, and of no service at all in building.

Another attractive tree is the *záhana* (*Bignonia articulata*), which grows to a considerable size in some places, and, as its name implies, has a curiously-articulated leaf, looking as if two or three leaves were joined together, base to point. Examples have been found with eight divisions of the leaf.

Spiny and Prickly Plants.—Like most tropical countries, Madagascar is tolerably prolific in spiny and prickly plants. One of these, a dwarf mimosa-like tree, of straggling creeping habit, and full of hook-like thorns, is called *tsiàfakòmby, i.e.,* " not passable by oxen," from its being extensively used to form fences and folds for the numerous herds of humped cattle. It belongs to the *Leguminosæ,* and has yellow flowers. Another tree of the same order is called *fàno*, and is frequently found growing over the ancient tombs of the Vazimba, the supposed aboriginal inhabitants of the central provinces. The seeds resemble in size those of a small french-bean, and grow in large pods or legumes, from fifteen to eighteen inches long, and about three broad, which look most conspicuous on the trees after the leaves have fallen. The seeds were used until very lately in the working of the *sikìdy* or divination, a practice closely interwoven with the idolatry and superstition of the people. They are also used medicinally.

A more unapproachable plant, however, than the *tsiàfakòmby* is the widely-spread prickly-pear (*Opuntia*) or *raikétra*, which forms the chief fortification of the Malagasy towns and villages. A dense thicket of this surrounds every village and homestead in many parts of the country, and a more formidable obstacle to the attack of an enemy can hardly be imagined. The trees attain a considerable thickness, and every portion of them, trunk, leaves, flowers, and fruit, is fully armed with clusters of sharp needle-like thorns, between two and three inches long; these, if carelessly handled, inflict painful wounds which inflame and are often difficult to heal. To an almost naked and barefooted soldiery, and without artillery, it forms an impenetrable barrier, which only rounds of chain and bar shot could clear out of the way. The prickly-pear is also of some service for food, the pears being a palatable fruit when carefully divested of their spiny covering. The larger thorns were formerly used as needles, and are still the ordinary pins of the Malagasy. It is perhaps not superfluous to remark that, except in old trees, there are no proper *branches* in the prickly-pear; all the thick fleshy leaves grow from the edge of the others, and the flowers and fruit also grow in the same position. They possess great vitality, so that a single leaf laid on the ground soon develops a number of tendril roots, takes hold of the earth, and rapidly increases.

Another prickly plant also very conspicuous in Imérina, and one of the most beautiful, is a species of Euphorbia (*E. splendens* and *E. Bojeri*), which is planted on the top of the

low earthen walls dividing plantations from the roads.
There are two varieties; one with a brilliant scarlet flower,
and the other with a pale flesh-coloured flower. Its native
name is *sòngosòngo.* It resembles some of the Cacti in its
prickly stem.

Among the trees found sparingly in the upper regions of
the island is one called *hàsina,* a species of pandanus, but
also much like a *dracœna,* with long sword-like leaves. This
sometimes attains a considerable size, growing not with a
single cluster of leaves, as is its habit when young, but
branching out into a wide-spreading tree. The young trees,
with their single head of foliage, are singularly graceful and
ornamental. The *hàsina* was formerly considered as sacred
by the people, being connected with idolatrous worship.

Grasses.—Although the central provinces of Madagascar
are very bare of wood, there are a great number of grasses,
some of which are very beautiful, and many others are of
value in the useful arts. In some marshy districts masses of
crimson grass are found, giving quite a peculiar appearance
to the landscape. It may be remarked in passing, that the
Malagasy word for "glory" is *vòninàhitra,* a word whose literal
meaning is "the flower of the grass." In some districts the
grass grows to the height of seven or eight feet, so that
travellers are quite hidden from view in the dense jungle.
In many places prickly grass (*tsévoka*) is found, preventing
the bare-footed bearers from straying an inch beyond the
narrow footpaths; and in others, a curiously barbed and
pointed grass called *léfon-dambo,* or "wild-hog's-spear," is also
a great annoyance to travellers, being strong enough to pierce
the skin. This *léfon-dambo* has the appearance of a handful
of grass tied in a bundle by two or three of the long wiry
blades. In some of the warmer districts of Madagascar
certain of the grasses have a very distinct and powerful
fragrance; and I have often felt that the scents, not less
than the sights and sounds, are among the surest signs of
one's being in a tropical country. But the grasses of Madagascar are very important to the people, as affording an
exhaustless supply of material for their household requirements. Fine straw mats, often beautifully woven in patterns,

...bidding plantations from the sea...
...some with a brilliant scarlet flower,
...pale flesh-coloured flowers. Its native
...It resembles some of the Cacti in its

...found sparingly in the upper regions of
...called *hofa*, a species of pandanus, but
...*vera*, with ... sword-like leaves. This
...is a considerable size, growing not with a
...trees, as is its habit when young, but
...into a lofty tree. The young trees
...of foliage are singularly graceful and
...tree was formerly considered as sacred
...was connected with idolatrous worship
...In the central provinces of Madagascar
...wood, there are a great number of grasses,
...of which are very beautiful, and many others are of
...useful plants. In some marshy districts masses of
...found, giving quite a peculiar appearance
...it may be remarked in passing, that the
..."is *vóninahitra*, a word which literally
..."the grass." In some districts the
...height of seven or eight feet, so that
...in them view in the dense jungle
...grass (*vero*) is found, preventing
...from straying an inch beyond the
...hairs, a curiously barbed and
...*lambo*, or "wild-hog's-spear," is also
...annoyance to travellers being strong enough to pierce
...skin. This *hy....* which has the appearance of a handful
...grass, seems to be held by two or three of the long white
...In some of the warmer districts of Madagascar
...and the grasses have a very distinct and powerful
...perfume; I have often felt that the scents, no less
...and sounds, are among the sure tokens of
...our past memory. But the grasses of Mada-
...important to the people as afford-...
...of material for their household re...
...in various ways often beautifully woven in patterns,

CHARACTERISTIC FORMS OF ANIMAL AND VEGETABLE LIFE IN MADAGASCAR.

(From Wallace's "Geographical Distribution of Animals.")

are part of the furniture of every Malagasy house; these
cover the floor, and often line the walls; and on the entrance
of a visitor, a clean one is always taken from the rolled-up
mats overhead and spread for him to sit down upon. This
straw is also platted into very neat hats and caps, which
vary in shape and pattern in different parts of the country,
and into a great variety of beautiful and durable baskets. In the Bétsiléo province the clothing of the lower
classes consists solely of a straw mat; and on the south-
eastern coast, similar mats, but made of a fine rush, are sewn
into a kind of sack, and thus worn by the coast tribes.
Small squares of mat are also used in these regions instead
of plates and dishes; and a variety of brushes are also made
from grass stalks. Several kinds of grass are used in many
parts of the country for thatching the native houses, the
long and tough stalks forming an excellent covering. Still
another purpose is served by grass in Madagascar. Owing
to the scarcity of wood in the central provinces, grass forms
the only fuel of the majority of the people. During the rainy
season it grows long and rank from the abundant moisture,
and then gets brown and dry during the six rainless months
of the cold weather. It is the work of the old slave-women
to go out and collect bundles of this fuel; and what is left
is generally set fire to towards the approach of the rainy
season, so that during the months of August, September,
and October the sky is lighted up at night with the glare
of burning grass in all directions, and visible at immense
distances all over the central provinces.

Reeds and Rushes.—Hardly less important than the grasses
are the reeds and rushes which grow in the marshes of Madagascar. Of these the *zozòro*, a species of papyrus, is the most
prominent and beautiful. This plant has a firm triangular
stem, with smooth shining skin and a pithy interior. It is
about an inch and a quarter each way, and grows to a height
of five or six feet in Imérina, with a head of long filaments
forming the flower. In the warmer parts of the country, especially in the Antsihànaka province, the *zozòro* grows to more
than double the height and size found in the colder regions,
and covers thousands of square acres of marshy land, growing

in water a foot or two deep. It is used for a variety of purposes: a number of the triangular stems are strung together by several strong tough twigs being passed through them, forming thus a kind of light door, which is used for the filling-in of the framework of houses, for doors and window-shutters, partitions, beds, and mattresses. The tough outer skin is used for making the stronger and coarser mats used for flooring, and is also platted into capital baskets. When the sovereign goes on a journey, the rivers are crossed not by canoes, but by rafts formed of great quantities of *zozòro* stems, this being the orthodox ancient custom. The paintings and carvings on the tombs and temples in Egypt indicate that the ancient Egyptians made rafts of the same materials, using the papyrus, which formerly grew plentifully in the Nile. The pith of the *zozòro* forms a good stuffing for pillows and mattresses, &c.

Another very useful rush is the *hérana*, a much smaller plant than the *zozòro*, and irregularly triangular in shape. It is extensively grown in the marshes to supply roofing material, as the great majority of the houses in the capital and its neighbourhood are thatched with *hérana*. The rushes are doubled over a stout twig, fifty or sixty of them forming one *ràvin-kérana*, as it is called. Bundles of twenty or thirty of these are sold in the markets; and when laid properly on a roof of good pitch, *hérana* forms a very neat and durable roof-covering. The roofs of the oldest style of native houses are very lofty and extremely high pitched, and in some of these the *hérana* rush roofs have lasted well for nearly a century. It is rough-looking when first done, but after having a shower or two of rain upon it, the ragged ends are all cut to a uniform surface, giving it a very neat appearance.

Vegetable Foods.—It is time to say something about those vegetable products of Madagascar which are used for food.

Standing at the head of these is rice, which is the staff of life to the great majority of the Malagasy tribes. *Mihìnam-bàry,* "to eat rice," is the native equivalent for the Eastern phrase "to eat bread," and for our English expression "to have a meal;" and all other food is only considered as *laoka,* that is, as an accompaniment to rice. The culture of the rice-fields accordingly occupies a large portion of the time of the people; and in the preparation of the ground, the bringing of water to irrigate the fields, and other necessary operations, a great amount of skill and ingenuity is displayed.

The rice-fields are of two kinds: first, those on which the rice is sown, and then those to which it is transplanted, and where it grows until it is reaped. The former are only narrow strips of ground along the banks of the rivers, or terraces on the sloping sides of the deep valleys; and to them water is conveyed from the nearest springs by means of aqueducts, often carried in a most ingenious fashion for a considerable distance along the curving sides of the hills. This is necessary from the fact that the rice is sown in the dry season, when there is no rain to afford the requisite moisture; for rice must be sown in water, and grown in water until it is ripe. Great skill is shown in the construction of these terraces; and there are few more beautiful sights than the hill-sides and valleys terraced from base to summit, often with nearly a hundred green steps.

The Hovas are very ingenious in rice culture, but they are far surpassed by the Bétsiléo in the southern central provinces. Not only are the valleys and hollows terraced, as in Imérina— the *concave* portions of the low hills and lower slopes of the high hills—but the *convex* portions also are stepped up like a gigantic staircase. These works display not only industry, but also some knowledge of hydrostatics, for I could not discover how the water was brought to some of the low hills which were surrounded by lower ground. Many of these were terraced up to their highest point, the lines of rice-field running round them in concentric circles, so that there was not a square yard of ground unproductive.

As soon as the rice-plants have reached a height of six or eight inches, they are all taken up and transplanted, plant by plant, into the rice-fields proper. These are much larger and more extensive pieces of ground, covering the surfaces of the broader valleys and alluvial plains. After being dug over, water is let into the fields, and after further working by the spade, and also by cattle being driven to and fro over the ground, the plants are stuck into the soft mud by the female slaves. The work is done with great rapidity, and yet it is difficult to understand how the enormous quantity of rice required for the consumption of a great population can be transplanted, every plant being placed separately in the ground. The Hovas maintain that the rice would not come to perfection unless thus transplanted. Some of the other tribes, however, do not take this trouble, but sow their seed sparingly on ground which has been merely trampled over by oxen while wet. And the forest tribes cut down and burn fresh portions of the woods year by year, and sow the rice in the ashes on the sloping hill-sides. West of the capital city of Antanànarìvo stretches a magnificent rice-plain, extending with its ramifications nearly twenty miles north and south, and more than ten miles east and west. When the rice is freshly planted, and again when it is harvest-time, it presents a beautiful spectacle: the villages on the low red-clay hills rising like islands from a green or a golden sea.

There are said to be eleven different kinds of rice known in Madagascar, and one or more of the fine large-grained varieties are reported to have been brought from South Carolina by a vessel accidentally touching at one of the ports of the island.

After rice, perhaps the next most important vegetable food of the Malagasy is *màngahàzo*, the common manioc or cassava, which is largely cultivated. The root consists almost entirely of a starchy flour, and forms an insipid food when boiled. Sweet potatoes, several kinds of beans, tomatoes, earth-nuts, onions, and the green leaves of a great variety of small vegetables, are also eaten by the people.

In the warmer parts of Madagascar a great variety of yams are found, some kinds growing wild. One species of edible root attains the size and thickness of a man's leg. The inside is white, and has a milky juice; it is soft as a water-melon, but without seeds, and is eaten raw. From the description given by Drury of this plant, which he calls *faungìdge*, it appears to be allied to that numerous class of juicy roots found so plentifully in Southern Africa, and without which many desert parts could not possibly be inhabited by the tribes which are found there.

A kind of millet (*ampèmby*) is grown to some extent; and of late years attempts have been made to cultivate wheat, but these have not as yet been very successful.

Several kinds of arum are cultivated for food, one of the most common being called *horirika*, the large green lily-like leaves of which may be seen in the fosses surrounding all the ancient villages in Imérina. Another arum (*A. esculentum*), called by the people *sàonjo*, has a hairy root much resembling the artichoke in taste. It is always eaten at a Malagasy housewarming, as well as at other times.

The coffee plant grows well in most parts of Madagascar, and in recent years large coffee plantations have been formed along the banks of the rivers on the eastern side of the island. These are chiefly managed by Creole traders, who, through their native wives, manage to get hold of land, and also employ slave labour, thus evading both their own country's laws and those of the Malagasy. Coffee promises already to become a very important article of export, and a source of wealth to the country.

The sugar-cane is another plant which also grows luxuriantly in Madagascar, especially in the Antsihànaka province, where it attains a height of twelve or fourteen feet. It is largely used as a sweetmeat, the cane being cut into short pieces for chewing; and in the central districts a considerable quantity is also made into a coarse brown sugar. Some few years ago European machinery was set up near Tamatave, and a very good sugar was produced. But the principal use to which the sugar-cane is applied in most places away from Imérina is in the manufacture of *tòaka*, a coarse spirit. In almost every village on the eastern coast a rude press for extracting the juice may be seen (and smelt). These presses consist of a long hollow trough, one end being solid for a foot or two, so as to form a slightly convex surface, with a channel cut on either side for the expressed juice to run into the trough. Over this is placed at right angles a rounded tree-trunk, seven or eight feet long, with two or three short handles fixed into it; this is turned backwards and forwards over pieces of cane laid on the convex surface, the juice being expressed by the mere weight of the round trunk. The freshly-expressed juice makes a pleasant drink; after a day or two it ferments, and is then still more agreeable, much like fresh cider; but it rapidly becomes too heady. The native still is as rude a contrivance as the press: an earthen pot with its cover fixed on with a luting of clay for boiling the juice, from which a piece of iron piping conveys the vapour through an old rum cask filled with cold water. In the central province there is, happily, a very stringent law against the manufacture or importation of spirits; but drinking habits have a fearful hold upon the ignorant coast tribes, further aggravated by the quantity of foreign rum imported by Mauritius merchants. There are said to be fourteen varieties of sugar-cane known in Madagascar.

Spirits are also made from a plant which grows plentifully in the country, the *séva* or *Buddleia Madagascariensis* (order *Solanaceæ*), which has long spikes of orange-coloured flowers; these are made use of in dyeing the coarser rofia fibre-cloths.

Of condiments there are quite sufficient to supply the needs of the Malagasy, who, however, do not use hot spices so largely as do many of the inhabitants of the tropics. Chillies (*sakày*) grow abundantly in many places, and their small brilliant scarlet pods contrasting with the glossy green leaves make them quite an ornamental shrub. Ginger (*sàkamalào*) is also cultivated to some extent. In the warmer parts of the island a spice, which is said to combine the virtues of nutmegs, cloves, and cinnamon, is procured from a tree called *ràvintsàra* ("excellent leaf"). The leaves, as well as the fruits and seeds, are fragrant, and are the produce of a magnificent tree.

In the interior of Madagascar a good variety of fruit is procurable, although many of them have been introduced into the island at a very recent period. Of the juicy sub-acid fruits we have oranges, citrons, lemons, and limes. These last grow wild and abundantly in the warmer parts of the country, and are most refreshing and wholesome. Mangoes are among the finest Malagasy fruits, and the tree on which they grow is one of the most ornamental. The mango-tree attains a great size on the north-western coast, some of the finest specimens being found at Mojangà. Besides these we have peaches, guavas, Chinese guavas, *bibàsy* or loquat, pine-apples, mulberries, pomegranates, grapes, and Cape gooseberries. Bananas are most plentiful, and of several varieties; the largest are called *òntsy*, and are more than a foot long. The trees attain a great size on the coast, and there are few more beautiful sights than a grove of these, with their smooth shining green stems eight or ten inches in diameter, and the canopy of graceful leaves twenty or thirty feet overhead. In some provinces a fine cloth is made from the fibres of the banana; the green succulent stems are also used as food for cattle, and from their containing a great deal of water they are used to put out fires. Figs and quinces have been grown to some small extent, and in the neighbourhood of the woods wild raspberries, very large and fine, are found in great abundance. Besides the foregoing, there is a considerable variety of wild berries and other fruits, which are esteemed by the people, although most of them are not much cared for by Europeans.

The most striking and characteristic tree of Madagascar is doubtless the traveller's tree (*Urania speciosa*), which is so plentiful in the island, and gives quite a unique character to the scenery of the maritime plains and the lower slopes of the outer belt of forest.

This tree belongs to the order *Musaceæ*, although in some points its structure resembles the palms rather than the plantains. It is immediately recognised as strikingly distinct from all other trees, even from the elegant palms, by its graceful crown of broad and light-green banana-like leaves, arranged, not as in almost every other tree and plant, *around* the stem, but at the top of its trunk, in the shape of a fan. The leaves are from twenty to thirty in number, and from eight to ten feet long by a foot and a half broad. They very closely resemble those of the banana, and when unbroken by the wind have a very striking and beautiful appearance. The trunk varies very much in height, according to the situation of the tree. On the coast plains, where, with the pandanus, it is the dominant form of vegetation and has plenty of room, its average height is from fifteen to twenty feet to the base of the leaf-stalks; but in the forest, where it has a crowd of rivals in obtaining light and air, it shoots up to heights of

eighty or ninety feet. The trunk is from twelve to eighteen
inches in diameter; but it is of a soft spongy texture, and
not of much service as timber. It grows at all heights from
the sea-level to an elevation of about 2000 feet, but is never
found in the higher plateaux of the island.

While travelling through the Taimòro country I noticed
that the fruit is seen on almost every tree, forming three or
four clusters of sheaths, about a dozen in each, much resembling in shape and size the horns of a short-horned ox. These
project from between the leaf-stalks, two in full bloom and
the other two generally dying off, or shedding the seeds, or
rather the seed-pods. These are oval in shape, about two
inches long, and yellow in colour, something like very large
dates, but with a hard woody fibrous covering. When ripe
they open and show each pod dividing into three parts, each
of which is double, thus containing six rows of seeds about
the size of a small bean. Each seed is wrapped in a covering
looking exactly like a small piece of light-blue silk with
scalloped edges.

In proceeding along the coast we had an opportunity of
testing the accuracy of the accounts given of the water procurable from the traveller's tree, about which I had always
felt rather sceptical, as somewhat of a "traveller's tale." In
fact, I had never before seen the tree where plenty of good
water was not procurable; but here there was none for several
miles except the stagnant water of the lagoons. We found
that on piercing with a spear or pointed stick the lower part
of one of the leaf-stalks, where they all clasp one over the
other, a small stream of water spurted out, from which one
could drink to the full of good cool sweet water. If one of
the leaf-stalks was forcibly drawn down, a quantity of water
gushed out, so that we afterwards readily filled a large cup
with as much as we needed. On examining a section of one
of the stalks, a hollow channel about a quarter of an inch in
diameter is seen running all down the inner side of the stalk
from the base of the leaf. This appears to collect the water
condensed from the atmosphere by the large cool surface of
the leaf, and conducts it downwards. The leaf-stalks are all
full of cells like those of the banana. After three hours'

walking along the shore in the heavy sand, with a hot sun overhead, we were glad to draw from these numberless vegetable springs, and thanked the Giver of these living fountains in that thirsty land. We afterwards found that in some villages the people supply themselves constantly from this source.

But a supply of water is only one of the many benefits the coast tribes derive from this beautiful tree. All along the east coast the houses are made of a slight framework, and filled in with the mid-rib of the leaf of the traveller's tree in the same way that the *zozòro* (papyrus) is used in Imérina, and looking exactly like the *zozòro*. The leaf-stalks are fixed together on long fine twigs, so as to make a kind of stiff mat. One of these forms the door on either side of the house, being shifted backwards and forwards, and kept from falling by sliding within a light pole hung from the framework. The flooring, which is always raised above the ground, is made of the bark of the traveller's tree, pressed flat so as to form a rough kind of boarding. And the thatch of every house is the leaf of the same tree, which forms a very neat as well as durable covering. The traveller's tree might therefore, with equal or greater propriety, be called "the builder's tree." The green leaves also are the ordinary plates and dishes of the coast people.

It has been generally believed that the traveller's tree was peculiar to Madagascar, but I find that it also grows in the Malay Peninsula. In a book entitled *The Land of the White Elephant: Sights and Scenes in South-Eastern Asia*, by Frank Vincent, jun., an American traveller (London: 1873), at p. 109, in speaking of the neighbourhood of Singapore, the writer says: "The road [leading from the town into the interior of the island] is very pretty, being lined by tall bamboo hedges and trees which, uniting above, form a complete shade; the beautiful *fan-palm*, or 'traveller's fountain,' as it is sometimes called, will deserve especial notice, with its immense spread of feathery leaves, constituting an exact semicircle."

The tree is not again mentioned by the writer, but a beautiful engraving is given of this "traveller's fountain," which seems identical with our Madagascar "traveller's tree," except that it has a larger number of leaves than is seen in the latter tree. There are *forty-eight* in the engraving, which is evidently from a photograph.

As far as I am aware, this fact has not been noticed by any other traveller, but it is another link of connection between Madagascar and the Malay Peninsula.

Plants used as Medicines and in the Arts.—The Malagasy have from time immemorial been acquainted with numerous roots, herbs, and trees which they believe to be efficacious in medicine and surgery. These are largely connected with that belief in charms which is the groundwork of their idolatrous worship; but many of them have real curative powers, and many others would probably prove on examination to be valuable additions to our *materia medica*. The castor-oil plant, with its beautifully-indented leaves and green fruit covered with minute papillæ, is very common in the native gardens, and also grows wild. The fruit or berry is pounded, and a thick green oil extracted for use by boiling. Aloes of great size are among the most ornamental vegetable productions of the interior. The great fleshy leaves considerably exceed in height the stature of a man; and when the plant blossoms, a great flower-stalk, straight and tapering as a mast, shoots up from the centre of the plant to a height of between twenty and thirty feet, with a crown of flowers, many hundreds in number. The juice is used medicinally, and a fine strong silky thread is prepared from the fibres of the leaves and flower-stalk. A much smaller variety of aloe (called *váhana*) is found plentifully on the bare summits of the hills. The leaves are edged with red, and it bears a tall spike of red and yellow flowers.

In travelling through the skirts of the great forest on the eastern coast, one passes continually through dense thickets of a plant called *longòzy*. This is a species of cardamom (*Amomum cardamomum*); the stem is a tall tapering rod, five or six feet high, with a number of long simple leaves. The fruit is a kind of scarlet pod, found near the base of the stem, and contains a sweetish acid pulp of a silky white appearance; but if one of the small purplish black seeds is accidentally crushed by the teeth, a most unpleasant burning sensation is felt for some minutes at the back of the mouth and in the throat.

Among the plants which are useful in Madagascar for other purposes besides food must be reckoned the gourds. These are found in great variety of shape and size, and are used instead of bottles, and for storing all kinds of liquids. A rude kind of guitar or banjo, called *lokànga*, is also made with a gourd; a long piece of wood with three or four strings is fixed to a gourd of a flat shape so as to give the resonance required; but the music produced is not of a very high order.

Tobacco is grown in considerable quantities by the Malagasy. It has not, however, been used for smoking until very recently, the native use of the fragrant weed being to take it in the form of snuff; and this again is not applied, as in most countries, to the *nostrils*, but is tossed by a dexterous jerk of the hand into the *mouth*, where it is retained for a few minutes under the tongue. This snuff is carried about in a beautifully-polished piece of hollow cane or bamboo. Hemp (*rongòny*) is also occasionally smoked by some of the more dissolute portion of the people, but its use is illegal.

For its more legitimate uses, however, hemp is grown to some extent, and is woven by the women into a coarse strong cloth for lambas, the national article of dress. Cotton is also cultivated, and a great variety of beautiful cloths are manufactured from it. The most favourite kinds are made in stripes with richly ornamented borders, in which silk is introduced.

Many of the dyes are procured from vegetable substances, the reddish brown used as the groundwork of many lambas being obtained from the bark of a large forest tree called *nàto*. Another vegetable dye, which is of some commercial importance, is the *orseille*, a lichen which forms the principal product of the sterile country at the south-west corner of the island, and grows in abundance on the bark of the spiny shrubs which are the characteristic vegetation of that region. Indigo, called in the native language *aika*, is cultivated by the Malagasy, and might probably, by the application of

European skill and capital, be so largely grown as to become one of the most valuable exports.

For the sustenance of the different species of silkworms the leaves of the mulberry-tree are used to some extent; but in the central portions of the island another tree is largely used for this purpose. This is the *tapia*, a small tree of which there are extensive plantations. The fruit, which is edible, is a long green pod containing a sweetish pulp.

The lichens growing on the bare rocks and hills of the treeless central provinces have not yet been collected in any complete manner, but from a few specimens obtained by the late Mrs. Pool, the Rev. J. M. Crombie remarks: "Judging from its climate and situation, there can be no doubt that Madagascar possesses a very rich and extensive lichen flora. Unfortunately, however, it is still in this respect almost entirely a *terra incognita*, nor does the present small collection throw much light upon its lichen treasures, though it affords some indications that these are both valuable and varied." *

Flowering Plants and Trees.—In speaking of Madagascar, as well as of most tropical countries, it is frequently remarked, "Of course there are very magnificent flowers there." It is a common mistake to suppose that in the matter of wild flowers the tropics are much richer than the temperate zones. But, as has been well shown by Mr. Alfred Wallace in his work on *The Malay Archipelago* (vol. i. 127, 128; ii. 294–298), the reverse is the case; and although there are, it is true, many beautiful flowers, they do not occur in great numbers, nor are they found in such masses as to give a character to the scenery. There is, for instance, nothing comparable to the effect of gorse, or heather, or clover, or even of the buttercups and daisies of an English meadow. It should be observed, however, that this remark applies chiefly to flowers *growing on the ground;* for in the forest

* *Jour. Linn. Soc., Bot.*, vol. xv. No. 86, pp. 409, 410. A list of the fifteen species is given, from which it appears that the lichens belong to the following six genera:—Thærophoron (1), Usnea (3, a species of Usnea, U. xanthophaga, is found in the Campbell Islands), Parmelia (1), Stictina (7), Ricasolia (this has special interest as being hitherto only known as inhabiting equinoctial America), and Physcia (2).

there are many *trees* which, when in flower, present grand masses of colour, being covered with scarlet, yellow, crimson, or purple bloom. No recent traveller has given more attention to the floral wealth of Madagascar, or described it with so much enthusiasm, as the late Rev. W. Ellis, who was an accomplished botanist, as well as an earnest missionary. Among the flowering plants Mr. Ellis mentions as seen on the eastern coast are species of acacia, solanum, vinca or *Catharanthus roseus*, gardenia, and many kinds of hibiscus; one of these latter (*H. tiliaceus*) grows to a great size, straggling over a considerable space, and covered with large yellow and claret-coloured blossoms. The aleurites or candlenut, common in Polynésia, is also seen on that coast, and also trees of large and shining foliage, like the magnolia, and large - leaved betonicas. Amongst Madagascar trees which have become naturalised in Mauritius, and "conspicuous beyond all the rest, is the stately and gorgeous *Poinciana regia*, compact-growing and regular in form, but retaining something of the acacia habit, rising sometimes to the height of forty or fifty feet, and between the months of December and April presenting amidst its delicate pea-green pinnated leaves one vast pyramid of bunches of bright, dazzling scarlet flowers. Seen sometimes over the tops of the houses, and at others in an open space standing forth in truly regal splendour, this is certainly one of the most magnificent of trees. Its common name is 'mille fleurs,' or 'flamboyant.' The Poinciana, and the large beautifully yellow-flowering Colvillia, as well as some fine and fragrant species of Dombeya, and other kinds, were introduced from Madagascar by M. Bojer, a German naturalist, in 1824."[*] A magnificent creeping-plant (*Crypta stygia*), with masses of purple flowers, has been introduced into the capital, as well as into Mauritius. Other flowering plants noticed by Mr. Ellis are heaths, species of petunias, gentians (*Tachiademus carinatus*, and *T. medinilla*), and others resembling *Stephanotis*, vanilla (*Dendrobium*), and Indian shot (*Canna indica*).

Another tree conspicuous for its beauty when in flower is the *Astrapœa Wallichii* or viscosa. The Malagasy name for it

---

[*] *Three Visits to Madagascar*, pp. 41, 57.

is derived from a word meaning "lightning," on account of the brilliancy of its flowers. Sir Joseph Paxton and Dr. Lindley have thus spoken of *A. Wallichii:* "One of the finest plants ever introduced, and when loaded with its magnificent flowers we think nothing can exceed its grandeur." * Mr. Ellis says of it: "I had seen a good-sized plant growing freely at Mauritius, but here it was in its native home, luxuriating on the banks of the stream, its trunk a foot in diameter, its broad-leaved branches stretching over the water, and its large, pink, globular, composite flowers, three or four inches in diameter, suspended at the end of a fine down-covered stalk, nine inches or a foot in length. These, hanging by hundreds along the course of the stream, surpassed anything of the kind I had seen, or could possibly have imagined." †

There are many fine orchids in the Madagascar woods: among these two species of *Angræcum* were brought into notice by Mr. Ellis, who was the first to bring specimens of them to England. One of these, the *A. sesquipedale*, has an extraordinarily long spur; some of those measured by Mr. Ellis being fourteen inches in length, thus nearly approaching the foot and a half to which it owes its name first given by Du Petit Thouars. This spur points to the existence of an insect with an extremely long trunk or sucking-tube for the fertilisation of the flower. The exquisitely white waxy flowers of these orchids are seen very frequently in the forests, masses of the thick fleshy leaves occupying the forks of the branches or any projecting part of the trunk, places which they share with the hart's-tongue and stag's-horn ferns. Mr. Ellis says he "found the trunk of a tree lying quite rotten on the ground, and *Angræcum sesquipedale* growing at intervals along its whole length, the roots having penetrated into the decayed vegetable fibre of the tree." In specimens which have been brought to England the pure waxy white flowers preserve all their delicate beauty for more than five weeks. Of another orchid brought to England by Mr. Ellis (*Epiphora pubescens*) Dr. Lindley says, "This little-known orchid is one that all lovers of what is beautiful and fragrant will eagerly welcome. Its scent equals the sweetest lilies of the valley, and its flowers are of the deepest golden yellow, most richly striped with crimson." *

One of the finest displays of flowers I ever saw in Madagascar was on the sea-shore near the mouth of the river Màtitànana. A considerable space of ground was covered with bushes of what I suppose were *orchis* plants, although the flowers exactly resembled those of an orchid growing on trees higher up the source of the river. Each bush had a score or two of branches, and each branch bore a number of large waxy white flowers, all in bloom, the whole forming a magnificent sight.

Vegetable Exports.—Many of the vegetable productions of Madagascar are of considerable commercial value. Of late years large quantities of gum-copal have been exported. This is obtained from more than one species of tree growing chiefly on the eastern coast. The forests are rich in gum-producing trees, and long lists of such are given in the works of early writers on Madagascar. The gum of certain trees has been used from time immemorial as incense, for in the worship of the charms or *ody* venerated by the Malagasy tribes, these were always invoked together with the fumes of fragrant gums ; and some have supposed that the most frequent name for the Supreme Being, *Andriamànitra*—that is, " The Fragrant One " —is derived from the use of incense in the ancient religious worship of the people.

Large quantities of indiarubber have also been exported from Madagascar during the past few years. Some of this is obtained from a liana or creeper (*Vahea gummifera*), but the greater portion comes from trees of a considerable size. But such a wanton destruction of the trees has taken place that unless some restrictions are placed upon the production, the trade will be wholly at an end at no very distant period.

From what has been already said it will be seen that the vegetable productions of Madagascar are very varied and abundant, and were European capital and skill to be introduced, large quantities of almost every kind of tropical pro-

* *Gardener's Chronicle,* May 28, 1858.

duce might be grown for export, and prove a source of
immense wealth. Rice is already exported in some quantity,
and coffee is being grown to a considerable extent, and its
production is yearly increasing; but sugar, indigo, tobacco,
and spices might also be produced in quantities practically
inexhaustible. The valuable timber of the immense forests
is also certain at some future time to form an important item
in the exports of the country, and a careful scientific exploration of the woods would doubtless bring to light other
vegetable products of commercial value. No such complete
investigation, however, has yet been made. Many years ago,
Sonnerat, a French naturalist, called Madagascar the land of
promise for the botanist, and Du Petit Thouars said that ten
years would not suffice to gain an adequate idea of the vegetable treasures of the island; but the jealousy of the native
government up to a very recent period, and the unhealthi-
ness of many parts of the country, have hitherto prevented
scientific botanists from attempting a thorough exploration
of the interminable woods. About forty or fifty years ago
Messrs. Bojer and Hilsenberg explored parts of the island, but
no complete or accessible record of their researches has been
published. M. Grandidier's great work on Madagascar, now
in progress, will probably do something to fill up the gap.

The Lace-leaf Plant.—This chapter may be concluded by
a description of a very interesting plant peculiar to Madagascar, and which is called by Sir W. J. Hooker " one of the
most curious of nature's productions." This is the Lace-leaf
plant, or water-yam; in scientific phraseology, *Ouvirandra
fenestralis.* This curious plant has an edible root, and grows
under water a foot or more deep; from this spring a number
of graceful leaves, which spread out just under the surface.
These leaves are nine or ten inches long and a couple of
inches wide, and their structure is most remarkable, for the
whole leaf is like a living fibrous skeleton rather than an ordinary leaf. The portions of the leaf between the veining are not
filled up, as in every other plant, but are open, so that the
whole is composed of fine tendrils in a regular pattern, so as
to resemble a piece of bright green lace or open needlework.
Mr. Ellis says, " It is scarcely possible to imagine any object

of the kind more attractive and beautiful than a full-grown specimen of this plant, with its dark-green leaves forming the limit of a circle two or three feet in diameter, and in the transparent water within that circle presenting leaves of every stage of development, both as to colour and size." The flower is a curious forked tuft, pink in colour, and rises above the surface of the water during the fructification. The ouvirandra grows in the streams along the eastern coast, but it is also found abundantly in the colder interior provinces in running water not many miles west of the capital. Mr. Ellis was the first to bring plants of the lace-leaf to England, and from these specimens have been obtained for the principal botanic gardens of London and its neighbourhood. For a long time this plant was supposed to be unique, but a few years ago another species was discovered in West Africa by a French botanist, and a third has since been found in Senegal, but these are said to be much less singular in appearance, the spaces which are open in the Madagascar species being partially or entirely filled up in the African ones.

The facts now given will be sufficient to show that Madagascar is a country of great interest to the botanist as well as to the zoologist; and it may be hoped that many more years will not elapse before its still unexplored vegetable riches shall have been thoroughly investigated by scientific travellers. There are probably many wonders and beauties of vegetable life still awaiting discovery, and yet hidden in the depths of those vast forests which form a green girdle round the island.

CHAPTER V.

ORIGIN AND DIVISIONS OF THE MALAGASY PEOPLE.

MALAYO-POLYNESIAN AFFINITIES—ALLEGED CONNECTION WITH AFRICAN RACES —EUROPEAN AND ARAB ELEMENTS—AFRICAN INFLUENCE ON WEST COAST —PRINCIPAL DIVISIONS OF THE PEOPLE—COLOUR, PHYSIQUE, AND LANGUAGE—DIFFICULT PROBLEMS RAISED BY VARIATIONS IN THESE RESPECTS —ATTEMPTED SOLUTIONS OF THESE—LIGHT AFFORDED BY TRADITION AND PHILOLOGY.

IT has already been pointed out, in treating of the animal life of Madagascar, that there are numerous most interesting questions raised by the very exceptional character of the fauna of the island, and that a considerable proportion of the living creatures inhabiting the country have very remote affinities, their nearest allies being found not in Africa, but in the Malay Peninsula and Archipelago, and even in still more distant regions. The same fact of dissimilarity between island and continent meets us when considering the Ethnology of Madagascar. For it may be confidently said that a considerable proportion of its inhabitants are not of African origin, but are unmistakably connected with the races which inhabit the Polynesian and Malayan Archipelagoes, and are thus the most western representatives of that very widely-extended division of mankind.

This fact, although denied by one or two writers whose opinion is entitled to respect, is now generally admitted by ethnologists. The grounds for this belief are found in the close connection between the languages of Madagascar and those of the Malayo-Polynesian races, and in the similarity of the customs, handicrafts, and mental and physical characteristics of these now widely-separated peoples. These resemblances will be noticed more in detail in succeeding chapters upon the language, customs, superstitions, art, and relationships of the Malagasy, and form a chain of evidence which is exceedingly strong, and which is confirmed by every recent accession to our information about the various tribes inhabiting Madagascar.

The Malay relationships of the Malagasy have, however, been disputed by Mr. Crawfurd, who, in *A Dissertation on the Affinities of the Malayan Languages*, maintained that the connection between them was very slight indeed, and endeavoured to account for the presence of the undoubted resemblances between them by the arrival of a few piratical proas driven by a hurricane from the Malay Archipelago, and bringing with them a few of the most necessary articles of food. The words for these, together with others, of an admittedly very important character, he thinks maintained their ground, while the immigrants themselves were absorbed in the mass of the population. But Mr. Crawfurd has largely underrated the connection between the two languages, as has been conclusively shown by the Rev. W. E. Cousins; and those who know the Malagasy will be disposed to place little reliance upon his opinion on this point where he says that they "do not bear any resemblance to" the Malays, and that "they are in fact negroes, but negroes of a particular description."

Another writer, Mr. C. Staniland Wake, in a paper read before the Anthropological Society (Dec. 14, 1869) on "The Race Elements of the Madecasses," has endeavoured to show that there is a much closer connection between the peoples of Madagascar and those of South and East Africa than had hitherto been supposed. This opinion he tries to prove by pointing out a number of resemblances between them in physical structure, hair, craniology, pastoral habits, political arrangements, and in religious notions and superstitions. No doubt some of these are entitled to be considered as of weight; and the quotations he gives of descriptions of a Hova and a Bétsimisàraka skull are very important confirmations of his opinion, *if they are indeed fair specimens of the craniology of these tribes respectively.* But as it is very difficult to obtain a Hova cranium, it appears to me that it is quite possible that the specimen described by Dr. Carter Blake and adduced by

Mr. Wake, although possibly obtained in Imérina, may have been that of a slave, either from one of the tribes distant from the Hovas, or even from an individual with a distinctly African admixture.

Those who have lived among the Malagasy in the central province know how carefully and religiously they preserve and bury the bones of their dead, so that it is one of the most difficult matters possible to obtain a skull of one of the free people; while violation of a grave is looked upon as the most heinous of crimes. Unless, therefore, there was most unmistakable evidence that the skull in question was really that of a pure Hova, little stress can be laid upon the evidence of a single so-called Hova skull. Could a series of crania be procured from all the principal divisions of the inhabitants of Madagascar, some most valuable information as to the affinities of the Malagasy would doubtless be obtained; but owing to the superstitions and habits of the people there seems little hope at present of getting light on this question from such a source.

Mr. Wake has, I think, laid too little stress upon some other points which tell against the supposed African affinities, such as the Malagasy non-use of skins for clothing, a material so universally employed in South Africa; their use of woven and beaten-out vegetable fibres, which connects them so closely with the Polynesian tribes; the use of the feather-bellows found among the Malays; their ancient knowledge of iron-smelting; the employment of the brotherhood-by-blood covenant, &c., &c. And the affinities which he believes he finds between the languages of South Africa and of Madagascar seem, in the greater number of the examples he adduces, to be of so obscure and doubtful a character that they have very little value as establishing any relationship. Mr. Wake takes his illustrations from Dumont D'Urville's Vocabulary, but in dictionaries of the Hova dialect, either French or English, or even the *Vocabulaire Sakalava et Betsimisara* of the Abbé Dalmond—much fuller and more correct works than D'Urville's—some of the supposed resemblances disappear entirely, while some of the words cited as connected with South African tongues—Kafir and Namaqua

—are found unaltered from the Malagasy form of them in one or other of the Malayo-Polynesian languages.

It must be said here that Mr. Wake does not deny *some* Malayan affinities in the Malagasy (indeed he devotes a long paragraph of his paper to an examination of the points of agreement between the Hovas and the Siamese, saying that " it is among the more civilised people of the Malayan Archipelago that we must seek for special Hova affinities "), but he thinks the African relationships as strong; so much so that he is inclined to suppose that many of the African races went *from* Madagascar to the continent, and that Madagascar, or some spot farther eastward, and now submerged, was the seat of man's primitive civilisation.

If, however, we take such a work as Mr. Alfred Wallace's *Malay Archipelago*, and examine the vocabularies given at the end of the second volume, we shall find that in the list of " Nine Words in Fifty-nine Languages " of that region, the Malagasy words are discovered in every one of the nine columns; and not only so, but in most of these nine examples words exactly like, or most closely identical with, the Malagasy are found in a great number of the fifty-nine languages. Thus, the Malagasy *afo* (fire) is found in twenty languages; *léla* (tongue) also in twenty; *fôtsy* (white), in thirty; and so on. Again, in the list of " One Hundred and Seventeen Words in Thirty-three Languages of the Malay Archipelago," the Malagasy words are found in more than eighty, or five-sevenths of the whole number; and also, as in the other list, often in not one only, but in many of these thirty-three languages. This remark applies to the Hova form of Malagasy, but it is highly probable that were the coast dialects more fully known many other similarities would be discovered. And it is also a fact that in the Polynesian languages, and in those of New Guinea, there are also numerous correspondences with Malagasy; so that the argument for the Malayo-Polynesian affinities with the Madagascar language is very strong indeed, and there is nothing yet produced on the African side which can be at all compared with it.

It will, however, be desirable to state in as brief a form

as is possible what we know positively about the Malagasy people ethnologically considered. But it must be premised that our information is still very defective, for no careful and systematic examination of the differences between the various tribes found in the island has yet been made; and in addition to the want of cranial observations we much need a series of photographs, both in full face and profile, of typical specimens of the different races, together with particulars as to their colour, hair, height, &c., &c.

From the long intercourse Europeans have now had with the people of the eastern coast and of Imérina, these are the best known of the various tribes; but there are in both cases certain extraneous elements intermingled, so that it is not quite easy to determine how far these have modified the original stock. On the eastern coast there is an undoubted European mixture in the population, arising partly from the intercourse which the pirates of the early part of the eighteenth century had with the people, and also from the Creole settlers and planters, who take native wives, and whose children become absorbed in the native population. There is also a certain amount of foreign blood derived from sailors and others who touch at the ports. When coming down to the east coast in 1867, after nearly four years' familiarity with the Hovas only, I was much struck with the lighter colour of the Bétsimisàraka women as compared with the Hova women.

In addition to this European mixture there is also an Arabian element in the eastern tribes, derived from the ancient Arab settlements, both in the province of Màtitànana on the south-east coast, and in the island of St. Marie's and the mainland opposite to it, farther north. It is possible, however, that this did not materially affect the mass of the people (although it has left ineffaceable traces of its influence on the language), since the white settlers became the princes and nobles of some districts, and kept themselves apart from the rest of the people. In some tribes these white chiefs are said to have been exterminated by the French, to whose settlement in the country they were strongly opposed; but, on the other hand, the chiefs of some of the Tanàla or forest tribes, living many miles inland, in the heart of the dense woods of the eastern side of the island, are said to derive their origin from the Arab settlers. In the *Antanānarìvo Annual* for 1877 (No. ii.) there is some information derived from the Tanàla people of Ivòhitròsa, a village situated at the edge of the high table-land of south-eastern Bétsiléo. In this paper it is said that the chiefs of Ivòhitròsa, together with those of other places in this same forest region north and south of them, are descended from those who "came from across the ocean, they were not natives of Madagascar." Then follow the names of the ancestors of the different tribes, Firàmbo being the father of the chiefs called Zàfiràmbo, &c. (*Zàfy*, be it remembered, is the native word for "descendant," and also for "grandchild.")

This account is confirmed by a short paper in the same publication for 1878 (p. 115), in which the Rev. W. D. Cowan describes a stone elephant which still exists at a village called Ambòhisàry on the east coast. This figure is made of soap-stone, and is in a good state of preservation; it is about seven feet long and four feet high. It is hollow, and evidently formed a receptacle for gifts and offerings. According to tradition this stone elephant was brought from Imàka (Mecca?) by Ramanìa, the ancestor of the tribe called Zàfira-manìa, who inhabit the district about Mànanjàra. This man is said to have been an uncle of Mohammed, and there are numerous details of his history preserved in Arabic books kept by his descendants, some of which were translated by order of Flacourt, the French Commandant at Fort Dauphin (1648–1655), and others by order of Benyowski (1774–1786). From other Arabs who arrived at about the same time as Ramanìa are said to be descended other ruling clans (or *andrians*) along the east coast of Madagascar. And of these clans Mr. Cowan says: "Having now met with representative chiefs of several of these divisions, I speak with confidence of their remarkable resemblance and distinctive character, which separates them widely from the people over whom they rule, and goes far to verify their traditions." I must, however, remark here that my own knowledge of these people, derived from a journey through the southern

Tanàla country and the south-eastern coast, does not confirm what Mr. Cowan here states. I could see *no difference* between the clans he names and the mass of the people. But as Mr. Cowan has had fuller and more frequent opportunities of observation than I have had, his opinion is entitled to considerable weight. At Ambòhipéno, near the mouth of the Màtitànana, some of the people, who call themselves *Zàfy Ibrahim* (" descendants of Abraham "), said to me in conversation, " We are altogether Jews; " but I could not detect any difference in colour, features, or dialect between them and the other people of the eastern coast. At the same time the Arab influence in this region is undoubted. At this very place M. Grandidier obtained in 1870 copies of Arabic books on various subjects. And here also a son of one of the former *òmbiàsy*, or diviners, gave me a paper with a number of Arabic words, equivalents for as many Malagasy ones; showing that, in some families at least, a knowledge of the language of their ancestors had not yet died out.

Farther north also, at the Isle of St. Marie's, and the adjacent mainland, the people call themselves Zàfy Ibrahim. If the traditions and written documents referred to above are correct in the main, this Arab element must have come into Madagascar about 1200 years ago (the Hegira or Mohammedan era was A.D. 662), and as the immigrants seem chiefly to have been *men*, for some are expressly mentioned as taking native women as wives, it is not remarkable that the foreign influence is so little prominent in the features and colour of the people. During all these hundreds of years the mixture with native blood has been assimilating it more and more every succeeding generation with that of the majority of the population, and climatic and other influences have also been working in the same direction.*

Besides this Arab influence exerted many hundred years ago

* It is perhaps not unworthy of remark, that the names of the Arab ancestors of the noble clans in the south-east of Madagascar seem derived from purely Malagasy roots, for Ramanla, Isàmbo, Imahàzo, Imanély, and Iràmbo are all good Malagasy words. Possibly, however, they have been somewhat altered from their original form to those more exactly resembling native words, a change of which there are numerous examples in the names of things of foreign introduction.

on the south-east coast, it is also found in operation to this very day on the opposite side of the island, the north-west, as will be noticed presently when speaking of the Sàkalàva tribes.

Among the Hovas, in the central province of Imérina, there is probably only a slight foreign (*i.e.*, extra-Malagasy) mixture of blood, although the whitest and most European-like natives are to be found among the upper and well-to-do classes; and in looking at some of these I have felt strongly inclined to believe that some not very remote ancestor of theirs was not a native Malagasy. Taking the population of Imérina as a whole, there can be no doubt that it is of a more mixed character than is the case in many provinces. For during the first half of the present century, when the Hovas were pursuing their career of conquest through the central and eastern portions of Madagascar, great numbers of the women and children of the conquered tribes were brought back to the capital and its neighbourhood, where their descendants now form a large proportion of the slave population. It is at the same time quite true that the free people do not intermarry with the slaves, and those free people who may become slaves for debt or other causes (*zàza-Hòva*) marry among themselves, and not with the slaves proper (*andévo*). And the *Andrians* or noble clans (with some strictly defined exceptions) marry from those of their own rank. So that there is a tendency from the habits of the people to keep the original stock of any tribe free from much foreign intermixture, for tribes and families, as a rule, marry among themselves in order to keep landed property together, as well as from a strong clannish feeling.

The people of the western and northern portions of Madagascar, loosely called Sàkalàvas, have *three* decided foreign elements mingled with them, or, at least, found among them. First, there are the Arab immigrants just referred to.* The Arabs have probably had intercourse with the country, and numbers of them have settled in it, for many hundred years past, although they seem to have kept themselves distinct to

* These people are called *Salàma* by the Malagasy; is this name derived from the salutation *salama* = Heb. *shalom?*

a great extent from the native population, and do not intermarry much with them, except they can get hold of an
heiress or a woman of high rank.   Then there is an Indian
element, there being a considerable number of Banyan
traders from Kutch and Bombay at some of the large towns
on the north-west coast, so that Indian dress, ornaments,
utensils, music, and customs meet one at every turn in these
places.   And as both Arabs and Indians are Mohammedans,
the towns of Màrovoày, Mojangà, Mòrontsànga, and some of
the islands, are much more like Arab or Hindoo places than
Malagasy ones.   The houses in these places are of stone,
with flat roofs and deep shady recesses ; there are mosques
for worship, and the cry of the *muezzin* is heard at the
appointed times of the day for Mohammedan prayers.

Then there is an African element, derived from the
numbers of slaves from the mainland who have been brought
into the country from time immemorial by the Arab slaving
dhows.   The emancipation of the African slaves two years
ago by the Hova government will doubtless do much to stop
this traffic, although, from the character of the north-west
coast of Madagascar,—full of bays and inlets, where a dhow
can easily evade the English cruisers,—it will probably go
on to some extent wherever the Hova authority is slight.
According to Sir Bartle Frere and other authorities, hundreds
of slaves were, until a short time ago, brought into the
country every year.   This infusion from the neighbouring
continent has doubtless had some effect on the language of
the western tribes, and probably added a darker strain to
their colour.

Having now looked at the foreign influences which have
been at work in various parts of Madagascar to modify the
original Malagasy stock, something may be said about the
chief differences to be remarked among the various tribes as
regards colour and physique.

Every traveller in Madagascar is aware that there are
very considerable differences in the colour, outline (as viewed
in front) and profile of the face, and stature of the people he
meets with in passing through the country.   He finds almost
every shade of colour, from a very light olive, not darker

than is seen in the peoples of southern Europe, down through
all gradations of brown to a tint which, although not black,
is certainly very dark. In the quality of the hair, too, there
is a good deal of difference; the lighter-coloured people having
usually long, black, and straight hair, while the darker tribes
have, as a rule, shorter and more frizzly hair, although it is
rarely, if ever, of the true negro woolly or tufted kind of
head-covering. This correspondence of colour of skin with a
certain kind of hair is, however, by no means invariable,
curling and frizzly hair being sometimes found with light-
coloured skin, and straight hair with dark skin. And even
where the hair is frizzly it is often long enough to be braided
in various fashions, so that the Sàkalàva and others of the
darkest-hued people have their hair arranged in a number
of long tails consisting of minute plaits, a kind of hair-
dressing hardly possible where the hair is rather a kind of
wool.*

In the contour of face and head also there is considerable
variety, many individuals approaching in this particular to a
European type; others having the high-cheek-bone Malayan
form of face; others again have some approximation to what
are considered as typical African features—broad nostrils,
somewhat prognathous in profile, and thicker lips, although
I do not remember to have seen any true Malagasy with
decidedly negro features.

Speaking broadly, the Malagasy may be divided into three
main groups: the Eastern, the Central, and the Western
tribes. Of these the Hovas (north central), and perhaps the
Bétsimisàraka (east coast) and some neighbouring tribes, are
the lightest in colour (although there are some Hovas as dark
as any of the more swarthy races); then come the Bétsiléo
(south central), Tanàla (forest tribes of the east side), other
eastern tribes, and perhaps the Bàra (southernmost central,
although our information as to these is not very exact);
while the Sàkalàva, all along the west side of the island, and

* Since writing the above, I am reminded by my wife (for ladies are closer
observers in such matters than men) that the Malagasy are accustomed to add
other hair than their own to these long braids. Still, I think the darker-
coloured races have long hair, as a rule, although it may be a little frizzly.

overlapping its north-east corner, are the darkest, together with some of the east coast and southern tribes.

As regards stature, the lighter races are probably a little below the average English height, with well-proportioned limbs and graceful and agile movements. I think, however, I have detected in some families of Andrians or nobles a superior stature to the majority of the people, a fact which may probably have arisen from the chiefs being able in former times to procure more abundant and nutritious food, from which circumstance also it is well known that the chiefs of many of the Polynesian islands are of much superior stature to their subjects. Some of, if not all, the darker-coloured people are somewhat taller and more robust than their lighter-tinted neighbours, with a fuller chest and more massive limbs.

The Hovas are noticeable for their well-shaped heads, with high foreheads, and often European cast of countenance. Their appearance gives one the idea of considerable intellectual capacity. In some I have noticed the slightly oblique position of the eyes, and a somewhat Chinese expression. Mr. Ellis's description of them in his *Three Visits to Madagascar* may be accepted as generally correct, when he says : "The foreheads were always well shaped, even when the space between the eyebrows and hair, as in some few instances, was comparatively narrow. The eyes were never large and projecting, but clear and bright, and the eyebrows well defined without being heavy. The nose was frequently aquiline and firm; it was, however, more frequently straight, and sometimes short and broad, without fulness at the end. Their lips were occasionally thick and slightly projecting; though seldom round and large, but often thin, and the lower one gently projecting (possibly from snuff-taking), with short curling upper lip. Their eyes are dark brown and hair jet black. Style of feature seems to mark the Hovas much more distinctly than colour and hair." The portraits given in the works cited in the footnote * will fully confirm the

* See *The History of Madagascar*, vol. i. pp. 116, 117; *Three Visits to Madagascar*, pp. 129, 137, 138, 413, 417; *Madagascar Revisited*, pp. 74, 220 ; *Tour du Monde*, 247e liv. pp. 211, 217, 219.

above description. The men have not much beard, but they wear moustachios, often growing rather thick, and clipped close.

Except that most of the other races of the central and eastern side of the island are darker in colour than the Hovas, much of the above description would apply to the finer examples of some of the other tribes as well. The children of the Tanàla people in the heart of the dense forest, of the Bétsiléo, the Bétsimisàraka, and the Sihànaka, are equally quick, bright, and intelligent with those of the Hovas, and, judging from the appearance of the few Sàkalàva I have met with, I should judge that they are not below the other tribes in mental qualities. I was always struck with the bold, free, martial appearance of parties of this tribe, who are occasionally seen at the capital. As is remarked in *The History of Madagascar* (vol. i. p. 129): "There is something in the very appearance of the Sàkalàva in his favour. His manly air and gait, his full countenance and penetrating look, declare him destined to something higher and nobler than he has yet attained." If I am not mistaken in my recollection of many of them, they have often an almost Roman shape of nose, thin at the upper part, although rather broad at the base. Captain J. C. Wilson, R.N., in some "Notes on the West Coast of Madagascar," * says the Sàkalàva are the finest race of savages he ever saw; strong, tall, and independent, somewhat like Africans, but better looking. He describes them as being good shots, of pastoral habits, and having clean and comfortable houses.

Mr. G. A. Shaw, who has resided amongst the Bétsiléo for seven years, says of them: "As compared with the Hovas, the Bétsiléo have a greater proportion of big men, and the average size both of men and of women is greater than in the north. The average height is not less than six feet for the men, and a few inches less for the women. They are large-boned and muscular, and their colour is several degrees darker than that of the Hovas, approaching in many cases very close to a black. The forehead is low and broad, the nose flatter and the lips thicker than those of their con-

* *Jour. Roy. Geog. Soc.*, vol. xxxvi., 1866.

querors, whilst their hair is invariably crisp and woolly. No pure Bétsiléo is to be met with having the smooth long hair of the Hovas. In this, as in other points, there is a very clear departure from the Malayan type." [*]

It has been said by some writers that there is a strongly-marked division between the light and the dark coloured races of Madagascar. As far as my own observation goes, I doubt the accuracy of this statement, and should rather say that the one type shades into the other by gradations almost impossible to be marked off in any exact manner either by tribal or geographical divisions. For instance, by some writers the Sihànaka are classed with the Sàkalàva, probably on account of their dark colour; but judging from their way of building their houses, and other habits, and from their dialect, they are a division of the Bétsimisàraka or Bézànozàno, who have come up from the coast and eastern districts. With them have become mingled a number of Hovas, but this mixed race is darker than either of the peoples composing it; and it seems probable that the great heat and moisture of their country, shut in as it is on almost all sides by forest, have tended to darken the colour of their skin. I fancied I could trace a distinctly different type of feature from the Hovas, but observations made during a single hasty visit are not very reliable.

There can, however, be no doubt that while from one point of view a three-fold division of the Malagasy tribes can be roughly made, taking another standpoint, that of language, they separate into *two* very distinctly-marked groups; the Hovas, or northern central tribes, forming one division; and the other comprising all the rest of the people, both of the east and west coasts and in the northern and southern interior provinces. We do not yet know with great minuteness the peculiarities of all the dialects other than the Hova, but we know sufficient to affirm that they all seem more related to one another than they are to the Hova. Most if not all of them appear to have a more nasal *n* sound than the Hova gives to have a broader and more open sound in some vowels, and to cut off many of the terminals of trisyllabic roots (*ka,*

---

[*] *Antananarivo Annual, No. iii. p. 79.*

tra, and *na*), while many words obsolete, or only used in special senses, in the central provinces, are still in common use among the outer tribes.

From this fact, and also from other circumstances, as well as tradition, there seems much reason to believe that the Hovas (and perhaps some of the lighter-coloured eastern tribes also) are the latest immigrants into the country, and that the other tribes have been inhabitants of Madagascar for a longer period. It seems certain that the Hovas have come into Imérina within a time to which tradition points back, and that they displaced an aboriginal race, the Vazimba (of whom more presently).

Here, however, come in two or three perplexing inquiries:

First,—Although there are considerable differences between the various tribes in colour, physique, &c., yet does not the substantial unity of language point, if not to a common origin, at least to a common *region*, from which they all came, although perhaps at somewhat widely-separated intervals of time? Is it possible that if they are of a radically distinct stock, there would not be very clear indications of at least two different languages in Madagascar? Yet we do not find such different languages; for although the dialects of some tribes are puzzling enough at first both to natives and Europeans from a distant part of the country, this arises chiefly from various pronunciations, the employment of words either obsolete or used in another sense elsewhere, and other minor differences, and certainly not because a distinctly different language is employed by such tribes. A glance at the personal names employed among the Sàkalàva, in whose dialect probably the greatest differences from Hova exist, shows that most of them are essentially from roots common both to them and to the Hovas. So it is also with the names of places; the structure of the language is the same; and although there is a small proportion of words in the Sàkalàva vocabulary which are not employed by the Hovas, it has not yet been shown that this is of African origin. At the same time there may very likely be some African infusion in the west-coast dialects, and possibly extending from thence into the interior. Remembering the proximity to

Africa, and the constant intercourse that has been going on from time immemorial, it would be strange if there was not some little connection between the languages of island and continent, and perhaps a few roots commencing with the consonants *ng* and *nj* are from a different stock to the great mass of the language.

Then again, if all the different tribes of Madagascar are from a common region, as one seems forced to conclude from the unity of their language, how is it that such differences exist in colour and physique, &c.?   Possibly, as seems suggested by what has been already remarked with regard to the Sihánaka, the colder climate of the highlands of the interior has to some extent modified the Hovas as regards colour, while moisture and heat combined have tended to darken the other tribes living in the lower and warmer regions of the country.   But although this may explain some of the variations in colour and physical conditions, it cannot be considered adequate to explain the many other differences found among the inhabitants of Madagascar.   How are these to be accounted for? and where did they originate?

May it not be that we have in Madagascar, as in the Malayan and Polynesian Archipelagoes, *two* races represented— one, an olive or light-brown people closely connected with the inhabitants of Eastern Polynesia (from the Sandwich Islands through the Samoan, Marquesan, Society, Paumotu, and other groups, down to New Zealand); and also a darker race, allied to the Melanesian tribes inhabiting Western Polynesia, from Fiji to New Guinea?   The mixed character of the words comprised in the Malagasy vocabulary seems to favour this suggested mixed origin.   Taking Mr. Wallace's " List of One Hundred and Seventeen Words in Thirty-three Languages of the Malay Archipelago," we find that *vòrona* (bird) is from the Malay and South Celebes languages; *ànaka* (child), besides being found in Malay, Javanese, and Celebes, is also used in Ceram, Sanguir (Philippines), and by the Sea Gypsies; *nio* (cocoa-nut) is found in Bouru, Amboyna, Ceram, and all over the Polynesian groups inhabited by the lighter-coloured races; *atòdy* (egg) is used in Mysol, Gilolo, and Ceram; and so on.   And an examination of Polynesian vocabularies would doubtless furnish fresh facts in the same direction. There is still, however, a residuum of a few important words whose origin has not yet been discovered.

Some of the facts pointed out by Mr. Wallace as to the limited area of some of these Malayan languages, such as the existence of very distinct dialects, and sometimes altogether different tongues, in neighbouring villages (see *Mal. Arch.* pp. 473–475, vol. ii.), seem very remarkable when compared with the substantial unity of language over so large an island as Madagascar, which has an area of more than 200,000 square miles. The same condition of things as exists in Malaysia is found also on the south-east coast of New Guinea, where the Rev. W. G. Lawes says there are from twenty to thirty distinct languages on a coast-line of only two to three hundred miles in length.

In Madagascar, on the other hand, we find a number of tribes scattered over a large area, many of. them with considerable tracts of uninhabited country separating them from other tribes, and yet strangely alike in language and in customs, and to a certain extent also in physical qualities.*

Considerations of language would lead one to infer that the ancestors of the Malagasy came from a rather wide area of the Malayan Archipelago; that then they remained together long enough in one part of Madagascar for their various languages to unite so as to become one tongue; and that subsequently they separated into the different tribes now inhabiting the country, their varying dialects as at present existing becoming gradually differentiated from the original stock, partly through the custom of *fady* or tabooing the words and particles occurring in the names of their chiefs (see chapter on Language), and also by other well-known influences which are constantly affecting and slowly changing human speech.

Then there is a third question which meets us: How did the ancestors of the Malagasy come from their distant homes

---

* These are: a somewhat flatter physiognomy than is found among Europeans, the men being usually better formed than the women, among whom there is a tendency to corpulency; having weak beards, generally plucked out when young; and somewhat colder blood and general temperature of body than Europeans have. See *History of Madagascar*, vol. i. p. 115.

and the islands where *their* ancestors dwelt? How did they contrive to cross the 3000 miles of ocean which separate them from the Malay Peninsula and Archipelago? This is certainly a difficult problem to solve. Still there are facts which may suggest a solution of the question. In the first place, it is well known that the lighter races of the Malayo-Polynesian region are adventurous sailors, and often make voyages of several hundred miles in their canoes. There seems little doubt that to this fact is owing the wide distribution of these peoples, north and south, from the Sandwich Islands to New Zealand (a distance of above 4500 miles), to say nothing of the 10,000 miles east and west from Easter Island to Sumatra. It is well known, both from tradition, language, and reliable native accounts, that some groups of islands in the Pacific have been peopled from others at great distances in somewhat modern times, and that considerable distances have been traversed by canoes, the occupants of which have sometimes made long voyages through being over-taken by hurricanes, and occasionally, although less frequently, through a spirit of adventure.

It is evident also that the coast tribes of Madagascar still possess much skill as sailors. Until the early part of the present century the people of the north-west coast used to make an annual piratical expedition to the Comoro Islands, and one of the articles in the first English treaty with Radama I. provided that these raids should be discontinued. Such expeditions, of course, required a considerable number of canoes of large size to take a sufficient force of fighting men; indeed, we know that these expeditions, which were carried on for forty years, became at length so formidable that the Portuguese authorities at Mozambique sent, in 1805, a corvette of fourteen guns to attack the piratical fleet. But the ship was becalmed and overpowered, and carried into a Malagasy port; and in the next year but one, another expedition of from 7000 to 8000 men seized a French slaver, which was also taken and destroyed. The last of these daring attacks was made in 1816, but it was repulsed with much loss, and afterwards met with storms, so that out of 6250 men in 250 canoes, not one is believed to have

survived.[*] Later writers also speak of the adventurous way
in which the people of the north-western islands put out to
sea in their outrigger canoes.[†] And on the south-east coast
the writer found that most ingeniously constructed boats
were in common use among the people, for going through the
heavy surf to the foreign vessels. (See chapter on Malagasy
Customs.)

When, therefore, we consider both the great distances
occasionally traversed in the Pacific, and the nautical skill
still evinced by the Malagasy, it seems less incredible than
it might at first sight appear, that even the 3000 miles
between the Malay Archipelago and Madagascar should be
crossed by canoes bringing the ancestors of the Malagasy
people.

It will perhaps be objected that in the Pacific there are
numerous groups of islands which would serve as intermediate
stages in the passage between such widely-separated lands—
as, for instance, New Zealand and the Sandwich Islands—and
that crossing the Indian Ocean in one voyage would be a
very different undertaking. This is perfectly true, but it is
not necessary to conclude that the passage across was made
in one voyage. If we examine a chart of the Indian Ocean,
we shall find that there are numerous groups of small islands
scattered over its area,—the Maldive, Chagos, Amirante,
Seychelles, Mascarene, and others—which would serve as
resting-places between the Malayan region and Madagascar.
And if we examine the chart more minutely, we find that
many of these islands have circling reefs, a pretty sure sign
(according to Darwin and other authorities) that they are
sinking land, and so are no doubt of much less extent now
than at an earlier period in human history. It seems highly
probable, therefore, that in past ages not only were these
islands of much greater size than they are at present, but
that there was also land where now a wide ocean rolls its
waves. As already mentioned in speaking of the fauna of
Madagascar, it has been supposed by many naturalists
of eminence (Wallace, Sclater, Bates, and others), that in

[*] See Guillain, *op. cit.*, pp. 199, 200 ; Owen's Narrative, vol. ii. p. 12.
[†] *Antananarivo Annual*, No. iii. pp. 23, 24.

recent geological periods the area of the Indian Ocean was, in part at least, occupied by a considerable extent of land, of which Madagascar, and the Mascarene, and other groups are the relics, the strange relationships of the animal life of these islands appearing to require some such link between Madagascar and the more easterly regions of the world. This supposition is borne out to a great extent by the deep-sea soundings recently made (although certainly not to the full extent of the supposed requirements), for an examination of the chart shows that there was probably a large island to the north-east of Madagascar, nearly as large as Madagascar itself, but of a longer shape, curving round to the north-west, something like a boomerang in outline, and with its north-western end about as far from the northern point of Madagascar as the latter is from the African coast (about 260 miles). Of this former island the Amirante and Seychelles groups form the relics of the northern portion, and the Cargados Garayos shoals and islets of the southern end. Then there would seem to have been an island considerably larger than Ceylon, about half-way between the boomerang-shaped island just described and India, whose position is indicated by the Chagos group; while the soundings indicate probably another long island about the size of Sumatra, lying in much the same contiguity to south-west India as Sumatra does to the Malay Peninsula. Of this island, the Maldive and Laccadive islets alone now lift their heads above the waves. South-east of these, a very deep sea, 15,000 feet deep, probably indicates a very ancient physical feature of this part of the globe, and shows that in all the more recent geological epochs at least, an ocean of profound depth has separated the region occupied by the islands just described from the Malayan and Australian regions. It appears to me that these former physical conditions of portions of the area of the Indian Ocean, give some probable clue as to the path along which Madagascar received from the far eastern archipelagoes the ancestors of its present population.

Still another question occurs, as to which again we can only put forward some slight hints towards a solution, viz, the question of date: At what period did these immigrants

—dark and light in colour—cross the space between the Malayan region and Madagascar?

The absence of any ancient writings and monuments leaves us little besides tradition and language to fall back upon. The former of these is vague and uncertain, but one or two probabilities may be gleaned from it, as well as from language.

We know little as yet about the traditions of the coast tribes, but Hova tradition points very clearly to their ancestors having come into the central province from the east coast.† In a native history which was published at the capital in 1873, a list of Hova chieftains and kings is given. The present sovereign makes the thirty-sixth on this list, but it is distinctly said that the first-named of these thirty-six was not actually the first, but that "the beginnings of the sovereigns who reigned here from the very first is still a matter veiled in obscurity," the accounts "being so mixed up with fabulous legends that the whole of them cannot be considered as reliable." Then follows a story deriving the origin of some of these chiefs from a son whom Andriamànitra (God) cast down to the earth to play with the Vazìmba (the early inhabitants of the central province). Now this list seems to give us some slight indications of a date, *after which* it is not probable that the Hovas arrived in the centre of the island, and it is most likely that it was considerably earlier. For if we look at a list of English sovereigns, we see that from William the Conqueror to our present Queen, their number is (curiously enough) exactly the same as that of these Hova chieftains. It is not quite certain that all these Malagasy princes reigned *successively*, but most of them no doubt did so; and therefore, supposing that the average length of reign was about the same in Madagascar as in England, probably the Hova incursion was not much, if at all, later than our Norman Conquest, and perhaps was much earlier than that event; while the date at which they arrived in Madagascar itself is lost in obscurity, as well as the probably much earlier invasion of the island by the other races.

Philology gives us a little additional light here, but only a little. The Rev. L. Dahle has pointed out, in a valuable article on "The Influence of the Arabs on the Malagasy

Language," * that the presence of Arabic names for the months and days taken from the constellations of the zodiac and the principal stars in these constellations, gives "some conclusions as to the time when the Arabic influence began to work its way here," and along with it the introduction of the terms in question, "at least as to the *terminus ante quem* it could not have taken place." Mr. Dahle adds that "about the end of the eighth century the Arabs already began studying astronomy, and translating Greek works on that subject, and consequently they can scarcely have introduced their astrology here earlier than the ninth century; probably it took place much later." It will be seen, however, that this refers not to the arrival of the Malagasy in the island, but only to the introduction of a certain element into the already-existing population.

As to the Malagasy language as a whole, the Rev. W. E. Cousins says: † "The fact that resemblances to the Malagasy, both in its vocabulary and in its grammar, are found in such widely-separated regions [the Malayan and Polynesian Archipelagoes], sometimes where they are wanting in the Malay itself, makes it probable, I think, that the Malagasy emigration must be placed far back at some period before the more cultivated languages took their present forms. We should also give due importance (1) to the absence of Mohammedan traditions in Madagascar, (2) to the presence of a few Sanscrit words, and (3) I think, too, to the richness of the Malagasy in derivative forms, as I judge that the Malagasy has a far greater variety of such forms than the Malay." Mr. Cousins also says that, from the examples he adduces of the affinities between Malagasy and the Malayan and Polynesian languages, he is "disposed to believe that the Malagasy represents an older stage in the common language now so widely spread over the Indian and Pacific Oceans, and has not been derived from what is at present known as Malay."

Thus, so far as philology goes, it seems to indicate that the emigration of the Malagasy tribes from the east occurred at a somewhat remote era in the history of the human race.

---

* *Antanànarìvo Annual*, No. ii. p. 82.
† "The Malagasy Language;" *Philol. Soc. Trans.*, 1878.

CHAPTER VI.

CHARACTERISTICS OF THE DIFFERENT TRIBES INHABITING MADAGASCAR IN ANCIENT AND MODERN TIMES.

HOVAS — BÉTSILÉO — BÀRA — TANÀLA — TANKAY — SIHÀNAKA — BÉTSIMISÀRAKA AND EAST-COAST TRIBES—ABORIGINAL PEOPLES BEFORE MALAY INCURSION : VAZIMBA—KIMOS OR QUIMOS—KALIO OR BEHÒSY—POPULATION—VARIOUS ESTIMATES—CHIEF TOWNS—TABLE OF PRINCIPAL TRIBES AND THEIR SUBDIVISIONS.

THE varieties in colour and physique found among the peoples inhabiting the different provinces of Madagascar have already been noticed in the preceding chapter; but as there are many other particulars which should be remembered in order to form a tolerably accurate notion of the people in their numerous divisions, we shall here note down some of the more important of them. Some information may then be given as to the traces found of earlier races in Madagascar before the arrival of the ancestors of the bulk of the present inhabitants; and also as to the probable amount of the existing population of the island.

1. *The Hovas.*—At the head of the Malagasy tribes stand the Hovas, who are now by far the most advanced of them all in civilisation, enlightenment, and intelligence, as well as in their political position. They occupy the central province of Imérina, and from this vantage-ground they now dominate a great part of the interior of Madagascar, all the eastern portions of the island, and parts of the north-west. For many centuries, however, the Hovas were only one among the many tribes inhabiting the country, and their power did not extend beyond their own central region; for in Imérina itself there were numerous petty independent sovereignties up to a comparatively modern period, and even within the present century

they were tributary to the Sàkalàva chieftains. But during the latter portion of their time of subjection to the western tribes, the kings from whom the present Hova royal family are descended were gradually consolidating their power by uniting the petty states of Imérina into one kingdom, so that an aggressive policy was begun by Andrianimpòina, father of Radàma I., and carried on by Radàma himself (1810-28). The Bétsiléo people in the south were obliged to submit; the neighbouring peoples in Imàmo and Vònizòngo were over-powered; then the Sihànaka to the north, and some of the east-coast tribes. A treaty made by Radàma with the English gave him additional power, through his obtaining European drilling and organisation for his troops, as well as firearms and ammunition. With these powerful aids to success he threw off all allegiance to the Sàkalàva, invaded their country again and again, and by a mixture of force and diplomacy obliged them to submit, so that Radàma from that time assumed the right of sovereignty over the whole of Madagascar, a claim which his successors have always insisted on. The same aggressive policy was carried on, often with great cruelty, in the south-eastern parts of the island by Rànavàlona I., who succeeded Radàma in 1828. But the Hovas have never been really masters of the whole of Mada-gascar, and probably a third part of the island to the west and south is independent, and their authority is only slight over many other distant parts of the country. It is most fully acknowledged in the central and eastern provinces.

There is no doubt that the Hovas have a greater ability than the other tribes for taking a leading position. They can rule because they can obey, and to this faculty of obedience to authority, organising power, and united action, they owe their present position in the country, as well as to their having had kings of such remarkable energy and intelligence as Radàma I. and his father.

For twenty-five years, during the reign of Rànavàlona I., the country was as much as possible isolated from all foreign influence; trade was shut out, and Christianity cruelly per-secuted. But since the death of that queen in 1861, great advances have been made by the Hovas, especially under the government of the present benevolent sovereign, Rànavàlona II., and her sagacious and powerful prime minister : education and civilisation have greatly progressed, and enlightened views on morals, humanity, and religion have, through the teaching of English missionaries, chiefly of the London Missionary Society, made wonderful advances, and are quietly revolutionising society in the central provinces, as will be detailed more fully in a concluding chapter.

It may be remarked also that the cooler, bracing climate of the country where the Hovas dwell has doubtless exerted considerable influence in making them what they now are. Imérina is the most elevated region of the interior of Madagascar, averaging about 4000 feet in height above the sea-level. The soil being generally far less fertile than it is in the warmer coast-plains, more energy and continuous labour are needed to procure the necessaries of life than is the case among most of the other tribes ; and all this has produced a more robust and self-reliant spirit among the Hovas, who have at length become, what was evidently their destined position, the dominant tribe of the island. Now that Christianity is beneficially influencing the political conduct of the Hovas, an extension of their authority over the whole of Madagascar would probably be very beneficial to the country.

The district which they inhabit is perhaps about eighty miles long from north to south, and about sixty miles from east to west.

2. The Bétsiléo.—Next to the Hovas should be mentioned the Bétsiléo, who inhabit the central portion of Madagascar south of Imérina. In industry, skill in agriculture and in manufactures, they are not behind the Hovas ; and although conquered by Radàma I., they are a brave and warlike people, the various divisions of the Bétsiléo being constantly fighting with each other in former times. They are divided into four principal tribes with numerous subdivisions (see Appendix), and their ancient towns and villages were built on the summits of very lofty hills. Morally, the Bétsiléo are said to be in advance of the Hovas, although lying and cheating are as rife among them as in other parts of Madagascar. They are extremely quarrelsome and litigious, often spending a great

amount of property in law-suits about some trifling matter.
Of this propensity Mr. G. A. Shaw gives some extraordinary
instances.* Drunkenness is also prevalent, but the people are
more simple and unsuspicious than the Hovas; the clannish
feeling is very strong among them, and they show much
family affection and hospitality. In former times their
government was very despotic, and there is still much
reverence paid to their chiefs, although these are shorn of
most of their former power. Curiously enough, the Bétsiléo
kings used to be called "the Hova," as if some feeling of
Hova superiority had impressed them even before being conquered by their northern neighbours. Their superstitions,
burial-customs, &c., will be noticed in other chapters.

The Hova authority being very firm among the Bétsiléo,
idolatry has been abolished, and a considerable number of
the population are under instruction, for the people have no
lack of intelligence. Indeed, next to the Hovas, no tribe has
made greater advances during the last ten years than have
these "many unconquered" of the southern highlands of
Madagascar.

3. _The Bàra._—Proceeding farther south, through the
centre of the island, we come next to the Bàra people, about
whom, until very recently, hardly anything definite was
known. But a Hova army having passed through part of
the country in 1873, some information was obtained from
the native officers about them.† In 1876 two English missionaries made a journey through the eastern part of the province; and in the following year a journey across the Bàra
country to the south-west coast (St. Augustine's Bay), and
attended with considerable peril while among a west-coast
tribe called Vézo, was made by the Rev. J. Richardson, who
has contributed some valuable information about the Bàra
and their country in his pamphlet, entitled "Lights and
Shadows; or, Chequered Experiences among some of the
Heathen Tribes of Madagascar." These people inhabit a
series of undulating plains divided by lofty ranges of hills,

* See *Antandnarivo Annual*, Nos. iii., iv., "The Bétsiléo : Country and
People."

† *Antandnarivo Annual*, No. ii., pp. 45-50.

forming the most southerly central portion of Madagascar.
The area of their country is perhaps about 20,000 square
miles. They appear to be in a much more uncivilised condition than most of the Malagasy tribes; they are divided
into a number of petty states which are perpetually at war
with each other, and the Hovas have hardly any authority over
them. They are distrustful, suspicious, and churlish, and not
very hospitable or friendly to strangers; they are also very
superstitious and immoral, purity and chastity being unknown, and in speech and manner they are rough and filthy
in the extreme. They have far less dexterity in manufactures than either the Hovas or the Bétsiléo, and they are
mostly ignorant of the use of money.

Mr. Richardson gives the following graphic picture of a
Bàra warrior:—"His hair is done up into knobs of fat, wax,
and whitening, numbering from ten to one hundred and
twenty; and on the crown is a chignon of the same
materials, about the size of, or larger than, a cricket-ball;
each knob is impacted against the other, and all have the
ring of a hard wax ball. On his forehead or temples he
carries his large charm or round shell, about the size of a
crown-piece, called a *fòlana*. Round his neck he carries a
number of beads of various sizes, and a few small wooden
charms. In his ears he will have rings or pieces of wood,
sometimes sticking in the lobe of the ear, and sometimes
hanging down like ear-drops. Hanging round his neck and
resting on his breast, he carries a circular charm about six
inches long, covered with innumerable small beads with two
or more long ones at the end. The stock of his gun, a
flint-lock, obtained from the traders on the coast, is covered
with brass-headed nails, varying in number from forty to
two hundred and twenty. His spear-heads—for he generally
carries two or more—are very bright and well-tempered; and
in the shaft, or where the shaft is inserted in the head, rings
of brass are worked in. His belt—which is sometimes six
inches broad—and powder-horn, his cartridge-box and tinder-
flask, are decorated with brass-headed nails to the number of
a hundred and twenty, and each one the size of a shilling, or
even a florin. Hanging from the shoulder, and resting on his

right side, he carries his scarf of charms. Round his loins he
wears a few yards of cloth, coloured or plain. Slung on his
gun are a pair of sandals, and thus equipped he stands ready
for any fight."

" *What he thinks :* Give me my gun, my powder and ball,
my spear; leave me my rum, my wives, my oxen, and my
king; let me rob, plunder, kill, and destroy anything or any-
body I please. Let me despoil every man, and carry away
any man's cattle, his wives, his children, his slaves, to my
heart's content. Let no man molest me; and then, who
cares who governs the country!" (pp. vii. viii.)

Neither education nor Christianity has yet obtained much
influence among this degraded people, but something is now
being done to enlighten the easternmost portion of the Bàra.

4. The Tanàla.—To the east of the two last-mentioned
tribes runs a line of dense forest, dividing the interior highlands from the lower maritime plains, and separating the
Bétsiléo and Bàra from the east-coast tribes. Here, amongst
these almost impenetrable woods, live the Tanàla, or forest
people, as their name implies (*àla*, forest). They stretch
over an extent of forest region about 200 miles long, but
only a few miles in width, many of their villages being
perched upon lofty hills amidst the trees. The northernmost
of the people acknowledge the Hova supremacy, and are
ruled by an energetic old chieftainess named Iòvana, who
lives at Ambòhimànga. Many of the southern Tanàla are
independent, especially those of the district called Ikòngo.
The people here have never been conquered by the Hovas,
having bravely and successfully resisted them more than
once; their chief town, of the same name, is situated on a
lofty and almost inaccessible mountain, about five miles long,
and more than a thousand feet high. As there are springs
of water at the top of this hill, and also rice-grounds, the
inhabitants cannot be overcome by famine; and the sides
of the hill are mostly precipitous, the only ascent being so
narrow and difficult that a very few men could secure it
against a considerable assaulting force. Another almost
equally inaccessible position is Ivòhibé, a detached and very
lofty conical mountain-fastness. These forest people are

very superstitious and addicted to charms and ordeals, but they are also most hospitable. Education and Christianity are making some way among Iòvana's people, and even in unconquered Ikòngo teachers have lately been allowed by the Tanàla king to settle among his subjects. The Tanàla people are probably closely allied with the neighbouring Bétsiléo and the coast tribes east of them.

5. *The Tankày or Bezànozàno.*—If we follow on the map the line of eastern forest and trace it northwards, we find that it divides into two, leaving a long narrow valley between the separated belts of wood. This open space is known as Ankày (from *hày*, a clearing), and the inhabitants are variously known as Tankày (or Takày) and Bezànozàno (probably from *zànozàno*, small trees, brushwood). The climate of their territory is hot and unhealthy, as it is enclosed by dense forest on each side, but the soil is very fertile. A considerable number of the men of this tribe act as bearers of goods from the coast to the interior, being extremely hardy and capable of enduring continuous labour. This work is chiefly carried on in the cooler season of the year. In many of their customs, and in their dexterity in weaving rushes and grass for mats, a material which is also used for clothing, the Tankày resemble the forest and east-coast tribes. They are very hospitable, a trait of character which seems common to all the peoples on this side of the island, as well as to the Hovas and Bétsiléo. In their marriage and funeral customs, dialect, and other particulars, the Tankày have many points of similarity with their Sihànakà neighbours farther north. They are darker in colour than the Hovas or the Bétsimisàraka, but more robust and strong in body. A very full and interesting monograph on this tribe and their country is given by the Rev. P. G. Peake in No. iv. of the *Antanànarìvo Annual*, pp. 31–43.

6. *The Sihànaka.*—Proceeding farther northward, still between the two lines of forest, we come to the country of the Sihànaka tribe, or "lake people," as their name implies, the largest lake in Madagascar, the Alaòtra, being in the district, and in former times was probably much larger than at present. About two-fifths of Antsihànaka is marsh, while

I

the rest is called *hay*, a word denoting that which is not forest or marsh, but the low rising-grounds between the two which are free from wood. There is some reason for supposing that these people are allied to the Bétsimisàraka tribes of the eastern coast, and that they advanced from the coast to the interior up the valley of the river Maningòry (by which the Alàotra communicates with the sea), and then settled on the edges of the plain, as their villages are most numerous around the north-eastern bays of the lake, while there is a large tract of fertile country to the south of them which is almost entirely uninhabited. In the early part of this century the Sihànaka were conquered by the Hovas, after a severe struggle, but for many years they have quietly submitted to Hova authority, and their two chief towns are garrisoned by officers and soldiers from the central province.

As may be imagined from its marshy character and its warm climate, Antsihànaka is a very unhealthy part of Madagascar, but it is exceedingly fertile, and most kinds of vegetable produce grow most luxuriantly, sugar-cane and the papyrus (*zozòro*) growing to double the height and size they attain in Imérina. The people are largely employed in tending cattle, immense numbers of which find rich pasture in the moist levels. Many of these herds belong to the wealthy people of Antanànarìvo: one noble is said to have nearly ten thousand cattle; there are others who have five thousand, many own a thousand, and the majority of the people have at least one hundred. Many of the Sihànaka also get wealth by catching and selling the abundant fish of the lake and other waters of the district. Until very recently all selling was done by barter, but now money is coming into use. In their rice-culture they do not dig the soil or transplant the young rice-plants, as do the other tribes, but drive their oxen over ground upon which water has been allowed to flow, and sow in the soft mud produced by the trampling of the animals. The rice is not stored in pits, as in Imérina, but in immense circular baskets, twenty to thirty feet in diameter, and about eight feet high. These are kept in their compounds or in the fields, and are roofed over. The people reckon their rice by the number of these stores, of which the richer Sihànaka have seven and eight.

In one of the villages in the dense papyrus thickets among the marshes to the south of the lake live a strange tribe of people, who seem quite isolated from the other Sihà-naka, and more barbarous in their habits, and have a distinctly different dialect. In the rainy season, when the water rises, it enters into the houses of these people; and they put together several layers of *zozòro* so as to make a kind of raft, so that as the water rises this raft rises with it. Upon these zozòro they make their hearth and beds; and there they live, rising and falling with the water, until the rainy season is over and they can live on the ground again. There are some curious stories about the simplicity of these people and their ancestors; for they have no intercourse with any one outside their village, except on a certain day, when they go out to sell the fish they have caught.

The Sihànaka are marked by their superstition, love of ornament, intemperance, and laziness. They think it shows a want of respect to visitors if they have no *tòaka* (rum) to give them. Nothing can be done, either at funerals or festivities, without drinking tòaka. But for four years past, the Rev. J. Pearse, with several Hova evangelists, has been living among them, and some progress has been made in education and in the knowledge of Christianity.

7. The Bétsimisàraka and other East-Coast Tribes.—If we cross from Antsihànaka over the lower line of forest, we come to the peoples inhabiting the plains of the east coast. These are often all loosely called by Europeans Bétsimisàraka, probably because the chief ports with which foreign vessels trade are in the territory of that tribe. But the Bétsimisà-raka, although one of the most important of these eastern peoples, and formerly perhaps the most numerous and power-ful of them, are only one of the many tribes found along the eastern coast. From the northern point of Madagascar down to the Bay of Antongil the people appear to be allied to the Sàkalàva, but south of that bay come in succession the *Bét-simisàraka* (of whom there are two chief divisions called respectively *Antéva* and *Vorìmo*), the *Bétàniména* (a little more inland), the *Taimòro*, the *Taifàsy*, the *Taisàka*, the *Tanòsy*, and the *Tandròy*, who reach down towards Cape St. Mary, the southernmost point of Madagascar. There are numerous subdivisions of these tribes, as shown in the tabular statement appended to this chapter, and possibly there are others not properly included in any of the above-mentioned peoples.

Of the east coast inhabitants the Bétsimisàraka are the lightest in colour, with straight hair, and have most affinity with the Hovas; the Taimòro are much darker and have frizzly hair; the Taifàsy again are lighter coloured than the preceding; and then the more southerly tribes are mostly dark, like the Taimòro. These coast tribes are, on the whole, gentle and docile people, although some of them made a strenuous resistance to the Hova invasion of their country; but since their conquest they have submitted quietly to the central government. Among some of these tribes, as the Taifàsy and Taisàka, there exists a much higher state of morals than is found among the Malagasy generally. The Arab influence in this part of the country has already been spoken of in the preceding chapter. Among the Bétsimisàraka there has been some little educational and Christian work going on; but among the more southern tribes hardly anything has been yet done for the people in this direction, the only advance being found in the neighbourhood of the Hova military posts at the chief towns and ports.

8. *The Sàkalàva or Western Tribes.*—The people who inhabit the whole of the western side of Madagascar, and who also overlap the northern and southern ends of the island, are commonly termed Sàkalàva, and are often supposed to be a single tribe of people. This is, however, a popular error, for the inhabitants of this extensive region consist of a number of separate tribes, all having their own name, and, until about 200 years ago, each having its own government. For more than two centuries the people of the west coast have been divided into two great sections or distinct nations, called respectively the Sàkalàva of Ménabé, or of the south, and the Sàkalàva of Ibòina, or of the north. But these two nations derive the name they bear in common from a small tribe coming originally from the south-west,

and living on the banks of a small river called Sàkalàva, from which they took their name. This tribe being endued with a warlike spirit, and led by chiefs of superior ability, invaded the neighbouring territory, and incorporated by successive conquests the different populations inhabiting the whole western portion of the island. The southern kingdom of Ménabé was first formed, and very soon afterwards the northern one of Ibòina, both by members of the same family of chiefs, so that the name Sàkalàva came to be loosely applied to all the peoples in the west of Madagascar.

For more than 170 years these western people were the most powerful in the island. Not only were the coast tribes subdued, but also some of the more inland races; the Sihànaka, the Bézànozàno, and even the Hovas, who then had little power beyond their own immediate territory. The Sàkalàva kings procured European arms and ammunition from foreign traders at the north-western ports; and there seems ground for believing that the chiefs who commenced the aggressions on the other tribes had European blood in their veins, a fact which has always given some supremacy in Madagascar. Their government was absolute, and the monarchy hereditary; and there was a class of feudal chiefs holding their land from the sovereign, and forming an order of nobles.

But towards the commencement of the present century, the supreme power in both the Sàkalàva kingdoms fell into hands much less vigorous and capable than were those by whom they were founded. Meanwhile the Hovas in the centre were rising into power, led by Andrianimpòina and then by his son Radàma I. The yoke of the Sàkalàva was soon thrown off, and pretexts for the invasion of their territory were found before long. Although his army met with severe loss again and again, as much through disease and famine as in actual fighting, Radàma never for a moment abandoned his purpose. Some of the chief positions were captured, and then policy came to the aid of the Hova king. By marrying the daughter of the Sàkalàva king of Ménabé, he induced him to acknowledge the Hova supremacy; and as each of the two western kingdoms left their neighbours to fight alone they were conquered in detail; so that in 1824 the greater part of the western side of the island was reduced to Radàma's authority.

During the reign of his successor, the cruelty of the Hovas caused a portion of the northern Sàkalàva to place themselves under French protection, and to cede some of their territory to France. The Bourbon Government accordingly took possession of the Island of Nòsibé, and in virtue of their treaty with the Queen of Ibòina still lay claim to territory on the mainland.

For some years past the Sàkalàva appear to have quietly acquiesced in Hova domination, although once or twice disturbances have occurred. The Hova authority, however, is slight over a great portion of the western coast, except in the neighbourhood of their chief military posts ; and the tribes in the south-west are virtually independent.

Owing partly to this fact, and also to their country being farther removed than that of other tribes from contact with Europeans, we know very little yet about the Sàkalàva, and much of their country is still unexplored. They have less settled habits than most of the other tribes in the island, being more a pastoral than an agricultural people; and they do not use rice for food to anything like the extent common with the people of the central and eastern portions of Madagascar, but live on the manioc and other roots. They are extremely superstitious, and have numerous curious customs and beliefs, as will be found detailed in succeeding chapters. Although, as noticed in the preceding chapter, there has been much Arab and Indian intercourse with the people of the north-west coast, the western tribes generally are the least advanced of almost all the Malagasy races. They have as yet been hardly touched by European civilisation, nor has education or Christianity made any progress among them ; but as a mission station has lately been formed at Mojangà, it may be hoped that some advance will soon take place. The Norwegian missionaries have also a station in the south-west, at a town called Mànja.

The Sàkalàva country is much warmer than the central and eastern portions of the island, and it largely consists of extensive plains at only a moderate height above the sea-level. These are, however, intersected by two or three chains of mountains which run in a very straight line north and south; and there is a good deal of land covered by forest. *

Traces of Aboriginal Peoples before the Malayan Incursion. —While considering the subject of the ethnology of Madagascar there is still one more point of considerable interest in connection with it, about which a few words may here be said. It is frequently asked whether there are any indications of the presence of an aboriginal race, an autochthonous people, inhabiting the country before the arrival of the Malayo-Polynesian tribes—dark and light—who have for so long formed the mass of the population of the island. I believe there *are* traces of the existence of such earlier inhabitants, although our information is scanty, and with regard to some of them, mixed up with something of the marvellous, so that it is rather difficult to disentangle fact from fable.

First, with regard to the central province of Imérina, for many hundred years inhabited by the Hovas,—there are numerous indications of the previous occupation of this part of the island by an earlier people called *Vazìmba.* The graves of these people (or what are believed to be such) are scattered over the bare downs of many parts of Imérina; these are small shapeless heaps of stone, and are regarded with superstitious fear by the people. It would be a valuable help in ascertaining something more definite about these Vazìmba could we open the graves, as we do the "barrows" of the Wiltshire downs and the Yorkshire wolds, and examine the contents; but such a test is at present quite impossible owing to the superstition of the people.

Tradition, however, supplies some little information about them, and there seems no reason to doubt that it contains a considerable element of truth. There are so many minute particulars preserved, together with the names of several of their ancient chieftains, and details of their sayings, &c., that it seems likely we have a substantial basis of fact on many points. According to the accounts handed down, the Vazìmba

* For fuller particulars of the Sàkalàva history, see an article by the writer of the above in the *Antananarìvo Annual*, No. iv., pp. 53–65; and also Guillain's *Documents sur . . . la Partie Occidentale de Madagascar.*

were a race of low stature; they had heads somewhat narrow and elongated; they were ignorant of the use of iron; and from their inferiority to the incursive Hovas in this respect they were obliged to flee before the superior weapons of their enemies. A remnant of this tribe is said by some French writers to be still existing in the Sàkalàva country on the west coast, between the rivers Mànambòlo and Tsìrìbìhina.[*] With all the other people of that side of the island they were conquered by the chiefs who founded the northern Sàkalàva kingdom of Ibòina. It is much to be wished that some competent traveller would visit this part of Madagascar to inquire into the habits, dialect, and traditions of the people living there. The names of six of the Vazìmba kings are preserved, and the last of these is said to have been driven westwards out of Imérina by the Hova king Andriamanélo. The natives say that the lake Itàsy, forty to fifty miles west of the capital, was formed by a Vazìmba chieftain, named Rapéto, damming up a river in the vicinity, and so the rice-fields of a neighbouring chief with whom he was at variance were flooded and have ever since remained under water.

From these accounts, together with the asserted different physique of these Vazìmba, their ignorance of the working of metal, &c., it seems highly probable that there was a race of different origin to the bulk of the present inhabitants, and occupying at least a portion of the centre of the island.

Since writing the foregoing I see, from an article on "The Bétsiléo: Country and People," by Mr. G. A. Shaw, in the *Antanànarìvo Annual*, No. iv. p. 5, that Vazìmba graves are known also among the people of the southern province. These, however, are not, as in Imérina, heaps of stone, but circles in the grass, where offerings are made to procure the removal of sickness. The same superstitious dread is felt at inadvertently treading on these graves or circles; this, it is believed, produces illness which is only to be cured by an offering made at the same grave where the offence had been committed.

Then there are also accounts (less easy to be credited) in some of the earlier French writers of another race of people

---

[*] See Guillain, *op. cit.* p. 18.

in the interior of Madagascar, who were called *Kîmos* or *Quimos*, and who were said to be of very short stature, averaging only three feet six inches in height. Of these people there are no such traces accessible to us as there are of the Vazimba; but the accounts given by Commerson, who was a scientific traveller and botanist, and Count de Modave (Governor at Fort Dauphin, 1768-70), are so circumstantial that it is difficult to believe there could be no residuum of fact on which they were founded.

These dwarfish people are said to have been lighter in colour than the majority of the inhabitants of Madagascar, they had woolly hair, very long arms, while the breasts of the women had hardly any prominence except when nursing their children. They are said to have been very bold in defending their own territory against an invader, using the spear and bow; they excelled in certain handicrafts, and were of ingenious and active disposition, with pastoral habits. A woman of this tribe was in the possession of de Modave, and is described both by him and by Commerson, in different accounts, as being about three feet seven inches in height, with the physical characteristics enumerated above.

The country of this pigmy race is described as being toward the southern centre of the island, on the twenty-second parallel of south latitude, and about 180 miles north-west from Fort Dauphin. This is a part of the island never yet explored by Europeans, and on the confines of the Bàra country. On the whole, one is disposed to conclude that we have here indications of the existence of an aboriginal race of people. Possibly these Kîmos were a race somewhat like the Bushmen of South Africa, who are also short of stature, and of a lighter colour than the tribes surrounding them.

Besides the foregoing, we hear vague accounts of another strange race of people in the western part of Madagascar. The Rev. W. E. Cousins gives the following particulars of these in the *Antanànarìvo Annual* (1875, p. 106):—"About a week's journey west of the capital is a tribe called the *Kalió* or *Béhòsy*. They live in a wooded country extending from Mojangà to Mahàbo. Their food is honey, eels, and lemurs. The lemurs are caught in traps and fattened. They are black, and in appearance are much like the Sàkalàva. They make network of cords, hence the name *Béhòsy*. They jump from tree to tree like monkeys, and cannot easily be followed, as the country is rocky. They are extremely timid, and if captured, die of fright."

From another paper in the same *Annual* (p. 76) it appears that these people live in the hills called Bémaràha, on the farther side of the great depression which bounds the high region of the central part of the island to the west, and about the nineteenth parallel of south latitude. These Béhòsy seem to resemble in some of their habits the "monkey-men" of Dourga Strait, New Guinea (see Wood's *Natural History of Man*, vol. ii. p. 224). It is much to be wished that some fuller information could be obtained about these singular people, for they appear to be lower in the scale of humanity than any other of the Malagasy tribes; and if what we hear is correct, are probably of a different stock to the rest of the inhabitants of Madagascar.

It may be remarked, in conclusion, that it unfortunately happens that those portions of the island where these abnormal races—Vazìmba, Kìmos, and Béhòsy—are said to be found, are those which are at present least known to Europeans. But we may hope that as we are becoming better acquainted with the country every year, no very long period will now elapse before these parts of it are explored, and that so further light will be thrown upon its ethnology.

A few remarks may be here made upon the subject of the amount and distribution of the *Population* of Madagascar.

It may be said at the outset that no very accurate information can be obtained on this point. The population is scattered over a great extent of country, large regions of which have never been even crossed by foreigners, much less carefully and minutely examined; and as the authority of the central Hova Government is but slight over a large part of the island, no reliable information as to the population of the island generally can be procured from this source. Besides this, no census of the kind employed in European countries has been taken, even in the central province where the Hova influence is most powerful; and the Government has shown some sensitiveness to anything approaching a collection by foreigners of statistics as to population, the birth and death rate, &c.

There are, however, some few facts and statistics available from other sources, such as the rough numbering of villages and houses in certain districts, and the observations of travellers in passing through different parts of the island, &c., from which some approximate estimate might be formed; although, with regard to some tribes, even these aids do not exist, and it becomes more a matter of guess than of calculation.

Madagascar as a whole is very thinly peopled, and large tracts of fertile country are wholly uninhabited. Many reasons may be assigned why the population is not large, and, apparently, has not increased since it was known to Europeans. Among these are the too-early marriages which are so common, the licentious habits of both sexes, and probably the intermarriage of near relatives, all tending to lessen the fertility of the women, so that large families are rare. Until the treaty made with England by Radàma I. (1820), great numbers of the Malagasy were sold as slaves, and carried away to Mauritius, Bourbon, and other foreign colonies. Then the superstition of the people, causing them to put their children to death if born on certain unlucky days, was a means of keeping down the population in all parts of the island, and still causes the destruction of a fourth of all the children new-born in some of the tribes. Then the *tangéna* poison ordeal used to cause great waste of life; and the people resort to charms for the cure of disease, instead of using the most simple medicines. For some five or six years past the small-pox has ravaged the coast, passing round from the north-west by the north to the south-east of the island, and has lately caused considerable mortality in some of the central southern provinces. Last year an unusual epidemic of malarial fever passed over the central parts of Madagascar, and occasioned great loss of life. To these causes may be added the frequent wars between the different tribes, and especially the great destruction of human life during the long-continued wars carried on by the Hovas during the first half of this century, to subdue the other peoples of the island, by which both conquerors and conquered suffered severe loss. Besides all these things, there is the unhealthy climate of a good deal of the coast and plain country, and the poor and insufficiently-nourishing food used by the poorer classes, so that their constitution is not fortified to resist disease; while in the colder parts of the island the want of warm clothing for the children adds considerably to the mortality of the young during the cooler months.

When all these opposing influences are considered, it is not wonderful that in some parts of Madagascar the population should be apparently decreasing, although, perhaps, this is not true of the country as a whole. But it is certainly not increasing to any extent, and in some provinces is evidently considerably less than it was a century ago. In reading Benyowski's Travels, it appears as if much larger bodies of men were called out for war in his time than could be mustered at the present day. But it may be hoped that, as in many of the Polynesian islands, the introduction of Christianity has proved to be the salvation of the inhabitants as peoples (as well as in other ways), and has put a stop to the rapid decrease which in some cases threatened their total extinction at no very remote period—so it will prove to be in Madagascar. In a large part of the island the destruction of life by the *tangéna* ordeal, and through the belief in unlucky days, has been put an end to, and the increase of intelligence and civilisation, as well as improved morals, will do much to check other causes of mortality.

Various estimates of the population have been made at different times. In Ellis's *History of Madagascar*, published forty years ago, we find the following table :—

The Hovas [north central]	750,000
The Sàkalàvas [west coast], including the Bezànozàno and the Sihànaka [east and north-east] . .	1,200,000
The Bétsiléo [south central]	1,500,000
The Betàniména and Bétsimisàraka [east coast] . .	1,000,000
Total . .	4,450,000

It is also stated that it had been ascertained that there were in the country nearly a million of houses, a little under

five per house being adopted as the average inmates of each
(vol. i. pp. 113, 114). But as the Hovas never conquered a
considerable portion of the south and west of Madagascar,
there could be little reliable information to be obtained about
those parts of the country. It is also said that " the amount
of the population is evidently less than the island has contained
at former and not remote periods of its history."

Some French writers have given a considerably lower estimate of the population, and from the intercourse which some
of these have had with the western coast, some reliance may
be placed upon their opinion as regards that portion of the
island. M. Barbié du Bocage reckons the entire population
at only three millions.[*]

In a paper read before the Anthropological Society of
London (March 1868), by Lieut. Oliver, R.A., on " The
Hovas and other Characteristic Tribes of Madagascar," he
gives a number, but says also, " of which it is impossible to
obtain accurate information."

1. Malay origin ?	1. Hovas	Fair	.	800,000
	2. Bétàniména	} Light Brown		1,500,000
	3. Bétsimisàraka			
	4. Bétsiléo	Brown	.	1,500,000
2. Aboriginal ?	5. Antsihànaka	} Deep Brown		300,000
	6. Bezànozàno			
	7. Southern tribes and	} Black	.	1,200,000
	8. Sàkalàvas			
		Total	.	5,300,000

This estimate is evidently largely in excess of the facts, as
may be seen from an examination of one item. From statistics I obtained in the Antsihànaka province, I reckoned that the
people there do not probably exceed in number from 40,000 to
45,000, while the Rev. P. G. Peake, whose district comprises
part of the territory of the Bezànozàno tribe, gives 45,900 as
their number, an estimate formed on the basis of the Government taxes on freeholds. Giving a few more to allow for the
strangers in the district, these two tribes together amount to
less than 100,000, or only a third of Oliver's estimate as
given above. It may be added that his division of the
different tribes, as regards origin and colour, is very arbitrary,

---

[*] *Madagascar: Possession Française depuis 1642,* p. 63.

and not borne out by facts, as will be gathered from the
statements in the previous chapter.

Later still another estimate has been made by the Rev.
Dr. Mullens, who made several journeys through the central
parts of the island in 1874 and 1875.

1. Bétsimisàraka, including Sihànaka, Tanàla, Tankay, and Ikòngo	300,000
2. Sàkalàva, North and South	500,000
3. Hovas and cognate tribes, including Bétsiléo (300,000) and Bàra (200,000)	1,700,000
Total	2,500,000

Probably the truth lies somewhere between this and the
three previously-given calculations; so that until fuller information can be obtained perhaps we may conclude that
the population of Madagascar is between three and a half
and four millions.[*]
It is no doubt true that large districts have been almost
depopulated within this century by war: on the north-west
coast the people having in some parts retired in a body to the
neighbouring islands, or gone away to the Comoro group.
On the other hand, in some parts of the country there seems
a denser population than had been supposed. Thus, in a
journey through the south-east provinces in 1876, I found
that in the valleys of some of the rivers were a great
number of populous villages placed very closely together.
And in notes of a journey taken by Mr. Richardson in the
following year, he says, "I am inclined to think that the
population of the Bàra province has been considerably under-
estimated. The two evangelists, who have travelled much
in Madagascar, north, east, and west, and Rabé, repeatedly
asserted that what they saw gave evidence that there were as

* Since writing the foregoing, I find my opinion confirmed in the main by an
estimate made by M. Grandidier (*Bull. de la Soc. de Géog.*, Avr. 1872, p. 378).
He says:—"It is impossible to obtain any exact account of the amount of
the population of Madagascar. At the same time, I believe that one cannot
reckon it at under four millions. The province of Imérina contains nearly a
million Hovas, and in the country of their neighbours and allies, the Bétsiléo,
there must be 600,000 inhabitants; nearly two millions inhabit the east of the
island; as for the Sàkalàva, Màhafàly, Tandroy, and Bàra, they certainly do
not reach, altogether, to the number of 500,000 souls." Against this last item,
see Mr. Richardson's estimate of the Bàra only, as given above.

many people in the Bàra province as in Imérina. I feel confident that there are far more people there than in the Bétsiléo; and I think that half a million is the lowest figure at which the population of the Bàra could be estimated. It may be more."

Of four of the Sàkalàva tribes occupying the south and south-west of the island, M. Grandidier reckons their numbers unitedly as 150,000. This district is, however, one of the least fertile portions of the western coast, and therefore probably thinly peopled compared with the provinces to the north of them. The small province of Angontsy (north-east coast) is given by another French authority as having a population of 9000.

The most populous districts in Madagascar are doubtless the central province of Imérina—especially within a circle of about twelve miles round the capital—and some portions of the Bétsiléo province to the south. In these parts of the country the extensive and fertile rice-plains provide food for the large number of populous villages, as well as for the chief towns of the two provinces.

There are few large towns in Madagascar. The capital, Antanànarìvo, is by far the most important place in the country, and has a population of above 100,000 people.

Fianàrantsòa, the capital of the Bétsiléo, has about 5000 people. Then comes Tamatave, the chief port of the eastern coast, with 6000 or 7000 inhabitants; and then Mojangà, holding the same position on the north-west coast, with about 14,000 people. There are very few towns besides with a population of as many as 5000, and the majority of the villages are small. Taking the places we saw in Antsihànaka, and omitting the two chief towns, we found that they averaged about forty-four houses each, but in many parts of the country the number is much smaller than this. In the Bétsiléo province great numbers of the houses are not gathered together into villages, but are scattered over the plains in groups of from three to six, and forming numberless little homesteads near the rice-fields.

DIAGRAMMATIC TABLE SHOWING THE DIVISIONS OF THE MALAGASY PEOPLE.

(FROM NORTH TO SOUTH.)

Western Tribes.	*Central Tribes.*	*Eastern Tribes.*
All loosely termed **SÀKALÀVA.**	**NORTHERN TANKÀY.** Zàna-tSihànaka. **SIHÀNAKA.**	**NORTHERN SÀKALÀVA.** **BÉTSIMISÀRAKA.** Northern Bétsim.

Tankàrana (extreme north).	**MAINTY.**
	Manìsotra.
	Manéndy.
	Tsiérandahy.
		Bétsim. proper.
		   Zàfin'Ibrahima
		   (on L. of S. Marie's).

Tàndrona.	**HOVAS.**	Bétàniména (a little inland).
Bóhìsotra.	Vònizòngo. Imàmo.	Antàiva or
Tsimìhéty.	Màrovàtana. Tsimàhafòtsy.	Antéva.
Tibòina.	Mandiàvàto. Tsimiambòholàhy.	Vorìmo.
Tsimilànja.	Vòromahéry.†	
Timiràha.	Vàkinankàratra.	Tàmbahòaka.
Béhòsy * or	**BÉZÀNOZÀNO** or	**TAIMÒRO.**
Tìmahìlaka.	**TANKAY.**	Antarày. Tapàsana.
Kalìò.	Taisàha.	Zafìn'Ibrahima or
Vazimba (?). *		Antaràva.
Tiména.		Tatsìmatra.
Antanàndro.	**BÉTSILÉO.** Mànandrìana.	**TAIFASY.**
	Isàndra. Ilàlangìna.	Zàfisòro. Zàsalàva.
Tiñherénana or	Mandrànosémina. Ilafarìvo. Ilàlangìnàivo.	Mahàzoarìvo (Sak. colony).
Zàfimanély. Andraivòla.	Andòharàno. Iàrindràno.	**TAISÀKA.** Zànafànfilàna.
Vézo or		Taìzàto. Tònilàza.
Màsikòra.	**BÀRA.**	Zàramanòmpo. Rànovào.
Tanòsy	(Many subdivisions, often called after	Zàraména. Lòhavòhitra.
Màhafàly (emigrants from S.E. coast).	the names of their chiefs.)	Zàzavao. Màsiànaka.
Kàrambòla.	Kìmos (?).	
	Tsiénimbalàla.	**TANOSY.**
	(In many maps a tribe so called is placed S. of the Bara, but nothing is known of them).	

TANDRÒY
(extreme point south).

CHAPTER VII.

CURIOSITIES OF THE MALAGASY LANGUAGE: WITH NOTES UPON
THE " HISTORY," " POETRY," AND " MORALITY " EMBODIED
IN NATIVE WORDS.

MALAYAN, NOT AFRICAN AFFINITIES—ONENESS OVER THE ISLAND—MUSI-
CALLY SOUNDING — PARALLELISM AND RHYTHMICAL STRUCTURE —
CURIOUS DEFICIENCIES AND FULNESS — PREFERENCE FOR PASSIVE —
DIALECTS—DIFFERENCES BETWEEN COAST AND HOVA FORMS—TABOOED
OR "FÀDY" WORDS—OBSOLETE WORDS—ADDITIONS FROM FRENCH AND
ENGLISH SOURCES—ARABIC INFLUENCE—EXAMPLES OF THE "HISTORY,"
"POETRY," AND "MORALITY" IN MALAGASY WORDS—WORDS INTRODUCED
IN RELIGIOUS MATTERS—ONOMATOPOETIC WORDS.

THE preceding chapters upon the origin, divisions, and characteristics of the different tribes inhabiting Madagascar may
now be followed by some account of their language, noting a
few of those curious features which distinguish it from our
western tongues, and especially showing (to borrow terms
from Archbishop Trench) how much " history," " poetry," and
"morality" is embodied in native words. (Some few particulars—it will have been observed—have already been
noticed in discussing the origin of the Malagasy people.)

At the outset we have the remarkable fact that although
Madagascar is, comparatively, so near Africa, the speech of
its people is not allied to that of any African tribe, and has
very few points of connection with the languages of the continent. Malagasy is, therefore, not of African stock, but is a
member of the great Malayo-Polynesian family of languages,
being, in fact, its most westerly representative. In Easter
Island, in the Pacific, we have its farthest eastern limit, so
that at the Equator these nearly allied tongues are spoken over
an area embracing more than half the circumference of the
globe. It seems very extraordinary that the peoples speak-

K

ing languages most nearly allied to Malagasy should be separated from Madagascar by a wide ocean more than 3000
miles across; yet such is undoubtedly the fact, for Java,
Borneo, Celebes, and the Philippines (in the Tagala tribes),
are the islands whose speech is most like that of the Malagasy.   And a glance at a comparative table of the most
commonly-used words in the Malay Archipelago and in Polynesia, shows that there is hardly a dialect which does not contain many words common to it and to the language spoken
in Madagascar.   (See pages 105 and 116.)

The Malay affinities of the Malagasy tongue have been
recognised by linguists for more than 250 years past; for
the *second* and *fifth* books published in Europe about Madagascar (only about a hundred years after its discovery) were
vocabularies of these two languages.*   And more minute
investigation of this subject by subsequent writers, from the
learned Reland, two centuries ago, down to Marsden, Baron
W. von Humboldt, J. J. Freeman, Latham, Van der Tuuk,
and Marre de Marin, has confirmed the early opinion of
Dutch and German authors, and made it certain that very
close relationships exist between the speech of the Malagasy
and those of the Malayan and Polynesian regions.†

Last, but far from least in importance in giving minute
information upon this point, comes one of the missionaries
of the London Missionary Society, the Rev. W. E. Cousins,
who, in a paper read before the Philological Society (*Trans.*
1878), has shown by a careful comparison of Malayan and
Malagasy that not only are a large number of words (at least
300) common to both, but that these words are of a very
important character, being those which are the most simple
and universally-needed words in all languages.   Among
them are the numerals, those for the parts of the body, for
the nearest blood relations, for times and seasons and the
aspects of nature, for many animals, birds, and plants, and for

---

* *Spraak ende woord boek in de Maleische en de Madagaskarsche talen;* Fred.
de Houtman; Amsterdam: 1603; and *Colloquia latino-maleyica et madagascarica;* Goth. Arthusius; Francfort: 1613.

† See Humboldt's *Kawi Sprache;* Dritt. Th. 8, 326; and H. N. Van der
Tuuk's *Outlines of a Grammar of the Malagasy Language;* Roy. Asiat. Soc.

many of the useful arts, the most common actions, and the
most necessary articles of daily use. He thus shows that
the theory by which Crawfurd sought to account for the presence of the Malay element in Malagasy is utterly inadequate,
and that sailors from a small fleet of piratical proas, driven
by a storm across the Indian Ocean, could never have so
radically influenced the language of the country to which
they came as strangers. Not only are there numbers of
words in Malagasy derived from Malayan roots, but in the
grammar and structure of both there is remarkable similarity,
and also in the particles, pronouns, and adverbs, &c.

Another curious circumstance connected with the language
of Madagascar is its substantial oneness all over the island.
It is well known that in many parts of Africa, in New
Guinea, and in other regions, the people of neighbouring
villages sometimes speak not merely varying dialects, but
even totally distinct languages. This fact makes it all the
more remarkable that in a vast island, nearly a thousand
miles long, a number of different tribes, often widely separated from each other, should speak only one language. This,
however, is the case; there are, it is true, a number of
dialects, but there are no traces of two or more different
languages of distinctly separate stock.

Compared with many languages, Malagasy is certainly an
easily-learnt tongue. This arises partly from the simplicity
of its grammar, and the absence of those inflections which
are so perplexing in many languages, there being no changes
for number, gender, or person. And it is also due partly to
there being no fresh character to learn, as there is in almost
all Asiatic tongues. The Malagasy had no written language
before Europeans taught them the use of letters, so, of course,
the Roman alphabet is used. Although some slight attempts
had been made by early Jesuit missionaries to prepare books,
to the missionaries of the London Missionary Society " belongs
the honour of having introduced the use of letters among the
Malagasy people," and of having given " the written form
of the language in use among them to the present day. The
two men who laid the foundation of this work were David
Jones and David Griffiths."

Like the majority of Malayo-Polynesian tongues, Malagasy
is a very soft and musically-sounding language, and has
been called by some the "Italian of the Southern Hemisphere." It has no harsh or guttural sounds, but abounds in
vowels and liquids. It is most pleasant therefore to listen
to a native orator, especially as in the more formal Malagasy
speeches the parts of every sentence are regularly balanced in
construction, forming a kind of rhythm very closely resembling the parallelism of Hebrew poetry. The arrangement of
the sentences in the poetical books of Scripture is, therefore,
quite in accordance with Malagasy usage in public speaking.
A large number of hymns for Christian worship have been
written during the last eight or ten years, and in these both
rhythm and rhyme have been successfully attained, so that
many of the classical hymns of England (such as "Rock of
Ages," "Hail to the Lord's Anointed," "There is a Land of
Pure Delight," &c.) have passed into Malagasy.

On first making acquaintance with the Malagasy tongue, one
is struck by some singular deficiencies in it; and chief of these
is its having no plural form, either in nouns or verbs, just as
if the plural of all our nouns was, as in the word "sheep,"
the same as the singular. But in other parts of speech it is
much fuller than English, as in some of the pronouns, and
especially in the adverbs of place, where there is such a
series of fine gradations of distance, from the speaker's point
of view, together with other minute distinctions, that it is
doubtful whether any but a native ever acquires an absolutely
correct use of them. And again, in certain subjects there is
great fulness, so that there are a number of words to express
the different ways in which a bullock's horns are curved, and
at least a score to denote the various modes of dressing the
hair.

On one point at least Malagasy is in great advance of
other allied tongues, viz., in the fulness of its numeral system.
It is a well-known fact that many peoples have no words for
any numbers exceeding those of the fingers of both hands,
and some do not even count more than the fingers of one
hand; but in Malagasy we have a complete numeral system
up to a million. This is certainly one proof (among many

others) of the mental capabilities of the people using it. The word for million is *tàpitrìsa*, literally "the finishing of counting;" the word for ten thousand is the same as that for night, *àlina.*

The preference for the passive instead of the active form of verb is also a marked feature in Malagasy; so that instead of saying, "I see it," a native would, nine times out of ten, say, "Seen by me it" (*hìtako ìzy*). There is thus, as in Hebrew, the constant use of the suffix pronoun, both with nouns and participles; and in the terseness and elliptical character of the language it has also several points of analogy with that ancient tongue.

Only two or three of the dialects spoken among the numerous tribes of Madagascar have as yet been carefully investigated, but collections of words are now being made and materials gathered for comparison. But there are quite enough differences both in vocabulary and pronunciation to make it difficult for natives from distant portions of the island to understand one another at first, for not only are many of the words themselves different in different places, but the style of speaking and pronunciation also varies very much, the vowel sounds being much more open and broad on the coast than amongst the Hovas. While there appears at first sight to be at least three clearly-marked groups of dialect, viz., the Hova, or speech of the central province; the Sàkalàva, or dialect of the western side of the island; and that of the Bétsimisàraka and allied tribes on its eastern side, closer examination seems to reduce their number to two, as the two latter have many points of similarity with each other and common differences from the Hova. As the Hova people - are the ruling tribe of Madagascar, and all native literature is printed in their dialect, it may be regarded as the normal form of the language, and probably will eventually become the standard of the Malagasy tongue, especially as the Hovas are scattered over a great many military posts in the island, as well as at the ports, and, of course, take with them their books as well as their own style of speaking.

It is very interesting to observe that all the coast dialects, in other words, those spoken in the warmer regions of Madagascar, are much more like the Polynesian languages than is the Hova, spoken in the colder highlands of the interior. Many of the coast words consist entirely of vowels, as in the Pacific Islands, and these doubtless represent the most ancient forms of the words.   But the Hovas seem to have a feeling after firmer and stronger sounds than these soft vowel-formed words contain, and so they insert an *z* in the middle of many, and add the syllables *na, ka,* or *tra* to the end of numbers of the two-syllabled words spoken on the coast.   Thus, the coast words *iàho, iahày, àia, ìa,* become izàho, izahày, àiza, and ìza in the Hova dialect ; and *vòla, fàsy,* and *éla* on the coast, become vòla*na,* fàsi*ka,* and éla*tra* in the interior.   These phonetic changes are doubtless connected with climate, in accordance with some still obscure laws of correlation between temperature and laryngal structure.   So much do the Hovas like a firm closing syllable that they add some of the terminals abovementioned to English words and names.   Thus, " sabre " becomes sàba*tra,* and two of my missionary brethren, named respectively Briggs and Jukes, are always transformed by the ordinary people into Birìngitra and Jukìtra !

Another case of dialectic difference among the Malagasy tribes is the strange custom, common to all the Polynesian languages, of considering the words forming the names of their chiefs as *fàdy,* or tabooed for common use.   Now in all this great group of tongues, proper names consist largely of names of common objects—animals, birds, insects, plants, trees, &c.   But if any of these happen to form the name, or part of the name, of the chief of the tribe, it becomes sacred, and must no longer be used for the name of that animal, bird, or tree, &c.   To this latter another name is given, often being a descriptive epithet, or a periphrasis for the ordinary name. Thus, the late Queen Ràsohérina was known before her accession to the throne in 1868 by the name of Rabòdo,[*] but on becoming queen she took the name of Ràsohérina.   Now

* It may be well to remark that in pronouncing Malagasy words the *a,* if accented, is sounded like a in "father," unaccented, as in "at ;" the *e* always like e in "fête" ; the *i,* if accented, like the ı in "marine," unaccented, as in "in" ; and the *o* is always like o in "move," except in the exclamation. *O* is always hard, and the other letters have one invariable sound, *s* being always s, and not like z.   The letters *c, q, u, w,* and *x* are not employed.

sohérina was the word used for the silkworm moth, but as soon as it was assumed as the name of the sovereign it could no longer be applied to the insect, which since then has been called *zàna-dàndy*, "offspring of the silk." So also with a chief in the western part of Imérina who was called Andria-màmba; *màmba* is one of the names of the crocodile, but in their chief's territory his dependants could not call the reptile by that name, but were always scrupulous to use the other word, *voày*. It is just as if in England we were unable to use all words in which the syllables of the names Victoria, William, or George occurred, and were forbidden to say "victory," "victim," "vixen," or "will," "willing," "wilful," or "geology," "geometry," "geography," &c., &c. What an endless annoyance should we not consider it; yet this is precisely the case in most parts of the Malayo-Polynesian countries and islands. It is easy, therefore, to see how very great an influence such a curious and inconvenient custom must have in altering the speech of different parts of Madagascar, and how changes must be continually going on to further separate one dialect from the other. It is doubtless a very important factor in the dialectic differences which occur in the country.

In the Journal of Mr. Hastie, formerly British Resident at the court of Radàma I., it is remarked that "the chieftains of the Sàkalàvas are averse that any name or term should approach in sound either the name of themselves or any part of their family. For similar causes the names of rivers, places, and things have suffered so many changes on the western coast that frequent confusion occurs; for, after being prohibited by their chieftains from applying any particular terms to the accustomed signification, the natives will not acknowledge to have ever known them in their former sense. This practice very much resembles the jealous monopoly of names by the kings and great chiefs of the Pacific Islands." *

In glancing over the pages of the Malagasy-English Dictionary (printed 1835), one meets with a great number of words which are now obsolete. Many of these were connected with the *sikìdy* or divination, and denoted certain arrangements of numbers in that curious superstitious practice, which

* Tyerman and Bennet's *Voyages Round the World*, 2nd edit., p. 276.

was worked something like a game at draughts. Others belonged to idol-worship, and are accordingly, like the idols themselves in the central provinces, a thing of the past, and will soon become, to the younger people at least, as much unknown as if they were foreign words. The dictionary of the first missionaries will thus be to succeeding generations a kind of museum, where alone they will find relics of the superstitions of their fathers; just as the people of many Polynesian groups can now only find in European museums the idols which their ancestors worshipped.

But while the language loses in some directions, it is constantly gaining in others, from its contact with Europeans, chiefly of the French and English nations. For the last 200 years the French have had considerable influence in Madagascar, and during the last sixty years the English have also powerfully affected the language, so that now scores of words derived from these two sources are naturalised in Malagasy, and form an integral part of the common speech. So that if through some strange catastrophe all other knowledge of the Malagasy people were lost, a complete vocabulary of the present day would give a large amount of information as to the influence exerted upon them by the two European nations.

The existence of a large class of words connected with the arts and appliances of civilised life would be an honourable testimony to what the French had done for civilisation in Madagascar; for we find in Malagasy the words chaise, la table, la bougie, l'armoire, and la clef, cheval, la selle, and la bride, bas, pantalon, épingle, and la mode, du thé, café, la bière, du vin, and la cuisine, la fenêtre, la cloche, la case, la sac, la soie, la vente, and cachet, with many others.*

But English influence would be no less marked in several directions. In government the Malagasy have adopted our words Prime Minister, Commander-in-Chief, and Secretary of State; while almost all the terms denoting grades of rank in the army and words of command are English, showing that

---

* These words are all altered in spelling, and in many the French article is also retained as an integral part of the word, as shown in the above list by the article being added to many of them; thus, la table becomes in Malagasy spelling *latàbatra*, la clef is *lakilé*, while épingle is *paingotra*.

they received from us all they know of military tactics and training. And the presence of such words as brick, square, rule, and many others used in building, and those for various tools, would also show that to English teaching the Malagasy owe the introduction of improved houses by the use of sun-dried brick, as well as instruction in building generally. But the influence of England would be most honourably shown by the fact that almost all the foreign words connected with education and literature are from us, such as school, class, and lesson, pen, copy-book, slate (and even black-board), book, gazette, press, print, and proof, capital, period, and names for all the stops, &c., grammar, geography, and addition, with many others, showing how much they owe to us for their intellectual advancement. And numerous words connected with religious belief and practices would also be lasting memorials that from England they have derived the greatest of all blessings, the knowledge of revealed religion; for we find naturalised in Malagasy such words as baptism, Bible and Testament, psalm and epistle, angel and apostle, martyr and virgin, patriarch and deacon, evangelist and missionary, demon and devil, and tabernacle, temple, and synagogue; while the English pronunciation of the name of our blessed Lord (written *Jesosy Kraisty*) is firmly fixed in the language.

All these words will form enduring records of the powerful influence that two western nations have exerted in civilising, enlightening, and Christianising this branch of the Malayo-Polynesian family of peoples.

A few ecclesiastical terms are also being introduced by the Roman Catholic and Anglican missions, but it is doubtful whether many of them will become naturalised like those already noted. And so also with a considerable number of words of Latin and Greek origin which are being taught in connection with the various sciences; from the difficulty of pronouncing most of these, few of them are likely to come into common use by the mass of the people.

While, however, history is now being embodied in the additions made to the language of Madagascar by two far-off European peoples, the language testifies to a very powerful influence exerted upon it many hundred years ago by one of

the most western Asiatic nations, the Arabs. It is well
known that during the Middle Ages these people were great
travellers and colonists, spreading far down the eastern coast
of Africa and into the interior; and before the tenth century
they also sailed across the Mozambique Channel to the Comoro
Islands, and then on the shores of Madagascar, both east as
well as west. From the time of Flacourt, one of the ablest
French commandants in Madagascar (1648–1655), it has
been known that the Malagasy words for the days and months
are of Arabic origin; this is obvious even to those unacquainted with the language, from many of them commencing
with the Arabic article *Al ;* as Alatsinàiny, Monday; Ala-
robìa, Wednesday; Alàhamàdy, the first month; Alàhasàty,
the fifth month, &c.

The subject has lately received minute investigation by
the Rev. L. Dahle, a learned member of the Norwegian
Mission, and his researches have brought out many interesting facts connected with the language, and thus thrown
light upon a remote period as to which no record or tradition
gives any information. The number of Arabic words in
Malagasy is not very numerous, being, as Mr. Dahle remarks,
" more significant by their *quality* than their quantity," and
so forming "instructive historical documents of the Arabic
contribution to Malagasy civilisation and superstition." [*]

In chronological, astronomical, and cognate terms, Mr.
Dahle shows that the Malagasy words for the days of the
week are closely identical with the Arabic words for those
days, being, in fact, just the numerals for the first five, while
Zomà, Friday, is *Dschuma',* *i.e.,* "congregation day," the sacred
day of the Mohammedans, while Asabòtsy, Saturday, is
simply the Hebrew *Sabbath,* slightly altered in its trans-
mission through the Arabic. But in the month-names, a
still more interesting fact is shown by Mr. Dahle, viz., that
the Malagasy words for these are the Arabic names, not
for the months, but for the constellations of the Zodiac.
These were doubtless introduced because of their use in divination, for the words for this practice, as well as those for witchcraft, fate, &c., are also shown to be of Arabic origin. Besides

* *Antanànarìvo Annual,* No. ii., 1876, pp. 75–91.

this, it is the custom in some parts of the country to reckon the days of the month, which are all lunar, not by sevens, but to give them separate names from the first to the twenty-eighth. Many of these Mr. Dahle discovered to be the Arabic names, slightly altered, of some of the principal stars in the different constellations of the Zodiac.

But it need only be further added here that some terms of salutation, many words for dress, woven fabrics, and bedding, the words for money and trading, terms referring to books and writing, and some sixty miscellaneous words, have also been identified as most probably of Arabic introduction. So that to the Arabs the Malagasy owe a considerable element in their language connected with civilisation, and by which they have been raised much above the semi-barbarous condition of many other branches of the Malayo-Polynesian race; while they have also received from the Arabs certain superstitions which they have engrafted upon their original charm-worship.

But besides the history now being embodied in the language generally by contact with Europeans, and that powerful influence exerted upon it many centuries ago by the Arabs, there are numerous separate words, in most cases of purely Malagasy origin, in which old customs and states of society are, as it were, fossilised and preserved unaltered up to the present time. A few examples of these may not be uninteresting.

The word for "gateway" is *vàvahàdy*, a compound of *vàva*, mouth, and *hàdy*, fosse; it is now applied to any gateway, whether there is an enclosing ditch or not, but the word is a memorial of a period, happily now passed away, when every considerable village in Imérina was an independent state, and when every Malagasy house was its owner's castle, enclosed in a deep fosse dug in the hard red clay, and with a rampart of earth inside that, through which a narrow opening or mouth, closed in time of war by a huge circular stone, alone gave access to the courtyard.

Another common word is also a memorial of the unsettled state of society before there was one central government, the word for "mountain," *téndrombòhitra.* This means literally "point of the town," and recalls the time when every elevated point was chosen for a village for security against an enemy. And so throughout the central provinces towns may be seen perched on hills several hundred feet high; in many cases, although there are no dwellings remaining, the deep fosses in the hard clay, often double and treble and even more in number, show where an ancient fortified town formerly stood.

This state of society, when height meant security, is also recalled in a common polite phrase always used by a Malagasy when you are approaching his house. A native always says, *Miakàra, Tòmpokoé!* meaning, "Pray, walk in," but literally, "Ascend, sir," although the house or village where he lives may be on level ground. But the old form of salutation remains although the circumstances have so much altered.

Another word also points back to a more primitive state of society than exists at present. A few years ago, a considerable number of stone bridges with circular arches were constructed over the chief streams in the neighbourhood of Antanànarìvo; these are all called *tetézana*, a word meaning literally "stepping-places" or stones, which, as in other countries, was doubtless the earliest and most primitive form of Malagasy bridge.

A memorial of a by-gone custom is preserved in the phrase *miléla-pàladìa*, *i.e.*, "to lick the sole" (of the foot). This is often used as an expression of extreme humility, and is not unfrequently employed in native prayers in public, especially by old men, accustomed to antique forms of the language. It is now only a figure of speech, but upon referring to the "Adventures of Robert Drury," who was a slave in Madagascar for fifteen years (1702–1717), we find him continually having to perform this act of homage to his master, and seeing it performed by others.

The names of some of the domestic animals and the most useful plants and fruits now found in Madagascar are proofs of their foreign origin. Thus, the domestic cat is called *sàka*, probably from the French *chat*, with the strengthening suffix *ka*; it is certainly quite a modern word. But the wild cat, possibly indigenous, is *kàry*. So also the domesticated swine is *kisòa*, probably a corruption of the French *cochon*; while the wild hog, closely allied to an African species of *potamochœrus* or river-hog, is called *àmbo*. The fine humped cattle of the island were probably introduced many centuries ago from Africa, for they are called òmby (or òmbé), doubtless the same word as the Swahili word for ox, *ngombe*. One of the most amusing words used as a name for a bird is that for turkey, *vòron-tsi-lòza*, which means "the *not* terrible bird." This name has doubtless arisen in this way : when first seen it excited some fear from its formidable-looking crest and wattles and its gobbling noise; but it was soon perceived that there was nothing to be afraid of, and so the apprehensions it at first caused being found to be groundless it was called voron-*tsi*-loza, "a bird *not* to be afraid of" after all.

So also, the peach, guava, and many other fruits, retain their foreign names, being unknown until the French introduced them; while, on the other hand, the word for the cocoa-nut, voa-*nio*, is the same as that used in the Pacific Islands, and points back to a very remote period, when the ancestors of the present inhabitants of Madagascar either brought it with them from over the sea, or found it growing in the country, and gave it the name by which they had known it in the far eastern Malayan or Polynesian islands.

One of the few words which has been retained in Malagasy very nearly in its original form is the widely-spread *salām*, the beautiful *shalom* (peace) of the Hebrew. It is, however, chiefly used in the sense of being in health.

Turning from the "history" to the "poetry" embodied in Malagasy words, we find many beautiful examples of this element in language.

And first of all, is the native name for the sun, which shines with such unclouded brilliance in Madagascar almost all the year round. It is called *màsoàndro*, the "eye of day," surely a most poetical term for the glorious orb which is

> "Not as in northern climes, obscurely bright,
> But one unclouded blaze of living light."

During more than half the year the sun rises in undimmed splendour, pursuing his course towards the zenith, and then to his setting, often in a cloudless sky, and so continually looks down upon the world like the eye of every day. From the absence up to a recent period of any clock or watch many native expressions for time are very vague, and it strikes a foreigner as very strange to hear a Malagasy say, even in the forenoon, if one is late, that "evening is the day" (*hariva ny àndro*), and even "night is the day" (*àlina ny àndro*), a figure of speech common in many eastern countries.

Then, a river is *réniràno*, "mother of waters," while a capital is *rénivòhitra*, "mother of towns." When the people in the nearly treeless highlands of the interior speak of the inhabitants of the more wooded coast plains, they call them '*ny ambàni-ràvina, i.e.,* "the (people) under the leaves." And when the whole people are spoken of they are termed *ny ambàni-lànitra,* "the (people) under the heaven;" but when the royal family are excepted, they are termed *ny ambàni-àndro,* "the (people) under the day." In another figurative expression the people at large are termed *bòzak-àman-àhitra,* "hay and grass," although it is not quite clear whether the comparison refers to their numbers, or to the light estimation in which "the masses" were held by former sovereigns.

A less ambiguous and very poetical term is the word for glory or honour; this is *vòninàhitra,* that is, "the flower of the grass." Many of the grasses in Madagascar are very fine, and it seems possible that their beauty suggested the idea, and perhaps also their transitory character, honour being so dependent in a despotic state of society upon the caprice of the sovereign. In some passages of Scripture, such, for instance, as 1 Pet. i. 24, where all the glory of man is compared to the flower of the grass, the exact similarity (in the Malagasy version) of the things compared has a curious effect on the ear.

From the aspect of the interior country during the dry rainless months, when "the beauty of the grass is as a fading flower," it being brown and parched, and all the rice-fields are bare, comes another descriptive word, the season being called *rirìnana,* that is, the time of being swept off or cleared away.

I have often thought, as I have gazed with intense delight

on the great fronds of the fan-palm standing out in bright green against the sky, that the native mind has caught a very striking feature of the beautiful tree in calling it *be-féla-tànana*, "many palms of the hand," comparing its green fans to enormous hands spread against the blue heavens.

As might be supposed, the complimentary terms and phrases in Malagasy are full of poetical figures. The comparisons used by the sovereign and addressed to the army, calling them "horns of the kingdom," &c., are mentioned in another chapter; but another phrase used of the people is also very common, and strikes our English ears as very strange. They are frequently styled the *mainty moldy*, "the black soot," the idea being taken from the long strings of soot which hang from inside the lofty high-pitched roofs of the old-fashioned Hova houses. These were never cleared away, for they were considered as a proof of an old and long-established family having inhabited that house, a kind of patent of respectability; and thus the word has become equivalent to what is ancient and venerable from age.

In the exaggerated and inflated Oriental style of addressing Malagasy sovereigns they were termed the "defence," the "glory," the "sun," and even the "God," of their subjects; while these latter were addressed by flattering titles, as the "walls of the rice fields," the "great lake" supplying water, the "cloth without difference back or front," "the water level, neither high or low," "the lip (or rim) of a vessel, one all round," and "the guinea-fowl all one colour," &c. The Borizano, or civilians, are complimented as "the spades with long handles to manure well (literally, apply soot to) the earth and the kingdom," "the hoofs to stand firm" (against an enemy), the "stones filling the hands of the people," and as being "the *grass* called tsirìry to remain upon the land, and not the *bird* called tsirìry to fly away from it," &c. While the "Ten ten-thousand men" or *Fòlo-àlin-dàhy*, the army, are styled "sharp spears and thick shields," "needles of the kingdom, and wetted thread to bind it together," "horns of the kingdom," and "bolts and covering of the land to keep together what Radàma gathered," &c. The sovereign styles the people, and they also call her, *rai-àman-drény, i.e.*

"father-and-mother," an expression continually applied to any friend or protector or superior.

Some of the salutations are very poetical. A frequent word of welcome is *arahàba,* probably derived from the Arabic, and equivalent to the Hebrew *rachab,* "to be enlarged," a phrase of which we have many examples in Scripture; as, "Thou hast enlarged me when I was in distress" (Ps. iv. 1); see also Gen. ix. 27; Ps. cxix. 32; Isa. ix. 5; &c. Then the common farewell is *Velòma,* "May you live," while to a superior it is proper to say *Traràntitra,* "May you reach old age."

Something may now be said about the "morality" which is embodied in many Malagasy words, a feature of the language of which there are many striking examples.

One of the most curious of these is the word for hypocrisy, *fihatsàrambélatsìhy,* which means literally "the becoming good by spreading a mat." The meaning of this, at first sight obscure phrase, is seen by remembering that the clay floors of the ordinary Hova houses are covered by the strong and neat mats made by the women. But as the Malagasy are, when untouched by Christianity, by no means as cleanly a people as might be desired, when a mat becomes dirty it is not usually removed, but merely covered over by a cleaner one; and so the process goes on until often there is a layer of four or five mats rotting on the floor, each one being dirtier than the one next above it. The habit of using the native snuff in the mouth, and rejecting it again in any convenient corner, the underside of the mat being often the most handy place, is an additional contribution to uncleanliness. When a stranger enters the house fresh mats are spread for him to sit down upon, and all looks nice and clean, but, let no one look underneath, for all sorts of filth may be hidden below! The house has merely become clean by "spreading a mat." And so the custom has suggested an ethical use of the phrase for conduct which is all clean and proper outside, but is merely a cloak for evil and impurity beneath.

Then there are two words connected with the marriage relation, which also are witnesses against some of the evils

of native society. One of these is the word for polygamy—
fàmporafésana, from the root *ràfy*, an adversary. So invariably has the taking of more wives than one shown itself to
be a fruitful cause of enmity and strife in a household, that
this word, which means "the making an adversary," is the
term always applied to it; and the root-word *ràfy* is just
that by which, in the Malagasy Scriptures, Peninnah, Hannah's
co-wife, is described (1 Sam. i. 6). The different wives are
always trying to get an advantage over each other, and to
wheedle their husband out of his property; constant quarrels
and jealousy are the result, and polygamy becomes inevitably
the causing of strife, "the making an adversary."

The other word, that for divorce, is an example of that
tendency in human nature to gloss over an evil by calling it
by a fine name. When a Malagasy wishes to divorce his wife
he has no need to apply to a law tribunal, like the Court of
Probate, or indeed to a court of any kind. He simply takes
a piece of money, sends it to his wife before certain witnesses with the words, "*Misaotra anao aho, Tompokovàvy*" ("I
thank you, madam"), and the thing is done! The wife has
no appeal, and yet this unjust and often cruel act he calls
by the fine sounding name *fisaoram bàdy*, which is literally
"thanking a wife," thanking her, in short, for the past, and
dismissing her as if he were doing her a kindness instead of
an injustice.

Among words which are like a covert satire upon the
effusive wordy loyalty so common in Madagascar is the
term *mànantsàfa Andrìana*, which really means "to inquire,
implying ignorance" (pretended), an expression which is
applied to those long inquiries about the sovereign and her
family, and the chief officers of state, which are used upon
every possible occasion by military officers of the Hova
Government, and by those having business to do with these
officials. These complimentary inquiries are amusing at
first, but become somewhat tedious when repeated over and
over again in the course of a journey upon meeting with
every petty official. They run somewhat in this way:
"Since you our friends are arrived, we ask of you, How is
Queen Rànavàlona, Sovereign of the land? How is Rajni-

L

laiàrivòny, Prime Minister and Commander-in-Chief? How is Rainimàharàvo, Chief Secretary of State? How is Rala-itsiròfo, Chief of the Judges? How are the Queen's relatives and the Twelve Wives? How is the kingdom of Ambòhimànga and Antanànarìvo? How are the cannon? How are the muskets? How are the Christians in Imérina? &c., &c. Finally, How are you our friends after your journey? and how is your fatigue?" &c., &c. And so the inquiry drags its wearisome length along; but it is all *mànantsàfa,* pretended ignorance, and pretended interest too!

Although slavery in Madagascar seems, and actually is, mild compared with that of many countries, yet, after all, the common word used in speaking of it is an unmistakable proof of the feeling with which it was regarded, at least in former times, when probably it was much more to be dreaded than now. To become a slave is in Malagasy to be *véry,* that is, to be "lost," a terrible phrase, which is still retained in ordinary use.

Another expressive word, throwing light upon the way in which buying and selling is carried on in Madagascar, is that for "bargain," *àdivàrotra,* literally, "a fought-out sale;" for, as in the East generally, a bargain is a long and tedious business, the seller beginning by asking many times the sum he is really willing to take, and the buyer offering as little in proportion, until, after an immense amount of haggling and talk, an approximation is gradually made and the purchase effected. The word for "paying" is *mandòa,* exactly the same word as is used for the act of vomiting!

A remark or two upon some of the words used in religious matters may conclude this part of the subject.

And first of these is the word employed in speaking of religion itself. Throughout Madagascar Christianity is universally known as the *fivavàhana,* "the praying;" so completely has the true religion become identified with prayer that when any one becomes a Christian they say of him, much in the same way as was said of one of old when he became a believer in Christ, "Behold, he prayeth!"

And then it is interesting to remark how in Malagasy, as in other languages, the Greek, for example, words which formerly had a wide and vague signification become specialised and limited. Thus the word for church and congregation is *fiangònana*, which originally meant simply an assembly for any purpose, but is now entirely confined to assemblies for religious worship. So also with the word for pastor, *mpitàndrina*, which is literally "one taking care of" or superintending, a word formerly applied to any superintendent, but now being gradually limited to denote the overseer or pastor of a Christian congregation; much, in fact, in the same way as the word *episcopos* was gradually specialised to mean an ecclesiastical overseer, a primitive bishop. And, still in the same line of things, just as by the influence of Christianity and by their use in the New Testament, many Greek words were purified and raised to a higher level, so it has been with many Malagasy words, such as those employed as equivalents for "grace," "faith," "justification," "righteousness," &c. These have now a fulness and meaning which they never conveyed to the Malagasy in their heathen condition. It is also, perhaps, worthy of remark that many native words have acquired the same double meaning that they have in our own language, one simply referring to physical qualities, and the other having an ethical significance. As with us, *méloka*, crooked, means also morally crooked, *i.e.*, wicked; *mahìtsy*, upright, means also upright in conduct; *màrina*, level, is also right and true; and *madio*, clean, is also used for moral purity and innocence.

Although in such widely-separated countries as England and Madagascar a great deal of difference of course exists in the modes of thinking, it is curious to observe how close a resemblance there often is between the idioms used in each. For instance, we speak of "stealing a march" on any one; the Malagasy say "stealing a step" (*mangàla-dìa*). We speak of "stealing a look," the Malagasy idiom is precisely the same (*mangàla-pijéry*). When overtaken by heavy calamity we say we are "overwhelmed by sorrow," and the Malagasy say they are "flooded in sorrow" (*dìfotr' alahélo*). While we speak of youthful people being "in the flower of their age," the Malagasy say they are in "the cream of it" (*hérotrérony*), just our own expression for the best of a thing. We speak of "high-handed" conduct, while the Malagasy say, Such an one "uses his arm" (*manao 'sàndry*). We speak of "going with the stream," and they say 'following the flow of water." The language is indeed very full of examples of short terse phrases and adages, proverbial in form, which give great force and point to native speaking; and an interesting chapter might be written upon Malagasy proverbs as illustrating native habits of thought, and the moral and religious notions of the people.

There is a large class of words of the kind called onomatopoetic, like our "whizz," "bang," "crack," &c., where the word is a close imitation of the sound it describes. Thus we find *héhy*, for laughing; *mibìtsibìtsika*, for whisper; *mitsìky*, for a giggling smile; *dòndòna*, for knocking; *éfonéfona*, for hard breathing; *dàbodàboka*, for splash, together with many others too numerous for further mention.

Enough has probably been here said to show that the language of Madagascar offers many features of great interest to the philologist, and that a careful study of its peculiarities throws much light upon the history and character of the people whose mother-tongue it is, and who can employ its musical sounds and poetical idioms with such effect. It has now received a further addition to its capabilities by embodying Christian truths, and by being used for the noblest purpose to which human speech can be applied, in the diffusion among the tribes of the great African island of that *filàzantsàra*, or "glad tidings," which is for every nation and people and tongue.

CHAPTER VIII.

CURIOSITIES OF MALAGASY NAMES: PERSONAL, TRIBAL, AND GEOGRAPHICAL.

LENGTH—NO FAMILY NAMES — PERSONAL PREFIX —DESIGNATION FROM CHIL-
DREN—UNPLEASANT NAMES—TABOOED WORDS IN CHIEFS' NAMES—ROYAL
NAMES — SÀKALÀVA CUSTOMS — CHRISTIAN NAMES — TRIBAL APPELLA-
TIONS—PLACE-NAMES—FOREIGN NOMENCLATURE IN COAST GEOGRAPHY.

ALMOST every one unacquainted with the Malagasy language
is struck by the length of many of the names, both of places
and people, but especially of the latter. Thus, to a European,
there seems an unconscionable length in such names as
Ravoninahitriniarivo, Rainivoninahitriniony, and Rabodonan-
drian-ampoinimerina! The last but one of these was the
name of the former Prime Minister; the last was the sacred
name of the persecuting Queen Ranavàlona. But such
names are of course compound words, being quite a little
sentence in themselves; and when analysed are seen to consist of a number of simple roots of two or three syllables, with
a good deal of meaning in them, and often with no little
poetry of expression as well. Thus, Ra-vònin'àhitri-ni-arìvo
is (omitting the *Ra*, to be explained presently) "the glory of
a thousand," the word for "glory" being, as was shown in the
previous chapter, literally "the flower of the grass." Then,
Rai-ni-vònin'àhitrì-ni-òny is "the father of the glory of (or,
the flower of the grass of) the river," or, in other words, the
father of a son named Ravòninàhitrìniòny. And Ra-bòdon'-
andrìan-am-pòin-imérina is "the simple one (or child) of
Andrian-am-pòin-imérina," which latter name means "the
prince in the heart of Imérina" (the central province).

There are, however, a great many Malagasy names which are much shorter and simpler than those given above, such as Rasòa, Ravélo, Raivo, Rabòdo, Randro, Ravòny, Razàfy, Razay, Ravao, &c.; and these are also combined in every conceivable way, as Rasòavélo, Rabòdosòa, Rasòandro, &c.

As among the Eastern nations generally, there are no family names in Madagascar, although there are tribal ones, something in the same way as among the Scottish and Irish clans. And so, as names are comparatively few, it is often puzzling to know "who is who;" there are so many Rakòtos and Ranàivos, Raivos, and Rasòas, as well as Rainisòas, Rainikòtos, &c., that continually some other appellation has to be added to distinguish persons from others of the same name, such as describing them as son, or brother, of such an one, who is better known, or giving their rank, as Government officials, or their position as deacon, or pastor, or preacher in the church. It is perhaps, after all, not much more puzzling than it is with us to discriminate the various Smiths, Browns, and Joneses of our acquaintance; nor so much so as in some parts of Wales, where every other person is a Davies or a Griffiths; or in portions of Scotland, where every one is a Campbell or a Macdonald.

It will have been noticed that all the above-given Malagasy names commence with the syllables Ra- or Raini-. The former is a particle which, added to any word, makes it a proper name. It is also prefixed to other words as a respectful way of addressing people: thus, children, *ankizy*, are addressed Ran-kizy; *anabàvy*, sister (of a brother), becomes Rànabàvy, &c. The word Andrìana, which is literally "prince," is also prefixed to other words in the same way to make a proper name, Ravèlo becoming Andriambélo, &c.; while a less respectful mode is by prefixing the particle I, as Ikòto, Inaivo, &c., a form also used for affectionate familiarity.

The names of animals, birds, insects, plants, and trees, or the words for any action or object, may be used as a proper name with these prefixes. Thus, two of the lads of noble family who were sent to England by Radàma I. for instruction were Vòalàvo and Totòzy, *i.e.*, Rat and Mouse; while the words for crocodile (*màmba*), wild-hog (*làmbo*), goat (*òsy*), dog (*ambòa* and *alìka*), &c., are all to be met with as personal names.

The other common prefix, Raini-, "father of," is commonly taken by men when they have a child born to them. Thus, for instance, a man may have been called all his life Rakòto, but if he has a child, say a girl, who perhaps is named Rasòa, he abandons his old name, and is henceforth known as Raini-soa, or "Father of Soa." Frequently also, although not quite so commonly, the mother of the child takes the name of *Rènisoa,* "Mother of Soa." There seems to be among the Malagasy a desire to be remembered rather by their children than by their parents; something indeed of the feeling of the old Romans as shown in the saying of the noble matron Cornelia, "Call me not Scipio's *daughter,* call me the *mother* of the Gracchi." Occasionally people who are not parents will change their name in this way, especially if they adopt other relatives' children, which is very frequently done. The Malagasy have strong family affections, and consider their brothers' and sisters' children as almost the same as their own, and their uncles and aunts as fathers and mothers, indeed, they call them so constantly, there being no single word equivalent to ours for those relationships. In one tribe of the Andrians, or people of noble birth, the ordinary rule of fathers calling themselves after their children is not followed; the clan of Andriamàsinavàlona forming in this point an exception to the practice of the Malagasy generally.

I had often been surprised in considering that there were in Malagasy many offensive names, such as Rafirìnga, "dung-hill," Rabézézika and Rabétay, "much dung," &c. The first of these is an extremely common name, and is that of the present governor of Tamatave, an officer of high rank. On inquiring, however, the reason of this, I was told that it is done from a superstitious idea which some have that a pleasant-sounding name may cause envy; just indeed from the same feeling that makes the people dislike that any one should praise their children for good looks. If you do this, remark-ing that an infant is pretty, or a fine child, they will reply, "No, it is ugly, or nasty," believing that they thus avert the consequences of the evil eye, which is, as is well known, a widely-spread superstition in the East. The idea seems to be that the envy of the evil powers is excited by any openly-expressed praise of human beauty or goodness, and that they will consequently attempt to injure those so praised.

In the preceding chapter on the Malagasy language, attention was called to the curious custom which the people of Madagascar have of considering as tabooed the words and syllables which form the names of their chiefs and sovereigns, and to the dialectic changes which this custom produces on the language. This sacred character of the sovereign's name accordingly makes it an offence to utter it lightly or carelessly. Instances have occurred at dinners and entertainments given to Europeans by Malagasy that the queen's name has been mentioned freely in conversation by the former; but they have soon been politely requested by their hosts to refrain from its frequent use as highly disrespectful to their sovereign. It is also considered indecorous to use the names of the royal palaces as a comparison of size or height, &c.

It should also be added that this respect for a royal name is also extended in a certain degree to the name of every one of any position in society; for in public speeches and *kabárys* a Malagasy will not mention the name of any one without first making an elaborate apology for doing so; and so also they do in speaking of the dead, avoiding, if possible, mentioning their exact name, and giving instead a complimentary periphrasis. So that the name stands for the person it represents, and is held to be as worthy of respect, much indeed as "the name" of Jehovah and of the Lord Jesus Christ are in Scripture frequently put for the persons of the Divine Beings, numerous instances of which will occur to every Biblical student.

The word "name" is also used by the Malagasy as an equivalent for position, influence, and fame. Thus, they say of a person who has done nothing to distinguish himself, *Tsy manan'andrana izy*, "He has no name," nearly equivalent in fact to our phrase, "He has made no name for himself."

It has been the custom among the Hovas at least, if not with the other tribes in Madagascar, for the sovereign to take a new name on his or her accession. Thus, the late queen, who was named Ràbòdo, became Rasohérina, and the present sovereign, who was known as Ramòma, was called Rànavàlona II. To these names is added the word *manjàka, i.e.,* "reigning," so as to become almost an integral part of the name; thus, Rasohéri-manjàka, Ranavàlo-manjàka, the last syllable of the first name being omitted for euphony.

The sacredness attached to the royal names among the Hovas is extended, after the death of the sovereign, to everything connected with their tombs and funeral ceremonies. Thus, they do not say of a king that he has died, but has "retired," *niamboho,* literally, "turned his back" upon his subjects, or, has "gone home to lie down," *nòdimàndry.* His corpse is not called *fàty,* the usual word for that of a subject, but *ny màsina,* "the sacred" (thing); and it is not "buried" (*alévina*), but "hidden" (*afénina*); and his tomb is not a *fàsana,* but *trano masina,* "the sacred house," in which is hidden the silver coffin, which is termed *làkambòla,* "the silver canoe." Everything, in short, is specialised by a name different from that applied to the same thing in connection with the people generally, whether nobles or otherwise.

The Sàkalàvas along the west coast of Madagascar have a different and very curious custom with regard to the names of their kings. After their death they give them a new name, by which from that time they are always known, it being considered as sacrilegious to speak of them by the name by which they were known while living. Thus, Andriandà-hifòtsy, a king of Ménabé, was afterwards called Andrianàni-narìvo, and Ravahìny, a queen of Ibòina, was known after her death only as Andriamamélonarìvo. The posthumous names of Sàkalàva chieftains almost all ended in the word *arìvo,* "thousand," and with the other portions of the name signified that the deceased monarch was loved by, feared by, or desired by, thousands (of his subjects). This custom appears to have been general among all the tribes of the west and south-west of Madagascar.

Since the wide acceptance of Christianity in central Madagascar many Scriptural names have been introduced, and some have become quite naturalised among the Malagasy, especially the names John and Jonah, slightly altered to follow the phonetic character of the orthography; the former becoming Rajaonina, and the latter Rajonà. So also we find Samuel, Daniel, Joseph, Boanerges (!), Japhet, Zechariah, and many others; and in all these the accent is carried forward a syllable, so that with the name-prefix the words become Rasamioéla, Radaniéla, Rajoséfa, &c. Women's names taken from Scripture are not so common; but the Latin form of Mary, Marìa, is also a native word, so that it enters into the composition of many names, as Ramarìavélo, &c. A few natives, chiefly elderly people, have had English names given to them at their baptism, which they use prefixed to their native names; and so we find such combinations as John Rainisòa, David Johns Andrianàdo, Joseph Andrianàivoravélona. But in recent times it has not been considered desirable to alter native names by any foreign element, at least among the Protestant missions. The Romish missionaries have given European names to their converts when baptized. so that numbers of the saints of the Roman calendar are represented by their Malagasy protégées.

Some of the compound names sound curiously enough: thus, one may find amongst school children, Ramoséjoféra, *i.e.,* *Ra*, native prefix; *mosé*, corruption of the French *monsieur;* and *jofera*, again a native name; and also Ramosévazàha, which might be translated, "Mr-monsieur-white-man" (or foreigner) !

Many of the tribal names are very poetical, and remind one of those borne by some of the North American Indian tribes. Thus, we have in the southern-central province, the *Bétsiléo,* "the many unconquered;" along the eastern coast are the *Bétsimisàraka,* "the many unseparated," standing shoulder to shoulder against an enemy; in the north-east-central district are the *Sihanaka,* "the lake people," from the nature of the country they inhabit; through the dense woods of the south-eastern side of the island are the *Tanala,* "the forest people;" while in the extreme north are the *Antankarana,* "the rock dwellers," so called from an almost impregnable rocky fastness in their territory. Then the central tribe of Hovas are subdivided into many smaller clans. The people in and around the capital city of Antanànarìvo are called the *Vòro-mahéry*, " the powerful birds," the birds known by that name being a species of large hawk or small eagle, and used as a kind of crest or emblem by the Hova Government. To the north of these are the *Tsimiambòholàhy*, "the men not turning their backs," *i.e.*, on an enemy ; farther north still, at Ambòhimànga, the old capital and sacred town, are the *Tsimàhafòtsy*, "those not turning pale" (with fear) ; while to the north-east are the *Mandìavàto*, those "treading the rock," standing firm.

In the names of two tribes on the eastern coast of Madagascar are preserved traces of the Arab settlements made several centuries ago in that part of the island, as already described in the chapter on the Origin and Divisions of the Malagasy people. These are the *Zafy Ibrahima*, *i.e.*, the grand-children or descendants of Ibrahim or Abraham ; and the *Zafy Ramania*, or, as some writers give it, *Zafy Rahimina*, or descendants of Imina, the mother of Mohammed.

As already mentioned in the preceding chapter, the custom of *fàdy* or tabooing certain words has had in some parts of Madagascar a most unsettling effect upon the nomenclature of places. But this remark does not apply to much of the central and eastern portions of the island ; and in the names of mountains, rivers, districts, and towns there is a field of research as yet unexplored, and which would probably yield some information as to the settlement of the country. A cursory glance over a list of villages shows many parallels to English place-names. Thus, we have Malagasy "Sunnysides" in Ambòhibémàsoàndro, "the place of much sun ;" "Oxfords" in Ampìtanòmby ; "Holytowns" in Ambòhimàsina ; "Stonebridges" in Antatézambàto ; while very numerous places called Ambòhimanjàka and Ambòhitriniandrìana are the "Kingstowns" and "Princetowns" of the central provinces, denoting the village of the headman of many small tribes at a time when the country was still divided with numerous petty kingdoms or chieftaincies.

Some interest attaches to the name of the largest lake in Madagascar, the Alaòtra, a sheet of water of about twenty-five miles long, in the Antsihànaka province. Among the Sàkalàva, Alaòtra means "ocean" or "sea," so that its name denotes the sea-like sheet of water. (*Cf.* the use of *Bahr* among the Arabs for lakes, in "Sea of Galilee" (or *Bahr et-Tabiriyeh*), and "Salt Sea" (or *Bahr el-Lut*). Alaòtra, according to the Rev. L. Dahle, is possibly the Arabic *Al-lutat*, "the dashing of the waves," the ocean; and the Arabs of the Comoro Islands and East Africa are known among the Malagasy as the Talaòtra, *i.e.,* "those from beyond the ocean."

An inspection of a map of Madagascar shows a curious contrast between the nomenclature of the interior and that of the coast-line. The former is purely native, as no European power has ever succeeded in retaining territory for long away from the coast; but the fringe of names along the sea-line has a considerable European element in it, and throws considerable light upon the successive periods during which the Madagascar coast was visited in early times by different European nations, as well as upon the attempts made by some of them to plant colonies in various parts of the island. Besides this, as all surveying and map-making has hitherto been the work of Europeans, and as the naval commanders who gave many of the names of prominent places were usually unacquainted with the Malagasy language, and consequently knew nothing of the native names of headlands, rivers, and bays, they give many of them European names in a very arbitrary fashion, in some cases, however, not the less embodying an historical fact or date. Thus, most of the prominent capes of Madagascar bear the names of saints—St. Mary, St. Vincent, St. Thomas, and St. Sebastian—showing the religious feeling of the Portuguese, the first European power who discovered the island, which for a considerable period was called by them and others Isola de San Lorenzo, after the saint on whose day it was first seen by Fernando Soares. The traces of the Portuguese are also left in St. Augustine's River and Bay, the shoal of Bonaventura, the Island of Juan de Nova, and the fine harbour of Diego Suarez, at the extreme north of Madagascar. We find another memorial of the same nation in the name of the chief inlet on the eastern side of the island, Antongil Bay, so called from Antonio Gil, a Portuguese, who first discovered it. Besides the names given above, numerous other saints' names are found in ancient maps, as St. Justina, St. Romano, St. Julian, St. Clara, St. Lucia, St. Roche, and others, but these latter have been disused by later geographers. The memory of the French occupation of Madagascar is retained in the words Fort Dauphin, to the extreme south-east; the island of St. Marie's, still held by them, on the east coast; Port Choiseul, Foule Pointe, and Louisbourg. And lastly, an English element in the map, but probably quite unrecognised by the natives, is seen in the names given by Captain Owen and others to various ports and islands; as William Pitt Bay, Liverpool Point, Port Croker and Point Barrow, and in Barren, Barlow, Crab, Murder, and Grave Islands; while Owen's surveying ships are both memorialised in "Barracouta" Island and Port "Leven."

Some of the foreign names given to places in Madagascar have been strangely altered by the Malagasy, both in sound and spelling, so that one hardly recognises in Tòamàsina, the native name of Tamatave, the San Tomaso of the Portuguese settlers; and still less in Fàradofày, the Fort Dauphin of the south, two centuries ago the chief French port and stronghold in the island.

In Madagascar, not less than in European and other countries, place-names will doubtless prove on careful examination to be one of the most valuable of ancient historical records; and while we sometimes ask carelessly, "What's in a name?" it will be seen that in Madagascar, as in other parts of the world, names form, strange as it may seem, more enduring and unmistakable records than tombs and temples, or marble and bronze.

CHAPTER IX.

CURIOUS AND NOTEWORTHY CUSTOMS AMONG THE DIFFERENT TRIBES.

ROADS AND TRAVELLING—CANOES AND BOATS—SLAVERY—RANKS OF SOCIETY —HOVAS OR COMMONERS—ANDRIANS OR NOBLES—ROYALTY—OATHS OF ALLEGIANCE—ROYAL PROPERTY—A MALAGASY KABÀRY—NATIVE ORATORY —OCCUPATIONS AND MODES OF LIVING—HANDICRAFTS.

Roads and Travelling.—One of the first things which strikes a stranger upon arriving in Madagascar is the absence of anything like a carriage or wheeled vehicle, and the consequent necessity for using *men* as bearers of passengers and goods, instead of employing horses or other animals. This arises in part from the conservative feeling of the Malagasy, who dislike innovation upon long-established usages, but still more from there being no roads, in our sense of the word, in the island; so that any wheeled vehicle would be almost useless except for very short distances on the level plains of the coast. The Malagasy, therefore, except people of the upper and wealthier classes, are accustomed to travel long distances on foot; and the men who are employed by the Government to take letters and despatches to distant places have wonderful powers of speed and endurance. Some of these have been known to travel from the capital to Tamatave on the east coast, a distance of about 200 miles, in four days; this journey, it must be remembered, being performed not over a smooth and level road like an English turnpike, but over rough and rocky hills, long descents slippery with mud, rapid streams without bridges, dense forest, and deep sloughs through which it is impossible to move rapidly. The endurance of most of the bearers also is no less remarkable. These are mostly young men who

begin to carry their master's children while they are still
mere lads. Thus they get inured to such work almost
from childhood, and although there are few middle-aged
men who can keep up the *pace* necessary for carrying people,
yet many retain strength and endurance enough for carrying
burdens until they are quite old and grey-headed.

The national carriage of Madagascar is the *filanjàna*, or
takon, as it is called on some parts of the coast. This consists of a couple of light poles of tough wood about seven
feet long, and kept together by iron rods with nuts and
screws; on the hindmost of these and from the poles is fixed
an iron-framed seat, covered with leather and stuffed, having
a back against which one can lean. To this many add a piece
of wood suspended by straps as a foot-rest, and leather pockets
at the side and back for carrying small articles. There is
no cover, but a stout sun-shade is strapped to one pole and
a piece of waterproof sheeting, as an apron for wet weather,
to the other; and thus equipped, one is prepared to explore
Madagascar from north to south and from east to west; and
in such a conveyance has the writer travelled many, many
hundreds of miles, either in the regular visitation of his
district or in making extensive journeys in various directions from the central province.

The *filanjàna* just described is a gentleman's palanquin;
the one used by ladies is usually a kind of oblong basket
made of platted sheep-skin, and borne on poles of the light
and strong mid-rib of the extremely long leaf of the *rofia*
palm. For long journeys these are usually fitted with a
covering of strong cloth on a light iron framework, often
with mosquito netting to keep out the various insect plagues
which are occasionally met with. Both kinds of palanquin
are carried in the same way, by four stout bearers, or, as they
are called, *màromìta*, a word which means "many fordings."
Every few minutes they change the pole from one shoulder
to the other, keeping up a short trot at a pace, on tolerably
level ground, of about six miles an hour; and when the men
are properly trained, the motion is much more smooth and
pleasant than might be supposed possible. If taking a
journey beyond an hour's duration, it is usual to have six

men, the extra two relieving the others every few minutes; but if out for a longer time, or for a day's journey, eight men are employed, so as to have a double set, who relieve each other at frequent intervals. This they do without stopping, the "leaders" running under the poles, and taking them from their companions while going at full speed.

From six to seven hours is an ordinary day's journey, although the bearers will frequently go eight or nine hours without much apparent inconvenience; and a good set of men will continue at such work pretty nearly every day throughout a journey which may take two or three or four months. The pay for each man is about 6d. a day, with 2d. for food; but although this seems small for each bearer, one is obliged to take so many men in addition to carry necessary articles that one cannot undertake a long journey without at least eight to a dozen men in addition to the personal bearers. There are no hotels in Madagascar, and so bed and bedding must be taken; in many parts of the country there are no inhabitants, so a tent must be carried; and although rice and fowls are generally to be obtained everywhere, yet tea and coffee, bread and flour, preserved meats, and other provisions are a very desirable addition to the produce of the country. And of course, in addition to all these, plates and dishes and cooking apparatus, necessary change of clothes, books for distribution, &c., all help to swell the list of articles to be carried about with one on a journey of any extent. The bearers of luggage have no change with others. Light packages are borne by a man on a pole, the weight at each end balancing the other; while boxes and heavier articles are borne by two men, or more, according to their bulk and weight.

And so, with a company of a score of men, more or less, long journeys of several weeks in duration are continually being made; and, as a rule, these Malagasy bearers are good tempered and willing, easily managed by a little tact and kindness, and made happy after any extraordinary exertion by a gift of some beef, over which they make merry as they surround their cooking fires in the evening, and soon forget the toils of the day's march in feasting and jollity. The luggage bearers are looked upon as somewhat inferior to those who carry people, for these latter have to be more agile and active, to go at a greater speed, and the whole set must be able to keep step and pace well with each other. In many of the luggage bearers, especially those belonging to the tribe called Bézànozàno, who are constantly carrying burdens to and from the coast, a curious bunch or callosity may be observed on the shoulders, a provision of nature by which a sort of natural cushion is gradually formed, protecting the collar-bone from any concussion, and the skin from abrasion.

Animals are, however, used to some extent for riding by the Malagasy. Oxen are often saddled and bridled, and having had their horns and tails cut short, are ridden at a short shuffling pace often as fast as a horse can canter. And during the last few years a considerable number of horses have been imported into the country. Many of these are Pegu ponies, which are hardy and sure-footed, soon adapting themselves to the rough paths and rocky ascents, up and down which they must often climb, more like a goat than a horse. Many of the natives are bold and daring riders, and about three years ago the Queen gave orders that all officers above a certain rank must be on horseback when escorting her in public, so that a great impetus was given to the practice of horse-riding. Only twice have I seen a wheeled vehicle in Madagascar; one of these was a small carriage belonging to the Queen, but which was *carried* by men, instead of being drawn by horses; and the other was an English cart, drawn by a yoke of oxen, one of a small number lately introduced by foreign traders, and used to convey produce along the grassy plains of the eastern coast.

Canoes and Boats.—One of the Hova kings of the old time, Andriamanélo, has, according to tradition, the credit of having introduced the use of canoes. Those employed in the rivers and lakes of Madagascar are hollowed out of the trunk of a tree, a kind called *varòngy* (*Calophyllum inophyllum*) being chiefly employed. The largest are about forty feet long, with a breadth and depth of nearly three feet. They are propelled with paddles, either of a spade shape or in that of

M

a spoon. These are *dug* into the water, the paddler sitting with his face to the head of the canoe. With three or four paddles and on smooth water these long canoes can be urged through the water with great speed, but as they have no keel they require careful ballasting. Very small canoes are used in the narrow channels along the sides of the rice-fields to convey the sheaves to the threshing-floors on the neighbouring high grounds.

Few things are more pleasant than a canoe voyage on some of the large rivers of Madagascar, always providing that you have a good canoe and a sufficient staff of paddlers. The men often beguile the time by singing their musical and often amusing canoe chants, in which one of them keeps up a recitative, usually an improvised strain, often bringing in circumstances recently happening, and very frequently introducing delicate flattery of the European employing them, how generous and rich he is, &c., and inquiring if there is not beef, and rice, and other food at the next stopping-place. To this all the rest chime in with a chorus at regular intervals, a favourite one being *Hé! misy và!* ("Oh, is there any?") In another one the chorus speaks of Tamatave as a great place for spending money, while the recitative brings in all the different villages on the journey from Tamatave to the capital, and ends with the north entrance to the palace at Antanànarìvo. In September 1877, I took a four days' voyage down the river Bétsibòka, encamping on the river-bank at night; and the heat and some insect plagues were the only drawbacks to a very delightful excursion, during which we glided over the smooth surface of the stream with the strong current, and the glorious vegetation—pandanus and palm and bamboo—swept past us like a continuous panorama, all glowing in the intense light and heat of the tropical sunshine.

A very primitive contrivance called a *zàhitra* is employed upon many of the rivers on the south-east coast. This consists of a number of bamboos lashed together at one end and spreading out in a fan form at the other. But when the sovereign has occasion to cross a wide river a kind of raft of *zòzòro* or papyrus is constructed, this being the ancient orthodox fashion for royalty. It will be remembered that the papyrus of the Nile was applied to similar uses by the Egyptians. Papyrus boats are frequently noticed by ancient writers. Plutarch describes Isis going in search of the body of Osiris, "through the fenny country in a barque made of the papyrus."* See also Isa. xviii. 2.

On the south-east coast of Madagascar, I was much interested to find that in the lagoons and river mouths, as well as for going out to sea to the foreign vessels, a most ingeniously constructed boat is employed instead of the ordinary canoes. These boats are called *sàry*, and are *built* of planks carefully fitted together, and with the ends rising rather high like that of a whale-boat. They are about thirty feet long by eight feet beam, and easily carry fifty people. But the strangest circumstance is that no nail or iron of any kind is employed in its construction, the planks are all *tied* together with twisted cord of *anìvona* palm fibre, a very tough and durable material, the holes being plugged with pins of hard wood. There is no framework to which the planking is fixed, but the seats act as stiffeners of the fabric, passing right through the sides. Strips of bamboo are used to caulk the seams, and loops of the same material also form rowlocks for the large oars or sweeps of European shape.

On the north-west coast again, the outrigger, a nautical feature never seen in Hova canoes, is largely used for the canoes of the Sàkalàva and Antankàrana, in fact they could not otherwise live in the rough waters of the broad bays and inlets of that coast. Some of these craft are quite different in construction from any Hova canoe, being made of very thin planking, and have a curiously curved piece rising from the head and stern. It seems possible that some of these canoes have been introduced by the Banyan traders from India; for, if I am not mistaken, some of them much resemble the boat in use at Madras and other Indian ports. Others, however, are probably coeval with these northern Malagasy tribes themselves. One kind of canoe much used among the islands and bays of the northernmost part of Madagascar is called

* *The Manners and Customs of the Ancient Egyptians*, new edition, by Samuel Birch, LL.D. London: 1878.

làkampiàra, the *fiàra* being a raised platform in the centre, intended for people to sit upon, or to place any luggage. One of these is described by Bishop Kestell-Cornish as being "twenty-six feet in length, and in breadth only twenty-five inches. It was formed of the trunk of one tree, and a plank on either side was added to give the necessary depth. There was an ingenious outrigger projecting some five feet on either side, and on the lee side bounded by a piece of timber shaped like the bottom of a canoe, which took the water when she heeled over, rendering her perfectly safe without materially checking her course. In so frail a structure it would be impossible to step a mast; they therefore work the sail by means of two sprits, which are stepped into holes which run along the keel line. If going before the wind, the sprits occupy the holes which are nearest together; if close hauled, those which are farthest apart." With a good breeze these canoes will go at a speed of twelve miles an hour.

The Malagasy along this coast are bold sailors, for these canoes put out in the open sea with the wind blowing very fresh; and it is clear that the people of the north-west have always been skilful navigators. From the long-continued and systematic piratical excursions they used to make, they must have been able to construct canoes of considerable size and with sea-worthy properties; and in keeping up such a custom they seem to have perpetuated the same predatory habits as those which are still common to the Malays of Borneo and other islands of the Eastern Archipelago.

Slavery.—Slavery is another institution in Madagascar which, together with many other things, makes the state of society very different from that in a European country. But when we hear of Malagasy slavery, we must not imagine gangs of men and women labouring in sugar or cotton plantations, under fear of the lash of a brutal overseer, and constantly liable to be sold away from their wives and children and sent to a distant part of the country. Slavery in Madagascar is really a "domestic institution," having much of a patriarchal character about it, and many analogies to that of the Jews and other Eastern nations, as described in Scripture. (See chapter on "New Light on Old Texts.") Although, of course, the innate injustice of buying and selling and holding as property one's fellow-creatures remains unaltered, practically, there is not, as a rule, much in the circumstances of the slaves generally to call for any great commiseration; for, on the whole, they are kindly treated by their masters, they are considered as a kind of inferior members of the family to whom they belong, and many of the slaves have a practical freedom of action to which the free population are quite strangers. They will join in the conversation of their masters at table and give their opinion with a freedom which strikes us as amusing, and which is utterly alien to our English habits with our servants. And then it must be remembered that in Madagascar there is not the colour prejudice, or the distinction of race between master and slave, which raises such an impassable barrier between the dark and white races in other countries where slavery exists; for the masters are often just as dark in colour as their slaves, and, as will be presently described, are, as regards some of them, of exactly the same origin.

The slave population in Madagascar is divided into three distinctly marked classes—viz., the Zàza-Hova, the Andévo, and the Mozambiques.

The first of these, the Zàza-Hova, are, as their name implies, of the same stock as the Hovas themselves, the mass of the population of the central province. But they or their ancestors have become slaves either from having been sold for debt, or as a punishment for political offences or for certain crimes. The cruel code of native laws up to about sixteen years ago denounced not only death for many offences, but also reduced the culprit's wife and children to slavery. And so a large number of persons are slaves whose fathers at a recent or more remote period were free people.

The second and largest division of the slave population, the Andévo or slaves proper, are chiefly the descendants of those who were captured in the numerous war expeditions carried on by the Hovas in various parts of the island, especially in the reigns of Radàma I. and Rànavàlona I. These wars were conducted with fearful cruelty: the men being, even after submission, often ruthlessly shot down or speared, while the women and children became the slaves of the conquerors, and were brought up to Imérina. They are, as a rule, rather darker in colour than the Hovas, and have a considerable variety of feature, as might be expected from their mixed origin.

The third division are the Mozambiques or African slaves, who have been brought into the country from time immemorial by the Arab slave-trading dhows. These have now been formally set free (in 1877), and the majority of them are actually so, although many of the female slaves remain with their former owners.

Slavery in Madagascar cannot be said to produce much of that feeling that accompanies it in some countries which makes all labour to be considered degrading, although there are traces of it to be seen now and then. Thus, it appears strange to the Malagasy to see us Europeans walking out for short distances unaccompanied by a servant or some attendant; for no free Malagasy, male or female, would think of going abroad without at least one follower at his or her heels. And so, if any of our native friends meet us alone, they will immediately offer and indeed insist upon escorting us on our way, thinking we do not keep up our dignity sufficiently by going alone. So again, no respectable Malagasy would carry with him any small article, such as a Bible or hymn-book; that must be taken by a slave boy or girl following them: and they wonder to see us carrying a map or a roll of drawings as we go to our schools or Bible-classes. There is great respect paid to seniority among the Malagasy; so that if two slaves who are brothers are going a journey, any burden must be carried by the younger one, so far at least as his strength will allow.

Ranks of Society.—The second of the three great classes into which society in the central provinces of Madagascar is divided is the Hovas or commoners, the mass of the free people. These are subdivided into a great many tribes and clans, who very seldom intermarry, but keep mostly to their own clan, and, as a rule, to their own family, cousins who are children of brothers very frequently marrying together, so as to keep property from being dispersed.

These so-called free people have, however, in some respects little freedom of action. They are divided into two great classes, the *bòrizàno* or civilians, and the *miàramìla* or military class. Both these are liable to be called upon to do any work for the Queen and Government, to cut and drag timber from the forest many miles distant, to make bricks and tiles, to quarry and build stone, and to perform all other service required of them, and all this without any payment. This compulsory labour is called *fànompòana*, a word meaning simply "service," and it appears to Europeans as the greatest hindrance to progress in the country, through repressing native talent and ingenuity. For, as all skilled workmen are liable to be impressed for an indefinite amount of unpaid work, they naturally do not care to be known as specially gifted. It is true there are few taxes, but *fànompòana* inevitably becomes very unequal in distribution, every one, if possible, shifting to his next lower in rank the burden he has to bear. There are no salaries paid to any Government officials (except school teachers), from the governors and judges down to the private soldiers; and although the customs and other sources of revenue bring in considerable sums, nothing is spent on harbours, lighthouses, or such public works. But it is said that the Government are intending shortly to commence the making of roads through the country, and a paved road has been already constructed from the palace to the residence of the chief minister, and this is to be continued through the city northwards; a European superintendent, of course salaried, being employed. As yet, in these matters Madagascar has hardly advanced much beyond its primitive uncivilized condition; although it may be hoped that the knowledge now being diffused, and the advance of intelligence, will ere long bring about beneficial changes in public policy. No doubt it would be a very difficult thing even for the Government to alter suddenly the old order of things, and to impose taxes instead of personal service; but a beginning has certainly been made; and through the building of the Memorial Churches and other mission buildings, in all of which fair and liberal wages were paid for all work done, the idea of payment

for labour has been impressed upon the public mind, so
that even the highest officers felt constrained to commence
making some small payment for work which hitherto they
had always claimed as having a right to demand.

The third class of Malagasy society is that of the Andrians or
nobles.　These again are divided into six classes or clans, some
of which are descended from different chieftains of Imérina,
formerly independent sovereigns, but whose dominions were
gradually absorbed by the ancestors of the present reigning
family.　Their descendants, however, have been allowed to
retain many of the privileges of their descent, being saluted
in different terms to the commoners, and having a right to
construct a different kind of tomb from that of the people
generally, and some of them having the distinction of carrying the scarlet umbrella, the mark of royalty.　Malagasy
nobility, therefore, is strictly a matter of descent, and not of
creation, nor has it ever been the custom to confer such privileges an Andrian possesses upon any one of a lower rank.
The present Prime Minister is not an Andrian, although his
family has been a privileged one and has possessed great wealth
and influence for several generations past.　It must not be
supposed, however, that the great majority of these so-called
nobles are marked off in any distinct way from the Hovas or
commoners.　Many indeed are very poor, so that it is almost a
proverb to say, " As poor as an Andrian;" and there is generally
little to distinguish them from others, except, perhaps, a somewhat more polite behaviour.　In certain villages almost the
whole population except the slaves are Andrians.　A kind of
non-hereditary nobility has arisen since the time of Radàma I.
in the giving of "honours" or *vònindhitra* to military and
Government officers.　This rank is reckoned by numbers; the
common soldiers having one honour, and so on up the various
grades, the highest being sixteen.　Of these last, however, there
are only three or four favoured individuals; but there are
many officers of fifteen honours, and a still larger number of
fourteen, and so the number of holders goes on increasing down
to the lower ranks.

There is nothing in Madagascar like the Hindoo caste,
except in some of the marriage restrictions.　Thus, most of

the clans of Andrians do not intermarry, nor can an Andrian marry a Hova, or a Hova marry a slave; neither do the three classes of slaves marry with each other; and tribes and even families generally marry amongst themselves (with certain exceptions as regards the descendants of sisters, who cannot intermarry down to the seventh generation), so as to keep landed and other property together. One clan of Andrians, however, the Zànakambòny, have certain privileges which they maintain with great tenacity; and there are various things they will not do, as mending a fence, associating with the other tribes, lending a mat or a drinking vessel, or eating from the same dish with other people. They are, accordingly, very superstitious, as well as proud, poor, and ignorant. They almost monopolise the craft of making tinware.

Royalty.—Royalty and chieftainship in Madagascar has many peculiar customs connected with it, a few of which may be here noted down. When a Malagasy sovereign succeeds to the throne an oath of allegiance must be taken by all persons of position and by representatives of the distant tribes, who come up to the capital for that purpose. These signs of allegiance are three in form—the *Léfon'òmby* or "spearing the calf;" the *Véli-ràno* or "striking water;" and the presentation of *Hàsina,* or silver coin.

In the ceremony of *Léfon'òmby,* a young calf is killed, the head and feet are reversed in position, spears are thrust into the carcass, and those who are to be sworn each hold a spear in their hand while one of the judges repeats a form of oath, imprecating fearful penalties upon the head of those who violate it, and hoping that they may in that case become like the mangled animal before them. To this they express assent by violently shaking the spears. This form of oath is chiefly employed for the more influential personages.

For those lower in rank the oath of *véli-ràno* is considered sufficient. In this ceremony the parties stand round a small pond of water into which there has previously been thrown the dung of a bullock, the flower of a certain grass, a musket ball, rice chaff, the wadding of a musket, branches of a tree called *àmbiàty,* a long grass, and a water flower. An oath of allegiance having been recited by one of the judges, assent is given by the persons to be sworn striking the water with boughs, a spear being also struck into the pool, and a musket fired over it. The writer has also seen this form of oath taken over water in a canoe, which is then violently shaken by the people who stand around it. At the accession of Rànavàlona I., another form of oath was devised, called *misòtro vòkaka.* In this ceremony a quantity of red earth having been taken from the tomb of one of the kings was mixed with water, and drunk by the common people, it being supposed that this would operate as a curse in those who violate the oath.

The third form of allegiance is by presenting the *hàsina* or silver dollar. While the other two customs are only observed at the accession of a new sovereign, this is repeated on every occasion when the Queen grants an audience either to a foreigner or to one of her subjects; it is also given at many other times, not to the Queen personally, but to governors or other officials who represent the sovereign. The piece of money presented is the dollar or *àriàry,* formerly the Spanish " pillar dollar," but in later years the French five-franc-piece; this is called *vòla tsi-vaky* (" unbroken money "), as distinct from the cut money used in trading. On presenting it, a wish or prayer is expressed that blessings on the sovereign may accompany the money offered. This offering of money seems analogous to that widely-spread custom which is alluded to in Ps. lxviii. 30, " Rebuke the company of the spearmen, . . . until every one submit himself with *pieces of silver.*"

A Malagasy sovereign never moves out of the palace without great state and ceremony, all the chief people of the kingdom residing in the capital accompanying her, and hundreds of soldiers and other attendants. Her presence is always known by a large scarlet umbrella being carried over her, and when taking the air in the verandah of the palace or in the gardens this sign of royalty is also seen above her head. In this scarlet umbrella there seems a link of connection with some of the African customs, many of the negro kings being distinguished by an immense ornamented umbrella being borne over them; and it will be remembered that the state umbrella of the King of Ashantee formed one of the trophies of the recent war in that country. The Nineveh sculptures also

show that the kings of Assyria when appearing in their state
chariots had a large and richly decorated umbrella carried
over them by an attendant.

In some of the songs sung in praise of the sovereign there
appears to be a trace of connection with the custom in some
Polynesian Islands, by which the king was always carried on
men's shoulders, as otherwise wherever he might walk would
become henceforth his own property. So some of the Malagasy songs speak of the Queen as *tsy mandìa tàny,* "not
walking on the ground," and indeed the sovereign is very
seldom seen except carried in the state palanquin, unless
when stepping from it to the "sacred stone." One of these
is in the centre of Antanànarìvo, and upon it the Queen always stands for a few minutes when returning to the capital
from a distance, being then saluted by the troops presenting
arms and by the discharge of cannon. The other sacred stone
is in a plain below the city to the west, and on that it used
to be the custom for the sovereign to stand at her accession,
a custom somewhat like that at an English coronation, when
the king or queen is seated in Edward the Confessor's chair
and upon the sacred stone from Scone.

Scarlet is (as with ourselves) the royal colour in Madagascar, and no one but the sovereign can wear a scarlet
làmba; and upon the death of a king or queen one of the
royal houses is completely draped in scarlet from the ridge to
the ground. When the scarlet umbrella is seen by the people
even at a great distance, they bow towards it and salute their
Queen. As in European courts, it is a great breach of etiquette
to turn the back towards the sovereign, and those who pass
in front of her bend down, stretching out both hands and
repeating the salutation, "Reach old age, sovereign lady, not
suffering from disease, live as long as the people" (or, "the
under the heaven"). And as a devout Mussulman turns in
the direction of Mecca whenever he prays, so does the loyal
Malagasy, in whatever part of Madagascar he may be, turn
towards the palace when drinking the health of his sovereign
on any festive occasion; and when any number of soldiers,
however small, at any of the distant military posts, are on
drill or are drawn up for any purpose, they turn towards the

palace and salute the Queen with music and drums, presenting arms in the European fashion. It is, therefore, highly improper to shoot in the direction of the palace when shooting wild fowl anywhere in Imérina, as it appears like a threat towards the majesty living therein.

In whatever assembly a Malagasy sovereign appears, she must always be seated in the highest place. And so, when the present Queen came to the opening of one of the Memorial Churches, she chose the gallery in the transept for her position; and at another church opening at which she was present, a temporary gallery was erected for her accommodation. And in her own chapel royal her throne, richly carved, and with a highly ornamented canopy of dark wood, is the highest place in the building (see engraving in *Sunday at Home,* March 1879, p. 200, where the royal seat is to the right, facing the pulpit). This custom is another of those numerous links of connection between Madagascar and the Polynesian Islands, for the people of these latter have precisely the same notion. In *Tyerman and Bennet's Voyages* (p. 118, 2d ed.), it is said of Tamehameha, King of the Sandwich Islands, that " if he were on board a ship in the cabin, and found that any of his subjects had walked, even inadvertently, on that part of the deck which was over his head, it would have cost them their lives as soon as they reached shore. When the British governor proposed to make him the present of a vessel, he desired it might be so built as not to require in the management that the sailors should ever step upon the cabin roof, as none of his people, by the law of his country, were allowed to be above him at any time." At the opening of any building, church or private house, a dollar is presented by the congregation or the owner to the highest military officer present, as an acknowledgment of the Queen's proprietorship of the land on which it is built, all the soil being theoretically vested in the sovereign.

One of the oddest occurrences to a foreigner newly arrived in Antanànarìvo is the respect paid to royal property when passing through the streets, for not only must every one turn out of the way before the sovereign, but also before anything belonging to her. When being quietly carried through the streets in a *filanjàna* one frequently sees, on looking a little ahead, the road completely cleared of people, even in a crowded thoroughfare; every one presses to one side or the other, and getting out of the way into any odd corner that may come convenient. All heads are meanwhile uncovered, and presently we see a native bearing a spear, followed by bearers of some small articles of luggage, the rear being brought up by another spear-bearer. These men, full of importance, shout out to the people, *Mitànilà! Mitànilà!* "Get to one side!" and none dares but obey, or a thrust of the spear would soon teach him proper manners. Sometimes the spear-bearer precedes a dozen men bearing water-jars, or half-a-dozen bullocks; but in every case—luggage, water, or cattle—it is royal property, and must be honoured by leaving a free road before it, and by uncovered heads. Should an unfortunate dog happen to cross the path, it is ruthlessly speared, and left wounded and dying on the road. This custom, again, is also found in Polynesia (as well as in Africa), for in the work just now quoted from it is said, "So stately was the royal etiquette during his [Tamehameha's] reign that whoever happened to meet the King's calabash of water as it was brought from the spring to the house, was required to unrobe and lie down upon the earth until the bearer of the vessel had gone by."

When there happens to be special work requiring to be done in connection with the royal courtyards, such as rebuilding or extending the lofty retaining walls, all ranks of the people, from the highest to the lowest, take a pride in doing with their hands some of the actual labour. Under the eye of their Queen, who sits on a raised seat looking on, the highest officers are seen with their làmbas girded round their loins, working harder than their slaves, carrying stone, digging or ramming earth, and doing whatever manual labour may be required. Much of the same kind of feeling exists in clearing the ground for the erection of their chapels, when every one—male and female, Andrians and slaves, officers and soldiers—will all labour with the greatest zeal; some digging, others bringing stone, others laying bricks, while their wives will mix the mortar and fetch the water required for the work.

There is a curious custom in connection with the administration of justice which seems unlike anything in our Western habits, viz., the use of the spear called *Tsi-tia-lainga*. This is a spear with a large silver blade, on which is engraved the name of the sovereign. Its name signifies "Hater of lies," and when any one of consequence is accused of any grave offence, officers are sent bearing this emblem of royal authority. They proceed to the house of the accused, and there in front of it they plant the spear in the ground by its sharpened lower end, after which no one can leave the house until the offence has been examined into, and inquiry made as to the truth or otherwise of the accusation.

For several other customs connected with royalty, see chapter on "New Light on Old Texts," first section.

A Malagasy Kabàry.—One of the most interesting sights that a foreigner can witness in Madagascar is a great *kabàry* or public assemblage for the purpose of hearing a message from the sovereign. These are usually held at Antanànarivo, in a large triangular piece of ground called Andohàlo, situated in the centre of the city, but sometimes in a much larger square plain called Màhamàsina, at the foot of the city hill to the west. On very great occasions every one of the population in the central province, even the children, except mere infants, are ordered to attend; and as there also come representatives from the distant tribes and provinces, a very large assemblage of people is gathered together.

From early morning, and before it is light, the people are thronging to the place of meeting to take their positions, and all the house-yards and buildings surrounding Andohàlo, and rising in somewhat amphitheatrical form around it, are also crowded with people. All sit on the ground, with a quiet order and power of endurance far exceeding what would be seen in a European crowd. Early in the forenoon, the discharge of cannon signifies that the high officers entrusted with the royal message have left the palace, and presently the roll of ·drums and the sound of military music announces their approach, lanes through the crowd being kept by lines of troops in their white uniforms. Soon they appear upon the scene, either on horseback or carried in their palanquins, and occasionally on foot. On important occasions the Prime Minister brings the royal message, he and the crowd of officers being clad in European uniforms, gorgeous in gold lace, and representing almost every kind of service, infantry, cavalry, naval, artillery, &c., both of the English, French, and other nations.

Waiting to receive them are lines of inferior officers, also clothed in every conceivable style of uniform, sometimes rather mirth-provoking to a European by their ill-fit and inappropriateness. (I have seen some in *policemen's* uniforms.) There also are the judges in their dark-red silk làmbas and Paris silk hats, and groups of the head-men of the different divisions of the people of Imérina, and those from distant tribes, these being clad in the native white or dark-red làmba, often richly ornamented with beads and coloured borders. At the upper part of the ground a space is kept clear by the soldiers, as well as an open area extending some little way into the mass of the seated people. After a short pause the Prime Minister rises, and giving the word of command to the troops, they present arms towards the palace and salute the Queen, the multitude uncovering and turning in the same direction, while all repeat the word *Traràntitra*, "Reach old age." The cannon are fired, and the national anthem played by the band. Then the officer next in rank gives the word of command for saluting the Prime Minister, who stands uncovered while the troops support arms and salute; and then this officer in his turn is saluted by the next in rank giving the word of command, and so on for two or three steps downward.

After these preliminaries, the Prime Minister advances to the front, draws his sword, and proceeds to deliver the royal message, which he usually does with great animation of gesture and fluency of language. Almost all Malagasy are born orators, and the Prime Minister is no exception to the rule, being indeed a very animated and lively speaker. In these royal speeches, after a short recital of her ancestry and mention of her predecessors, the subject of the message is approached, and the new laws and regulations are announced, the whole speech often occupying an hour or more in delivery. At the conclusion of each important paragraph the question is put in a loud voice, *Fa tsy izày va, ry ambànilànitra?* " For is it not so, ye people ? " (or, " Ye under the heaven)," that is, " Do you not agree to my wishes ? " To which there is a united shout of *Izay!* "So," in a sharp quick burst of sound which is very exciting.

At the conclusion of the message the Prime Minister resumes his seat, and then, after a slight pause, the representatives of the different classes of the people, the clans of nobles, the heads of the various tribes, far and distant, the officers of the army, the native-born Arabs and the Europeans, commence replying to the royal communication. The precedence of all these is strictly followed; and when replying three persons at least of each class advance a little into the open space, and after saluting the Queen and repeating a number of the usual complimentary phrases, they express in vague and general terms their assent to the words they have heard, and, *mànomé tòky*, give assurance of fidelity and loyalty, presenting at the same time the *hàsina* or silver dollar. On some occasions, when popular feeling has been aroused, these speeches in reply are more lengthy, the orator turning to face his companions at the end of his rounded periods, and demanding in a loud voice in the usual *Fa tsy izày vā!* to which the assenting shouts of *Izay!* are again given in reply. Occasionally the speaker will throw off the làmba or outer dress from his shoulders, girding up his loins, or sometimes throwing his làmba on the ground, seize a spear and shield, and with immense energy and violent gesticulation leap about, brandishing his weapons with fury against an imaginary enemy of the Queen ; while his auditors will become so excited as his oratory continues, that at last they will leap to their feet in an enthusiasm of loyal zeal, waving swords and spears amid shouts of *Izay! Izay!* I remember seeing the Snider rifles also thrown up in the air by the soldiers and dexterously caught again, and even an Armstrong cannon lifted up bodily with its carriage and carried about in a fashion that would have astonished a European officer of artillery.

All this speech-making is necessarily a lengthy proceeding, so that by the time all the different ranks and classes have replied, and royal and other salutes given, it is generally late in the afternoon before the vast assembly breaks up, most of the people having squatted on the ground for eight or ten or perhaps twelve hours.

On very special occasions the sovereign comes in person to deliver her speech, when, of course, the pomp and ceremony is much greater, a large covered platform being erected for her and her attendants; but the main features of the ceremony remain the same.

It will be gathered from what has been already said that, in common with many people who have only recently had a written language, the Malagasy are ready and fluent speakers, although they certainly have also the power of saying a great deal without conveying any clear idea of what they mean. It is often most difficult—in fact, next to impossible—to get a simple answer, Yes or No, or to make them come to the point; there is such a cloud of words, complimentary phrases and vague nothings, that one often wonders what it really is they are driving at. It is extraordinary to an Englishman, who holds it as a maxim that "time is money," to see how a company of people will meet together to talk day after day, the whole day long, for a week or more. This may be often seen after the death of any person in good circumstances; the whole family and connections will assemble, generally in the open air, and all day long for days together they will dispute and argue and speechify over the division of a very small amount of property. This power of talking is not confined to adults, for even young lads will sometimes make speeches with the greatest confidence and assurance; and in ignorant districts, where few people can read, an intelligent lad with a little smattering of knowledge has sometimes been put up in the native chapels, not only to read a chapter, but also to pray, and he has occasionally even held forth in a most edifying manner, much to the admiration of his elders.

Occupations and Modes of Living among the Malagasy.— When inquiring about the habits of the Malagasy, English people frequently ask, "How do they live?" "How do they

N

subsist and get a living?" To such questions it is not very easy, even for foreigners who have lived long in Madagascar, to give an entirely satisfactory reply; for it often puzzles us who live among them to know how great numbers of people gain a livelihood and procure necessary food and clothing. On the other hand, it must be remembered that the state of society in a country like Madagascar, even in the partially civilised central province, is utterly different from that of a European country with its complex civilisation and classes of society in great dependence one upon another. There is no great working class or masses of people living solely by being employed in manufactures or in agriculture. There are no such extremes of abject poverty and enormous wealth as we find in England. The great mass of the people are in pretty much the same easy circumstances: every one is engaged more or less in agriculture, almost every woman is skilled in some handicraft, strictly so called, especially weaving, and almost every man can do a good deal in the simple building required to put up a dwelling; every person, the slaves included, has his rice-ground, so that if he will only work he can always procure the necessaries of life. And as the population, except in the near neighbourhood of the capital, is small compared with the extent of the country, land for planting edible roots and vegetables may always be obtained by those who will take the trouble to cultivate it.

Then, again, the absolute wants of daily life are few: rice, with the manioc root and sweet potato, is the staple food; cattle, sheep, and poultry are abundant; very little clothing is worn, and of this an industrious woman can weave the rofia, hemp, and cotton stuffs which are required, and the very young children go almost or quite naked until a few years old. A house can be put up with little actual money outlay; the red clay of the ground on which it is built forms the walls; the coarse grass growing at no distance from the village makes the thatch; no glass is needed for the windows, or boarding for its floor, which is simply the ground itself with a thin layer of cow-dung plaster, and covered with the strong and neat mats also made by the women; so that the wood for the roof-framing and the door and window shutters is almost the only thing requiring money expenditure. Of course all this refers to the poorest class of native houses; the well-to-do people often expend considerable sums on their houses; and during the last ten years the capital has been almost entirely rebuilt, good substantial houses of sun-dried brick, with tiled roof, European arrangement of rooms, stair-case, fire-places, &c., have replaced hundreds of the old native houses with their single large room, and lofts in the high-pitched roof.

In Antanànarìvo and its neighbourhood there are, however, many changes now passing over native society. Trades and occupations are beginning to more sharply define the different classes of people, and an increasing number are being chiefly occupied in one distinct pursuit. The large number of build-ings which have been erected within the last few years have trained a great class of skilled artizans, masons, bricklayers, plasterers, carpenters and joiners, tilers, glaziers and painters. Then there are bootmakers and tailors, straw-hat manu-facturers, leather workers, blacksmiths and coppersmiths, gold and silver smiths, and potters. Then there are a large number who gain a living by selling all kinds of things in the markets, and there are a good many who go down to the coast and purchase European goods, cloths and hardware, &c., and bring them up to the interior for sale. Besides this, there is an increasing number of people who are engaged in educational work, as well as in printing and bookbinding at the mission presses. Since the reopening of the country to Europeans in 1862, the establishment of large missions in the capital, and the erection of the Memorial Churches and other important buildings, has brought a large amount of money into the country, a fact which is slowly altering many of the old usages, and is raising prices generally. There are no banks in Madagascar, so money is generally stored in a hole within the house, and it is also lent at high rates, seldom at less than at 50 per cent. per annum.

Handicrafts.—As remarked just now, the Malagasy are skilful in all handicrafts; indeed, their long taper fingers seem naturally fitted to perform all kinds of delicate and minute work. And in speaking of *manu*factures among them, the word denotes strictly that which is its literal meaning, "done by *hand*," and not by machinery, as the vast majority of our so-called manufactures are produced. Almost every Malagasy woman, from the sovereign down to the slave, can spin and weave; the spindles are simply a long piece of the tough wiry bark of the *anìvona* palm, to which is fitted a circular piece of bone to fix the cotton wool or silk cocoons; and the looms are the rudest possible contrivances, these being only four stout pegs stuck in the rough earthen floor of the house with some slight connecting pieces, a few hanks of yarn, of course a shuttle, and a long piece of smooth wood to tighten up the woof, and that is about all. And yet with these simple means the women contrive to produce strong and durable and often very beautiful stuffs made from hemp, rofia-palm fibre, cotton, aloe and banana fibre, and silk.

In platting mats and baskets, the ingenuity and dexterity of the women is also very apparent. In the coarser of these the tough peel of the *zòzòro* or papyrus is employed, and in the finer ones a variety of the numerous beautiful grasses of the country are used. The smallest of the fine straw baskets are minute boxes of about three-quarters of an inch cube, in which the plait is like the finest thread, and both the basket and its cover have a double thickness of straw.

But in metal-work the men are no less ingenious and skilful than the women. All kinds of iron, copper, and brass *wrought* work can be produced with as neat a finish as can be desired; and the goldsmiths make minute silver chains of wonderful fineness, as well as filigree silver ornaments something like Maltese work. In one of the royal palaces is a set of large silver vases of classic design, all made by native workmen from one sent from Europe. There are many indications that there is no lack either of manual skill, or of ingenuity, contrivance, and inventive genius among the Malagasy, and with the gradual lightening and eventual removal of the *fànompòana* or forced service system, great results for the future advancement of the people may be expected.

CHAPTER X.

CURIOUS AND NOTEWORTHY CUSTOMS AMONG THE DIFFERENT TRIBES—(*continued*).

HOUSES, THEIR STRUCTURE AND ARRANGEMENT—THE HOUSE AS A COMPASS AND SUNDIAL—TOWNS AND VILLAGES—FIRE BY FRICTION—POTTERY AND SUBSTITUTES FOR IT—KISSING OR NOSE-RUBBING—TATTOOING AND OTHER ADORNMENTS—MODES OF DRESSING THE HAIR—CLOTHING —USE OF VEGETABLE FIBRES FOR DRESS—FEMALE ADORNMENT— WEAPONS.

Houses, and their Structure and Arrangement.—The structure and arrangement of a native house in Madagascar varies considerably among the different tribes throughout the island, and is perhaps not unworthy of notice as closely connected with the habits and customs of the people.

A Hova house of the old style is always built with its length running north and south; it is an oblong, the length being about half as much again as the breath, and the window and door always on the west side so as to be sheltered from the prevailing south-east trade-wind; for, as there is no glass, there would be much inconvenience in facing the windward side. There is frequently another window at the north end of the house, and often one also in the north gable. The material is usually the hard red clay found all over the central provinces of the island. This, after being mixed with water, is kneaded by being trampled over thoroughly, and is then laid in courses from a foot to two feet in depth, and about a foot and a half or less in thickness. Each layer is, of course, allowed to become hard and firm before the next is laid. It is well beaten on either side as it dries, and if properly laid and of good material there are few cracks, and it makes a very substantial and durable walling; and although we should think an earthen house a poor dwelling, yet these clay houses are warmer than the timber ones, and are probably quite as durable as the majority of cheap brick houses in England. There is something similar to such construction in the "cob" houses seen in Devonshire and the western parts of our own country. The boundary walls of the compounds are also made of the same hard clay, and it is remarkable how many years such material will last without much damage, although exposed almost daily for five months every year to the heavy rains of the wet season. The better class of houses are of timber framing, the walls being of thick upright planks, which are grooved at the edge, a tenon of the tough *anìvona* palm fibre being inserted so as to hold them together. Several lengths of the same fibrous substance are also passed through each plank longitudinally at different heights from the ground, so as to bind them all firmly together round the house.

The roof in both clay and timber houses does not depend for its stability on the walls, but is mainly carried on three tall posts, which are let into the ground for some depth and carry the ridge-piece. One of these posts is in the centre, and one at each end close to the walls inside the house. This is a wise provision, as the roofs are generally of very high pitch, and in violent winds would need much more support than could be given by being merely placed on the walls. The gables are always thatched with the same materials as the roof, either of long grass or the rush called *hérana.* The ridge covering is of another kind of grass, and is fastened down with laths of split bamboo, and further secured by layers of clay. At each gable the outermost timbers cross at the apex, and project upwards for about a foot or two, the extremities being notched and often ornamented with a small wooden figure of a bird. In the houses of people of rank the *tàndro-tràno* or "house-horns" are three or four feet long, while in some of the old royal houses they project ten or twelve feet, the length being apparently some indication of the rank of the owner. In some tribes these gable ornaments, which have become only conventional horns among the Hovas, are carved in exact resemblance of the pair adorning the head of a bullock.

The interior arrangements of a Hova house are very simple, and are almost always the same.

Let us, following Malagasy politeness, call out before we enter, "*Haody, Haody,*" equivalent to, "May we come in?" And while we wait a minute or two, during which the good woman of the house is reaching down a clean mat for us to sit down on, we notice that the threshold is raised a foot or more above the ground on either side, sometimes a couple of feet, so that a stone is placed as a step on either side to go up and down. Entering the house in response to the hospitable welcome, *Màndrosòa, Tòmpokoé,* "Walk forward, sir" (or madam), we step over the raised threshold. In some parts of Imérina a kind of closet, looking more like a large oven than anything else, is made of clay at the south-eastern corner, opposite the door, and here, as in an Irish cabin, the pig finds a place at night, and above it the fowls roost. Very near the door the large wooden mortar or *làona* for pounding rice generally stands, and near it are the *fanòto* or pestle, and the *sahàfa* or shallow round wooden dish in which the rice is winnowed from the husk removed by pounding. At about the middle of the eastern side of the house are placed three or four globular *sìnys* or water-pots, the mouths covered with a kind of basket to keep out the dust. Farther on, but near the west side, is the *fàtana* or hearth, a small enclosure of about three or four feet square. In this are fixed five stones, on which the rice cooking-pots are arranged over the fire. And over this is sometimes fixed a light framework upon which the cooking-pots are placed when not in use. There is no chimney, the smoke finding its way out through window or door or slowly through the rush roofing, and so the house is generally black and sooty above, long strings of soot hanging down from the roof. The north-east corner of the house is the sacred portion of it, and is called *zòro firaràzana,* where any religious act connected with the former idolatry was done, and near which the *sampy* or household charm was generally kept in a basket suspended to the wall. In this corner is the fixed bedstead, which is often raised up some height above the ground and reached by a notched post serving as a ladder, and generally screened round with mats or coarse cloth.   West of this, close to the north roof-post, is the place of honour, *avàra-pàtana*, "north of the hearth," where guests are invited to sit down, a clean mat being spread as a seat, just as a chair is handed in European houses.   The accompanying diagram will show at a glance the arrangement of an ordinary house in Imérina.   There is little furniture in a native house: a few rolls of mats, half-a-dozen spoons in a long basket fixed to the wall, some round baskets, and perhaps a box containing làmbas for Sundays and extra occasions; a few common dishes of native pottery, and perhaps two or three of European make; a horn or a tin *zìnga*, for drinking water, very likely a spear or two,—these, with the rice mortar and pounder and winnower already mentioned, and the implements for weaving and spinning,

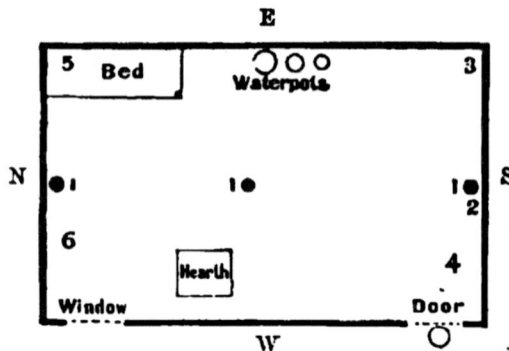

Diagram of Hova House.

111 Roof Posts.	4 "Place of Pounding Rice."
2 "Place of Tying the Calf."	5 Sacred Corner.
3 Fowls' Corner.	6 Place of Honour for Guests.

constitute about the whole household goods in the dwellings of the poorer classes.   The smooth earthen floor is covered with coarse mats, and sometimes the walls are also lined with finer mats; in the roof an attic is often formed for a part or the whole length of the house, and is reached by a rude ladder.   This upper chamber is frequently covered over with a layer of earth and used as a cooking-place, with much advantage to the cleanliness of the lower part of the house, which is thus kept free from smoke and dirt.

This arrangement of house is much varied among the other tribes.   These latter do not need to keep to the north and south direction, although the Hovas retain it in most

parts of Madagascar to which they remove on military service
or for other reasons; and while in a Hova village the houses
are generally built in rows, all looking one way, among the
Tanàla, Bétsimisàraka, and other tribes the houses are arranged
on all four sides of a square, with the doors on two or three
sides, and often no windows. The houses in the warmer
portion of the country usually have the floors raised some
little height above the ground, the flooring being made of the
bark of the Traveller's tree spread out flat. The walls are of
a slight framework, filled in with the mid-rib or stalks of the
leaves of the same tree, and the roof is thatched with the
leaves themselves. The door on each side of the house is of
the same material, and a short pole being slung from the low
eaves the rude door is slid backward and forward, thus, by
this primitive contrivance, dispensing with any joinery or
iron work.

The majority of the houses in the Bétsiléo province are
much smaller than those of the Hovas; in a village where the
writer once stayed the largest house was considerably less
than his tent (eleven feet square), the majority being much
smaller than this, and so low that one cannot well stand upright close to the side walls, which are sometimes only about
three feet high. The houses have two openings, one of which
is called a door and the other a window, but as they are
both a considerable height above the ground a stranger would
call them both windows, and say they had no door at all.
In the above-mentioned house the threshold was nearly three
feet from the ground, and as the opening was only about two
and a half feet square it required considerable agility to enter
the building, and rendered dignity out of the question. The
window is a very small hole about eighteen inches square at
the north end of the house, nearer the east than the west.
"Exactly in front of the door is the cooking-place, behind
which is the stand, often richly carved, for the large water-
pitchers in the south-east corner. Over the fire-place is the
invariable frame for drying the rice and wood for fuel, over
which again are the joists supporting the plaited bamboo
flooring of the store-room and sometimes sleeping-room. The
bedstead, at times quite an elaborate affair, is between the

doorway and the north-west corner.   The bedstead is generally
made of wood reaching from the ceiling to the floor, and
panelled all round, except a small opening, very like the door
of the house, through which the occupant creeps when he
enters or rises.   They are doubtless very warm and—lively.
Suspended from the centre of the ceiling is a round piece of
board, with a hook or hooks hanging down below, to which
articles likely to be devoured by the rats are hung, whilst
other articles are put into baskets and ranged on a shelf
which runs the whole length of the north and east sides of
the house, a foot from the ceiling.   When it is remembered
that all these things are packed into a space of nine or ten
feet by seven or eight feet, one may well wonder how in
such a house from six to a dozen people can find room to eat
and sleep, yet it is managed somehow." *

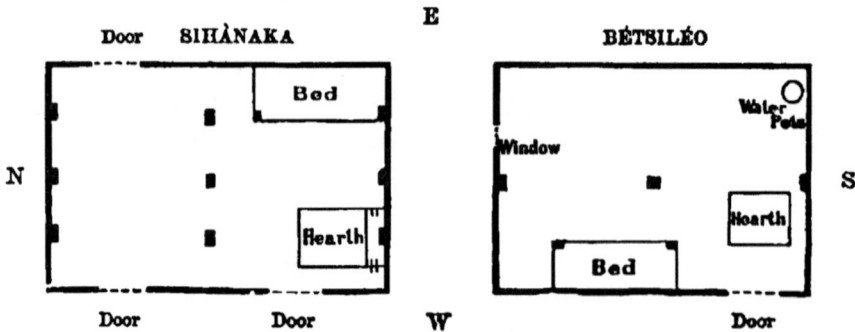

The Sihànaka houses, like those on the east coast, have
not one post only at each end of the house to support the
ridge, but three, with a sort of cross piece covering them.
And instead of one door and window on the west side, the
Sihànaka make two doors, these with high thresholds, dividing it into three equal parts, and a low door on the eastern
side, just where the fixed bedstead is placed in Imérina.   The
bedstead is at the south-east instead of the north-east corner
and the hearth at the south-west corner instead of towards
the north, as in the Hova houses.

Among the people of the southern-central provinces, the
Bàra, and those adjoining them to the west, Mr. Richardson
says that the houses are built with doors always facing the west,

* "The Bétsiléo: Country and People;" by G. A. Shaw, *Antananarivo
Annual*, No. iii. p. 83.

and four-square. "There is no dressed wood used in building, the various parts are tied by bark or held together by wooden pegs; there are no iron nails used. The corners are made of round poles, as are also the ridge and gable posts. The size of the houses varies, from the smallest scarcely five feet square, to sixteen or eighteen in the case of the kings. The height of the walls is never as much as six feet, and sometimes less than three. The walls and gables are made of bamboo, or the stalks of a long grass called *véro*. These are held together by cross pieces of the same material. In houses of the better kind there is an outer and inner wall, and long grass is fixed between the two. The inside is plastered with cow-dung, is open to the roof, and roofed with very long grass. The bed of the Bàra is always on the west side, with the head to the doorway; the Tanòsy bed is generally in the same position, while that of the Màhafàly is against the south wall. Among the Bàra there is no special place for the hearth. A shelf of bamboo is fixed against the south wall; and on the walls and suspended from the ridge pole are pegs for hanging powder-flasks, belts, charms, &c. The following simple diagram will show at a glance the style and differences of the houses in the three tribes."

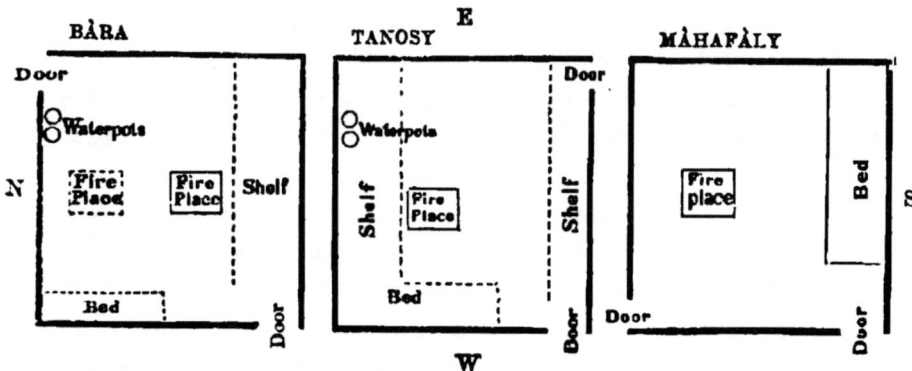

"The beds are sometimes raised a foot or more; they are constructed of round poles, and are sometimes surrounded by a mat like curtains, a rush mat being the only mattress. The north door can never be used by the Bàra while the father and mother of the couple who inhabit the house are living

A king may also have another door on the west side at the north corner. The doorways mostly reach the ground in the worst kind of houses, but are about a foot or more from the ground in the better kind. They are very small and narrow : my tin boxes are fourteen inches wide, but it was only on one or two occasions that we could get them into the houses without turning them on the side, the depth of the boxes being ten inches." *

A native account, written by a Hova officer, gives much the same information as to these Bàra houses in a somewhat different part of the country they inhabit; for he says their houses are about nine feet long, and only about six wide, and the height only just so that a person can stand in them : and the doors are so narrow that one is obliged to wriggle in sideways, as well as to stoop. Not only so, but they make their cattle-folds adjoining the house, so that the dung spreads all over the house, and it becomes almost unbearable in-doors.

The Native House a Compass and Sundial.—Owing, probably, to the invariable north and south arrangement of Hova houses, it is common to use the points of the compass in speaking of the position of things in a dwelling, rather than to describe them as "left" or "right." Articles placed on the table or on a shelf would be defined by them according to their north and south, or east and west positions.

From the invariable position of Hova houses, and the usual absence of clocks and watches, there has arisen the habit of describing the different hours of the day by the parts of the house where the rays of the sun touch on his course from east to west. Thus, about nine o'clock in the forenoon is *mitatào hàratra*, "to come (that is, the sun) above the purlin" (of the roof). Noon is *mitatao vovònana*, "to come above the ridge," *i.e.*, when the sun is vertical, just as at nine o'clock it is at an angle of forty-five degrees or about square with the slope of the roof. Then at about one o'clock is *mitsìdik'àndro*, "the peeping in of the day," *i.e.*, when the sun begins to shine in a little at the open door as he commences to decline from the zenith. Towards two o'clock is called

* *Lights and Shadows; or, Chequered Experiences among some of the Heathen Tribes of Madagascar*, pp. iv. v. Appendix i.

ampitotòam-bàry, i.e., " at the place of pounding rice," when the rays reach farther into the building, and touch the part where the rice-mortar usually stands. Three o'clock is *ampàmatòra-jànak'òmby,* " at the place of fastening the calf," *i.e.,* when the rays reach the middle post, where the animal is tied up at night; while at about half-past four o'clock is called *tàfapàka,* " touched," when the sun's rays reach the east wall of the house. So that the arrangement of their houses furnishes them with a tolerably correct method of ascertaining the time in the after part of each day.

Malagasy Towns and Villages.—Perhaps the reader may be inclined to ask what kind of place a Malagasy town or village is.

The old towns of Imérina are often picturesquely situated on the summits of hills; around them are lines of deep fosses, often three or four deep, one after the other, and crossed over by a narrow causeway. Within the innermost of these trenches, which are sometimes thirty feet deep, and perhaps twenty wide, an earthen rampart is often formed of the material dug out of the fosse, and this is pierced by a rude stone gateway, inside which there is a great flat circular stone, which runs in a groove, and used to be drawn across the opening in time of war. These deep fosses are not filled with water, but they often form the orchard of the inhabitants, being thickly planted with banana, peach, and mango trees, as well as the *horìrika,* an edible arum, and other vegetables; for their depth gives a certain amount of moisture. Some of these great trenches look almost like a railway cutting, and must have cost immense labour to the early inhabitants in the old time when almost every considerable village was the head of a petty state or independent kingdom. The fosses round the old deserted towns are fine places for collecting ferns and other plants.

All round the summit of the old towns are a number of *avìàvy,* a tree much resembling an English elm. The highest part of the town is generally occupied by the *làpa* or chief's dwelling-house, a lofty timber building, often with its ridge and long gable horns rising sixty feet above the ground. This, with its smaller houses around it, is usually enclosed within a strong rough wooden palisading, forming a square or *ròva*. In one part of this is generally seen the great square tomb of the chief's family, a stone structure in two or three stages, diminishing as they ascend; and if he is an Andrian or noble, it has a small timber house surmounting the stonework. In this courtyard there often grows an immense *amòntana* tree, rising high over the *àviàvy* trees, and forming a great dome of foliage, ever green, and with large glossy leaves.

The rest of the houses are scattered in rows over the space within the fosse; the sanitary arrangements are of the most primitive kind, so that the sights and scents are often the reverse of pleasant. At frequent intervals between the houses, and closely adjoining them, are the *fàhitra*, a kind of shallow square pit, and here the oxen are kept to be fattened for the New Year's festival. And here, being fed regularly with succulent green food, roots, and sugar-cane, they grow to an enormous size, so as to be hardly able to waddle up out of their den. In some of the old towns, a shallow space of ground of considerable extent and surrounded with raised banks is seen, in which, until recently, bull-fights took place. This used to be a favourite amusement with the Malagasy, but it has now happily fallen into disuse. The language contains a considerable number of words for various charms, which were supposed to act so as to disable an opponent or to strengthen a favourite animal, and so formed part of the "turf" vocabulary of former times. Frequently in one part of the little town there is a cattle-fold, where a huge layer of powdered cow-dung makes a deep slough of mud in wet weather, and supplies material for clouds of penetrating dust in the dry season.

But since there has been one settled Government in the central province throughout the present century, the great majority of the villages of Imérina are now built on the level ground, and are, consequently, far less picturesque than the old towns on the hills. Many of these, especially in Imàmo and Vònizòngo, are distinguished by two or three fine *amòntana* trees. To the north of Imérina, among the tribe called Sihànaka, the villages have no fosses, but are surrounded by a dense thicket of prickly-pear, which makes an impervious barrier to an enemy. The roads leading to the gateways are narrow and winding; and the gate consists of a number of round poles hung from a cross-bar at the top, each of which must be lifted up before one can pass through. In many cases the gateway has a low wall built round it inside, so that it seems made rather to deny entrance than to facilitate it, for a visitor has to climb over it in a most awkward and undignified fashion. And on the borders of the uninhabited land, where marauding parties of Sàkalàva frequently appear, the gateway is often a long low tunnel, in some cases fitted with three pairs of strong wooden gates, which are carefully barred at night.

In the Bétsiléo province the old towns are built on yet loftier and more inaccessible hills than even in Imérina; but the plains are often dotted over with numbers of detached homesteads or *vàlas*, each enclosed in a green ring-fence of a species of thorny mimosa, which is as effectual a barrier as the prickly-pear itself.

The Bàra towns are described by Mr. Richardson as "arranged more for the convenience of the cattle than for the comfort of the people." Like the Sihànaka villages, they have defences of prickly-pear, with similar gateways of poles hung from a cross-piece. Among all the tribes of the eastern and southern portions of Madagascar the number of houses in a village looks much larger than it really is, from the fact that about a third of what appear to be dwellings are rice stores, *tràno àmbo* or "elevated houses." These are neatly made little houses, but raised up five or six feet from the ground by four stout posts. Just under the flooring a sort of collar, a foot to eighteen inches in diameter, is fitted to each post, these are saucer-shaped, with the concave side downward, and cut quite smooth, so that an adventurous rat or mouse, wishing to feast on the rice deposited in the little room above, finds it an insurmountable obstacle to ascending higher than the top of the post. These rice-houses are also used for storing clothes and other valuables.

Fire by Friction.—Like every semi-civilised people (and, indeed, like almost every barbarous people as well), the

Malagasy are skilful in producing fire by friction. Choosing
two pieces of a particular kind of wood, they cut one to the
shape of a round stick with a pointed end; the other is a
flatter piece in which a slight hollow or groove is cut. Taking hold of the pointed stick, the operator twirls it rapidly
round first one way and then another, until the friction produces smoke and then fire, which is communicated to a little
tinder placed close to the point. Gently blowing upon the
spark which is produced, the tinder bursts into flame, the
whole operation only occupying a few minutes. There are
special words for this mode of obtaining fire: *mamósitra*,
which is also used for the boring of a hole by an insect to
deposit its eggs; and *miràingy*, the piece of wood being called
raingy.

Pottery, and Substitutes for it.—Mention has been made
of the earthen water-pots which stand in Hova houses. The
largest of these, the *sìni-bé*, or "big water-pot," is about two
feet in diameter, and globular in shape, and is the store-pro-
vision of water for daily use; the smaller kind, used for
bringing water from the springs, are less than half these
dimensions, and are carried on the head. These jars are
made of a blue clay, but are not very well burnt or durable,
for the Malagasy are not quite so skilful in pottery as in
some other handicrafts; although there are some dishes and
water-bottles made of a bright-red clay, which resemble
Samian ware in colour, and appear to be of excellent material.
Flattish clay vessels are made for cooking rice, and are fitted
with a cover; and the plates for eating rice have usually a
foot or stem to raise them a few inches above the ground.
A special kind of vessel made for cooking the beef at the
New Year's festival is rather elegant in shape, much like
some of the Anglo-Saxon pottery now and then found in our
own country.

All through the warmer parts of Madagascar, the leaves of
various trees form the usual plates and dishes of the people;
and among the Hovas the fresh green leaves of the banana
are largely used as plates for rice. The leaves of the
Traveller's tree serve the same purpose on the coast, but
especially the thick tough leaves of the pandanus; these can

easily be folded into a hollow form so that they will hold gravy or other liquid. For spoons they use a piece of leaf from the Traveller's tree or banana, doubled up so as to easily convey food to the mouth. This kind of spoon is also made for eating rice at the palace at the New Year's feast, it being dexterously tied up with a fine tendril. In other parts of the country small squares of mat are used instead of dishes, the edges being turned up so as to retain rice or other food.

Kissing or Nose-rubbing.—The Malagasy are, as a rule (like the Malayo-Polynesian peoples generally), very undemonstrative in matters of affection, and even if they feel deeply do not often show it by any outward sign. Kissing, in the Western and Oriental sense, is almost unknown, at least up to a comparatively recent period. It is, as the nearest word for it seems to imply, a pressing or rubbing of noses, *mandraka,* from the root *orana,* of nose (the *ka* and *na* being frequently interchanged). This in a colder country would be a decidedly unpleasant habit, nor, as it is, is it specially agreeable to have a nose pressed upon one's hand. The people are, however, beginning to understand our kiss with the lips, and often kiss our hands, although the kiss given and taken on the lips is hardly ever seen between natives, old or young. They have learnt the shaking of hands from Europeans, and it is often a rather trying ordeal to go through with a large congregation, especially on a hot day, and as many of the hands which are pressed upon one have not touched soap and water for a long time. The old and now obsolete custom of kissing or licking the foot of a superior has been mentioned in connection with Malagasy words (see p. 156).

Tattooing and other Adornment.—One of the most striking customs of the Polynesian Islanders, that of tattooing, is never seen amongst the Hovas. But there are traces of it among the Bétsiléo people, and probably among some of the other southern tribes as well. It is chiefly seen among the women, who frequently have a kind of collar tattooed upon their necks and breast. At a little distance this appears like an elaborate lace pattern or vandyking, and when looked at more closely, it is seen to include some of the same ornamental patterns as are used upon the memorial stones and richly-carved wooden

o

posts which are erected near tombs in many parts of the Bétsiléo province. Neither the face nor other parts of the body seem to be adorned in this fashion, but only the neck and upper part of the chest, the lines appearing as a dark indigo blue on the olive or brown skin.

It is also the custom in some other tribes to make marks, which are intended to be ornamental, by slight incisions in the skin; while another kind of adornment (?), called *tòmbok' àfo*, consists of scars burnt in the skin,—so much pain will people suffer for fashion's sake. The Hova women are also accustomed to put a plaster of white paste on the lips and face, which when removed is supposed to enhance their charms by making them fairer; and a spot of dark colour is often put on the cheeks with the same intention, much, indeed, as did the beauties of a hundred and fifty years ago in our own country, the contrast of the round black patch with the skin heightening the effect of their fair complexions. The Hova girls are also fond of staining their finger nails with the petals of red flowers, a practice quite the reverse of pleasing to our European tastes. The young men frequently allow the nail of their little fingers to grow to a great length, an inch or an inch and a half, keeping it from breaking by a frequent use of oil. The teeth are kept white, not only by the sensible practice of rinsing the mouth with water immediately after a meal, but also by the application of a black coating called *laingo*, which after peeling off leaves them of a beautiful whiteness. Among the Tanàla or forest tribes the people use this black substance as an adornment, which gives them an unpleasant appearance as they open their mouths; all the teeth, however, are not thus disfigured, but chiefly those at the back, leaving the front ones white, while in some cases the lower teeth are alternately black and white.

Modes of Dressing the Hair.—A few words may be said about the various ways of dressing the hair among the different Malagasy tribes.

This is a very important operation among the people, although it is not a business which they perform every day. Before the time of the first Radàma the Hovas, both male and female, all wore their hair long, either hanging in a great

number of little platted tails, or with these plaits folded up
and formed into a series of little knots, and symmetrically
arranged round the head. But as soon as Radàma had adopted
the military tactics of the English he had his hair cut short,
and ordered that all his officers and soldiers should adopt the
same fashion. This command produced quite a disturbance
among the women of the capital, who assembled in great
numbers to protest against the King's orders. But after being
surrounded with troops the leaders were cruelly speared, and
with hardly less cruelty the rest were kept three days without food or shelter, to teach them not to meddle with political
matters. From that time until the present the short hair,
with a slight tuft or topknot over the forehead, has been the
mark of the military class, while the *bòrizàno* or civilians
have their hair platted and arranged as already described, just,
in fact, as the Hova women have. But the law is continually
allowed to fall into disuse, and the men generally like to keep
their hair short, and wear the broad-brimmed straw hat which
is used by the military.

The Hova women have long and straight glossy black hair,
but there are a number of people who have stronger and
crisper curling hair, which is called *ngita*. No one dresses
her own hair; this is always done by another, and the
mistresses will often do this service for their slaves. It is
generally a matter of two or three hours' work, the operator
having a couple of vessels at her side, one filled with water
and the other with melted fat or suet. Holding a small
bodkin-like instrument of bone in one hand, and a kind of
brush made of strong grass stalks in the other, the hair is
symmetrically arranged on each side in from twenty to thirty
braids, there being always one on the crown of the head.
This is extremely neat in appearance, although a little stiff
and formal. When mourning or at a funeral, the hair is
always unbraided and allowed to fall dishevelled over the
shoulders. At the death of a sovereign the whole population,
male and female, are obliged to shave the head and keep it
shaved during a certain period, often extending over several
months.

Young children have their hair cut very short, it being

left in a series of rings all round the head; and the day when
a child's hair is first cut is made quite a festive occasion for
the friends and relations, who are invited to eat rice, and who
offer congratulations and wishes for the child's long life.

Among the Sihànaka and Sakalàva the hair is platted in
numerous little tails hanging all round the head; while the
Bétsimisàraka and other east-coast tribes have it generally
arranged in five large knots, one on the crown of the head,
and the others in front and at the back on either side. Some
of the south-eastern people have a rather elegant style of
coiffure. It is done thus: the hair is platted in very fine
braids, and then twisted into thin flat circular coils of from
two to two and a half inches in diameter; these are symmetrically arranged, in two rows, one overlapping the other,
the upper one completely encircling the head from the forehead to the back of the neck, and the other ending below the
ears. The whole has a very becoming effect, quite a "dressy"
look in fact, and certainly much more pleasing in its general
appearance than the *chignon* and some styles adopted in
Europe. At no great distance from these people is another
tribe, many of whose women have their hair arranged in two
rows of little balls. Behind the head they carry fastened
into the hair a piece of hollow wood ornamented with brass-
headed nails, and in this they keep needles and other small
property.

The Bàra people have a still more curious style of hair-
dressing than those already mentioned. Mr. G. A. Shaw
thus describes it: "Once a month, and in some cases once in
six weeks, the hair is washed, and then rolled up into a great
number of knots, varying in size from that of a marble to
that of an orange, and always round. After being carefully
rolled up and tied or sewn, as the case may be (for these
people, like their more civilised sisters, are given to making up Nature's deficiencies with hair from other sources),
it is then thickly coated with bees-wax melted into fat, so
that when cold each knob is firmly cemented to those adjacent
to it, and all appearance of hair is gone. When freshly done
it looks like lumps of grey clay stuck on their heads, each of
which when struck gives back a sound like striking a piece of

hard wood. It is a marvel how, having no pillows, they can sleep. I asked one woman how she could do so, and she assured me that without the lumps they cannot sleep well, and that it is comfortable to feel the hard lumps under the head when lying down." * Mr. Richardson gives much the same description, with this in addition: "Her hair (that of a Bàra belle) is done up into knobs as in the case of the men, but the chignon (a large lump at the top) is bedecked with beads and representations in brass of oxen, which are inserted by a long pin; and in addition there is another large knob exactly over the centre of the forehead, round which are fixed three armlet rings, and to the top and sides from four to twenty brass-headed nails, and a few silver and long coral beads are inserted. The two knobs of hair on each side of this 'top-knot' are also decorated with brass nails."

Clothing.—Among the Bétsiléo, Tanàla, and the tribes of the south-east coast, large use is made of mats for clothing. These are of grass, *zozòro* or papyrus peel, and *hàzondràno*, a tough kind of rush. These mats are sewn into a kind of sack, which is kept in its place by a girdle of coarse cloth made from the bark of trees. This use of bark for cloth is, doubtless, one of the many proofs of the connection between the Malagasy and the Polynesian peoples. All these latter, it is well known, are most skilful in the manufacture of beautiful and delicate materials from the bark of the hibiscus and other species of trees. The bark cloth of the Malagasy tribes is not, however, to be compared with these Polynesian fabrics; it is rough and brown in colour, and coarse and fibrous in texture, bearing the marks of the grooved mallet heads with which it is beaten out, and has little strength except in the direction of the fibres. Some of the pieces I obtained must have been taken from trees of considerable size, while one specimen had been stripped off the trunk without cutting it lengthways, so that it formed a long bag.

It may be here remarked, also, that the absence of any employment of *skins* for clothing by the Malagasy may be considered as a pretty conclusive proof (amongst many

* *Antanànarivo Annual,* No. ii. p. 106.

others), that the peoples of Madagascar have never had much connection with the African races. These latter, as is well known, make large use of the skins of a great number of the animals, both wild and domesticated, found in Africa, under the name of *karosses;* while the Malagasy, as far as is known, never make the least use of such material, except that very occasionally a cap made of the round hump of the cattle may be seen. It is quite true that wild animals are much fewer in Madagascar than in Africa; but, on the other hand, the herds of fine cattle are numerous, and sheep are also plentiful, but their skins are never used as articles of dress.

This is the more remarkable, inasmuch as during two or three months in the year there is a decided need for warm clothing in the cool highlands of the interior provinces of Imérina and Bétsiléo; and it has often occurred to me, as I have seen the people shivering in the chilly morning air of the winter months, with nothing on but a thin cotton or hemp làmba, that in this unaltering conservative habit of dress there is certain evidence that the Hovas and other inland tribes were originally inhabitants of a warmer region where thick clothing was never needed. For centuries they have been living in the cool elevated plateaux of the interior, from 3000 to 5000 feet above the sea, where warm clothing is a necessity to Europeans in the cold season, and yet, with the unchanging habits of a semi-barbarous people, they go on without any change from the light covering that was sufficient for their ancestors when they dwelt in the warm maritime plains, or, previously to that, in the sunny isles of a tropical ocean. Thousands of animals are killed every year whose skins in Africa would be all used as cloaks and coverings, and yet it seems never to have occurred to the Malagasy to employ them for such a purpose. Of course the above remarks as to the non-use of thick clothing apply chiefly to the mass of the poorer people; the upper and wealthier classes see the advantage as well as the comfort of warm dress in the winter months, and even the poor are beginning to use flannel and other thicker fabrics for themselves and for their children. A large amount of infant mortality has, doubtless, resulted from the way in which young children are usually exposed to the cold with little or no clothing.

While speaking of native dress, two or three particulars may be here noted as to the clothing of the forest tribes and those on the south-east coast. The former, both men and women, wear but little clothing above the hips, but the women of the upper classes, at least, are rather highly ornamented on their heads, necks, and arms. A fillet of small white beads, an inch or so wide, is fastened round the head, and secured by a circular plate of tin on the forehead. From their neck hangs several necklaces of long oval white beads and smaller red ones. On the wrist are silver rings, and a broad bracelet of small black, white, and red beads; and on every finger and thumb are rings of brass wire. The poorer women wear hardly anything but a mat sewn together at the ends so as to form a sack, which is fastened by a cord round the waist. Those who are nursing children have also a small figured mat about eighteen inches square on their backs, and suspended by a cord from the neck; this is called *lòndo*, and is used to protect the child from the sun or rain, as it lies in a fold of the mat above the girdle. In the valley of the Màtitànana, we noticed a comely girl who was so highly ornamented as to be conspicuous among her companions even at some distance. Round her head she had the fillet of white beads, and from it depended a row of small beads like drops. On each side of her temples hung a long ornament of hair and beads reaching below her chin; several beads hung from her ears, and a number of white and oblong beads were worked into her hair at the back. Round her neck she had no less than six strings of large beads, and another passing over one shoulder and under the arm. On each wrist were three or four silver rings, while on every finger and thumb were several coils of brass wire. Her clothing was a piece of bark cloth fastened above the hips, over an apron of mat; and on one toe was a brass ring. Thus she was got up " from top to toe," and made a most striking appearance.

Weapons.—The ancient weapons of the Malagasy were the spear and shield, and these are still the chief means of attack and defence with many of the tribes of the eastern and southern provinces. (See chapter on "New Light on Old Texts.") The use of the bow and arrow is not nearly so common in Madagascar as in many semi-civilised countries, the introduction of fire-arms among the Hova and Sàkalàva having probably rendered the earlier weapons almost useless. But there are words for them in the Hova dialect, *tsipìka* and *zàna-tsipìka* (" bow," and " child of the bow "), showing that the things were once used, and they are still found in use among some of the northern tribes. In some parts of the island, the boys use a long hollow bamboo as a blowgun. These are fitted with a light arrow, and are used for killing birds and small animals, much in the same way as it is employed by the Indian tribes of the Orinoco.

As far as our present information goes, there seems no trace of a stone or flint age in Madagascar, nor have any of the primitive weapons made of such materials yet been discovered. But tradition speaks of a time when the Vazìmba, the aboriginal inhabitants of Imérina, had no iron weapons, but made spear-heads of hardened and burnt clay, in shafts of bamboo. But a Hova chief named Andriamanélo, having made spears of iron, overcame the Vazìmba with these superior weapons. These latter then said, "Come, let us flee, for Andriamanélo makes 'flying iron.'" Iron has doubtless been worked from a very remote period, for it is found in great abundance and purity in Madagascar; and it is affirmed that the progress of the Hovas from the coast to the interior may be traced by the remains of the smelting-furnaces they constructed at different stages of their route. Iron is smelted by means of a bellows, consisting of two cylinders formed from the hollowed-out trunks of trees and fitted with pistons of cloth or feathers, similar to those used by the Malayan peoples. Old men say that in ancient times the strong tough fibre of the *anìvona* palm was also used for spears, and this would doubtless make a rather formidable weapon. The sling is used in some parts of Madagascar, and boys are skilful in its use.

CHAPTER XI.

CURIOUS AND NOTEWORTHY CUSTOMS AMONG THE MALAGASY TRIBES—(*concluded*).

CIRCUMCISION OBSERVANCES—BROTHERHOOD BY BLOOD COVENANT—ROYAL ANCESTOR-WORSHIP AMONG THE SÀKALÀVA—TOMBS AND FUNERAL RITES.

Circumcision Observances.—The reader of the Hebrew Scriptures would suppose that any notice of circumcision in Madagascar should be considered in connection with the religious observances of the Malagasy, since it holds such a prominent place in the Jewish religion, and among Mohammedan peoples. But among the Malagasy tribes it appears to have little, if any, religious significance, and to be regarded rather as an initiation into the community, since no one who has not undergone the ceremony can be a soldier, or be considered as properly qualified for Government service. The children who undergo the ceremony are said to be made "men," to be "consecrated" or established. Circumcision appears to prevail throughout all the various tribes inhabiting the island, and in their main features the observances connected with it are much the same, although there are curious varieties of custom on some particular points.

Among the Hovas, it was a time of the greatest festivity, exceeding that of any other time, but also of shameless licentiousness. It is not observed when every male child reaches a certain age, as amongst the Jews and other Semitic peoples, but every few years, at a time appointed by the sovereign for the ceremony to be observed by the people generally, who have children still to receive the rite.

The ceremonies last over several days, and in the case of children of the royal family are somewhat fuller than when the people observe the "custom of their ancestors," as it is especially termed.

After proclamation has been made for a great *kabàry* or assembly of the nation to meet, they are ordered to repair and clear the roads for the sovereign to visit six of the ancient towns in the central province, and are admonished to "kill the rats," *i.e.*, to put all sorcerers to death. After this has been done, notice is given of the day for the ceremonies to commence, and the first of these is the dressing or "parting the hair" in a special way. This is for the fathers and mothers of the children to be circumcised, the sovereign being attended to while seated on a sacred stone in the centre of the capital city. It is worthy of notice here that this and many other of the ceremonies at this time, are performed by the *vélondrày aman-drény*, that is, by people whose father and mother are still living; persons from Alasòra, the town from which the reigning family originally came, a place about five miles south-east of the capital, performing the ceremonies for the sovereign. A cow of a red and white colour is sacrificed, with prayers and supplications for blessings on the children, that they may overcome their enemies, and have long life. Oxen are then killed, with dancing and rejoicing, and firing of cannon.

After this, preparations are made for fetching water, which is called at this time "sacred" or "consecrating water;" the fathers and mothers of the children meanwhile having their hair done in the fashion called *sàlotra*, a platting into numerous small plaits, lengthened with false hair, and each plait folded round a small piece of wood.

A dance called *sòratra* is then arranged, the people standing in lines, and the sovereign taking part. He then pulls down the southern wall of the house where the circumcision is to be performed, after which it is extended southward, and then handsomely lined and furnished. This, together with everything else done at this time, appears to have some symbolic meaning.

Then comes the ornamenting the gourds in which the sacred water is to be fetched. These gourds are those shaped like a bottle, and are bound round with three bands of certain kinds of grass and bark, and joined together like a net, and ornamented with pieces of silver. The gourd is then pierced three times with a spear. These things are taken charge of by the *vélondrày aman-drèny*, who also procure a number of other things required for the various ceremonies.

The day of fetching the sacred water is the most important day of all. The fetchers carry the gourds on their heads, and are accompanied by a number of men armed with shield and spear. They are received with shouts of " What water is this ? " To which they reply, " Sacred water, joyful water," and are saluted much in the same way as the sovereign is received. The water is then carried seven times round the house before being brought into it. The mothers of the children then plait small baskets of the *sandrìfy* leaves, one for each child, in which he is to hold the unripe bananas which are to be thrown away as a *fàditra* or piaculum.

When evening comes, the house is lighted up in a special way. The stem of a banana tree is fixed upright in the north-east (the sacred) corner of the house, to serve as a stand for a lamp. This is made in an earthen dish, with a number of minute arrangements, all fixed by custom, and of prescribed materials. Dancing and singing is kept up all night, and these festivities are continued for two or three days at the sovereign's pleasure ; during the day the dance called *sòratra* being performed, and cannon and muskets fired.

Another preliminary ceremony also takes place at night, this is the " measuring of the children." This is done with a fine bamboo called *vòlotàra ;* they are first measured from the ground to the loins, then up to the shoulders, and lastly, the whole height of the child. Then follows a formal blessing of the children, which is done as follows :—some of the sacred water is put in the shallow wooden dish used for winnowing rice, and with it honey, a large silver chain, and a reed called *fantàka* with the leaves still fresh. The children are sprinkled with the water, while a blessing is invoked as follows :—" The lad is not a child ! He is a man breasting the stream ; not caught in crossing, not taken in a net! The lad is a banana tree north of the town,* the leaves not broken, the young shoots untaken! The lad is not a child! He is a *soròhitra* (a bird) on a rock; thrown at, not hit; throwing, hitting (his enemy)! His cattle cover the plains! His money fills a large tomb!† His slaves crowd his country house!" with much besides of a like figurative character.

On the morning following the above-mentioned ceremonies (the morning of the day of the circumcision itself) water is again fetched, but this time it is termed "strong water." For each child a strong and powerful man is appointed, who fetches water in the same kind of gourd as the "sacred water;" and, as on the former occasion, is accompanied by others bearing shield and spear. Following these again are the fathers of the children, who take the baskets already platted by the mothers to fetch the unripe bananas which are to be a *fàditra*.

Having obtained the water, the bearers return at the top of their speed. Their attendants cry, "Children of the eagle," to which the water-carriers reply, "Lay their eggs on the rock." Upon arriving at the gate of the town, strange to say, they are assailed with stones by the people inside. Making their way through these opposing forces, they arrive at the *làpa* or chief house, where the children to be operated on are seated on a drum placed *north* of the hearth, and opposite the window. Just before the circumcision is effected the sovereign says to each child of his own family, "Be a man to overcome, my lad! May you obtain! Reach old age! Live long! Conquer the land, my lad! Be master of the kingdom!" As soon as the operation is over, the children are taken to be warmed and comforted at a rush fire made in the south corner of the house, after which they are taken home.

The children of the sovereign's relatives and of the people generally, are placed on a drum to the *south* of the hearth and opposite the door. They are also saluted with a benediction:

* That is, the leeside, sheltered from the prevailing south-east winds.
† The tombs are commonly used as repositories of money.

"Be a man to overcome! May you obtain! Be strong with the gun! Be strong with the spear! Reach old age!" &c.

After the children's wounds are healed, the sovereign visits the six ancient towns to give thanks at each of them; oxen being killed, and dancing and festivities kept up at each place.

It will be seen from these particulars that the ceremonies here described have reference chiefly to the children of the royal family. Those observed at the circumcision of children of the nobles and of the people generally are, however, very much the same as those for children of royal blood, and need not be further particularised. It will be remarked how very important the ceremony is considered, from the numerous and minute observances which have grown up around it in the course of the centuries during which it has been celebrated by the Malagasy.

A word or two may be added as to some particulars in which the practices of the other tribes in the island with regard to circumcision differ from those of the Hovas.

Among the southern Tanàla or forest people, if the child' of a reigning prince, or the child of his relations, should commit any impropriety during the ceremony, the child by that act loses caste; and it is henceforth no prince, but is called a "child of the knife" (*zának' àntsy*).

"In former times, on the circumcision of a young prince, the people had to be assembled, and a clever spearman was appointed to carry the child to the place of circumcision; and there was another spearman who hid himself somewhere about, and when the one carrying the child just emerged from the house, this one hurled a spear at him who was carrying the child. If he was struck and yet the child was unhurt, the child lost caste and was no longer a prince. If the man and the child were both struck, and both killed, nothing was thought further about it. Should both the man and the child escape unhurt, it was a proof that the child was a prince." "Just before the time of circumcision the mother of the child had to fast from several things. Should she be guilty of disregarding any of the tabooed things or acts, she made her child lose caste. The diviners (*òmbiàsy*) perform the operation and they use a curved knife; some wash the wound with milk." *

Mr. Richardson says that, among the Bàra people, "the diviner is consulted as to the fitting time for the ceremony. He comes with his knife; a good bullock is selected, killed, and divided with a spear into two equal parts, from the tip of the nose to the tail. The spear is then thrown over the ridge of the house, and the diviner runs after it; the half of the bullock and the spear become his." Two or three other curious particulars are given in the footnote. †

Among the Sàkalàva generally, according to M. Grandidier,‡ the circumcision itself is performed without any public rejoicings, on account of the risk attending the operation, for not unfrequently the child does not survive it. After a favourable result, a thanksgiving feast called *savatsé* is celebrated. At this time (and at this only) a *bull*, and not an ox, is sacrificed, the child being placed upon the animal during the invocation. Among some western tribes the operators are women.

It may be here remarked that, since the adoption of Christianity by the people of the central provinces of Madagascar, there has been no general observance of the ceremony in the fashion of former times. The rite has been administered in a very quiet and unostentatious fashion, so that for several years past no European has seen the numerous minute observances already detailed as preceding the circumcision in heathen times. It has been felt that so much of evil was mixed up with the ceremonies that they are being allowed to fall into disuse, as inconsistent with the profession of Christianity now made by the Hovas and neighbouring peoples. Among the heathen tribes there has, probably, been little alteration in the ancient customs.

---

* *Antanànarìvo Annual*, No. ii. p. 93.

† Apud Hovas præputium infantis in folio bananæ involutum vitulis datur; apud incolas quosdam oræ occidentalis in haustu alcoholico infant bibendum datur. Apud gentem Bàra pater præputium in flumen vicinum projicit; apud gentes Sàkalàva pars præcisa ex tormento [gun] vel cuspidi hastæ affixa emittitur super tectum patris. Si hasta rectà in terram cadit, indicio est, ut illis videtur, puerum animosum futurum esse.

‡ *Bull. de la Soc. de Géog.*, Avril 1872, p. 397.

Brotherhood by Blood Covenant.—Another peculiar custom of the Malagasy may be here noted, viz., the practice of making brotherhood by persons partaking of each other's blood. This is termed *fàto-drà, i.e.,* "bound by blood," and is found with certain variations in almost every tribe; and is intended to make those who enter into the covenant to become as brothers, devoted to each other's welfare, and ready to make any sacrifice for the other's benefit, since they thus become of one blood. The ceremony consists in taking a small portion of blood from the breast or side; this is mixed with other ingredients, stirred up with a spear-point, and then a small portion swallowed by each of the contracting parties. Imprecations are uttered against those who shall be guilty of violating the solemn engagement thus entered into. Now and then Europeans who are not over-scrupulous, and to whom it has been a matter of great importance to keep in good terms with some of the powerful chiefs, have consented to make this covenant. The French traveller, M. Grandidier, became a brother by blood with Zoména, a chief of the Tanòsy in the south-west of Madagascar, in order to gain his good-will and help in proceeding farther into the interior from the Onilàhy, or St. Augustine River. But in this case the blood was not taken from the contracting parties, but from an ox sacrificed for the purpose. He thus describes the ceremony, which he terms the *famakí.* The diviners having previously fixed upon a favourable day, at the appointed time the people assembled together on the east side of the King's house. "Zoména and I were seated together on a new mat. An ox was brought and thrown on the ground, where its four feet were tied together. A prince of the family of Zàfiraminìa cut the throat of the victim, reciting at the same time some prayers, and received the first blood drawn in a calabash filled with water. After adding a pinch of salt, a small quantity of soot, a leaden ball, 'une grosse manille d'or,' he placed it before us." [In some cases the blood is mingled with brine, pimento, pulverised flint, earth, and gunpowder, and rum instead of water.] " I took the ramrod of my gun, and Zoména seized his spear, and we then dipped the points into the consecrated liquid. The principal chief of the village, continuing to strike with a knife the weapons which we each held in the right hand, delivered a speech, in which, after having celebrated the praises of the high contracting parties, he enumerated the obligations which the covenant of blood imposed, and called down upon us the greatest misfortunes if we should ever perjure ourselves. My servant Cravate, while this was going on, did not cease to wet the point of the spear with the liquid. Then Zoména, filling a wooden vessel with the sacred beverage, put it to my mouth and made me drink the contents, then struck me on both shoulders, on the back and on the breast, with the empty vessel. I repeated the same ceremonies, and the *famake* was completed, we were brothers in blood. My new relatives addressed to me their congratulations, and a crowd of princes and princesses, some calling me their son, the others giving me the name of father or of brother, came to take my hand." *

Of this custom amongst the Bàra, Mr. Richardson says : "To friendships formed by two persons drinking a little blood taken from an incision in each other's bellies, they depend for success in plundering, gratifying their lustful desires, and as a protection from being plundered by others."

In the "Memoirs and Travels of Count de Benyowsky," a Polish noble who, in 1776, so gained the confidence of the people on the eastern coast as to be made by them their *Mpanjàkabé* or supreme king, there is an account (vol. ii. p. 267) of the oath which he took on receiving the allegiance of the chiefs and people, this oath being a kind of blood covenant. Oxen were killed by Benyowsky himself, one or more, according to their number, for every rank of the people, the chiefs taking a drop or two of the blood, and pronouncing an oath. And after this, to quote his own account: "I was again conducted to the circle of the *Ròhandrìans* [or principal chiefs], who made a second oath with me, which was performed in this manner: each person made an incision, with a razor, under the left breast, as I did likewise myself; and each mutually sucked the blood of the other, at the same time pronouncing the most horrible maledictions against whoever

* *Bull. de la Soc. de Géog.*, Fev. 1872, p 144.

should violate his oath, and benedictions in favour of those who should continue faithful to their engagement."

From a native account of the *fàto-drà* as observed among the Hovas, and contained in a small book edited by the Rev. W. E. Cousins, I translate the following:—"And these are the observances customary in the blood covenant: They procure seven roots of grass, and a grasshopper with its neck twisted, and dung from a calf whose mother is dead (or lost), and water from a spring drying up, an old bone, and a single gun, and these are placed in a rice winnower, together with a spear without a foot, and set in one side."

After an invocation to God and the four corners of the earth, and some supernatural being named Andriampàtitra, these are addressed as witnesses of the covenant about to be entered into by such-an-one and such-an-one, who, although not of the same parents, are united in friendship and affection by these things. An explanation is then given of each of the articles brought, as follows:—"The seven roots of grass are brought to show that if they do not observe [the covenant], the sevenfold death will overtake them. The grasshopper with twisted neck is brought also as a warning that, if the covenant is not observed, their necks will be twisted so they cannot see what is before them. The dung of the calf bereft of its mother is brought as a warning that, if they do not preserve this friendship, may they have no descendants, no posterity to inherit. The water from the drying-up spring is brought to warn them that, if they do not keep friendship, their lives will dry up in a similar way. The old bone is brought to show that, if they do not be friends, may their bones be scattered with none to bury them. The single gun is brought as a sign that if they do not be friendly then may they be killed by a gun in the war, while as to their corpses, devour them, O hawks and all birds, that they may not come to the home of their fathers; and the spear without its foot is brought to show that if they do not preserve this friendship and relationship, then may they be killed by this (spear) in the hand; and if they do not die by the hands of others, may they die by their own hand, whether going north or south, or east or west; therefore are ye invoked,

O four corners of the earth to observe this ; therefore observe,
O Andriampàtitra."

After some further maledictions and benedictions, the
wooden dish containing the above-mentioned things is over-
turned, and water is poured over the hands of the contracting
parties above the dish.

Royal Ancestor-worship among the Sàkalàva.—Closely connected with this subject are some customs of the Sàkalàva
which may be here mentioned. Among the southern division of this people, the corpse of a king is. wrapped in an
ox-hide and suspended in the deepest recesses of the neighbouring forests. After some months the chiefs meet together
and search for the remains, that is to say, one of the vertebræ
of the neck, a nail, and a lock of the hair. The remaining
portions are interred with much ceremony. They sometimes
offer human sacrifices on this occasion; the bodies of the
victims are placed under the royal bier, for a sovereign
cannot rest in the earth like his humbler subjects. They
enclose the relics in a crocodile's tooth, and then carry them
to the sacred house where the relics of former kings are preserved.

The possession of these relics constitutes the right to the
royal authority. A legitimate heir who should be dispossessed
of them would lose all authority over his people; and a
usurper, on the contrary, would ascend the throne without
opposition. (See Grandidier, in *Bull. de la Soc. de Géog.,* Avril
1872, p. 402.)

At Mojangà, a principal seaport on the north-west coast,
at the mouth of the Bay of Bémbatòka, is a sacred house
called *Zómba,* where the relics of the former kings of the
northern Sàkalàva are preserved with religious care. The
eastern part of the house is partitioned off from the rest, and
inside this portion are suspended four small boxes containing
the royal relics. These are a span in length and three inches
wide, and contain the hair and finger and toe-nails of the
deceased king. A cover or hat of gold is placed on one, the
other three having a similar cover of silver. Around them
are placed spears, knives, and hatchets.

On every Friday the Sàkalàva meet there to sing and pray

to the royal ancestors; and on a certain day every year, all the people assemble from the surrounding country. There is a general killing of oxen, which are hunted about before being slaughtered; after which they enter the house. But there are numerous tabooed things to be observed, since no one can enter who has any disease, or who wears blue serge, or trousers, or shoes. Slaves are not allowed to enter, as they would, in that case, become free people. The gates to the courtyard surrounding the house, on the east and west respectively, have each their proper use, only the nobles and the attendants using the eastern one, and the common people the western, for it is believed they would die if using the other. The ceremonies on the special day of worship consist of prayers, which are led by one who is a descendant of the ancient kings, and the burning of a fragrant gum, and the anointing of the relic boxes and other royal property with a honey-like juice and white earth. All this is followed by blowing of shells, beating of drums, dancing and singing, in which some work themselves into a frenzied state, during which they are believed to be inspired by the spirits of the departed kings, and their words are received as oracular utterances.

The Tombs and Burial Customs of the Hovas have been described in various books upon Madagascar, but it will be necessary to give a short account of them here, not only to give completeness to the subject, but also to show in what respect they agree with and differ from the usages of the other tribes, which are less known, and some of which are very curious and noteworthy.

It may be remarked, at the outset, that all the different peoples inhabiting the island expend a large amount of time and trouble and money upon their tombs and burial observances. This care arises in great part from their religious notions, for they believe that their departed friends become *divine*, in a certain sense, and are able to benefit their descendants. And so they offer prayers to them in connection with the Supreme Being, and at certain seasons anoint the headstones of their tombs with blood and fat as offerings to their spirits.

The Hovas.—The majority of the Hova tombs consist of

a small vault or chamber, sunk for about half its depth below
the surface of the ground, and forming a cube of from eight
to twelve feet. The four sides of this vault are made of rough
slabs of the hard blue basalt rock found so extensively all
over the certain portions of Madagascar. These slabs are not
hewn, but are detached from the surface of the rock by heat.
Small fires of cow-dung are kindled and kept burning for
several hours on the line along which it is wished to break off
the slab; then being suddenly withdrawn, the unequal con-
traction of the rock, and the employment of heavy crowbars,
causes immense slabs, from four or five to ten or twelve inches
thick, to be detached. These heavy pieces of rock are dragged,
by the simple force of numbers, from the place where they are
quarried to the spot where the tomb is to be constructed; the
owner getting the assistance of all his relatives and the people
of his tribe, as well as those of the village where he resides,
if he is a person of any consequence. No money payment
is made for such services, but quantities of food have to be
cooked and many bullocks killed during the many days it
takes (often at long intervals) to drag these massive stones
to their destination. And as everybody helps every one else,
a considerable portion of the time of the people is spent in
such services, it being one of the most frequent causes of in-
terruption to Bible-classes and other instruction. One of the
most common sights on the chief roads is to meet two or three
hundred men and women and slaves, all dragging by repeated
jerks at the rough ropes attached to the stone, which is fixed
to a rude sledge. One or two persons who act as fuglemen
stand upon the stone, and with violent gesticulation and
flourishing of a handkerchief, encourage the people to pull;
but as the roads are of the roughest kind, while the stones
have often to be taken across country, up and down hills, and
across rice-fields, &c., the progress made every day is often
only two or three hundred yards; so that a considerable time
elapses before the four side stones, the smaller ones for
shelves, and then the great *rangolàhy* or covering-stone over
the whole, are all brought to their destined position.

It will be seen, therefore, that building a tomb is a costly
and lengthy operation; but upon nothing is expense more

cheerfully lavished; for a Hova will frequently live in a house that has not cost ten dollars to erect, while he will freely spend a hundred or two upon his tomb. This he begins to make as he advances in life, and gets a family around him; and in the case of large and costly tombs several years often elapse before the whole is completed, at least as regards the external ornamental stonework.

In a few places in Imérina large numbers of ancient tombs may be seen in one spot, as at the northern and southern extremities of Antanànarìvo, where they line the sides of the road for a considerable distance. But in the case of well-to-do people, the family tomb is usually constructed in a spacious square enclosure near their ancestral village, or in the neighbourhood of their rice-fields and landed property. This is surrounded by a lofty wall of clay, while on three or four sides of the square are built rows of small houses, where the slaves and dependants live, the tomb being in the centre. But in some cases the tomb is in the courtyard of the house where the owner resides, while the royal tombs are all in the palace-yard, either at Antanànarìvo or Ambòhimànga, and so also are those of the chieftains of old times in the ancient towns throughout Imérina.

The stones being brought to the spot where the tomb is to be constructed a deep trench is cut, into which they are lowered, on edge, after being roughly trimmed to a tolerably regular shape. At the west side, where the entrance to the vault is always formed, a small low doorway is broken through the stone, and the earth in the centre is removed. Then shelves of the same hard blue rock are fixed round three sides of the chamber, and finally the great stone covering all is placed on the top. A superstructure of earth and stone is formed, generally in two, and often in three, steps or stages. In the ancient style of tombs the stones were merely fixed neatly in the earth, without mortar, and the top was often covered with lumps of white quartz. In the more costly modern tombs the exterior is formed with regular masonry, and massive cornices and mouldings at each stage; while in some few there is elaborate architectural enrichment in pilasters with carved capitals, copied from drawings of the classical styles, and occasionally having a sort of open square arcade surmounting the tomb. One of the most remarkable structures of this kind is the immense family tomb of the Prime Minister in the north-west suburbs of Antanànarìvo. This is a spacious vault with numerous chambers opening out from it, and about sixty feet square. It is surrounded by a massive verandah of stone columns and flat segmental arches, and a flight of steps leads up to the roof, about fourteen feet high. Upon this is an open arcade of columns and arches, and steps lead down to the interior, which is entered by a massive door of brass. The doors leading into the tombs are often of stone, the hinge being a tenon cut out of the stone and turning in hollows above and below. At two of the angles of this great tomb are elegant columnar structures carrying the lightning-conductors.

The dead are not enclosed in coffins in Imérina, but are tightly wrapped up in a number of dark-red silk *làmbas*. In some cases these are very numerous. Four or five years ago the senior officer of the native army, an aged general named Rainingòry, died; and as he was believed to be about 100 years old, the Queen gave orders that he should be wrapped in a hundred làmbas, of which number she herself sent about thirty. The corpse thus bandaged is laid upon one of the stone shelves in the vault. Funerals usually take place in Imérina on the day after decease, or at least upon the second day after, according to the time of death. The house where the corpse is laid is lined with the richest silk làmbas belonging to the family, or sometimes only with white calico, while the corpse is deposited in a small tent, either in the house or in the courtyard. When carried to the grave it is sometimes covered with a uniform coat and cocked-hat, if the deceased were an officer; and I have occasionally seen bonnets and other articles of female dress surmounting the bier of a Hova woman. The attendants carry small paper fans, of diamond shape, to keep away flies, and these are stuck into the ground at the head of the grave.

The tombs of the sovereign and of the highest ranks of Andrians have a small and neatly-finished wooden house erected on the top of the stone structure. This exactly resembles a dwelling-house, except that it has no window or hearth, from which fact it is called *tràno manàra,* "cold house," as well as *trano màsina,* "sacred house." In this house valuable property is often deposited, and when King Radàma I. was buried, and also the late Queen Rasohérina, an immense quantity of costly articles of dress and furniture and other valuables were placed in their tombs, as well as chests of money. Their coffins were made of plates of silver formed from dollars hammered out, while many thousands of dollars were also put into the coffin as a bed for the deceased sovereign. There is, to European ideas, a prodigal and painful waste of money. (For other curious facts connected with the subject of royalty, see the chapters on the Language, and "New Light on Old Texts.")

In former times it was usual to erect poles near the tombs in Imérina, and upon them to fix the skulls and horns of the bullocks killed at the funeral feasts ; but this custom is now falling into disuse, although still kept up by other tribes. In many places a massive upright slab of rough undressed basalt is erected as a memorial of distinguished personages.

The Bétsiléo.—The Bétsiléo people in the southern central district of Madagascar have some strongly-marked differences, both in their tombs and their funeral customs, from those of their neighbours in Imérina. One of the most prominent facts in connection with their burial memorials is the existence of a considerable amount of decorative carving in the curious and elaborate timber-posts erected over or near their graves, and also, to a less extent, in the massive stones set up as memorials in the same situations. On the road from Antanànarìvo to Fianàrantsòa, I was much interested when coming to an old town called Ikangàra to find a large collection of these burial memorials. They were well worth examination, as in a small space there were grouped together many different kinds of tombs and monuments, some forty or fifty in number, and of the following kinds :—

1. The largest tombs—there were two of them—were of small flat stones, built in a square of some twenty to twenty-five feet, and about five feet high. But around them was a railing of carved posts and rails, those at each corner with a

vase-shaped top; these were connected by a transverse rail, and this again was supported on each of the four sides by upright posts which finished under the rail. All the upright timbers were carved in patterns.

2. Another kind of tomb was formed by a square structure of flat stones, four or five feet high, and perhaps a dozen feet square; but on the west was a square enclosure of four carved posts with the vase-shaped heads, connected by lintels, and with an intermediate upright. This structure was about four feet square, by seven or eight feet high, and in the centre was a single carved post.

3. A third kind of monument was a massive block of granite, from eight to ten feet high, and from eighteen inches to two feet square, with carved posts at the four corners and touching them. On the top these were connected by carved cross pieces, and upon these the skulls of the bullocks killed at the funeral of the person commemorated were placed. Many of these horned skulls remained in their original positions.

4. Another kind of memorial was a massive square post of wood, about twenty feet high, and fifteen inches square, carved on all four sides from top to bottom. There were four or five of these immense posts here. In one case there was a pair of them, as if intended to form a kind of gateway.

5. Still another kind was an oblong block of dressed granite, with an iron hooping round the top, in which were fixed a dozen or more pairs of slender *iron* horns. There were two of this kind of monument at this place, and we afterwards saw others on the road.

6. Besides the foregoing there were numerous specimens of a smaller carved post with the vase-shaped head, and a small open staging near the top, on which were fixed upright sharp-pointed pieces of wood. These were for placing the ox-skulls upon.

Many of these memorials were sorely weathered and defaced, and others were falling, or had fallen, and were rotting away. But there was a great variety of carving, and the patterns almost endless, and many of them were well worth preserving and carefully copying.

On the road-side were a number of the more simple tombs, of a kind that seem peculiar to the Bétsiléo. They consist of a plain square, almost a cube, of thin undressed stones laid very evenly. Proceeding farther south we were struck by the number of tombs and carved monuments on the road-side all the way to Ambòhinamboàrina. The most common form was the plain square tomb just described, and the upright *vàtolàhy*, about two feet square, and from eight to ten feet high. While the *tsàngam-bàto* in Imérina are all of rough undressed slabs of blue rock, these in Bétsiléo are of fine-grained hard white granite, in massive blocks, and dressed to a beautifully smooth face. They are often in couples, and in one instance there were two stones, with an elaborately carved post between them. But the combinations of the different kinds of monument were very numerous; there was something new every few yards; and all over the plain, near every little cluster of houses, we could see these white memorial stones.

South of the Matsìatra river there were very few of the upright memorial stones, and none of the carved wood pillars. All the tombs, which were very numerous, were the plain cube of undressed flat stones, and I was surprised to find that the majority of them were hollow, many having trees, species of dracæna, mimosa, and others growing out of the circular opening in the centre, and overshadowing the whole tomb, a sight never seen in Imérina. From this it appeared that the chamber in which the corpses are deposited does not project at all above the ground, as it does in the Hova tombs; and I afterwards ascertained that this chamber is excavated at a considerable depth beneath the square pile of stones, which is therefore not a grave, but only marks the position of one far below the surface. I noticed also that there was in most cases a long low mound of earth, extending from one side of the tomb to a distance of from thirty or forty to eighty feet and upwards. This, it appears, marks the line of a long tunnelled passage gradually descending from the surface to the deeply-sunk burial chamber.

Mr. Richardson says about Bétsiléo tombs: "They are very

deep in the earth, some of them being as much as sixty feet deep, and are approached by a gradually-descending passage opening some forty or fifty feet distant from the tomb. The tombs of the rich are sometimes fifteen or sixteen feet square, and are quite on the surface of the ground; the four walls and roof are formed of five immense slabs, which are brought from great distances, and involve almost incredible labour. I measured one such stone, and found it to be 18 feet long, 10 feet wide, and nearly 3 feet thick in some parts." Mention is also made of a circular memorial stone, 12 feet in circumference, and nearly 20 feet high above the ground. This was said to have occupied four years in making and dragging to the place where it is erected. Mr. Richardson also describes other tombs as having "the skulls of all the oxen killed at the funeral regularly arranged on the cornice. I have seen one," he says, "now rapidly falling into decay, on which were no less than 500 such skulls. The most symmetrical that I ever saw was a new tomb, on which on the outer square were arranged 108 skulls of oxen in most regular order; every other skull being that of an ox whose horns had grown downwards. There were also two other squares of skulls arranged behind this one." *

In the same paper Mr. Richardson gives a detailed account of the strange ceremonies he once witnessed at the funeral of a child of noble birth. This is too lengthy to be given here in full, but one or two of the chief features of the proceedings may be briefly described. One of the earliest portions of the ceremonies was the killing of a couple of oxen; these, however, were first *wrestled* with, a man to each, and being thrown down after a hard struggle, the forelegs of each were dexterously, but cruelly, turned over its head and locked behind the horns. As soon as the first blood was drawn, a portion was taken to the child's grandfather to be tasted. During these proceedings a procession of women, carrying the property of the deceased, kept entering the house by the south door and leaving it again by the west door. The corpse was placed in a long box covered with coloured cloth and with a roof-like top; upon this were arranged about thirty

* *Antananarivo Annual.* No. i. pp. 74, 75.

solid silver rings of various sizes. A constant wailing, drumming, fiddling, and shell-blowing was kept up during the whole of the time.

But the most curious part of the Bétsiléo burial customs is yet to be described : it is a very disgusting one, but is not peculiar to them, being, as will be seen, common to other tribes, with certain variations. "The third day after death the body swells ; it is then taken from the coffin and rolled upon planks until it becomes all of a pulp. On the fourth day another ox is killed, and the skin from that and those killed previously are cut into long strips. The corpse is then held upright against the beam of the house, an incision is made in the heel of each foot, and all the putrid liquid matter is collected in a large earthen pot or pots ; and when nothing scarcely is left but skin and bone, the corpse is strapped to the beam and there left." The curious beliefs of the people as to the worm supposed to come from the corpse will be more appropriately described in the chapter treating of Malagasy Superstition and Folk Lore.

The Sihánaka.—The Sihánaka tribe have also certain burial usages peculiar to themselves. In a tour which I made round their territory in the year 1874, 1 noticed a somewhat different kind of memorial from any seen among the Hovas. At the entrance of almost every Sihánaka village two or three tall and slender trunks of trees are fixed into the ground, rising to a height of from thirty to fifty feet. To the summit of these lofty poles the fork of a tree is fixed, the points being sharpened so as to resemble an immense pair of horns. These are erected by the children of deceased persons, who fetch them from the forest, choosing wood of a hard and durable kind. Besides these, were frequently clusters of shorter poles bearing the skulls and horns of bullocks, as was formerly the custom in Imérina ; at some villages these were very numerous, one place being called Màrosalàzana, "Many poles," evidently from there being a group of twenty to thirty such poles at its entrance. In several instances small tin trunks, painted oak colour, were fixed on one point of the fork ; and in others, numerous articles, the property of the deceased, such as mats, baskets,

&c., were placed on a wooden railing near the poles.   This is done probably from an idea that it is improper to use anything belonging to the dead, the same notion indeed that leads to the burial of royal property among the Hovas, as already described.

The mourning ceremonies among the Sihànaka often continue for a week; the house being filled with men and women, who weep, and sing funeral chants, and play barbaric music. One man goes round the house chanting a dirge, which is replied to by those in the house.   Accompanying all this there is a good deal of drinking of spirits and eating of beef, oxen being killed every evening.   On the first day of watching the corpse, a great many oxen are brought up into the village; these are all killed by spearing.   Every one then takes what meat he pleases, excepting the heads, which are placed on poles near the grave.

On the day of the funeral a number of oxen are taken on the path along which the corpse is to be carried; and as it approaches, one after another of the animals are speared, and their carcasses laid on the ground so that they may be stepped over by those who carry the corpse.   If the grave is at some distance, this is done many times before the procession reaches it.   This custom of carrying a corpse over the bodies of newly-slaughtered animals was formerly observed by the Hovas, especially at the funerals of their kings; not only oxen, or rather bulls, being killed, but also some of the finest horses belonging to the sovereign (see *History of Madagascar*, vol. i. pp. 251, 252).

The Bétsimisàraka and other Eastern Tribes.—Among the Bétsimisàraka and other tribes on the east coast, there are certain customs which show a clear connection with those common in Polynesia.   The inhabitants of many of those islands do not, in their heathen state, bury their dead, but place them on an open stage or framework, leaving the corpse to decompose and pollute the surrounding atmosphere.   Much the same practice exists on the eastern coast of Madagascar. Of the Bézànozàno people, who are near neighbours, to the west, of the Bétsimisàraka, Messrs. Jukes and Lord say: " Near several of the villages through which we passed we noticed burial-places. Most of them consisted of mounds of earth surrounded by shallow trenches. Trunks of trees hollowed out and shaped like troughs contained the dead bodies, and were placed on the top of the mounds. These troughs or coffins were fitted with movable lids. A number of small platters made of banana leaves, and containing native spirits, were deposited on or about the mounds. The Bétsimisàraka and Bézànozàno tribes seem never to bury their dead underground, but simply enclose them in wooden coffins and expose them on mounds, or place them on a rude kind of trestle fixed in the ground."

Another traveller, the Rev. J. A. Houlder, thus speaks of the customs of the inhabitants at the head of Antongil Bay : "The people hereabouts do not bury their dead out of their sight. They put them in rude coffins made of tree trunks, and arranged in some kind of order, like the tombstones in a European churchyard. These receptacles for the dead are usually placed in some obscure spot, in a thick shady wood, or a part of the great forest. But little care is taken to conceal the coffins, and no thought is apparently bestowed on the extreme danger of depositing the decaying bodies of the dead near the dwellings of the living."

The Tanàla.—Among the Tanàla or forest tribes in the neighbourhood of Ivòhitròsa, in the south-east of Madagascar, the corpse of a person of importance is kept for a month before burial. The face is exposed for three days; the body is then covered with a red cloth or *làmba,* some silver is put into his mouth, and rings upon his hands, but none are put upon his feet, that honour being reserved for kings. A month is passed in watching the corpse, fat being burnt to overcome the effluvium. The burial procession is accompanied with firing of guns and loud wailing. Upon arriving at the grave, a man stands up and cries out, addressing the spirits of the dead previously buried there,—"This is what you get, but you must not follow after his progeny, his grandchildren, his brothers; this is the one you have got."

The corpse of a king is buried on the day of his death; his decease is not published abroad, but some guns are broken and put along with the corpse. An image of the king is then made; it is covered with cloth and hung up in the east corner of the house. The heads of his wife and children are shaved. After six weeks, this image is thrown into the River Màtitànana, and the same customs are followed as described above on the burial of a subject. Every ox in the kingdom that bellows at that time is killed for the benefit of those who are burying the image. The corpse is buried in a wooden house in the forest; the coffin is made of *nàto* wood. The lid is roof-shaped, and two horns are placed straddle-wise on each side. When this decays, a new one is made, and new cloth is substituted; and all the kings of one family are buried in one house, but each one has his own coffin.

Some of the forest tribes, however, in common with the people near to them on the south-east coast, do not bury their dead, but throw them into a large hole or pit in or on the border of the forest. This place is called *kibòry*, and each village has one for its inhabitants; the corpses are not covered with earth, but are wrapped in a coarse matting made of rush. Hardly any graves or memorials to the dead are seen in travelling through the forest, or in the Taimòro or Taisàka country; but at a village called Iàboràno, we saw something of the kind in four poles placed in a line, the outer ones higher than the rest, and the inner ones pointed in a peculiar fashion. These appear to serve the same purpose as the upright stones in Imérina and Bétsiléo.

In passing through the great forest farther to the north, we saw a Tanàla funeral, and a curious, although saddening, sight it was. Some time before we met it we heard a good deal of noise and shouting ahead of us, and supposed that the forest people were dragging an unusually heavy piece of timber. On getting nearer, however, we found fifty or sixty people, men and women, and a number of men carrying something, which, on coming closer to them, we found was a child's coffin, made of a piece of the trunk of a tree hollowed out, and with a rough cover of wood fastened on with bands of a strong liana. This was being carried with a barbarous kind of chant, but without the slightest sign of mourning on the part of any one. Amongst these Tanàla people funerals are called *fàndroritam-pàty* (literally, "the stretching out of the corpse"), and it seems that the corpse in its coffin is pulled about, first in one direction and then in another, by different parties of those following it, and is finally thrown into some hollow in the woods where the moisture may soon cause decomposition.

With regard to the people of Ikòngo, in the southern Tanàla, Mr. G. A. Shaw says: "They make no tombs, but bury their dead in the forest, with no other mark than a notched tree to keep the spot in remembrance. The carrying of the body to its last resting-place is accompanied with yelling and screaming; but I saw no ostentatious mourning and weeping, as with the Bétsiléo. At certain places on the road the body is placed on the ground, and a series of games is commenced, in which wrestling and the spear-exercise form a prominent part. Burying is called 'throwing away the corpse.'" *

The Bàra.—Of the Bàra tribes, Mr. Richardson says: "At death guns are fired, and a horrible wailing is set up; a third of the deceased's oxen must be killed before 'the ghost is laid.' At the death of a king half of his oxen must be killed, and his wives must cut off all their hair; and the ghost is not laid until his successor has captured a town, or has fought against one to the shedding of blood, either his own or some one else's, friend or foe. They dig no graves; the corpse is put into the ground naked, and stones are piled around and over it, making an oblong structure from a foot to three or four feet high. In the neighbourhood of the Isàlo, the bodies are taken and buried in the caves." This custom of cave-burial was also followed by two of the chief divisions of the Bétsiléo. "Natural crevices in the sides of enormous precipices were selected, and made larger and more suitable by men let down by ropes from above. The body was then lowered in the same way, and deposited at the innermost extremity of the hole, the entrance filled up with stones, and on the stones were fixed the skulls of cattle killed during the funeral festivities. In some of the bold, smooth, rocky heights dozens of these tombs may be counted, each with its bleached ox-skulls

* *Antanànarìvo Annual,* No. i. p. 66.

shining in the sun. At the foot of these rocks a guard is constantly kept, and no one is allowed to enter the enclosure containing the houses of the guard." [*]

The Sàkalàva and Allied Tribes on the West and North.—
Of the last of the great divisions of the people of Madagascar, the numerous tribes commonly known under the name of Sàkalàva, we do not yet know very much. But with regard to one of these tribes, those called Antankàrana, at the extreme northern end of Madagascar, the Rev. R. T. Batchelor has supplied some information, from which it will be seen that the strangely-repulsive custom observed by the Bétsiléo in the south is also common in the extreme north. He says: "The corpse, after being sewn up in an ox-hide, is bound tight with cords so soon as the friends of the deceased think it time the obsequies should be commenced (which is not so soon as might be wished), in order that great quantities of beef and rum may be consumed by the mourners. This marks the second stage in the mourning. Several times every day these cords are drawn tighter, and this process is continued until nothing but the bones remain. These are then carefully laid in a canoe, with its two ends cut square, and covered in. When this has been done, the burial takes place. The coffin is conveyed amidst continuous musket-firing to the family cemetery, a solitary and unfrequented spot on the sea-shore; and an Antankàrana will travel a very long distance in order to assist at these burial customs. A cup and a plate are placed by the side of the coffin, and every now and then the friends go in large numbers, and taking rice and rum with them, hold a feast in these cemeteries, and believe that the spirits of their dead ancestors and relations come and join them. Studious care is taken that these coffins are renewed before they have rotted away." [†]

A French writer, M. Guillain, also says: "That before placing the corpse in the bier, the Antankàrana subject it to a species of mummification. The corpse, placed upon a stage of bamboos raised some feet above the ground, is covered with aromatic substances, and with hot sand, which is frequently renewed.

[*] *Antanànarìvo Annual,* No. iv. p. 8.
[†] *Ibid.* No. iii. p. 30.

When it is perfectly desiccated they envelope it in linen bandages, and then carry it to the place of burial, which is usually situated upon a small islet, or on some steep cavernous mountain. The first ceremony of drying the corpse is succeeded by a most revolting custom; for at the end of several days decomposition produces a putrefying liquid, which is received into vessels placed under the framework on which the corpse is deposited. Then each one of those present holds his hand so as to receive a portion of the horrible liquid, with which he rubs his whole body!" *

Another quotation, this time from one of the earliest English books upon Madagascar, must complete these descriptions of the burial customs of the Malagasy. In the narrative of Robert Drury, describing the customs of the south-western tribes (1702 to 1717) there occurs the following account :—" In the first place, they pitch upon a tree for a coffin; after that, a cow or an ox is killed and some of the blood sprinkled upon it, imploring, at the same time, their forefathers, and the demons and demi-gods, to aid and assist them. When the tree is down, they cut it about a foot longer than the corpse, and split it directly lengthwise, and dig both parts hollow, like two troughs. It is then carried to the house, the corpse being, in the meantime, washed and wrapped up in a làmba, or frequently in two, and sewed together. There is frankincense, or a gum very much like it, burning all the time in the house. They seldom keep the corpse above one day, especially in hot weather. They put the corpse in the troughs, closing them together, and carry it upon six men's shoulders. Every family has a burying-place of their own, which no one dare infringe upon or break into; nor does any one indeed attempt it. This is enclosed and fenced round with sticks. When they come near the place, the corpse is set down, and then they make four fires, one at each corner, on the outside of the burying-place. On these fires they burn the ox or cow which was killed before for that purpose; they divide it into quarters, which are all consumed in the flames. After this they

---

* *Documents sur . . . la Partie Occidentale de Madagascar.* Paris, 1845, p. 158.

Q

sprinkle frankincense upon the coals, and spread them **all**
about. This being done, the chief, or eldest of the family,
goes close to the entrance of the burying-place, and halloos
aloud several times; after a short pause he calls upon all the
dead that are there deposited, commencing at the eldest and
proceeding to the last, and each one distinctly by his name,
and in the conclusion tells them that there is a relation come
to lie amongst them, and that he hopes they will receive him
as a friend. Then the gate is opened, and two or three persons are sent in to dig the grave, which is made, for the
generality, seven or eight feet deep; and the corpse is placed
in it, and covered over with earth without any further
ceremony. None are permitted to enter here but some of the
nearest relations and the bearers, and the door is immediately
shut fast again. They generally visit this burying-place once
a year to clear it from weeds and make it clean, but never
enter it until they have first burnt a cow or a bullock before
it." (Pages 225–227, edition of 1807.)

CHAPTER XII.

RELATIONSHIPS, AND THE NAMES USED FOR THEM, AMONG THE PEOPLES OF MADAGASCAR, CHIEFLY THE HOVAS.

AS ILLUSTRATING MORALS, MARRIAGE CUSTOMS AND RESTRICTIONS, AND SOCIAL AND FAMILY LIFE.

THE subject of relationships and marriage customs among primitive peoples has excited much interest and received considerable attention from ethnologists during the last few years. And as there are several facts connected with this subject as found among the Malagasy tribes, which have not, I believe, as yet been brought into public notice, it may, perhaps, be of some service to note them down as a slight contribution to a fuller knowledge of the state of society among the less-known races of mankind.[*]

When a foreigner begins to study the Malagasy language, he finds in many classes of words strange deficiencies as compared with English, while at the same time there is in other groups a much greater fulness and minuteness of distinction than exists in his own or allied languages.

This remark applies fully to the names used for relationships among the Hovas, if not also to those employed by the other Malagasy tribes.

The words for " father," *ray*, and " mother," *rény*, are used with a very wide signification, and are applied not only to the actual father and mother, but also to step-father and step-mother (who are also called *raikély* and *rénikély*, " little father," and " little mother "), and to uncles and aunts, with their wives and husbands ; so that it is almost impossible to get to know the exact relationship people bear to one

---

[*] My attention was first drawn to this subject by the perusal of a paper by my friend, C. Staniland Wake, Esq., M.A.I., upon " The Origin of the Classificatory System of Relationships used among Primitive Peoples " (*Proc. Anthrop. Inst.*, Nov. 1878).

another without asking, " Is he the father who begat him ? "
or, " Is she the mother who bore him ? " (It may not
be unworthy of remark here that the same word, *mitéraka*,
is used both for begetting and for bearing children.) Consequently there are no single words in Malagasy corresponding to our " uncle " and " aunt ; " one must say
" father's brother," or " sister " or " mother's brother," or
" sister," as the case may be. And so it naturally follows
that there are also no single words for " nephew," or " niece ; "
these are all *zànaka*, " children," and if more minutely
described are distinguished as children of their father's or
mother's brothers or sisters.

Ray, " father," does not seem to take the sense it has in
many Semitic languages of " maker " of a thing, but it is
used in a wide sense as an elder or superior ; and in addressing an elderly man it is common to call him *ikàky*, a word
which, together with *dàda*, is the more familiar and affectionate word used by children in addressing their parent ;
the latter word being perhaps more commonly used by sons,
and the former by daughters. It is singular, however, that
rény, " mother," does take the sense of author of a thing :
thus, *réniràno*, a river, is literally " mother of waters ; "
rénitantély, a bee, is " mother of honey ; " *rénivòhitra*, a
capital, is " mother of towns ; " and *rénivòla*, capital, principal,
is " mother of money." And also, the four first months of
the four quarters of the year are called *rénivintàna*, " mother
of fate," or fortune, these being the principal months. In
the same manner, the word for child, *zànaka*, is used as the
converse of *rény*, " mother," or " originator of a thing." Thus,
zàna-bòla is interest or usury, literally, " offspring of money,"
while *mizànaka*, is to be at interest ; *zànakàzo* is a word for
the pieces of wood cut from a tree, " offspring of the tree ; "
zàna-tòhatra, the rungs of a ladder, is " offspring of a ladder ; "
and *zana-tsòratra*, vowels, are " offspring of writing." The
words *aba* and *baba*, *ada* and *daday* and *angy*, are also used
for " father," while *ngahy* is a respectful term for an elderly
man or any superior.

In the same way, *rény*, " mother," or its more common and
familiar form, *nény*, is also used in a wide sense as a respect-

ful way of addressing an elderly woman. The word *éndry* is also used, almost exclusively so in some tribes, for mother, and also *ima*, and *jàry*, probably the same as *zàry*, which means "made," "formed," "created."

There is no exact equivalent for our word "parent." The compound phrase *rai-aman-drény*, *i.e.*, "father together with mother," is applied to any superior, elder, or patron, male or female, and is given as a title of respect by the sovereign to the people, and by the people again to the sovereign. In some of the early editions of the Malagasy Scriptures the Fifth Commandment was wrongly translated, "Manajà ny *rai-aman-dreninao*," instead of "Manajà ny *rainao sy ny reninao*," and has accordingly, at least on one occasion, been preached from by a native whose knowledge was not equal to his zeal, as containing a command to honour the Government and the great people of the country.

In the Sàkalàva dialect, a man is *johàry*, which in Hova means chief, president, or governor, "the lord of the creation," in fact; while "woman" is *baréra*, a word which in Hova means "to brood over," as a bird over its young.

Then the word for "child," *zànaka* or *ànaka* (the latter is a more affectionate and respectful word used in direct address), is used in an equally wide sense for children actually borne or begotten, for step-children, and for nephews and nieces, for which last relationship, as already remarked, there are no distinct words. The word *zànaka*, in like manner with its complements *ray* and *rény*, is used in a wide sense in addressing or speaking of a younger person. "Son" is *zànaka-làhy*, and "daughter," *zànaka-vàvy*.* "Boy" is *zàza-làhy*, and "girl," *zàza-vàvy*; while a girl who is an only child is called by the curious compound *vàvilàhy*, literally, "male-female." (*Làhy* and *vàvy* are "male" and "female," or "masculine" and "feminine.") A child dying under two years of age is termed *ràno*, the word for "water," and used also figuratively for anything soft and delicate.

A girl is in many tribes called *zàza-ampéla*, that is, "spindle-

---

* My friend Mr. Wake wrote to me: "Have you ever thought of the amusing fact, that while *anak* means 'small' in so many languages, in Hebrew the *Anakim* were sons of the *giant!*"

child," or simply *ampéla;* for every Malagasy woman can spin as well as weave. So that we have here a close analogy with our English word "spinster," which recalls the time when our great-grandmothers and their mothers before them could all use their spinning-wheels.

Adoption of relatives' children being very common, owing no doubt to a great extent to the somewhat large proportion of people who have no children, there are several words denoting the different relationships arising from this *fànan-gànan' ànaka* (literally, "raising up children"), as it is termed. Thus *zàza-làva* (literally, "tall children") are children of near relatives united by adoption, so as to be treated as children of the same parents, and to inherit equally. *Zàza mòmba reny* ("children of a barren mother") are step-children who live with their mother and step-father.

To die without posterity is looked upon as a great calamity, and is termed *màti-màso*, "dead as regards the eye." And the Malagasy have a practice similar to the Levitical law of the Jews, viz., that if an elder brother die childless, his next brother must marry the widow to keep his brother in remembrance; the children of such marriages being considered as the elder brother's heirs and descendants (see Deut. xxv. 5, 6). This is called *mitòndra lolòha* (*mitondra*, to carry, *lolòha*, a family under the protection of the elder son or guardian); and he who thus preserves heirs for his elder brother is said to *mamélo-màso*, "make to live the eye," while, as above stated, he who dies heirless, dies *màti-màso*, "dead as regards the eye."

Fàra is a word for "offspring," "heir," or "progeny." "*Maròa fara aman-dìmby*," *i.e.*, "Be numerous in offspring and descendants," is a frequent marriage benediction or salutation; and *faraina* ("last life") is a word applied to the youngest child. There is also a special word for the last child when the mother is again pregnant, *aizana*. Foster-child is *miolo-nòno*, "suckling together with."

The words *Kòto* and *Kétaka* are applied to children who have had no name given them; and although meaning little more than "lad" and "lass," are often retained for a considerable time as the only names, with the prefix *Ra-* (see chapter viii.).

It may not be out of place to say something here about the words used for "tribe," "nation," and "family," among the Malagasy. For "family" the word *mpianakavy* is used, of which the word *anaka* (child) is evidently the root, but whether the terminal is the verb *àvy* ("come" or "come from") is doubtful. For "tribe" there is the word *fòko*, a somewhat wide term, meaning also family, class, or clan; and frequently combined with *òlona*, people, and *firenéna*, nation. This last word, however, has not the wide meaning which our "nation" has, as it often means only a clan or tribe; and it is evidently derived from the root *rény*, mother, which fact, taken in connection with the practice of inheriting through the female rather than the male line, is not perhaps without significance. But we still need more minute inquiry among the natives of Madagascar upon all these subjects.

In the words for "brother" and "sister," there are distinctions we do not possess, viz., *rahalahy* for brother's brother, *anadahy* for sister's brother, *rahavavy* for sister's sister, and *anabavy* for brother's sister.

These words again are used for "cousin," for which relationship there is no single or equivalent term; and so much is the near kinship of brothers' and sisters' children recognised that, as with the words father and mother and child, it is difficult without close inquiry to find out what actual relationship there is between members of a family. There are, however, the compounds, *zana-drahalahy*, child of a man's brother; *zànak'aina* (*aina* = life) and *zanak'anabavy*, child of a man's sister; *zana-drahavavy*, child of a woman's sister; and *zanak'anadahy*, child of a woman's brother.

The words "brother" and "sister" are also used widely for any person whom one meets and desires to act towards in a friendly manner, generally with the polite prefix *Ra-*, as *Ranabavy, Ranadahy*, a form also used for Such an one, Mr. So and so (*Ranona*), and also with the word *ankìzy*, children, as *Rankìzy*, and with other words as well. (This last word, *ankízy*, is also used to denote "servants," being thus somewhat analogous to the French *garçon* and to the German *kellner*.)

From the (until lately) common practices of polygamy and divorce, half-brothers and sisters are much more numerous among the Malagasy than in European nations, but there is no distinctive word for this half relationship, except that they say that such an one is *miray ray*, "of one common father," with another, or *miray tam-po*, "of one common mother," or literally, "joined from the heart." There are special words for an elder or younger brother or sister, viz., *zòky* and *zandry*, words also applied widely as "senior" and "junior" generally;* and there are also words for brother-in-law, *zaodahy*, and sister-in-law, *zaobavy*. *Zazampimihìra* are brother and sister whom the father claims as his own before divorcing the mother. *Zazasary* (literally, "image of a child") is a natural child, a bastard.

Marriage between brother's children is exceedingly common, and is looked upon as the most proper kind of connection, as keeping property together in the same family (the marriage of two persons nearly related to each other is called *lòva-tsi-mifìndra*, *i.e.*, "inheritance not removing"); and there does not seem to result from such marriages any of those consequences in idiocy and mental disorder of the offspring which are frequently seen in European nations as arising from the marriages of first cousins. It is possible, however, that to this marrying in and amongst tribes and families is due, in part at least, the sterility so frequent in Malagasy women, although this is no doubt also largely caused by the too early marriage of young peoples, and the licentiousness allowed until very lately among the young, and even among mere children.

Marriage between brothers' and sisters' children is also allowable on the performance of a slight prescribed ceremony, supposed to remove any impediment from consanguinity; but that of sisters' children, when the sisters have the same mother, is regarded with horror as incest, being emphatically *fàdy* or

---

* *Saònjo mihòatra akòndro*, *i.e.*, "The arum exceeding the banana," is a phrase used to express preferment given to a junior brother by his senior.

tabooed, and not allowable down to the fifth generation, that is, to the great-great-great-grandchildren of such two sisters. So when a man divorces his wife he calls her *anabavy,* " sister," implying that any intercourse between them is henceforth impossible.

There are also special words for the eldest, middle, and youngest children of a family, both male and female. Thus, the eldest son is termed *Andriamatòa,* the eldest girl, *Ràmatòa ;* the middle sons, *Andriandivo* or *Randivo,* the middle girl, *Raivo ;* the youngest son, *Rafàraldhy* (last male), and the youngest girl, *Rafàravàvy* (last female). Except the two first of these words these are often retained as proper names, either alone or combined with others ; and the two first are frequently prefixed as a complimentary addition to the names of elderly men and women, whether they be the eldest of their brothers and sisters or not, and they are also used as a complimentary form of address to men and women generally.

Grandchildren are *àfy* or *zàfy,* a word also used widely for "descendànts ;" and for tribal names, as *Zafin-dralambo, Zafin' Ibrahim, Zafimanélo,* &c. (*taranaka* is also a word nearly equivalent, and used for "posterity, generation "); great-grandchildren are *zafiafy,* great-great-grandchildren are *zafimafy,* great-great-great-grandchildren are *zafin-dohàlika,* i.e., "descendants of the knee," and great-great-great-great-grandchildren are *zafim-paladìa,* "descendants of the sole of the foot." *Zàfindorìa* is a word used for a very distant relation ; *dorìa* is a word denoting "everlasting," probably through the Arabic from a Semitic root of the same meaning.

The words for grandfather and grandmother are exactly equivalent to our own: *raibé* (*bé,* great) and *rénibé ;* * but there appear to be no distinctive terms for any relationships further back, all previous to grandparents are known by the general term *ràzana,* ancestors. To all ancestors a kind of divinity is ascribed, for they are spoken of as *lasan-ko Andriamanitra,* "gone to be gods," and they are invoked in prayers immediately after the Supreme Being.

* In Sàkalàva the words for grandfather and grandmother are *dàdilàhy* and *dàdivàvy,* both, but especially the latter, very curious combinations.

In the ceremonies of the circumcision, the parent or other person who carries the child to be circumcised, and also the circumciser, is called *rainjaza*, "father of a child;" so that he and a woman who acts as mother, and is called *reninjaza*, are a kind of godfather and godmother.

For "father-in-law" and "mother-in-law" there is one word, *rafòzana*, but unless this is defined by the gender suffixes, the word generally means "mother-in-law," and there are proverbs in the language which warn people about the desirability of being on good terms with one's mother-in-law, speaking of it as being far more important than even agreeing with one's wife! * *Vinanto* is the word for "son-in-law" and "daughter-in-law," and is often further defined by the gender suffixes.

For "husband" and "wife" there is but one Malagasy word, *vady*, and it is not customary to add to this the masculine and feminine suffixes, *lahy* and *vávy*, the meaning being gathered from the connection. (These words are, however, often used alone to distinguish the husband or wife.) *Vady* is also used in a wide sense for pairs or things which fit to each other. (In several tribes, by euphonic change of consonants, *vady* becomes *valy*; *valy* in Hova means an answer, or anything replying to or corresponding with another.) Until the spread of Christianity in the central provinces of Madagascar introduced a higher idea of the marriage relation, the idea of *love* between husband and wife was hardly thought of among the Hovas. Marriage indeed was compared to a knot so lightly tied, that it could be undone with the slightest possible touch.† There was no lack of strong affection between blood relations—parents and children, brothers and sisters, grandparents and grandchildren; but the marriage state was regarded chiefly as a matter of mutual convenience, each party carefully retaining separately his or her property. Married people never address each other by any endearing epithet, but the wife is called by the husband *Rafòtsy* or *Ramatòa* (this,

---

* *Ny vady no tiana, ka ny rafòzana no malala;* "The wife is liked, but the mother-in-law is loved."

† *Ny fanambadiana tsy nafehy, fa nahandrotra;* "Marriage is not (a thing) tied fast, but tied in a bow."

however, being confined to the first wife), while he is called by her *Tòmpokolahy* ("sir," or "my lord"), or *Rainjanaka* or *Rainianaka*, that is, "father of a child." Marriage is called *fanambadìana*, "the state of having a partner," and the word for wedding is *fampakaram-bady*, apparently from the root *akatra*, "ascended, got, or fetched." A widow is *mpitòndra-téna*, "one who carries one's self;" she is also called *ampéla-bàntotra* (*ampéla*, spindle, *vantotra*, middle-sized). An orphan is *kambòty*, and another word was also used, but now nearly obsolete, *asòrotànitsisàtry*. *Asòrotany* is the name of the fourth month, most of which is unlucky; *tsy satry*, "is not wished," or "not intended."

Among the Hovas a marriage is celebrated first at the house of the bride's father, and then at that of the bride-groom's family. The young couple sit together to eat rice and other food with one spoon from the same dish. A hand-some silk làmba is thrown round them both, and the marriage becomes legal and binding by presenting a small sum of money to the bride's parents or guardians. This is called the *vòdi-òndry*, lit., "sheep's rump," and no doubt used in former times to consist of that portion of a sheep.

Among some, at least, of the Malagasy peoples there are certain marriage customs which seem connected with the widely-extended practice of taking a wife by force from her father's family. Thus among the Sàkalàvas when a young man wishes to obtain a girl as his wife, his courage and suitable qualifications are tested in the following way:—Placed at a certain distance from a clever caster of the spear, he is bidden to catch between his arm and side every spear thrown by the man opposite to him. If he displays fear or fails to catch the spear he is ignominiously rejected; but if there be no flinching and the spears are caught, he is at once proclaimed an "accepted lover." It is said that a similar custom prevailed among the Bétsiléo,[*] and probably further research would reveal something like it in other Malagasy tribes. A betrothed girl is *fòfombàdy*, a bespoken or engaged wife, and it is considered quite proper that such should

---

[*] See *Antanànarìvo Annual*, No. ii. 1876, p. 22.

co-habit with their future husbands before they are actually married. *Màtifàhana* is a word used for breaking an engagement to marry, "a breach of promise."

Among the Sàkalàva tribes marriage between a brother and sister was not forbidden by the laws. One of the kings of Ibòina, the northern of the two great Sàkalàva kingdoms, a chieftain, named Andriamàhatindy, is said to have married his youngest sister, and to have had by her six daughters. Such marriages were, however, preceded by a ceremony of sprinkling the woman with consecrated water, and reciting prayers asking for her happiness and fecundity, as if there was a fear that such unnatural unions would call down upon the parties the anger of the Supreme Being.[*]

It should, however, be observed that such marriages were usually made because of the difficulty sometimes occurring of finding a wife of equal rank with the chief or king. There was also often a jealousy of any claimant to the supreme power, on account of the brother of the chief being, of course, older than the chief's own children. Thus the founder of the southern Sàkalàva kingdom of Ménabé sent away his younger brother to the north, but gave him at the same time a body of soldiers. With these he followed the example of his elder brother, and before long, by the conquest of several tribes, founded the northern Sàkalàva kingdom of Ibòina.

Lawful marriages are termed *hény*, an imperative verb implying "ought," "should," behoveth."

Although gross immorality was common among the Hovas, and is still so among the Bétsimisàraka and other tribes, amongst whom the very idea of purity seems unknown, there being no word for virgin or maid (for *mpitòvo*, which is commonly used as an equivalent for these words, means only an unmarried girl), there are some other tribes, more isolated, as certain of the eastern peoples, where a higher standard of morality prevails, girls being kept scrupulously from any intercourse with the other sex until they are married; and this notwithstanding the slight use of clothing, unmarried girls merely wearing a cloth or mat round the loins, while the upper part of the body remains uncovered. But amongst

---

[*] See Guillain, *op. cit.*, p. 26.

other tribes, on the contrary, as the Bàra and some neighbouring races, there is a shameless and open indecency of speech
and behaviour which would shock the Hovas, although many
of them would, in secret, act quite as immorally. Thus there
is a Hova word, *sàodrànto* (*saotra*, "divorced;" *ranto*, "traded
in"), to express the leave given to a wife to have intercourse
with another man during her husband's prolonged absence
from home. On the other hand, there are certain ornaments
worn by a wife during such absence to denote that her person
is sacred. Then there are also phrases, such as *miàro-
vàntotra*, to express refusal to allow a near female relative to
be taken for immoral purposes, showing, as is well known
from other evidence, that the opposite of this was a not
infrequent practice. It also used to be usual among the
Hovas for the most shameless licentiousness to be allowed by
custom on certain occasions, such as the birth of a child in
the royal family; but Radàma I. prohibited this, owing to
the urgent remonstrances of Mr. Hastie, the British resident,
who threatened to proclaim to the world what vileness was
carried on in his dominions. Radàma, who earnestly wished
to be well thought of by Europeans, was so affected that he
gave peremptory orders to stop such practices, and even put
to death some persons of high rank who were found to have
been guilty of disobedience. Such days were called *àndro-
tsi-màty*, "days-not-dead," that is, not involving death for any
offence (*History of Madagascar*, vol. i. p. 150).

A wife is sometimes called *andéfimàndry*, "the one lying
beyond," close to the wall; a second wife is *vàdy kély*, "little
wife," while if there are three or more wives, the wife or
wives between the first and the last are called *masày*, a word
whose meaning is not clear. * The wives of chiefs among
the Sàkalàva are termed *bìby*, a word which in Hova means
"animal." A present made to a first wife upon marrying a
second is called *ìso-pandrìana*, a corruption of *ìso-pandrìana*,
from *ìsotra*, "cleared, removed," and *fandrìana*, "bed." The
privilege (?) of having twelve wives was reserved by the

---

* A French writer, M. Désiré Charnay, says that among the Bétsimisàraka:
"Les sœurs de ces trois femmes [d'un chef] appartiennent de droit à l'époux
jusqu' à ce qu'elles soient mariées." (*Tour du Monde*, x. liv. 247 ; p. 208.)

Hovas to the sovereign, and Andriamàsinavàlona (who is fifteenth on the list of Hova princes, the present sovereign being the thirty-sixth) is the first recorded in native accounts as having exercised this right, the names of the twelve wives being preserved. These *Roàmbinifòlo Vàvy*, or " Twelve Wives," had a recognised place among the great people of the kingdom, and their advice was always asked in all matters of importance. There are still (or were until very recently) some two or three aged ladies in the palace who are the survivors of Radàma the first's wives; but their influence is now a thing of the past, for since 1828 there have been (with eighteen months' exception) only female sovereigns. Among some of the other tribes polygamy is carried to a much greater extent than it was with the Hovas, some chiefs having from twenty to thirty wives; and one of the Bàra kings, Ivóatra, is said to count his wives by the hundred !

The power of divorce is legally in the husband's hands, although a wife can practically divorce herself in many cases. But in some cases the husband can divorce his wife so that she cannot marry again, and can also make certain restrictions as to children and property after she is divorced, a power expressed by the word *hàdindràno*, whose literal meaning is not very clear (*hàdy* is trench, *ràno*, water, or possibly it is *tràno*, house). Among the Tanàla, if a woman of noble birth marries a commoner, he cannot divorce her, but she can divorce her husband. As to the significant native words for poly-gamy and divorce, see chapter vii.

Money or property is occasionally given on the separation of husband and wife, to prevent the woman becoming the wife of another man, except by consent of the husband. This is called *tàha*.

If a wife is divorced as to be unable to marry again, "she is often treated personally with extreme cruelty, and during the formal process of being divorced receives, first, a *black fowl*, expressive, it is supposed, of the wish of her husband that she may ever be to all others a repulsive object; second, a *walking-stick*, indicating that for the future she is to have no home, but is to be an outcast on the roads; third, a small *piece of money*, signifying that she is to be dependent on what is given by others; and fourth, a piece of *white gun-wadding*, to signify that she is to continue in that state until her hair is white with age" (*History of Madagascar*, vol. i. p. 174).

The Sihànaka have a curious custom with regard to widows. Upon the death of any man of position or wealth, on the day of the funeral the wife is placed in the house, dressed in all her best clothes, and covered with her silver ornaments, of which the Sihànaka wear a considerable quantity. There she remains until the rest of the family return home from the tomb. But as soon as they enter the house they begin to revile her with most abusive language, telling her that it is her fault that her *vìntana* or fate has been stronger than that of her husband, and that she is virtually the cause of his death. They then strip her of her clothes, tearing off with violence the ornaments from her ears and neck and arms; they give her a coarse cloth, a spoon with a broken handle, and a dish with the foot broken off, with which to eat; her hair is dishevelled, and she is covered up with a coarse mat, and under that she remains all day long, and can only leave it at night; and she may not speak to any one who goes into the house. She is not allowed to wash her face or hands, but only the tips of her fingers. She endures all this sometimes for a year, or at least for eight months; and even when that is over, her time of mourning is not ended for a considerable period; for she is not allowed to go home to her own relations until she has been first divorced by her husband's family.

The word *hàvana,* meaning strictly "relative," is also used widely and vaguely for friends and acquaintance; a "distant relative" is called *hàvan-tetèzana,* literally, a "relative (reached by) stepping" (over intermediate links). A sarcastic native proverb describing "cupboard love," says: *Hàvako raha misy pàtsa, fa raha lany ny patsa, hàvan-tetèzana, i.e.,* "He's my relative while the *pàtsa* last [a minute fresh-water shrimp, much liked as *laoka* or accompaniment to rice], but when the *pàtsa* are eaten, he's quite a distant relative." The proper word for friend is *sakaiza,* but this again cannot be used between persons of the opposite sex, as it implies a paramour in such connection.

Hàvan-tsi-aina ("a relative without life") is a word used for an unkind relation; and a curious word for near relations, or consanguinity, is *àtin-kàvana*, or *ati-havana*, *àty* meaning "liver," or the "inside" of a thing. *Làfy*, which also means "side," is another word for relative.

It is a matter for great satisfaction that during the last few years, owing to the influence of Christianity, great changes for the better have passed over society in the central provinces of Madagascar. The marriage relation is every year being raised in the estimation of the people; a much higher standard of morals is being formed; polygamy may be said to be at an end, and divorce is very much less frequent than it used to be; and an enlightened public opinion is gradually shaming out many of the immoral practices which formerly passed unreproved.

A word or two may be said in conclusion as to class distinctions, and the marriage restrictions which keep separate different ranks of society. As already described in chapter ix., the Hova population consists of three great divisions: the nobles, the *Hovas* * or commoners, and the slaves, and these classes, with few exceptions, cannot intermarry.

The nobles are divided into six clans, from the third of which the sovereign can take a wife. Some of the ranks of nobles can intermarry with certain of the inferior ranks, and only those of the highest ranks can marry a commoner.

The second great class, that of the Hovas, the mass of the free people, is subdivided into a considerable number of tribes and clans and families, and these, as a rule, do not intermarry with each other, but keep to their own clan, and largely to their own family. A free man cannot marry a slave, except by redeeming her first; should he divorce her she continues free, much in the same way as according to the provisions of the Mosaic law (Exod. xxi. 7-10; Deut. xxi. 11-14).

There is among the Malagasy much strong family affection and tribal and clannish feeling, and one of the most dreaded evils that can befall any one is to be *ariana*, or cast off by

---

* This is a restricted use of the word, for, of course, all the free people, with the nobles, and the first class of slaves as well, are Hovas, as distinct from the other tribes inhabiting the country.

his family or tribe, so as to become an outcast. This family affection is even extended in some degree to the slaves born in the family, who are looked upon as inferior members of it, and who take pride in its prosperity. The young slave children and infants are often nursed by their owners with almost as much affection as are their own children; while the old slave men and women are called *ikáky*, and *inény*, "daddy," and "mammy," much in the same way as the elderly free men and women of the family.

There is also with this family feeling a great mutual politeness and a strict adherence to certain forms of expression towards each other, there being proper modes for a man to address another of superior, of equal, or of inferior rank to himself, each being different; while there are similar terms proper for a woman to address members of her own sex; and still others for women to use to men, and for men to women, and for brothers-in-law to address each other.

The subject treated of in this paper has as, yet received but little attention, but there is doubtless much of value awaiting research and careful inquiry. I trust that others will more thoroughly investigate the question, and that thus further contributions may be made to our knowledge of the primitive races of mankind.

CHAPTER XIII.

NOTES UPON MALAGASY ART IN DECORATION AND MANUFACTURE.

HOVA ART: HOUSE DECORATION—CHURCH ADORNMENT—TEXTILE FABRICS—
STRAW PLAITING—METAL WORK—POTTERY—BÉTSILÉO ART: CARVING
ON BURIAL MEMORIALS—HOUSES—AND UTENSILS.

IF we look at any illustrated book describing the inhabitants
of Polynesia we shall find that every group, and sometimes
every solitary island, has its peculiar style of ornament,
special to itself, and easily distinguishable from that of other
groups and islands. Their canoes and paddles, their clubs
and spears, houses and beds, dishes and spoons, pipes and
snuff-boxes, are all ornamented, sometimes most elaborately
and beautifully. And this decoration extends to their own
persons, in the practice of tattooing, and also to their clothing, as seen in the patterns woven into the cloth or matting
of their dresses, or stamped upon the bark cloth they procure
from various trees.

Hova Art.—But among the Hovas, in the centre of Madagascar, there is very little ornamental art, and in the great
majority of the articles which they construct for daily use,
there is a remarkable absence of the elaborate and varied
carving which is employed by most of the Malayo-Polynesian
tribes. It is true that many of the large stone tombs built
of late years in Imérina have some architectural pretensions,
and decorative carving is employed on them, but the details
are copied from drawings of European buildings, and can in
no respect be considered as examples of indigenous art.

There are, however, some few indications of a feeling for
decoration among the Hovas which it may be worth while
to note down, before proceeding to speak of the much more

abundant decorative carving found among the Bétsiléo in the southern central provinces.

There is in Imérina, as in Madagascar generally, nothing which can be called an architectural style, for there are no buildings of any size except the royal palaces at the capital. But still the Hovas have a style of house peculiar to themselves, both in construction and shape, and these give a distinct character to the appearance of the purely native towns. The capital city of Antanànarìvo has been almost entirely rebuilt within the last ten or twelve years, and its old timber houses replaced by buildings of sun-dried brick, on European models. But about fifteen or sixteen years ago, it was crowded with the old-fashioned houses, most of them of wood, with lofty and extremely high-pitched roofs, and finished at the gables with the crossing timbers called " horns," the extremities of which projected above the ridge to a height of from two or three to five or six feet, and in the case of the royal houses even to twelve or fourteen feet. Towering above these, on the summit of the hill, were the two chief royal palaces ; the principal one an immense timber structure with lofty roof, and arched verandah in three tiers surrounding the building. To the north-east of this was the second palace, of similar design, but only two stories in height, and about two-thirds the size of its loftier neighbour. The great palace has, however, during the last ten years been surrounded with a massive stone verandah, with lofty corner towers, and with Corinthian engaged columns, all the details being excellently worked out under English superintendence in the classic styles, so that it no longer presents the peculiar Malagasy type of construction.

In the interior ornamentation of these royal houses (as well as of some few of those belonging to the upper classes), there seemed to me to be a certain distinct style prevalent. This is chiefly seen in the painted decorations of the upper parts of the walls, and sometimes of the ceilings, which both in the colouring and large bold style of the patterns always reminded me somewhat of Assyrian ornament, as shown in decoration of the palaces at Persepolis. I am sorry that I am unable to confirm this by illustrative sketches, for the few state occasions on which foreigners are admitted to the palace were not favourable times for minute examination; but the general impression I received as to the style of ornament was as already stated.

The only stone structure of any size erected by the Hovas (apart from European design) is the large family tomb of the Prime Minister. This building, in many of its details, in the outline of its elegant and somewhat minaret-like columns for carrying the lightning conductors, and in the curious series of semicircular mouldings forming so marked a feature in their decoration, as well as of that of the corner piers, always reminded me somewhat of Indian structures, and as having some little resemblance to certain features of buildings seen in the Punjab and North-west Provinces. (I do not for a moment mean to say that any comparison can be drawn between this Malagasy tomb and the wonderful creations of the Moguls, but there are undoubtedly some points of resemblance in detail.)

As regards the timber houses of the Hovas, there is hardly a trace of any ornamental carving, except the occasional use of a notched zigzagged or minute semicircular edging to certain pieces of timber, as the " horns " and in the windows in the roof.

In interior decoration, however (apart from the palaces), we occasionally meet with examples of tasteful ornamentation, which show that here and there a certain amount of artistic feeling is to be found. The walls of some of the village churches in Imérina sometimes display considerable taste, as well as ingenuity, and show that with a little guidance, and a few hints and suggestions for conventionalising somewhat more the natural objects employed in decoration, the native talent might be trained to produce a very appropriate adornment for the walls of sacred and other buildings. It is true that occasionally the native artist has introduced figures and scenes decidedly (though not intentionally) comic in their effect: soldiers, sportsmen, animals, and birds being depicted. But in many cases the walls are painted with a diaper of groups of leaves and flowers, giving them the appearance of a well-papered surface, while the doors and windows are bordered by bold lines and running sprays of leaves and flowers. In a church at Ambòhimànga the windows were all surrounded by groups of palm-like trees, while on the key-stones of the arches over windows and doors were painted groups of flowers, many of them most tastefully designed and coloured.

I was much struck by a piece of wall-painting which I found six or seven years ago in a country church some twenty miles to the west of the capital. The ornamentation covered about two-thirds of the wall behind the pulpit, and had it been the custom in our churches to place our communion tables "altar-wise" against the end wall, the painting might have been taken for an elaborate altar-piece or "dossal." There were, however, no figures, or even attempts at representing such natural objects as leaves or flowers, but only combinations of lines and circles, and curves and zigzags, in a variety of colours. But the most noticeable feature was that, both in the forms employed, and in the key of colour pervading the whole, there was a remarkable resemblance to the style of ornamentation which may be seen in the mediæval wall-painting still remaining on the stonework of a few of our ancient Norman and Gothic churches in England. In fact the whole formed an elaborate diaper, and the colours employed, mostly the native clays of various shades of brown, buff, chocolate, and black, with sparing use of the primary tints, were at a distance all blended in a kind of neutral tint or purple haze. Indeed, the untaught native artist had unconsciously succeeded in accomplishing what more laboured attempts often fail to do. The chief difference between this Hova decoration and the mediæval examples was the absence, in the former, of any distinctively sacred emblems or monograms. But the similarity of things so far apart both in time and locality struck me as curious and suggestive.

In the different cloths which the Hova women weave from silk, cotton, hemp, and other materials, a good deal of taste and ingenuity are shown. In these woven stuffs stripes are largely employed, and in the coarser and cheaper fabrics made from the fibre of the rofìa palm, the colours are obtained from vegetable dyes and from various coloured earths. A very favourite style of *làmba* is what is termed *àrindràno*. In these the body of the stuff is of cotton woven into a strong twilled substance, the groundwork white, and with a number of narrow stripes of black, in which coloured threads are mixed. A broad black border runs along each edge in the length of the làmba, and each has a coloured pattern of tasteful design in the centre. The most striking examples of native design are, however, seen in the silk làmbas. These are of considerable variety of pattern and colouring (within certain conventional limits), often extremely rich and elegant in their effect, and with a peculiar kind of square leaf or flower introduced into the stripes, and various combinations of small diamond-shaped patterns.

Another thoroughly native style of ornament is seen in the dark-red làmbas worn by the chief men of many districts, and in which fine metal beads are woven into the stuff in a variety of patterns across the ends of the làmba.

In silver work, the native silversmiths are very ingenious and skilful. With a few very rude tools they produce filagree work, and excel in making minute and delicate silver chains of wonderful fineness. They are very quick in imitating any pattern given to them, and will make perfect copies of European jewellery with such exactness that it is difficult to tell which is the original and which the copy. This manual dexterity shown by the Hovas extends to all kinds of metal work; they are equally skilful in working iron, copper, brass, and tin.

Considerable artistic feeling is also to be seen in the beautifully fine mats and baskets which the Hova women plait from the straw of various grasses. In some of these patterns are formed by the straw being dyed in red and black; but in the majority of the straw work there are elaborate and tasteful designs formed without colour, and so as to be only seen on a close inspection.

In pottery the Hovas do not show so much inventive power as in their textile productions. Except in one class of work, the few articles which they manufacture are devoid of all ornament. The exception to this usual absence of any artistic feeling is in the earthen pots called *vilàny nòngo*, which are made for cooking the beef eaten at the New Year's festival. These vessels are circular, and somewhat flattened, and are frequently ornamented with a series of lines and zigzags, very closely resembling those on the early fictile productions of the Germanic races.

Bétsiléo Art.—Having for many years seen little of any Malagasy tribe except the Hovas, and having often wondered at the almost entire absence of decorative carving amongst them, I was greatly interested when taking a journey in 1876 into the southern central province of Bétsiléo to find, very soon after leaving the territory of the Hovas, that their neighbours to the south employ carving very abundantly, both in their houses and their burial memorials. There is among these Bétsiléo people a decided and special style of ornament, used not only in their dwellings and tombs, but also in many of their household utensils, as spoons, gourds, dishes, &c.; and a kind of tattooing is also very common among them, in which personal adornment some of the same ornamental details are also introduced.

I first noticed something new in the tombs in the tract of country between Isàndrandàhy and Ambòsitra (about four days' journey south of Antanànarìvo). Within two or three hours' journey of the latter place, I observed that the upright stones placed near the graves were not the rough undressed blocks or slabs common in Imérina, but were finely dressed and squared, and ornamented with carving. During my stay at Ambòsitra, I walked to the top of the rising ground on the western slope of which the village is principally built. Here there is an old *amòntana* tree, and a memorial to one of the early kings of the Bétsiléo. It is a piece of timber seven or eight inches square and about ten feet high, having pieces of wood projecting from a little below the top so as to form a kind of stage. Each face of the timber is elaborately carved with different patterns arranged in squares. Some of these are concentric circles, a large one in the centre, with smaller ones filling up the angles; others have a circle with a number of little bosses in them; others have a kind of leaf ornament; and in others parallel lines are arranged in different directions. The narrow spaces dividing these squares from each other have in some cases an ornament like the Norman chevron or zigzag, and in others something similar to the Greek wave-like scroll. The whole erection with its ornamentation bears some resemblance to the old Runic stones, and the memorial crosses in Ireland and parts of the Scottish Highlands. The north face of this memorial post was quite sharp and fresh, but the others were worn by the weather, and the carving was filled up with lichen.

Not very far from this memorial there were some others, consisting of two pairs of posts, each with a lintel, like a gateway, except that the opening was filled up by a large flat upright stone. These posts were carved much in the same style as the single one just described, but were not so massive, and were more weathered. The tops of the posts were carved into a shape somewhat resembling a vase. I then remembered that we had passed a newly-set-up memorial stone carved in three large squares, with much the same kind of ornament as these posts had in wood.

On the journey from Ambòsitra to Fianàrantsoà (the capital of the Bétsiléo), at about two hours' distance from the former place, we passed a tomb by the road-side with a carved wooden post similar to those at Ambòsitra. Some of the carving was similar to what we had already seen, but there were other graceful forms which were new, and some of the compartments were like the English Union Jack. But it was on the following day, when passing over an elevated line of road between Nandihìzana and Ambòhinamboàrina, that I was most astonished and delighted by the profusion with which these carved memorials were scattered all along the road-side, as well as in all directions over the tract of country visible on either hand. At one ancient town especially, called Ikangàra, we found a large number and great variety of these specimens of native art in tombs and memorial posts, as already described in the chapter on Malagasy Tombs and Burial Customs.

I regretted that our journey being made chiefly for the purpose of seeing districts farther south than the Bétsiléo, we were unable to visit some of the more important old towns in their province, where there is said to be a great deal of the peculiar carving, not only in the tombs, but also in the dwelling-houses and furniture. We did, however, see two specimens of this native art as used in building : first, just before entering the Tanàla country, and again, immediately on leaving the forest on our return home. The first example was at a village called Ivàlokiànja; in the house where we stopped was the first example I had seen of decorative carving in Malagasy houses, the external faces of the main posts being carved with a simple but effective ornament of squares and diagonals. There was also other ornamentation much resembling our national flag. The gables were filled with a neat platted work of split bamboo. The other example was at a small hamlet called Ifandrìana. The three centre posts of the house in which we stayed were all covered with carving of much the same character as that used in the memorial posts already described, but it was not quite so well executed. The nearly square window-shutters had each a circular ornament carved upon them, much like the conventional representations of the sun, with rays proceeding from a centre.

One of the most perfect examples of the carved memorial post we saw the same day, in the morning, at the picturesquely-situated village of Ivòhitràmbo. This village is perched like an eagle's nest on the summit of a lofty cone of rock, on the edge of the interior highland, and overlooking the great forest, the country of the Tanàla tribes, above which it towers about 2500 feet. This memorial was close to the village, and was very perfect, the carving very sharp, and the stage near the top in good preservation, with about thirty ox skulls and horns still in their places. In many cases, figures of oxen and men are carved in some of the panels or compartments of these memorial posts, but the ornament is chiefly conventional.

Of Bétsiléo ornament, Mr. G. A. Shaw says : "It is a significant fact that the *simple* designs are almost identical with the same species of ornamentation in Polynesia." *
On a carved hatchet handle from Mangaia in his possession

* *Antanànarìvo Annual*, No. iv. p. 11.

are some patterns precisely like those on the Bétsiléo spoon handles.

Before leaving the subject of Bétsiléo art, it may be remarked that gourds, fifes, tobacco-boxes (a piece of finely-polished bamboo), and other articles are often very tastefully ornamented with patterns incised on the smooth yellow surface, the lines being filled in with black. These patterns consist of lines, zigzags, scrolls, and diaper grounds, often very artistically arranged.

It may be hoped that those who reside in the province will carefully examine these interesting examples of indigenous art, and describe and copy the most characteristic examples. Hardly anything but photography and the autotype process could adequately reproduce the many varieties of elaborate carving that are to be found; but much might be done by a few careful measurements and sketches. Many of the finest specimens of carving in the memorial posts are being fast obliterated by the action of the weather, and if not secured within a few years the patterns carved upon them will be past recovery. And it is very possible that the influence of foreigners (whether intentional or not) will eventually lead to the discontinuance of this primitive style both of memorial and of ornament. As examples of indigenous art, therefore, it is highly desirable that they should be copied as soon as possible; and perhaps it might be practicable to secure a few examples of the best carved pieces of timber themselves, and have them carefully deposited in some place of safety for reference and preservation. Apart from their intrinsic interest, these carvings may prove of value in showing links of connection between the Bétsiléo and some of the Malayan races, and thus afford some light towards a better understanding of the ethnology of Madagascar.

CHAPTER XIV.

MALAGASY FOLK-LORE AND POPULAR SUPERSTITIONS.

ANIMALS—BIRDS—FABULOUS ANIMALS—TREES AND PLANTS—LUCKY AND
UNLUCKY DAYS AND TIMES—ORDEALS—FOLK-LORE OF HOME AND
FAMILY LIFE—LUCKY AND UNLUCKY NUMBERS, ACTIONS, ETC.—SICK-
NESS AND DEATH—WITCHCRAFT AND CHARMS.

THE Folk-Lore of the various tribes inhabiting Madagascar has
been as yet but slightly studied, and no one has up to the
present time made any systematic examination of the curious
superstitious beliefs which are found in the island. But as
there exists a considerable amount of information on these
points scattered through different books—notes of journeys,
miscellaneous pamphlets, and magazines published only in
Madagascar—which are inaccessible to the general reader, it
will perhaps be worth while to collect these together in the
present chapter, in the hope that attention may be directed
to the subject, and that those who reside in the island may
be led to inquire more minutely into the noteworthy facts
which still invite research.

That there is a reason to suspect the existence of much
more that is curious in Folk-*Lore* may be inferred from the
fact that within the last three or four years a large number
of most interesting Folk-*Tales* have been discovered, of the
existence of which, for the most part, we who had resided in
the country for several years had no suspicion. But as these
Folk-Tales are sufficiently important to require a separate
chapter to themselves, we shall not refer to them now, but
endeavour, by grouping our information under various heads,
to show how much there is of interest in the Folk-Lore,
properly so called; while the following chapter will be
devoted to the idolatry and religious beliefs and practices of

the people of Madagascar, and the notions they entertain about a Supreme Being.

Animals.—It may, perhaps, be convenient to commence by describing some of the superstitions which exist among the Malagasy as connected with animals.

As is the case almost throughout the world, <u>serpents are held in great dread,</u> although, unlike most tropical countries, Madagascar is singularly free from noxious reptiles of this order. In the greater part of the interior there are no venomous snakes, and there are probably only two or three species at most which are harmful in the warmer coast plains. But curiously enough, with this dislike of the reptile there exists also, as in other countries again, a belief in its connection with the healing art; for one of the chief idols of the central province, which was the god of healing and of medicine, was held also to be the patron of serpents, and to be able to employ them as the agents of his anger should any one become obnoxious to him. And so, when this idol, Ramàhavàly, was carried abroad, his attendants used each of them to carry a sepent in his hand, which, as it writhed and twined about him, inspired terror in the beholders.

There is a curious belief about a species of serpent called *màrolòngo,* which inhabits the mounds made by a white ant called *vitsikàmbo.* Mr. Grainge, in his notes of a visit to the north-west coast, says : " We noticed a large number of earthen mounds, varying from one to two and a half feet in height ; these were the nest of a large ant, credited by the people with uncommon sagacity. We were told that they make regular snake-traps in the lower part of these nests, easy enough for the snake to enter, but impossible for it to get out of. When one is caught the ants are said to treat it with great care, bringing it an abundant and regular supply of food until it becomes fat enough for their purpose ; and then, according to native belief, it is killed and eaten by them." " There is no doubt," says another resident (Rev. R. Toy), " that the belief is most universal among the natives. I have been assured most confidently over and over again that it is a fact that snakes are kept and fattened by the ants as above described." Perhaps we have here a piece of natural history, and not a fanciful notion; for a similar belief is related by Mr. Bates in *The Naturalist on the Amazons*, as held by the people with regard to a species of serpent found in the Amazons valley.

A much more formidable reptile in Madagascar than the serpent is the *crocodile*, which swarms in every river and lake, and is not a little destructive to human life. About this creature, accordingly, a good deal of fable has been evolved from the imagination of the people; and from their dread of its power, they will never kill one except in retaliation for one of their friends or neighbours who has been destroyed by a crocodile. They believe that the wanton destruction of one of these reptiles will be followed by the loss of human life, in accordance with the principle of *lex talionis*. The inhabitants living in the neighbourhood of the lake Itàsy, to the west of the central province, are accustomed to make a yearly proclamation to the crocodiles, warning them that they shall revenge the death of some of their friends by killing as many *voày* in return, and warning the well-disposed crocodiles to keep out of the way, as they have no quarrel with them, but only with their evil-minded relatives who have taken human life. On the principle of "taking a hair of the dog that bit them," a crocodile's tooth is worn as an amulet or charm, and silver ornaments made in that shape formed a chief part of the adornment of the people in former times (see frontispiece to *History of Madagascar*, vol. i.), while a golden crocodile's tooth formed the central ornament in the royal crown. From this dread of the supposed supernatural power of the crocodile, it is invoked by prayers rather than attacked; even the shaking of a spear over a stream is dreaded as likely to give offence to the reptiles and provoke their vengeance the next time the offender ventures on the water; while to throw dung into the water was a heinous offence.

Mr. Grainge mentions that along the river Bétsibòka the people believe that "crocodiles live chiefly on stones, stealing cattle, pigs, and people merely as a relish to the harder fare. Also, that smitten by the charms of the pretty little divers and other water-birds, they choose their mates from among

them, and so crocodiles' eggs are produced." * Among the
Antankàrana, in the extreme north of Madagascar, the people
believe that the spirits of their chiefs pass into crocodiles,
those of inferior people being transformed into other animals ;
and doubtless this belief leads to their being unmolested
except in the cases already mentioned. A similar belief is
also held by the Bétsiléo.

The belief in a kind of transmigration of souls is also connected with other animals besides the crocodile. The pretty
species of lemur called Babacoote, is believed by the Betàni-
ména tribe to be an embodiment of the spirits of their ancestors, and therefore they look with horror upon killing
them. They have as much repugnance to killing the harmless and timid little Aye-aye, so interesting to naturalists,
although it is not quite clear that it is from the same notion
respecting them. Accordingly, it is very difficult to obtain
one, as the natives believe that any one killing an Aye-aye
will die within the year, and that evil will follow from their
even seeing one of them. Dr. Sandwith, who procured the
first specimen sent to England, from which the creature was
described by Professor Owen, was only able to overcome this
dread by offering the large sum of fifty dollars for a single
animal.

The spirits of those who die unburied are believed to be
doomed to associate with, if not to become, wild cats, owls,
and bats. And there is much the same opinion with regard
to the spirits of certain criminals, especially those who are
killed for supposed sorcery. The above-mentioned animals
are therefore all of evil omen, and in most parts of the
country the people look with horror upon the keeping of a
wild or native cat, those who have one in their houses being
regarded as familiar with the black art. This cat is called
kàry, and is a beautifully marked animal, with stripings of
black on a grey ground. The European cat, on the other
hand, which is called *sàka*, is rather prized, and fetches a
good price in the markets.

There is also in many parts of the country a dislike to
goats, and also to pigs. Repeated proclamations have been

* *Antanànarìvo Annual*, No. i. p. 16.

made about the latter animals, ordering their removal to a distance of several miles from the capital city, and some tribes and families will not eat their flesh, considering it unclean.

The most valuable and plentiful of all the animals found in Madagascar, the large-humped *buffalo*, has some curious legendary history connected with it. A king called Ralàmbo, the eleventh on the list of Hova sovereigns, is held in memory as the first who ventured to use it as food. It is said that before his time it was called *jamòka*, a word which is still in use as an adjective, meaning " gentle, easy, not harsh." But since then it has been called *omby*. This name is said in the story to be derived from the circumstance that Ralàmbo said, " *Omby, omby !* " (" Enough, enough !"), when the folds were filled with cattle. But it looks very much as if the story were invented to account for the word, which is most likely the same as the Swahíli *ngombé*. It has been conjectured that before Ralàmbo's time the ox had retained (in that part of Madagascar, at least) the semi-sacred character which it still bears among many nations, as with certain Himalayan tribes, the Veddahs of Ceylon, the Kaffirs, and some peoples in the valley of the White Nile. The correctness of this supposition is confirmed by the fact that amongst several Malagasy tribes the office of killing an ox is one which belongs only to the chief, who was, it must be remembered, a sort of high priest among his people. Thus, Drury says, " Few in this part of the island [south-west provinces] will eat any beef unless it is killed by one descended from a race of kings. My master and his brother, to execute these high offices were sometimes obliged to go five or six miles to kill an ox." Among the Taimòro people, on the south-east coast, the writer found the same custom to prevail. At a large village called Ambòtaka we were told that no bird or animal must be killed for food except by some one belonging to the family of the king. A relic of this custom still remains among the Hovas, for at the Fandròana, or New Year's festival, the fattened oxen to be killed are driven into the royal courtyard to be blessed by the sovereign. An ox without blemish is killed, and the hump being cut off is brought to the sovereign to be tasted, as a

sort of first-fruits. After this the people take their cattle
home and kill them. Connected with this doubtless is the
fact that in many Malagasy tribes they do not kill oxen,
although they have them in great abundance, unless at
funerals or other very important occasions. The Sàkalàvas
of Ménabé never kill a red bullock for food except in case
of absolute necessity, and then it is not slaughtered in the
ordinary manner, but with all the forms made use of when
sacrificing animals. A tribe in the Angàvo valley are said to
eat none of the flesh, but only the blood, of the oxen they
kill. In former times the Bétsiléo killed oxen only at reaping
times, while the Tanàla kill chiefly at planting time; but on
these occasions there is evidently some religious significance
in this bullock killing. The Tanàla offer a great deal of the
flesh upon altars in their fields.

Another noteworthy circumstance connected with the ox
is that the rump is the royal share of every ox killed. As
Dr. Davidson has pointed out, "The very name anatomists
give to this part is suggestive. It is called the *sacrum*, or
sacred part—the part devoted to the gods in Greece and
Rome. But tracing this up to a higher source, we find that
in the Levitical law, this part was specially directed to be
offered" (Lev. iii. 6–11); see *Sunday Magazine*, 1873, p. 674.

It is also worth notice that the same part of a fowl (*vòdi-
akòho*) is the proper portion to be given by children or in-
feriors to their parents or superiors; while the same portion
of a sheep is what is given by a man to the father and mother
of the girl whom he marries. This is now always a money
present, but it retains the original name, *vòdi-òndry*, and
makes a marriage legal and binding.

These three animals, it may also be observed, are those
esteemed by the Malagasy as proper to be sacrificed. These
sacrifices were sometimes holocausts, but more frequently what
are called meat-offerings in the Mosaic law, being feasted
upon by the offerers; while the blood and fat, as representing
the life and the best part of the animal, were alone offered.
These portions of the victim were smeared upon the upright
stones of the tombs as offerings to the ancestors, and also
upon other sacred stones and places.

Mr. Richardson says that the following curious notion in connection with oxen exists in some parts of the country:— " The top of a large ant-hill is frequently taken off and thrown at the rump of an ox that persists in returning to the town where it has been bought, and it is a belief firmly held by the cattle dealers that the animal will never return to its former owner after the operation."

The buffalo, being by far the largest and most powerful land animal known to the Malagasy, is continually used in their poetical and figurative language as the emblem and embodiment of strength and majesty, much as the bull was employed by the ancient Assyrians, and the lion by Western Asiatic and European nations. Thus, the kings were saluted as *Ombelàhy,* " bulls ; " and the same expression frequently occurs in forms of benediction at the circumcision and other festivities. In some tribes the chief is saluted as *Bìby,* a word usually meaning " animal " or " living creature," but probably intended as a figurative way of saying that he possesses all the power of the noblest animal forms. Bull-fighting was formerly a favourite Malagasy amusement, and numerous charms were used to make a favourite animal victorious.*

In the rejoicings connected with the ceremonies at the circumcision the ox has a prominent place. In the songs which are sung the animal is called by a special name, *Vòrihàngy,* instead of the common name, *òmby.* And every portion of the animal is apportioned to a particular person ; every one taking part in the slaughter of the ox having his proper share, as well as the old, the newly-delivered, the visitors, &c. This song is a kind of chant, with a chorus which is repeated at the end of every line, while the name of the ox (*vòrihàngy*) is also repeated in every stanza. Thus, leaving out the repetitions, the horns, the hoofs, the tongue, the ears and eyes of the animal, are each celebrated as having their special office ; while the brain is the share of the newly-delivered, the head to the beater of the drum, the neck to the owner of the axe, the hump to the children

---

* In digging out the foundations for a new palace gateway, a few years ago, the remains of one of the former Queen's fighting bulls were discovered, carefully wrapped up in a red làmba.

s

undergoing the ceremony, the shoulder to the fetchers of the
sacred water employed, the sirloin to the circumcisers, the
breast to the visitors, the ribs to make bodkins for parting
the hair, the dewlap to the blowers of the conch shells, and
so on, until every part of the creature has been appropriated,
and all concerned in the ceremonies or the killing have had
their proper share of the meat.

Another ancient saying as to the uses of the ox thus
apportions the different parts of the animal : "Its horns to
the maker of spoons, its teeth to the plaiters of straw, its
ears to make medicine for a rash, its hump to make fat, its
rump to the sovereign, its feet to the oil-maker, its spleen to
the old men, its liver to the old women, its lights to fathers
and mothers-in-law, its tripe to the owner of the rope, its
neck to the owner of the axe, its haunch to the herald, its tail
to the weaver, its suet to the soap-maker, its hide to the
drum-maker, its head to the chief orator, its eyes to make
beads, its hoofs to the gun-maker," &c.

Birds.—Turning from the quadrupeds to the *birds,* it has
already been remarked that owls were considered of ill-omen ;
and no one who has heard the unearthly screech of some of
the Madagascar owls can wonder that they should be held in
disfavour by a superstitious people.   Their name, *vòrondòlo,*
means "spirit-bird," and they are popularly supposed to be
embodiments of the departed spirits of evil men.   But there
is another bird which is also looked upon with dread should
it fly across the path a person is taking.   This is the *Tàkatra,*
a bird which builds a very large nest resembling an immense
heap of hay or grass when viewed from below.   No business
of importance would be undertaken by a Hova in former
times were his path crossed by one of these birds ; and if it
crossed the path before the chief idols these were obliged to
return to their houses.   It was also believed that any one
destroying the nest of the *tàkatra* would be seized with
leprosy.

Among the Tanàla people the diviners foretell events " by
means of good and bad birds, according to their notes, or the
way they take in flying, and they profess to know whether
they bring good or evil.   They look upon the kite as being a

bird of much evil omen. Should its droppings fall upon the head of any one, he is watched as sure to die; the people mourn for him and kill oxen to ward off the impending death." *

Then again, the laying by a fowl of an unusually large egg is regarded as ominous either of some extraordinary good or evil, while an unusually small egg is feared as foreboding evil. Something of the same feeling comes up in the name given to a small insect which attacks the young rice-plants. It is called *Ondrikélin' Andriamánitra*, "God's lamb;" it appears to be regarded as an instrument of divine anger for men's wickedness.

The fables respecting animals and birds are numerous, and sometimes very amusing, as giving ingenious reasons for their respective habits, likes and dislikes, &c. Thus there are conversations between "The Crocodile and the Wild Hog," "The Wild Hog and the Rat," "The Wild Hog and the Chameleon," "The Hedgehog and the Rat," "The Kingfisher and the Great Moth," "The Sìtry and the Antsiàntsy" (two species of lizards), "The Wild Cat and the Rat," "The Hawk and the Fowl," "The Fly and the Ant," &c., &c.

Fabulous Animals.—But besides these well-known animals the native imagination has pictured several wonderful creatures which have no existence except in the fancy of some story-teller of a past age. Among these is the *Songòmby*, a beast said to be the size of an ox, but of wonderful swiftness, and addicted to human flesh. Then there is the *Tòkan-dia* or *Tòkan-tòngotra* ("the single-footed"), a creature whose fore and hind legs are said to be each joined, so that it has only two feet altogether; also a beast of incredible swiftness, eating men, and only going abroad by night. Then there is the *Làlomèna*, a beast with red horns and as big as an ox, but living in water. But besides these fabulous stories there are others of strange serpents, described as of marvellous power, which very possibly have a basis of truth, since it has been ascertained that there is a species of boa in the western part of the island which drops from trees upon oxen and passing travellers.

But there is another creature also spoken of by the

* *Antanànarìvo Annual*, No. ii. p. 98.

Malagasy, especially by the Bétsiléo, in which there seems to be a curious mixture of fact and fable. This is the *Fanàny* or the *Fanànim-pitolòha* ("the Fanàny with Seven Heads"). This creature is variously described as a lizard, a worm, and a serpent, and is believed to come from the corpse of those of noble blood, and to be, in fact, an embodiment of their spirits. After the completion of the revolting practice of treating the bodies of such people (by so compressing the corpse that a putrid liquid exudes from the foot), the pots containing the liquid portion are taken great care of, for the corpse cannot be buried until a small worm appears in one or other of them. Two or three months are said to frequently elapse before this takes place. After the worm has increased in size the body may be buried; while the earthen pot with the worm is placed in the grave, but in it is also fixed a long bamboo reaching up to the outer air through an opening at the top. After six or eight months they say that this worm climbs up the path prepared for it and comes into the village. It is then like a lizard in appearance, and called *Fanàny.* The relatives of the deceased proceed to question the creature, asking if it is Such an one, and believe that they get an infallibly correct answer by its lifting its head. Thus assured, they make assurance doubly sure by fetching a plate off which the deceased ate his or her last meal, and in this plate the blood from an ox's ear, together with rum, are poured. The *fanàny's* drinking these liquids leaves no doubt as to its identity. A clean cloth is then spread, upon which the creature steps, and it is borne into the village with feasting and rejoicing. It is finally carried back to the tomb from which it emerged; there it remains (so they say) and becomes the guardian deity of the people living near, and grows to an enormous size.

The Rev. J. Richardson, from whose account the foregoing description is taken, says that, although he has never seen the *fanàny* itself, he knows for certain that the bamboo and earthen pot in the tomb, &c., are arranged as described. He adds: " And I have heard from the lips of the chief prince of one of the tribes, when his mother was dead, " She has not yet appeared in the earthen pot, and so I cannot bury her body." Of this prince's mother I know that for nearly three months from the time of her decease, as also the decease of her sister, and until the *fanàny* appeared, the people in the whole district were not allowed to dig or plant. There was danger of a famine, and the Hova authorities were obliged to interfere and hasten the appearance of this *fanàny*." *

In a native account of this marvellous creature it is said to have seven heads, whence its name, and each head has horns. At its death it swells to the size of a mountain, so that the villages near are uninhabitable from the effluvium; while there are other equally apocryphal stories of its ascending up to heaven, and of its taking refuge in the sea, where only it could have space to move about. The narrator says that the *fanàny* seen by him was the size and had the appearance of a small water snake called *tòmpondràno*. He confesses that he saw only one of its seven heads, but the people accounted for this deficiency by saying that the specimen he saw was still young. Evidently the doctrine of development was urgently needed in this case.

Trees and Plants.—There are several *trees* which have a somewhat sacred character among the Malagasy. Among these are the *Fàno*, a species of mimosa, which is frequently found growing over and around the tombs of the Vazìmba. The tombs of these ancient people were held in extreme veneration, and also the tree growing over them; the seeds were commonly used in the working of the divination or *sikìdy*. Another tree connected with idol worship is the *Hàsina*, a species of pandanus. The name of the tree implies its sacred character, *màsina* being the adjective used to describe consecrated or sacred things.

Another tree called *Zàhana* (*Bignonia articulata*), an evergreen with dark glossy leaves and pink flowers, is one frequently seen growing in Imérina as ornamental timber. But "there is an old superstition regarding it, and still believed in by many, to the effect that any one planting it in his grounds will meet with an early, if not sudden, death."

In the southern parts of Madagascar, among the Bàra and

* *Antandnarìvo Annual*, No. i. p. 74.

Tanòsy, the Tamarind tree (one of the finest of the trees growing in the island), and also the Baobab, have each a sacred character. In this latter tree there is a certain part considered as specially belonging to God. Portions of the tree are coloured black, white, and yellow, bound with mats, and decorated with charms.

Among the Sàkalàva, a tree called *Hàzomànitra* ("fragrant wood") is planted at the birth of the first child, as a witness that the father acknowledges it as his own.

The Malagasy do not, like the Polynesians, make much use of flowers in their festivities; but it was formerly the custom that those who accompanied the Queen, on her return from the ancient to the present capital, should all be decorated with flowers. The effect produced by several thousands of people, with their heads or head-dresses all adorned with flowers, was often extremely pleasing. Some flowers used to be considered as acceptable offerings to the idols; thus, a pink-petalled flowering plant, called *Vonénina*, was proper to be brought to the tutelar deity of the reigning family, while the other idols had also their appropriate flower offerings.

Flowers were also carried in the joyful procession which was formed of the friends and relatives of those people who had been cleared of guilt by the *tangéna* ordeal, and were then termed *madio*, "clean," or cleared of blame. These were fastened to small wands, and carried in the hand.

In the times when bull-fighting was common, the owners of the bulls held a plant called *Tsivalondriana* in their hands to ensure victory. Concerning a hard-wooded tree called *Hàzotòkana*, the Malagasy used to believe that if any part of it were brought into the house the rice-pans would be broken. And formerly, the root of a plant called *Vàrikitia* was brought by the father of a newly-born child (if the first-born), who held it over his head outside the house, then dashed it on the ground westwards, with the idea that the child was in some way or other benefited thereby.*

An edible arum, called *Sàonjo*, is always eaten at a Hova housewarming. But occasionally, possibly on the principle that "one man's meat is another man's poison," some of the

* Rev. R. Baron, in *Antanànarivo Annual*, No. iv. p. 115.

most nourishing vegetables are *fàdy*, or tabooed, by certain individuals or families. Thus, I was once warned that I could not.enter a certain house if I had amongst my property any arrowroot prepared from the manioc root, as that was *fàdy* to the owner of the house.

Lucky and Unlucky Days and Times.—Leaving now the natural objects, animal and vegetable, with which superstitious notions are associated in Madagascar, something may be said about *days and times*. The wide-spread belief in lucky and unlucky days is common to all the tribes in the island. The Malagasy month is, of course, a lunar one; indeed, the word for moon and month are the same. In some parts of the country there seems little use of a sevenfold division of time, but the days from one new moon to another are called by twelve names. These are the very same as the month names, and include two or three days respectively, which are distinguished as *vàva*, *vònto*, and *fàra* or *vòdy* ("mouth or opening," "swelling or increase," and "end or close") of that name. The Hova names for the months are all of Arabic origin, while those used on the coast are compounds of native words; but curiously enough, although these words, with slight variations in their form, are the same on both the eastern and western sides of the island, they are not synchronous. So that while the order of the twelve names is the same, the month Vòlambìta, for instance, is four months later in the east of Madagascar than on the western side of it. From the double meaning of month names, a very complicated system of lucky and unlucky times was formerly in use among the Hovas. Thus, out of the twenty-eight days of the month, twelve only are lucky. The *vàva* or first days of some months were especially disastrous to the children born on them, in some cases to the offspring of the people generally, and in others, to those born of the family or in the household of the sovereign. These were usually put to death by placing the new-born infant's head, face downwards, in a shallow wooden dish filled with lukewarm water. In certain cases, however, this fate might be averted by making prescribed offerings, or by undergoing an ordeal, as will be presently described. On the other hand, some days were considered as favourable for planting, commencing house-building, going on a journey, or a war expedition, &c.

Each tribe, however, has customs peculiar to itself. Thus, among the southern Tanàla we found that eight days in each month were considered unlucky, viz., those called Tsàratà, three days, Alakaòsy, two days, and Alijàdy, three days; and that children born on those days were put to death in the manner above described, so that a fourth of all who are born are destroyed.

Then we also learned that with them every day throughout each month has its *fàdy* or food which must not be eaten when travelling on that day. Thus, on the first day silk-worms must not be eaten; on the second Indian corn is prohibited, and so on successively, with sugar-cane, bananas, sweet potatoes, rice, yams, honey, earth-nuts, beans, *kàtsaka*, and *vòamàho.*

Among the Sihànaka tribe the people of a village called Anòrohorò are said to be almost like wild men, and are extremely superstitious, being addicted to astrology and the observance of days. Among them the twelve months have each their qualities of good or bad, and the month is also divided into the same number of parts; each day, even, they divide into a number of parts from morning to evening. And if a stranger comes to them on a day which they consider unlucky, or on one of the divisions of the day or of the month which is of bad omen, they will not allow him to enter the village, but make him remain outside, and there they bring him food. Should he, however, persist in coming in they say he will certainly come to harm, either dying in the town, or being so ill as to lose his senses, or will be lost and not find how to advance or retreat, becoming hopelessly adrift among the rushes on the water. For as this village is situated in the midst of a dense thicket of papyrus, there is no road to it except by canoe.[*]

Among the Bàra, if a child is born on a day which is unlucky to either its father only or its mother only it is not put to death, but if born on a day of evil omen to both parents it is buried alive in an ant-hill. The unfortunate

[*] *Antanànarìvo Annual*, No. iii. p. 61.

infant thus destroyed is called *nébo*, a term also employed as indicating the strongest reproach.[*]

Among the Tanàla one of the months called Faosa is extremely unlucky. "No one works on that month, no one changes his place of abode or goes about. If any one happens to be in the fields when the month comes in there he remains. Almost all children born in that month are buried alive in distant forest; but should the parents determine to let one live, they fetch the ômbiàsy or diviner." This functionary makes an expiatory bath, consisting of certain grass, herbs, and other articles placed in water, in which the child is bathed. This ceremony puts an end to the child's evil days, and the water and its contents are buried.[†]

Among one clan of the Sàkalàva all children born on Tuesdays are put to death, while almost every family has a day similarly ill-omened to their newly-born offspring.

The month called by the Hova Alakàosy was esteemed very unlucky; and among them and other Malagasy tribes the waning of the moon is an unfavourable time for any important undertaking. Among the Antankàrana the dead are only buried immediately after the new moon appears.

Before the destruction of idolatry in Imérina in 1869 every idol had a day sacred to it, on which day those who were especially its votaries abstained from work. Until quite lately the Sunday or Thursday were the lucky days for the Hova sovereign to go on a journey or commence any undertaking.

Ordeals. — Reference was just now made to a certain ceremony by which a child might be preserved from death, although born on an unlucky day. There are, however, many different ordeals in use among the Malagasy tribes, of which a short description may now be given.

Foremost among these is the well-known one of the *Tangéna* or poison ordeal.

The Tangéna is a small and handsome tree growing in the warmer parts of the island, and the poison is procured from the nut of its fruit. This in a small quantity acts as an

---

[*] *Lights and Shadows*, App. i. p. 5.
[†] *Antananarivo Annual*, No. ii. p. 100.

emetic, but in a larger dose as a virulent poison. The chief use of the tangéna ordeal was for the detection of witchcraft, by which the African races " understand the use of poisonous drugs for evil purposes." Dr. Davidson remarks * that the word "is in fact equivalent to the Φαρμακεία of the Greeks ; and as the terms Φαρμακὸς and *veneficus* were applied by the ancients to signify alike a physician, a sorcerer, and a poisoner, so in many of the African languages the same peculiarity obtains. This arises from the fact that among these and other primitive races the physiological effect of drugs, whether poisonous or medicinal, are ascribed to some magical power, either inherent in the substance itself or imparted to it by sorcery. Medicines are thus employed as charms both for causing and curing disease."

The use of *some* poison as an ordeal in Madagascar is probably of very ancient date, but it seems possible that the tangéna itself has not been used for a very long period. It was used chiefly for the detection of infamous crimes when ordinary evidence could not be obtained, such as witchcraft and treason ; and it was believed that there was inherent in the fruit some supernatural power, a kind of " searcher of hearts," which entered into the suspected person, and either cleared him of guilt or convicted him. The mode in which it was administered was by giving a portion of two nuts rubbed down in water or in the juice of a banana, the culprit having previously eaten a little rice and swallowed three small square-shaped pieces of a fowl's skin. Tepid water was after a few minutes administered to cause vomiting, and the proof of innocence was the rejection of these three pieces uninjured. But even if the ordeal was fairly administered, there was an amount of risk of poisoning ; and as it was frequently used to get rid of obnoxious persons, by a little management it could easily be made to yield an unfavourable result.

One of the most remarkable things in connection with this ordeal was the implicit faith of the people generally in its supernatural power, so that they would often demand of the authorities that it should be administered to them to clear

* *Journal of Anatomy and Physiology*, vol. viii. p. 97.

them of any possible suspicion, and this notwithstanding the certainty that some would fall victims to their credulity. As whole villages sometimes took the tangéna, the mortality caused by it was very great, and it was a fearful means of destruction with an appearance of fair dealing.

I have been told by native friends who had been obliged to take the ordeal during the persecution of Christianity that they were not freed from suspicion even after the pieces of skin had been rejected, but that for a day or two afterwards they were closely watched, and dared not even spit to get rid of the bitter taste caused by the poison. In that case they would have been put to death all the same. Happily, this absurd and cruel custom is now at an end in those parts of the island to which the Hova authority extends; for, by the Anglo-Malagasy treaty of 1865, the use of the tangéna ordeal was abolished for ever in Madagascar. There can, however, be no doubt that it is still believed in by numbers of the people. This was shown unmistakably quite recently (April 1878), for the prevalence of a very fatal epidemic fever led many of the people in a village only a few miles distant from the capital to resort to the tangéna, several dying from its effects. The Government, however, promptly interfered, and punished severely all the inhabitants of the place.

Among the Tanàla, or forest tribes, some other ordeals are in use, and it is curious that two of these are called *tangéna*, with another word added, as if the word had become equivalent to "ordeal" in meaning.*

One of these is termed *Tangén-Janahàry*, i.e., "the Creator's ordeal," and is administered as follows:—Water is heated in a pot, and as the water begins to boil some pieces of quartz, called *vàto vélona* (i.e., "living stones"), are slung in the water, so as not to touch the bottom of the pot. When this is done, the accused person is ordered to take the stone out of the pot, putting his hand under the stone, and bringing it out lying on the palm of his hand; he must then put the stone into cold water. He is then carefully watched until the next day, and should his hand not blister he is declared innocent. Yet if the accused himself should be the first to declare his

* *Antananarivo Annual*, No. ii. pp. 94, 95.

hand unblistered he is accounted guilty, and if accused of stealing he must pay the stipulated fine. The hand not blistering, and the accused having waited for others to declare him innocent, his accuser must give him one slave, and he is set free.

Another ordeal is that of *Tangém-bóay*, the "ordeal by crocodile." In this test the person suspected of wrong-doing is taken to a river in which there are many crocodiles. The people are assembled there. A man stands behind the accused and strikes the water thrice, and addresses the crocodiles, begging them to show whether the culprit is guilty or otherwise. He is then made to swim across the river and back again, and if he successfully accomplishes this, and is not hurt by the crocodiles, then the accusers are fined four oxen; the swimmer gets two, the king one, and the councillors one.[*] It may be presumed that few escape this ordeal with life.

Still another ordeal is called *Kodéo*, a word of obscure meaning. In this ceremony the accused is set upon a rice-mortar, and he is made to mutter. A man then approaches holding a large stick, with which he thrice strikes the earth, and thrice cuts the hair of the accused, throwing it to God, who is invoked to show his guilt or innocence by certain signs. Should the person be guilty it is said that he at once begins to tremble, to be purged, and to vomit; and some of them, although they do not die as they sit there, do not escape, for the lightning, it is said, soon strikes their houses. If, although guilty, he finds favour with his judges, they invoke God's mercy for him and purify him by lustration. Should the person be innocent he is sprinkled with water, in which silver rings have been allowed to stand, to make him well.

The drinking of the *Vòkoka*, or water mixed with earth taken from the tomb of a former sovereign, as a test of allegiance, may also be regarded as a species of ordeal.

Another ordeal must be mentioned which was formerly in use in Imérina. In the case of children born in the month of Alakàosy it was possible to avert the necessity of actually

---

[*] For a romantic story founded on this custom see *Chambers's Journal*, p. 309, December 1, 1849, "The Trial by Caïman," by Percy B. St. John.

destroying them by placing them at the entrance of the cattle-fold of the village, the oxen being driven over the spot where the hapless infant was laid. Should it happen that through any freak of the animals the child was avoided by them and so escaped death from their hoofs, it was considered to have overcome the evil fate, and its life was spared. It was usually sent away into some sequestered village, and not acknowledged as its father's offspring until some time had elapsed. It was believed that these children who escaped through this ordeal would live to be extremely rich. It is said that the present Prime Minister of Madagascar was thus exposed as an infant, having been born in the ill-fated month, but he escaped injury, and so has lived to be the most powerful chief minister the country has ever had as its ruler.

There is still one more custom in use in Madagascar having the character of an ordeal. This is called *Ràno-àn'-òrona,* "water in the nose," and is a test which is made by putting water in the nostrils, this being supposed to cause the guilty party to sneeze. So that if a person accuses another of theft the accused will say, "Come, let us both put water in our nostrils, if you dare test it, and see whether I stole or not ?"

Folk-Lore of Home and Family Life.—A few words may now be said about some popular Malagasy beliefs and superstitions having reference chiefly to home and family life.

The mention of sneezing just now reminds us that the world-wide superstition of some evil influence being at work when any one sneezes is equally prevalent in Madagascar. Thus, when a child sneezes its mother or nurse always repeats the common benediction, "*Hotahìn' Andriamànitra hianao,*" "God bless you," exactly as is done in Europe and other parts of the world.

When a child loses one of its first or milk-teeth the tooth is thrown over the house, a practice closely corresponding to what is common in some parts of England. Toothache is believed to be caused by a small worm in the offending tooth, and so the sufferer is described as being *maràry òlitra,* "poorly through the worm."

There is a common belief that the first spittle produced

after waking in the morning has medicinal virtue in healing a sore ear or eye. It is then called *ròra mafàitra*, " bitter or disagreeable saliva." And when a Malagasy passes anything with an offensive smell, as, for instance, a dead dog on the roadside, he always spits, as a kind of antidote. (Perhaps, however, this should not be regarded as a superstition, but as a sensible sanitary precaution.)

On entering a house, especially a royal house, it is improper to use the *left* foot on first stepping into it; one must " put one's best (or right) foot foremost." Then again, it is improper to lean against a chief's house, and it is highly indecorous to sit upon any royal property, such as cases of goods, &c.

In many parts of Madagascar it is common when giving a present of food for the donor to taste part of it himself, as an assurance that it is given in good faith and may confidently be eaten without any suspicion of its being poisoned. Much the same feeling is expressed in old forms of salutation, as *Sàrasàra tsy ambàka*, the two latter words meaning " not deceived, overreached, or beguiled." This is no superfluous assurance in some portions of the island, for the Bàra are said to live in such constant suspicion and dread of an enemy that they never wash in their houses, but only in the open air. And even then they only wash one side of the face at the time, leaving one eye open, and one hand grasping gun and spear.

Mention has been already made (Chapter X.) of the arrangements of a Hova house, and the sacred portion of it at the north-east corner, where, in time of war, the women sing the *ràry*, a chant or invocation imploring victory for their husbands and friends. The following is one of these chants :—

> " Although they have many guns,
> Although they have many spears,
> Protect Thou them, O God."

The *ràry* is also made use of at other times, as when there has been injury caused by hail, lightning, or waterspouts.

In this north-east corner the fixed bedstead always has its head towards the north, for the Hovas invariably sleep with their heads towards the north or east. Even in their tombs the dead are also laid in this direction, never with the head towards west or south. The entrance to the tomb is always on the western side. Other tribes, however, are not so particular as the Hovas about the position of their tombs.

In building a house the first corner-post set up is always at this sacred part of it. Several kinds of plants are attached to its base, and on the top is fixed a piece of silver chain, a sort of assurance that the owner will always have money in his dwelling. In the case of a royal house the post is sprinkled by the sovereign with sacred water brought from a special spring, and an invocation is pronounced imploring a blessing on the building.

Lucky and Unlucky Numbers, Actions, &c.—In the building of a house for the late sovereign all the measurements were regulated by the Queen's own *réfy*, or fathom, that is, the space between the tips of her fingers when the arms were extended; and the smaller dimensions were according to her span, a most awkward and troublesome fettering of the European architect in making his drawings. Besides this, no dimension was, if possible, of the unlucky numbers six and eight. These are considered as of bad omen, because *énina*, six, is the same in sound as the root of the word *manénina*, to regret, or feel remorse; while *válo*, eight, is similar in sound to *miválo*, to abjectly beg pardon, and also to *fàhavàlo*, an enemy. The word *fàhatélo*, third, is also used for enemy, possibly on the principle that "three are no company," so that it also has some disfavour attaching to it, as has also the word *fàhasìvy*, ninth, in some tribes, at least, amongst whom it is used to denote a malignant kind of spirit or ghost. It is probable that some, if not all, of these ill-omened numbers derive much of their discredit from their position in the columns of arrangements of numbers in working the divination or *sikìdy* (see next chapter).

Mr. Richardson says that the Bàra have a strong dislike to the singular number. "They will take nothing singly. You must offer two, and sometimes they will spend an hour or two in matching two beads. They call two 'one person' (*iraìka amin' olo*). If you offer one they always ask, '*Aìa ny vàliny?*' (Where is its partner?)" Perhaps, however, this love of the plural arises from nothing more than their covetous habit of mind, in short, by an apparent paradox, from their love of "Number One."

But of course some numbers are lucky, especially twelve, a number which appears in many connections. Thus the sovereign has *twelve* wives; there are *twelve* capital crimes, and *twelve* men who are appointed executioners for such offences; while in the proclamations *twelve* royal ancestors are often spoken of, and also the *twelve* ancient towns in Imérina, or, as they are usually on hills, they are called the "twelve sacred mountains."

The left hand and side appear to be regarded as more appropriate in circumstances of mourning than the right. Thus, after leaving off mourning for a deceased relation, the youngest son or daughter puts a little grease on the left side of the neck by the little finger of the left hand, a custom known as *mitendrilo.*

There are numerous acts and customs which are *fàdy* or tabooed in different parts of the country. Thus in some villages it is forbidden to enter with burdens carried by one man only; all must be borne by two men. Then "there is a belief prevalent among the carriers of burdens that if a woman should stride over their poles, the skin of the shoulders of the bearers will certainly peel off the next time of taking up the burden. A cooking-pot may not be used for ladling water out of a stream, or be put into a pool; an infringement of this is looked upon as a sure precursor of a wet day." Similar weather is expected should a man die on a journey and be buried on the downs where he dies.*

Of the river Fanìndrona in Bétsiléo, Mr. Shaw says, that although it is a splendid river, "on account of the superstition of the people deterring them from putting a canoe on it, is one of the greatest obstacles to travelling to and from the capital in the wet season. In one itinerating journey the only way of getting the writer's goods across was by balancing them upon the native water-pitchers, and a man swimming on each side propelling the cranky vessel forward. And

* Rev. J. Richardson, in *Antananarivo Annual,* No. iii. p. 84.

although scarcely a year passes without one or two being drowned, yet no inducement is sufficiently strong to overcome their superstitious dread of allowing a canoe to be used." *

Mention has been made in the chapter on Malagasy *Names* of much that is curious in connection with them, but there are two or three facts that may be perhaps more appropriately considered as illustrations of folk-lore. For instance, it is often difficult to get persons to tell you their name; if asked, their attendants or slaves will reply for them; indeed in some places it is *fàdy* for a person to pronounce his own name. Mr. Grainge says, "Chatting with an old Sàkalàva while the men were packing up, we happened to ask him his name, whereupon he politely requested us to ask one of his servants standing by. On expressing our astonishment that he should have forgotten this, he told us that it was *fàdy* for one of his tribe to pronounce his own name. We found this was perfectly true in that district." †

There is a custom called *Tatào*, which consists in placing on the head a portion of the rice, honey, and meat eaten at the New Year's feast. But it is also employed on other occasions; thus, when crossing a stream which is dangerous either from the strength of the current or the number of crocodiles in it, those who have passed in safety take a handful of the water and put it on their heads, apparently as a sign of thanksgiving. This practice seems to be a relic of some ancient form of worship. Among the Bétsiléo the word *tatào* is applied to heaps of stone and rubbish, called by the Hovas *fànatàovana* (see next chapter).

Sickness and Death.——It will be readily supposed that amongst the Malagasy there are many strange observances and beliefs connected with death. Some of these have been already described in the chapters on their Burial Customs, and on their Language, but there are others more strictly belonging to the present subject.

At the death of a sovereign there are a number of things which become *fàdy*, and must not be done for a specified

* *Antanànarivo Annual*, No. iv. p. 77.   † *Ibid.* No. i. p. 24.

T

time, usually extending over several months, and in some
cases lasting a year.   Thus at the death of Radàma I. not
only was almost every one ordered to shave the head, but also
to use no showy dress or ornaments or unguents, not to ride
on horseback, or be carried in a palanquin ; not weave silk, or
make pottery, or work in the precious metals, or manufacture
sugar ; no carpentry work was to be done, or writing, or
plaiting of straw ; no salutations were to be used, or musical
instruments played, and dancing and singing were prohibited ;
no beds, tables, or chairs were to be used, and no spirits were
to be drunk.*   At the decease of the late Queen Ràsohérina
in 1868 it was ordered that no musical instrument should
be played, that there be no building in clay, or manufacture
of pottery, that no one lie on a bed, or spin, or prepare silk,
and in case of death the corpse was to be buried without any
killing of bullocks or the usual ceremonies.

The trouble the Malagasy take about their tombs is partly
accounted for by their belief that the spirit of the departed is
unrestful if the body remains unburied.   There also exists a
general belief throughout the country in pollution as connected with death.   Thus no one who has been at a funeral
can enter the palace or approach the sovereign unless a
month has elapsed, and no corpse is allowed to be buried in
the capital city, or to remain in it beyond a very short time.
The rough bier on which the body is carried is thrown away
in the neighbourhood of the grave as polluted ; no one would
dare to use it even for firewood, but it is left to decay with
the weather.   Besides this, after a funeral the mourners all
wash their dress, or at the least dip a portion of it in running water, a ceremony which is called *àfana*, "freed from,"
and is supposed to carry away the uncleanness contracted
from contact with or proximity to a corpse.

Among the Sàkalàva such is the dread of death that when
it occurs in one of their villages they break up their settlement, and remove to a distance before rebuilding their slight
houses.   They seem to believe that the spirit of the deceased
will haunt the spot, and do some harm to those who stayed

* *History of Madagascar,* vol. ii. p. 398.

where it had lived in the flesh. This perpetual fleeing before death, of course, prevents the population from becoming settled in its habits, and produces a most unsubstantial style of house-building. The same notion is also found among the Bàra.*

Something of the same superstition prevails in other tribes. Thus the Sihànaka do not pull down the house or go away from the village, as do the Sàkalàva, but they leave it, and allow it to fall to pieces of itself. Such deserted dwellings they call *tràno fòlaka*, "broken houses." †

These same people, when taking a corpse to the grave, have an earthen dish filled with burning cowdung carried on a man's head, and this is placed at the headstone. They say that the reason of this is that the dead person may be able to get fire should he chance to be cold.

"When the corpse has been placed in the grave a man knocks at the door of the tomb, or on the stone covering it, should there be no door, and calls out, 'O thou, Such an one, whoever it is that has bewitched you, let him not hide, let him not be concealed, but break him upon the rock, that the children may see it, that the women may see it;' and all there also join in the adjuration." ‡

Among this same tribe, should any one happen to be seriously ill, he is taken secretly out of the village and conveyed to some out-of-the-way place, where no one is allowed to see him except those who nurse him. §

It is said that among the southern Tanàla the people are accustomed, when any of their relatives are ill and become insensible, to take and place them in a part of the forest where they throw their dead; and should the unfortunate creatures so cast away revive and return to the village, they stone them and kill them outright.

Among these same Tanàla, they call sudden death *fòla-mànta* ("broken-unripe"), and "such deaths are ascribed to witchcraft. The diviner is fetched, and he consults the oracle; and wrapping up some grains of black sand, places them on the head of the corpse, saying, 'He who is caught

* *Antanànarìvo Annual*, No. ii. p. 46.   † *Ibid.* No. iii. p. 66.
‡ *Ibid.* p. 65.   § *Ibid.* p. 63.

carrying his cloth (*i.e.*, his dress) within a month is mine.' They think that the black sand will make the person who bewitched the deceased to go about naked; and, therefore, should such a one be caught at such practices during the month he is killed." *

Witchcraft and Charms.—It will be inferred from the above, what indeed is the fact, that those who practise witchcraft are accustomed to go about naked, but this is, of course, done by night, and the *lámba* or outer dress is carried on the head. To dance on tombs is said to be another action commonly done by *mpámosávy* or sorcerers.

Although to practice sorcery was a capital crime, it appears to have been very prevalent; indeed the sorcery which consists in a use of charms of various kinds is still practised almost all over the island. When it was wished to do injury to any one, a basket containing various small articles, each having a symbolic meaning, was laid at his door. Shortly before the revolution in 1863, Mr. Ellis had such charms betokening evil to him laid at his door or window for more than a week. "This charm consisted of a small basket, three or four inches in diameter and depth, in which were two pieces of granite stone, called 'death stones.' A hole was burned in the basket, which indicated calamity by fire. Amongst the contents were hedgehog's bristles, parts of scorpions or centipedes, hair, earth said to be from a grave, and other strange ingredients." †

Charms or *ódy* (*óly*, in some parts of the country) are used for all sorts of purposes: thus there are *ódifáty*, a cordial for exhilarating in circumstances of extreme sorrow or danger; *ódifitía*, a philtre or love charm; *ódimahéry* or *ódirátsy*, a malignant charm, &c. There were also certain charms thrown towards an enemy before a battle as a means of ensuring victory. And as soon as one goes away from the Christianised portions of Madagascar one meets with numbers of charms worn by the people, and designed to protect from various evils or to procure certain benefits. Thus, among the Bàra, Tanàla, and east-coast tribes, every one carries

* *Antanànarìvo Annual*, No. ii. p. 98.
† *Madagascar Revisited*, p. 271.

charms round his neck. These are small pieces of wood, some being smeared with animal oil, and others with castor-oil, those belonging to rich people being ornamented with beads and anointed with fat. Occasionally these charms are tied round their knees, or fastened round the chest; some are small pieces of wood shaped like a little canoe; others are lemur's bones, both from the hands and feet; others are small wooden figures of men; others are figures of women, or of oxen, with a variety of other small objects. "This lemur's foot," said the people, "we call *tsimòkotra*, and it is a charm against fatigue; and the meaning of this little canoe is, that we shall not be upset, and if we swim we shall get across safely." And the little human figures they call a charm for obtaining spoil and getting plenty of slaves; and the figure of a woman is to aid in obtaining women; and as to the figure of an ox, they say of it that those who possess it will get abundance of cattle.* There are other charms also called *sàmpilàhy* or *òdi-bàsy*, that is, charms against a gun. These are pieces of a bullock's horn, from three to five or six inches of the tip; they are ornamented with tin, or with small beads worked in patterns; the cavity is nearly filled with the ashes of certain trees or plants of supposed magical power, and mixed with fat or bees'-wax; in this composition are stuck a number of large needles. These *òdi-bàsy* are supposed to render the wearer invulnerable, being an unfailing protection against a musket-ball.

Mr. Richardson says of these Bàra people: "The charms are very numerous;" and in addition to the gun-charm just described, "the men wear from two to twenty-nine (the greatest number I counted), others on the head, or slung from the shoulder and across the breast." "They have unbounded confidence in these charms, and will not part with them except on exorbitant terms." "Should you show a man that his charms are useless, he will only agree to the belief that you have a more powerful charm than his own, and which he is prepared to buy at any price." According to the same authority, the Bàra have many prohibited acts

* *Antananarivo Annual*, No. ii. p. 63.

(*fàdy* or tabooed), for which fines are imposed.   Thus, "for
sitting or reclining on another person's bed, a fine of one ox,
or to be shot.   For striding over a person, or for striding
over the foot even, the same.   For brushing a person's face
or any part of his body even with any part of your clothing,
the same.   For using spoons, plates, or drinking vessels belonging to another person, the same.   Children while young
are exempt from the penalties ; but when a child arrives at
an age when he may be trusted with a spear, he is given in
charge of his mother, who takes him from home for a month,
and instructs him in his duty to his fellow-men, especially
urging him to beware of incurring a fine, or running the risk
of being shot.   On his return, should he commit any of the
above offences the father will pay the fine, but disinherit his
child ; and on the second offence will drive him from the
place."

Of the Bétsiléo charms, Mr. Shaw says that they consist " for the most part of pieces of wood about a span in
length, cut from various trees, some growing only, it is said,
in distant places, and hence costing considerable sums of
money ; " and that he has in his possession between twenty
and thirty *òdy*, of each of which he had ascertained the use.
Some are believed in simply as medicine, the sticks being
rubbed on a stone, and the dust thus grated off eaten by the
sick.   One is used as an antidote to any poison an enemy
may have placed in the ford ; while others are efficacious for
curing cuts and open wounds, delirium, sudden illness, as
protection from thieves, lightning, crocodile, &c. *

Among such customs may be counted one found among
the Sihànaka.   In a certain place is a small hole, into which,
if you can pitch a stone, you will be rich and prosperous.
Among these people also, as amongst other tribes, a white
earth is plastered over the face as a cure for certain com-
plaints.   The Hovas are also accustomed to put patches
of this substance on their faces on some festive occasions.
Thus, at the coronation of Queen Rànavàlona I., her
majesty's forehead was marked with this white clay, which is

---

* *Antananarivo Annual,* No. iv. pp. 5, 6.

called, probably from this use of it, *tàny ràvo*, or "joyful earth."

The charms which were used to procure victory in the bull-fights have already been mentioned; and many charms are also employed to secure a favourable result in the *tangéna* ordeal.

There is a curious custom formerly in use among the Bétailéo, and still practised by other southern tribes, which is called *Sàlamànga*, a kind of incantation to induce the "spirit of evil," which they believe possesses every one who is ill, to leave the body in which it has entered and pass into other bodies. Mr. G. A. Shaw, in his *Notes of a Journey to Ikòngo* (South-east Madagascar), and also from information he has kindly supplied me with, gives the following particulars of the ceremonies employed:—" To compass this object many forms are gone through under the direction of a diviner. On the roof of the house were placed pieces of white wood, pointed and painted in cross-bars of black and red, and stuck in the thatch near the ridge, so as to resemble the horns of the old-fashioned Malagasy houses. About three feet from the door was planted a forked branch of a tree, also resembling horns, having the bark peeled off from the joint upwards. Those in the roof were to induce the spirit to ascend them and so leave the house. That near the door is to prevent any stranger, or any one coming from a house of mourning, from entering the house, as that would break the spell. Then twice every day a dance is performed. The *òdy* or household charms are brought into the courtyard, and placed on the wooden rice-mortar together with a dollar. A cloth or mat is spread over this, and upon the whole the sick person is seated, dressed in a most curious fashion. One had on, among other ornaments, a conical fool's cap, decked with leaves and flowers, and a great tassel at the tip. Then drums and bamboos were beaten, and the native guitar, banjo, and flute played, the whole village forming a circle round the sick person and clapping hands, while the women and girls sang a monotonous refrain. Then a woman of rank appointed for the occasion began to dance, while another, seated behind the sick persons, began to beat a worn-out spade, suspended by a string, with a hatchet, quite close to their ears, making a horrid din. I thought as I stood by that if it wanted anything to make an indisposed person downright ill this would be a good recipe. The idea of this is to drive the *àngatra* (evil spirit) possessing the sick person into one of those dancing. But the two sick persons sat perfectly motionless, while the drums were beaten louder and louder, and more and more voices and hands joined in the chant and the clapping until it reached a perfect shriek; when I was rather astonished by seeing the two sick girls jump up and commence dancing round the inside of the circle formed by the performers. All this goes on twice, and sometimes three times, a day, and if the sick persons are not speedily cured appeal is made to the diviners, who tell them that not enough rum has been brought, or enough beef, or that the persons dancing are not of high enough rank, or anything else for an excuse."

NOTE.—Since the above was written I notice in the 4th No. of the *Antanànarivo Annual,* p. 41, the following items of curious superstitious practices related by the Rev. P. G. Peake of the Bezànozàno tribe : —" At the funeral, if the heir is young, the fruit of a very bitter creeper (*hòfika*) is cooked for him, that he may learn to bear hardship and have a foretaste of endurance, lest he consume foolishly his possessions. If a person of consequence dies, the horns of the gable-ridge of the house are broken off, and the appellation *An-tràno jòloka* ('at the house of humiliation') is given to it."

CHAPTER XV.

MALAGASY IDOLATRY AND RELIGIOUS BELIEFS AND OBSERVANCES.

IDOLS AND THEIR WORSHIP—SACRIFICES—ATONEMENT AND EXPIATION—ALTARS
AND SACRED STONES AND PLACES—DIVINATION—AMBRÒNDROMBÉ, THE
MALAGASY HADES—NEW YEAR'S FESTIVAL.

THE subjects of the preceding chapter and the present one are
so closely connected that it is impossible to draw a rigid line
of distinction between them, for curious superstitious notions
are mingled with all the religious beliefs and practices of the
Malagasy. But as a matter of convenience, they may be considered under the separate headings given to the present and
preceding chapters.

Idols and their Worship.—The Malagasy occupy a middle
position among heathen nations : on the one hand, they have
never sunk so low as some of the South African peoples, the
Australian aborigines, and other tribes, who appear to have
lost all idea of a God or a spiritual existence, and have, therefore, no words for such ideas ; and, on the other hand, their
idolatry has never been developed into a system, with an
elaborate mythology and an organised worship, such as is
found in such fulness in India and other Eastern countries.
In Madagascar there are no temples or regular worship, and
nothing like shrines, pilgrimage, penance, asceticism, and self-
torture, and there is no priesthood, properly so called. The
people undoubtedly have the religious instincts far less developed than is seen among the Hindoos and many other
Asiatics. The idolatry of the Malagasy generally is indeed a
fetishism or worship of charms, such as are described in the
last chapter. But among the Hovas there had grown up, in
comparatively modern times, an idolatry somewhat different
from the charm-worship common to the people of the island

generally, and of this a few particulars may not be without interest.

When Europeans first went up to the interior province of Imérina in the early years of the present century, they found a number of idols held in veneration by the people, in addition to the household idols or *sàmpy* common to every house, and those held in special veneration in different villages and districts. Of these idols, some fifteen or sixteen in number, four were especially famous, and were regarded as the protectors of the kingdom and the sovereign. These four were, however, nothing more than charms, some of them, if not all, having, according to tradition, been brought from distant parts of the island, and seem, through some accidental circumstance, to have acquired fame for their supposed supernatural powers.

First in rank and estimation was the idol Rakélimalàza (*i.e.*, " Little (yet) renowned "). This was especially the protector of the kingdom, and was supposed to make the sovereign invincible, to protect from crocodiles, from sorcery, and from fire.

From a drawing given to me by a native friend whose family was the hereditary guardian and keeper of one of these chief idols, it appears that Rakélimalàza consisted simply of three small pieces of the wood of some sacred tree, wrapped round with white silk. It was kept at a large village called Ambòhimànambòla, distant about six miles east of the capital; and it, like the other chief idols, had a house appropriated to it. The office of idol-keeper was hereditary, and was one both of honour and profit, those who held it having several privileges belonging to no other subjects, such as the right of carrying a scarlet umbrella, the badge of the royal family, and in some cases of being not subject to the punishment of death for any offence. The principal idols were usually kept in a box, and were occasionally anointed with castor-oil and other unguents, a ceremony having apparently some religious significance. At none of these idol-houses, however, was there any regular worship, but they were visited by those people who desired to obtain certain benefits, offerings of money or of fowls, sheep, and other animals being brought to the idol-keeper. The idols were also taken abroad on special occasions, being at these times usually fastened to the top of a slender pole, so as to be visible from a distance, although the idol itself was generally hidden from view by a covering of scarlet silk or velvet, striped with dark-blue cloth.

Each idol had its special *fàdy*, that is, certain things or acts which were distasteful to it, and which must not be touched or practised by its votaries. The *fàdy* of Kélimaláza were as follows :—Pork and shellfish were forbidden, and also to taste food which was still being cooked, or which was taken off the fire at a different side to that at which it had been put on. Should the bird called the *tàkatra* cross its path when carried abroad, it must be carried back ; and should this bird fly over the idol's house, a red ox entirely of one colour must be killed as an expiation. It could not be taken abroad on Friday or Saturday, and two species of grass, called *hòròndràno* and *ténona*, were forbidden to be taken into its house. Its keepers were not allowed to eat beef killed at a funeral, and no person who had recently attended a funeral could enter its house ; and its keepers were obliged to dress their hair in a special manner, parted back, and not arranged in a knot near the forehead. And, finally, all who entered its house must step in with the right foot.

Next in rank to Kélimaláza was Ramàhavàly, the Malagasy Æsculapius ; this was kept at a village a few miles north of the capital, and was regarded as having power to cure diseases. To effect this, small pieces of wood which had been fastened to the idol were sold to those who required them, and were regarded as of undoubted efficacy. The name means "able to answer," or "able to revenge," and, as already mentioned, when speaking of the superstitions connected with animals, serpents were regarded as the agents of this idol's anger if he were offended. Very extensive and extraordinary powers were attributed to Ramàhavàly, not only over disease, but over the elements of nature, the seasons, and futurity ; and not only were serpents his agents, but he was said to be able to twist the neck öf those who offended him, so that they faced backwards, a reverse which

no earthly power could remedy. From the native drawing it
appears that this idol consisted of two small rude wooden
figures of lizards, ornamented with coral beads and pieces of
silver. And from an interesting account of the burning of
this idol given to me by a Malagasy friend, it seems that
the idol had several coverings of different kinds of cloth, the
outer ones profusely ornamented with silver and beads, and
made respectively of dark-blue cotton, of native silk, and of
scarlet cloth. Together with the idol itself, there were burnt
twenty-six large and small baskets, all filled with leaves and
pieces of wood used as charms; and nine wooden boxes filled
with charms to be used as fillets for the head, necklaces, or
armlets, and supposed to give the bearer certain protection in
battle.* The tabooed things and acts of this idol were onions,
and funeral beef; vegetables to be cooked must not be put
to boil inside the house, but out of doors, and the rice about
to be eaten must not be mixed up in the middle of the
cooking-pot. No serpent must be killed, nor could any
attendant at a recent funeral enter the idol house; it could
not be carried abroad on Thursday, and those who sought its
aid paid fourpence and a cock to the keepers as a fee.

Next perhaps in importance was the idol Rafantàka. This
was kept at the old capital and sacred city of Ambòhimànga,
about eleven miles north of Antanànarìvo. From the native
drawing already referred too, it appears to have been simply
the curved tusk of a wild-boar, to which was attached a long
ribbon-like piece of dark-red native silk. At each end of
this was a kind of fringe made of coral beads and small
pieces of silver. The *fàdy* or tabooed objects and actions of
Rafantàka were the following:—Onions, kidneys, the herb
called *àna-mafàitra*, tripe, and funeral beef, and food tasted,
or removed, while cooking, in an improper way from the fire.
It was forbidden to take into its house the rolls of twisted
grass used to place under anything carried on the head, or the
rush called *vòndrona ;* and the reed called by the same name
as the idol, *fantàka,* must not be burned, or the wood called
haròngana. Chaff must not be scattered, and if the idol's house
were crossed by a *tàkatra,* an ox with horns growing down-

* See *Sunday at Home,* April, 1879, pp. 213–216.

ward must be killed. The worshippers of the idol took an offering of dark-blue cloth and a silver ring, and money to about the value of about threepence, and were sprinkled with water by the idol-keepers.

The fourth of these principal idols, that called Manjà-katsirða (*i.e.*, "Not two sovereigns"), was the tutelar deity of the sovereign, and was kept in a house in the palace-yard at Antanànarìvo. From the native drawing it has a very exact resemblance to a common bottle-gourd, but I believe it was really nothing more than a small bag of sand. This curious god was taken in one hand of the sovereign at her first public appearance after her accession, the idol Rafantàka being held in the other; and standing upon the sacred stone or rock, she invoked the protection of these two idols for herself and the kingdom.

Among the other idols of Imérina was one of which a word or two may be said. This was Rànakandrìana, which was kept in a cave on the steep side of a lofty rocky ridge, a few miles north-west of the capital. This cave was a kind of Delphi, and was resorted to by those who desired answers to questions they put about various benefits they sought for. It is quite true that audible answers were given to such inquiries, but, as might be supposed, it was the voice of a man, and not of a god, which replied. Two brothers were the idol-keepers; and one of them, previously concealed in a cavity in the rocks, gave such answers as he deemed would be acceptable to the votaries.

Of the other idols, some were believed to be able to protect against hail; others to bring travellers safely home again; and others to punish theft. Many were the curious antipathies they were supposed to entertain; one of the most foolish of these was the dislike to houses with walls made of non-combustible materials, so that until about nine or ten years ago no stone, brick, or earthen building could be erected either in the capital city or the other principal towns of the central province.

These idols have, however, now all passed away. On the 8th and 9th of September 1869, they were committed to the flames by royal command; and on the following days the whole of the charms and *sámpy* throughout the central province of Imérina were also destroyed. In almost every village a heap of curious and worthless looking objects which had long been regarded with reverence were collected together, and, to the horror of many of their worshippers, met with the same fate as the principal gods.

In the other parts of Madagascar the idolatry of the people seems never to have reached the development it had attained among the Hovas; it was, and indeed still is, more of a household, and occasionally, a tribal, worship of charms, and every man was priest in his own house. Speaking of the people in the south-west of the island, Drury (1702–1717) says: "There are no people here who pretend to be greater favourites of the Supreme Being than other men, and to have a particular commission to interpret and declare His will. No one here yet has been so presumptuous as to attempt this; and if any one should be so hardy, he would meet with but few to credit him. Every man here, the poor man as well as the rich lord, is a priest for himself and his family, and expects the demons should answer his requests in his dreams." In another part of his narrative he describes this household worship, which consisted of placing the family idol or *òly* (*òdy* in Hova and other dialects) upon a forked stick, burning a fragrant gum under it, and invoking the Supreme Being and some inferior divinities.

A native account of the Sihànaka tribe relates that an old man of the district said: "We had no religion except making offerings (*sòrona*) and sacrifices (*fànalàmboàdy*), while our country was still separate from the Hovas; but when the country was conquered by Radàma I., then were first brought here the idols called Itsimàhalàhy and Ramàhavàly. But notwithstanding that," said he, "we regarded their worship only as Government service which must be performed, for we did not see the meaning of it; for the only idol (or charm) we Sihànaka made use of was a charm for preserving cattle, and that we did not worship, but it was taken by the herdsmen into the pastures with them." [*]

Sacrifices.—Sacrifices were offered by the Hovas, and are

---

[*] *Antananarivo Annual,* No. iii. p. 66.

still offered by the people in those parts of the island which are uninfluenced by Christianity. These consist of oxen, which in many cases must be entirely of one colour, and of goats, sheep, and fowls. In certain cases the whole animal was burned; but in most instances the fat only was burned and the blood poured out, as representing the best portion of the victim and its life; while the flesh was eaten by the offerers, forming thus a meat-offering. Sacred stones and places were also anointed with the fat and blood; the graves of the Vazìmba and the upright headstones of family tombs being thus honoured. A gum called *émboka* and a fragrant wood called *havòzo* were also burnt on some occasions; and a kind of lustration, by sprinkling water upon the worshippers by the idol-keepers and by those who acted as sacrificers, was a frequent part of the religious ceremonies in use. Among the Hovas the sovereign acted on some occasions as a high priest; thus, Radàma I. is described by the Rev. J. J. Freeman, in 1828, as burning a small piece of fat before each of the seven small wooden houses covering the tombs of the royal ancestors in the royal courtyard at Antanànarìvo. This was done at the New Year's festival.

It is worthy of remark that sacrifices of thanksgiving are called *fanalamboàdy*, that is, "the accomplishment of a vow," while others offered to obtain benefits are called *sòrona*. This latter word is also used, probably from its connection with the burning of the flesh, for the simple feeding of a fire with fuel.

In one province of the island, the Vangaindràno district on the south-east coast, human sacrifices were formerly offered. These were made every week, Friday being the proper day, and those of high rank were considered the most appropriate offering; the victims were speared and left to be devoured by wild dogs and birds.

Atonement and Expiation.—Closely connected with the Malagasy customs as regards sacrifices was the practice of making a *fàditra*, a kind of expiatory or atoning offering for certain offences, or to avert threatened or dreaded evils. This *fàditra* often consisted of most worthless objects, such as ashes, the husk of a fruit, the gourd or pumpkin, or the water with which the mouth had been washed out; or it was sometimes a piece of cut money, or a sheep. Whatever it might be, the evil desired to be removed was first recited over the *fàditra*, with the wish that it might be removed by its means. If ashes were employed, these were blown so to be driven away by the wind; if cut money, it was thrown into deep water, so that it could not be found again; if a pumpkin, it was dashed violently on the ground; while if a sheep, it was carried to a distance on a man's shoulders, who ran with the utmost speed, imprecating on the victim all the evils it was intended to carry away.

In the early part of the reign of the first Rànavàlona, one of her favourites, foreseeing a speedy reversal of the royal favour, "applied to a diviner, and inquired what would be his fate. The diviner told him he would die a violent death, for his blood would be shed. He asked how he might avert the doom. The diviner gave him little reason to expect that anything could avert it, but directed him to mount a bullock, carrying on his head a vessel full of blood, and as the animal moved along he was to spill the blood on his head, and then send it away into the wilderness. This was done, but the doom was not averted." A few days afterwards he was cruelly killed in his own house.[*]

Another remarkable occurrence, but with a happier ending, may be related as a further illustration of the belief the Malagasy held, in common with many other nations, that "blood maketh an atonement." In the reign of a former Hova sovereign, named Andriamàsinavàlona, the first one who united the whole central province of Imérina under his authority, he was told by the diviners that a human sacrifice would be the best to make when setting up the first corner-post of his new palace. Upon his announcing this to the people assembled to witness the ceremony, the whole multitude fled precipitately from the palace-yard, and many even from the city. But a man named Ratrìmofòloàlina, living at a village a mile or two to the west of the capital, when he heard of the King's wish, went up to the palace, and offered to the King to give his life for his sovereign's benefit, and

[*] *Narrative of the Persecution*, p. 21.

allow his blood to be shed as an offering to sanctify the new royal house. His offer was accepted, the corner-post was raised, and he was fastened to the top, and prepared himself to die. But the King gave private instructions that his ear only should be cut, and that at the same time a quantity of water dyed with a red bark should be sprinkled over the post, so that the people thought that Ratrìmofòloàlina was really killed. But he was soon brought down again, his bonds cut, and then the King in the fulness of his gratitude offered him anything he should chose: oxen, fighting bulls, an estate, money, or to be made a prince. He chose, however, something different, and the King agreed that to the latest generation the descendants of the man who had offered his life for his sovereign's benefit, should never be put to death for any offence, or be placed in irons, or punished for any theft of the sovereign's property. From that time, therefore, the clan descended from Ratrìmofòloàlina has been known by the name of Tsimàtimanòta, *i.e.*, " Not killed (although) transgressing."

Altars, and Sacred Stones and Places.— Although the Malagasy have no temples they have sacred places, where certain sacrifices are offered, and which may be considered as a kind of altar. Of these, the headstones of their tombs, rude undressed slabs of blue granite or basalt, are the most prominent, being, as already mentioned, anointed with the blood and fat of the animals killed both at funerals and on other occasions, especially at the New Year's festival. In numerous places, other stones may be seen anointed in a similar way. Some of these are in the bed of streams, being thus honoured to propitiate the spirits supposed to dwell in the water or around it. Other stones are anointed by women who wish to obtain children.

Among the forest tribes (Tanàla), Mr. Brockway describes the following kind of altar as seen by him :—" One outside the forest was a perfect altar, upon which no tool had ever been lifted, and was about two and a half feet high. Three stones (the tripod) were firmly fixed in the ground, and a large flat one covered these; the whole finding a back-piece in a

vàto-tsàngana, a large upright stone." * Among these same
people, but farther south, I met with an altar consisting of a
long flat stone supported by several smaller ones. Another
kind was made by an upright stake fixed in the ground with
a number of bamboos arranged round it, forming a cone-
shaped structure; in front of this several stones were placed;
and upon this rude altar the heads of cattle, fowls, &c., were
thrown as offerings. Here also the people come to pray for
the blessings which they desire, especially for children.

Among the Bàra people there are said, by Mr. Richardson,
to be three kinds of sacred places. The first are the fetish
tamarind trees found near some of the towns. Surrounding
the trunk of these trees, some of which are very large, "are
laid small baskets, mats, fan-palm leaves, locks of hair,
&c. &c.; and on the surrounding branches similar articles are
hung, evidently placed there in making a vow, or as a thanks-
offering for some benefit." Then come the sacred posts outside the towns. The commonest kind of these are "about a
foot in diameter, and rise to the height of six feet or more.
The lower part is round; about a foot from the ground two
grooves are cut in the post, leaving a piece about the size of
a man's head; above this the post is cut in the form of an
immense four-sided stake tapering to a fine point. They are
sometimes three in number, and in exposed places are surrounded by a fence of *véro* (a very tall grass) or bamboo.
Some of these posts are much shorter, and are rudely carved
to represent a man, but mostly a woman. These are the
guardians of the town." The third kind are "the sacred
posts in the King's enclosure, which are generally of the same
character as those outside the town; but more frequently
they consist of about half-a-dozen sticks about the thickness
of an ordinary walking-stick. The bark of the upper part is
peeled off in circular rings, showing the white wood, and these
are smeared with blood, mostly the blood of oxen killed to
propitiate the deity. There is a bent spear, also smeared with
blood, stuck in the centre of these sticks, and the whole is
enclosed in a fence of bamboo."

In another part of the Bàra country, a native account de-

* *Antanànarìvo Annual,* No. ii. p. 60.

scribes the people as paying a kind of adoration to a tree called *bontóna*. An ox-skull is suspended to the branches, and to it numbers of charms are fastened. In another district the largest tree had a figure of a woman fixed to it. On being asked the meaning of this, the people replied, " This is the tree of adulterous desires, for here those pray who want women, or are about to marry."

Among the sacred places of the Hovas, the stones and graves of the Vazìmba formerly held a prominent place. These Vazìmba, as already mentioned in the sixth chapter, are believed to have been the aboriginal inhabitants of the central province. There are numerous traditions about them, some of which are doubtless fabulous, for certain of the Vazìmba chieftains were elevated by the popular imagination to the rank of demigods endowed with marvellous powers. After the expulsion of the Vazìmba from the central province, their tombs became sacred places, and their spirits the objects of a special worship and dread. Oxen, sheep, and fowls used to be sacrificed at their tombs, and the stones were rubbed with fat, as a means of obtaining good from them, or averting their anger. It was believed that to tread on their tombs was especially offensive to them, and that those offending were struck with pain and disease, or made blind.

The Vazìmba were supposed to be of two kinds, the kindly-disposed and the fierce and cruel. Some are said to inhabit the water, the lake Itàsy being especially their abode, while others are terrestrial in their habits. They were believed to appear to those who sought their aid, in dreams, warning them and directing them. This appearance was called *tsìndrimàndry*, *tsindry* meaning " squeezed," " impressed," and *màndry*, " lying down." One famous Vazìmba called Ranòro had, like the chief idols, his *fàdy* or tabooed things. Salt was one of his antipathies, and was forbidden to be brought near the water he inhabited. If, however, salt was carried past the lake it must not be mentioned by its usual name, *sìra*, but must be called *fàrào*, otherwise it would be all dissolved and lost; while the people he inspired must term it *sakay màmy*, *i.e.,* " sweet pepper" (or chillies), or they would be violently shaken by the offended spirit. Onions, shellfish, and funeral meat were also very offensive to this Vazìmba. A marvellous story is told in a native account of a slave-girl who was inspired by Ranòro, and after offending him was struck blind, but was restored to sight by a wash made of a blue flower called *nifinakànga*, of sassafras (*havozo*), and a tree called *fànazàva*. After this she was taken by him into the river Ikiòpa, where she remained, so they say, three days under the water.

It is said in this same account that the Vazìmba in the lake Itàsy were accustomed to show themselves every day on a rock in the midst of the water, but if any one approached too near they disappeared. They were clothed in a red làmba; possibly the presence of scarlet herons or flamingoes gave rise to this story. Other Vazìmba are said to appear on the margin of the sea; most probably these were seals, some species of which are well known to have a remarkable resemblance to human figures at a little distance. As was said of the Lares and Lemures in European countries at the introduction of Christianity, so the Vazìmba are reported to have all disappeared from the central provinces since the idols were burnt, and to have gone into the sea to the west of the island.

Among the Tanàla people there is also a belief in a kind of water-sprite or mermaid, called *Andriambàviràno,* "water-princess." "She is said to be white, and her hair is green and long. It is only in deep water, where there are many long weeds, that she is to be seen; she possesses water-cattle with long hair, and these oxen also live in the water. The people think there is land below the land in which they live, but they do not profess to know anything about it.*

Another kind of sacred place frequently seen in Imérina by the roadsides is what is called *fànatàovana.* This con-sists of a heap of stones, sticks, grass, and other rubbish on which persons passing usually throw something to express the hope of a safe return.

Divination.—Among the superstitions of the Malagasy,

* *Antanànarìvo Annual,* No. ii. p. 100.

divination held a very important place. Among the Hovas this was called *sikìdy*, a word which has been shown by the Rev. L. Dahle * to be most probably of Arabic origin. This fact, together with the additional one that the words for fate, *vìntana*, sorcery, *mosàvy*, and possibly some other words connected with these practices, are probably derived from the same language, leaves little doubt that the practice of divination is of foreign origin, and was introduced into Madagascar many centuries ago by the Arab settlers, both on the east and west coasts. And this is further confirmed by the fact, that many of the words employed in working the oracle are also evidently of Arabic origin, from their commencing with the Arabic article *Al*. According to native accounts, this form of divination was supernaturally given to their ancestors; but probably the stories told were invented to give greater authority to the decisions of the diviners, who were accustomed to invoke the names of the ancients to whom the art was said to be first communicated and who transmitted it to posterity.

But it will be asked, What was this *sikìdy?* and how were its decisions ascertained? It was a "mode of working a particular process by means of beans, rice, straw, sand, or any other objects that can easily be counted or divided. Definite and invariable rules were given for working the process and deciding upon the result." A number of lines were drawn resembling the divisions of a chess-board; the first set had sixteen columns one way and four the other, the second set four columns each way, and the third set four by eight. Taking a handful of beans from a heap, the diviner withdrew two, then two more, and so on until only two or one bean was left, which he placed on the first square at the top of the right-hand corner. All the spaces were filled up in a similar way. Then by certain fixed combinations of numbers from the second table, the third one was filled up; and as each column, read in different directions, had a special name and significance, the coincidence in numbers between different columns was supposed to point out what was to be done in case of real or imaginary, present or apprehended,

* *Antanànarìvo Annual,* No. ii. p. 80.

evils.   It will be seen, therefore, that there was a mixture of
chance and of fixed rules in the working of this oracle.   In
Ellis's *History of Madagascar* (vol. i. chaps. xv., xvi.) will be
found diagrams of these tables, with minute particulars as
to the methods employed in ascertaining the decisions.   In
illness, in buying and selling, in going on a journey, in dread
of any calamity, recourse was had to the *sikìdy*, and implicit belief placed in its direction, as of divine origin.   The
first Queen Rànavàlona had recourse to the divination for
the directing of almost every action and event of her life.
"She could scarcely venture to take even an ordinary meal
of rice without having it worked ten or a dozen times.   First,
the diviners must decide from what class of the people the
rice is to be obtained; then, in what direction it may be
fetched; then, who is to fetch it, in what kind of basket;
who is to cook it, with what fuel; in what dish to serve it
up; on which side it is to be served out; what may be eaten
with it, drank with it, &c. &c.   All this is thought needful
to guard against witchcraft and sorcery." *

To avert the evils pointed out by the *sikìdy* various offerings, of the kind already described and called *fàditra* and *sòrona*,
were made.   These offerings had generally some verbal connection with the particular evil to be averted.   Thus, for evil believed to come from heaven, a herb called *tsikòbondànitra*,
"stirred up by heaven," was presented; if from sheep, a small
fish called *ondrìndràno*, "water-sheep," was offered; while if
death was feared, a piece of disintegrated granite called *vàto
màty*, or "dead-stone," was the fàditra.   In other cases there was
a different kind of connection between the evil and the remedy;
thus, if fire was the origin of the evil, then the scarlet flowers
of the *sòngosòngo* (*Euphorbia splendens*) was offered.   When
it was wished to bring home a person from a distance, a reed
was erected upon a mountain in accordance with the instructions of the *sikìdy*, and this was called *mandìnga-làvitra*,
"to raise up afar off."

The Hova diviners were acquainted with the science of
casting nativities, and those who practised this art were called
mpanandro, i.e., "makers of days."   It was not, however, done

* *Narrative of the Persecution*, p. 60.

by astrology, for the *vìntana*, or fate of persons, depended upon the age and situation of the moon at their birth.

Among the Tanàla tribes, however, there appears to be an astrology, strictly so called. Some of their diviners " look at the little stars that are visible about three o'clock in the morning in the eastern sky, and from which they foretell any calamity that may be hanging over any person or town. They also know from them who will die and who will live; and before the time of their death comes they are able to give them something to ward it off and make them live longer. These star-gazers are the chiefs of the diviners. Some others look into a glass or a white plate, and they say they see there what will make people ill, and give medicine to ward off the calamity. The diviners in the Taimòro district are said to have a large book, and on looking into this book they are able to foretell what will kill any one, and what will ward off death." So runs the native account; but the " book," and the looking into a glass or white plate, seem so unlike indigenous Malagasy customs that I strongly suspect they are derived from the Arabs, who are known to have settled in the south-east coast of Madagascar, and to have advanced inland, becoming chiefs of some of the forest tribes, as well as of others on the coast. (See chapter v.)

Ambòndrombé, the Malagasy Hades.—The old ideas of the Malagasy concerning the state of men after death seem very confused and obscure. Sometimes the dead were spoken of as *làsan-ko-rìvotra*, " gone into air," or as having become nothing; and yet there was doubtless a belief also in their continued existence, as they were prayed to and invoked on all religious observances, and were said to have gone away and "become God " (*làsan-ko Andriamànitra*), a noteworthy phrase, implying something of a pantheistic idea. In a remarkable speech attributed to Andrianimpòinimérina, father of the first Radàma, who died in the year 1810, he told his friends and family that he was " fetched by God," and was " going home to heaven." And a phrase used in speaking of the dead, who are said to have *nòdy màndry*, which means literally " gone home to rest," also seems to imply a return from the grave, as it is often employed when people spend the night at a place and return home the following day.

A belief in ghosts is found all over the island. There are several names for these shades, as *matòatòa, ambiròa* (with many variations), and *lòlo.** The Bétsiléo, Tanàla, and probably other southern tribes, have also the words *kinòly*, a grotesquely horrible being, more like an animated skeleton than anything else, and also a curious word, *fàhasivin' ny màty*, which is literally, "ninth of the dead," or simply, *fàhasivy*, "ninth." The word *àmbiròa* (or *àmeròy*) is also used by the Tanàla to denote the spirits of the living. These *fàhasivy* are said to appear in dreams, and are propitiated by offerings of an ox.

The spirits of the dead are believed to go to Ambòndrombé, a lofty mountain covered with forest on the eastern edge of the highland of the Bétsiléo country and dividing it from the lower Tanàla territory. While travelling in the southern part of the island in 1876, I was much interested to have this Malagasy Hades pointed out to me when near the Hova fort of Imàhazòny. It had the appearance of a long regularly-curved mountain, stretching like the outline of a bow from north to south, and many miles distant to the east. The summit is often covered with clouds, and thus, from its height and almost inaccessible character, it has been invested for ages past with an atmosphere of dread. No one resident in the surrounding country would dare approach it, and strange stories were told of the firing of cannon and making of salutes whenever a royal ghost arrived to take up his abode there.†

About three years ago, Mr. G. A. Shaw solved the problem raised by the strange sounds reported to be heard from Ambòndrombé, by a personal examination of the dreaded mountain. He was unable to induce any Bétsiléo to accompany him or bring hatchets to cut open a path, but some of his bearers were bold enough to follow him, and after three hours' hard work, cutting away the undergrowth and creepers, he reached the summit.

He describes the mountain in the following terms:—" I

---

* *Lòlo* is also the word for "butterfly:" a curious analogy with the similarly double meaning of the Greek ψυχη.

† See *Antanànarìvo Annual*, No. i. pp. 95-97 ; No. ii. p. 99.

found that Iaràtsa [another name given to it] consists not of
one hill, as it appears at a distance, but of a large group of
hills, some six or seven in number, with very deep gullies
between them. These gorges have a general north and south
direction. The northern end of the gorges or valleys is open,
but at the south three hills, or one large hill with three tops
—I could not tell which—blocks up the southern end except
at the south-west corner, which is open to the west. This
peculiar arrangement of an isolated block of hills is, I think,
the first cause of the strange sounds which are the origin of
the superstitious fears connected with this place. The eastern
hill is one of the highest, if not the highest, in Bétsiléo, and
the wind, generally easterly, meeting this obstruction, rushes
with furious force round the north end, and over the top
into the three longitudinal valleys, out of which there is no
outlet except the narrow mouth at the south-west end. In
this way a species of natural trumpet is formed. And certainly while there I noticed that when there was scarcely a
breath of wind in my camping-ground, there was often the
roar as of a furious tempest going on above us. The hills
are more thickly covered with forest than any other part I
have seen in Madagascar, but I could discover nothing else,
such as caves, &c., that by an echo could have given rise to
the weird tales so fully believed in by the Bétsiléo. I quite
think from what I heard that the wind is the great ghost
raiser at Ambòndrombé." *

The Fandròana or New Year's Festival.—The observances
connected with this principal feast of the Hovas have been
described by more than one writer, but as any account of the
religious usages of the Malagasy would be incomplete without some mention of this national festival, a short summary
may be here given. It is to be noticed that the Fandròana
seems to be a *Hova* observance, and is not kept by many of
the tribes away from the central provinces of Madagascar.

First as to the *name* of the festival. This is derived from
one of the principal ceremonies observed, that of bathing,
fandròana meaning a "bath." Native tradition relates that

* *Antananarìvo Annual,* No. ii. p. 57.

the king named Ralàmbo first instituted the observance of
the festival, the same chieftain who is celebrated as having
discovered the excellence of beef.

The first ceremonies are held on the last day but one of
the old year. The great people of the kingdom meet the
sovereign in the principal palace, and a red cock is then
brought by the chief diviner. Its neck is wrung, and the
blood being caught in a banana leaf, is carried to the sovereign; this blood he takes with the nail of the left-hand little
finger and with it touches his forehead, neck, stomach, arm-
pit, finger-nails, and toe-nails; the rest of the assembly following the example. This blood is allowed to remain on.

On the following day the great people assemble again,
wearing the handsome red silk *làmba,* and in the morning the
royal tomb-houses in the palace-yard are swept and furnished
with mats. In the evening they assemble again for the royal
bathing in the great palace. Native music of the old style is
played, together with that of more modern European fashion,
and the representatives of the six royal clans, and of those
from the commoners and the army, present the dollar of allegiance. A fire on a temporary hearth of red earth is prepared in the middle of the great hall, and numerous pots of
rice are put on to cook. Then the Queen proceeds to bathe;
this she does in the north-east (the sacred) corner of the
house, in a silver bath, being screened from view by làmbas
held up by her attendants. The cannon are fired and a royal
salute given. After bathing the Queen takes a horn of water
in her hand and sprinkles those present, pronouncing a benediction and asking for a blessing on the new year, in certain
prescribed formulæ. She then goes to the open door to the
west and sprinkles those outside. The rice mixed with honey
is then partaken of by the Queen and the assembled guests,
the spoons being made of banana leaves tied up with fine
tendrils of some plant. Several salutes are fired, and the
assembly disperses at between ten and eleven o'clock. The
new year is then supposed to have begun, it being called the
first of the month Alàhamàdy, and the new moon of that
month. Since the accession of the present sovereign, however (1868), the festival has been held at the time of *full*

moon of the month, and prayers and the singing of one or two hymns have been added to the former observances.

On the following morning takes place the ceremony of blessing the oxen of the people, and killing an ox without blemish for the sovereign, as already described in the previous chapter. The rump is roasted near the head of the royal ancestors' tombs, and the sovereign eats, invoking a blessing; then, together with the royal family and heads of the royal clans, she enters the chief palace and eats, a small portion of the rice being placed on the head, with the invocation, " Blessed, blessed (be) God the Creator! thousands of us have reached the year, the family unseparated!"

In the evening there is more feasting, the four chief palaces being entered one after another by the sovereign and her guests. Sunday and Thursday were the proper days for the principal ceremonies of the feast. If the oxen were killed on Thursday the chief feast was on Sunday, but if the killing was on Sunday, the feasting, dancing, and singing was on Thursday. A red-and-white ox was killed both at Ambòhimànga, the old capital, and at Antanànarìvo, the present capital, the animal at the latter place being killed by the sovereign in person, and that at the former place by one of the royal family. A few days after all this takes place at Antanànarìvo, the sovereign and court go to Ambòhimànga to feast and eat *jàka* there, and offer prayer at the tombs of the royal ancestors. Among the ceremonies is the placing of a rush, dipped in the blood of the ox, at the door of the royal tomb-houses, while the hump is deposited inside the house. So much for the Fandròana ceremonies as observed by the sovereign. A few words must next be said as to the observances of the festival amongst the people generally.

Proclamation is made beforehand of the time of the feast, and the people are forbidden under pain of death to kill any animal, except poultry, five days before and after the appointed day for killing oxen. The fat is ordered to be brought to the royal soap factories, and the hides are asked for for making the soldiers' caps and belts. A poll-tax of a minute sum is ordered to be paid, and also the royal share (the rump) of each ox killed; and if any one dies during the first days of the month the mourning and full funeral ceremonies are to be deferred until it is past.

A great deal of visiting of friends and parents and superiors takes place, and small pieces of money are given as *jàka*, or substitutes for the preserved meat so called; and good wishes and benedictions are exchanged.

One of the most pleasing of the Fandròana ceremonies is the lighting of small fires just at dusk on the two evenings next before the royal bathing. These fires are called *harèndrina*, and the first of these is for the sovereign, the second for the people, but there is no difference in them. The fires are made by small bundles of dry grass being fixed to the end of bamboos; these are lighted, and are carried about and waved by the children, amidst a general shouting and rejoicing. Looking from the summit of the capital over the surrounding country, the sight is a very beautiful one; all around, in every direction where there are villages or houses, these dancing lights are seen through the dusk, thickly massed in populous places, and scattered thinly where there are few inhabitants, while a general murmur rises through the air. It seems probable that this custom is a relic of some observance connected with the worship of fire in remote times. Those, however, who have had a death in the family during the year do not make these fires, nor do they kill oxen, or bathe.

On the night when the fires are lighted for the people, there is a general weeping at cock-crowing for the dead who have not lived to see the new year. On the eve of the new year every one bathes in warm water; each household meets together, and a little of the water is placed on the head with the proper benedictions. At this time also all slaves return to their masters from wherever they have been, either trading, or doing work for them or for others, for they have each to provide a bundle of firewood for the cooking of the special food eaten at the Fandròana. Every wife also must be with her husband at that time, or it is considered that she is as good as divorced.

For several days there is much feasting and visiting; all are dressed in their best clothes and ornaments; and all when eating place a portion of rice on their heads, repeating a benediction, similar to that already quoted, with the words, " Salutation, reached is the year."   As in the case of the royal tombs, a rush dipped in the blood of the ox killed at the feast is hung up over the door of the house; this is said to be as a protection of house and life, and for sanctifying the house.   The hump is carried to the family grave, and the headstone anointed with the fat, while prayers for blessings and prosperity are made to the spirits of their ancestors.   A particular kind of dish is much liked at this time, and is prepared from the inner portions of the oxen killed, and stewed in a special kind of earthen dish.   The slaves take meat and cook it out of doors, and after feasting, dancing and singing together with native music is kept up, the highest personages often joining in the festivities.

The oxen killed at this time have generally been fattened for several months previously, and are usually very fine and fat animals.   Portions of the meat are sent to all friends and relatives by those who kill one or more oxen.

It will be understood that the above description applies to the customs observed before the general reception of Christianity nine years ago.   The prayers to the ancestors and offerings at their tombs are not presented at the present time.

CHAPTER XVI.

NEW LIGHT ON OLD TEXTS: ILLUSTRATIONS OF SCRIPTURE FROM MALAGASY CUSTOMS.

ROYALTY AND GOVERNMENT — FAMILY LIFE — MARRIAGE — BENEDICTIONS, CURSES, AND SALUTATIONS—DRESS AND FOOD—WEAPONS—HOUSES AND TOWNS—TOMBS AND BURIAL—ROADS AND PATHS—SYMBOLIC ACTS AND FIGURATIVE LANGUAGE—AGRICULTURE—SLAVERY—TIME.

It has been often remarked that "the Bible is an Eastern book;" and perhaps it is impossible for those who have never lived in any but a temperate climate to fully appreciate, not merely the figures and allusions in which the Scriptures abound, but the whole Eastern feeling and atmosphere in which they are steeped. The researches of a host of travellers and of residents in the East have, however, now enabled those who stay at home to understand the Oriental colouring of the Bible far more clearly than it was possible to do only a few years ago; and some of the most trivial, and at first sight unimportant, details are found to contribute most essentially to the vividness of the narratives and teachings of the Scriptures.

But although the Book of God is, of course, most clearly seen in the light derived from Palestine and Egypt, Assyria and Persia, *all* tropical countries and peoples have more or less affinity with the land and peoples of the Bible; and illustrations of Biblical customs may be derived from almost every mission-field. This subject has already been treated of in some missionary works, but it has by no means been exhausted; and, as in the course of several years' labour in Madagascar, I have frequently been struck by the close analogies between native customs and those described and referred to in the Scriptures, it may not be uninteresting to note down a few of them. They will afford, I venture to think, not only some new light upon Bible customs and allusions, but also be of service as illustrating the habits of the Malagasy people.

Royalty and Government.—It is not very easy for a foreigner to immediately understand the absolute character of a government like that of Madagascar, where every person, from the highest to the lowest, is a servant of the sovereign, and where no one can take any step in life—change his residence, built a house or a tomb, go on a journey, be married, or even be buried—without reference to his immediate superior in rank, or directly to the head of the State. But all this is much more like the state of society described in the Bible, like the autocratic character of the Jewish monarchy, to say nothing of other monarchies referred to in the sacred records, than is our own social and political system. And, therefore, such sayings as, "The king's wrath is as the roaring of a lion, but his favour is as dew upon the grass" (Prov. xix. 12); "The wrath of a king is as messengers of death;" &c., are in thorough harmony with Malagasy ideas.

It should, however, be understood that there are many influences now at work in the spread of Christianity, and the growth of European ideas, to modify the absolutism of former times. What this was may be gathered from an incident related of Queen Rànavàlona I. Soon after the promulgation of the laws against Christian worship, some of the people came to certain of the missionaries and asked if they did not tremble at the word of the sovereign? They replied that they were indeed grieved that the Queen wished to prevent the knowledge of the Word of God, but that they did not tremble, because, after all, the Queen was only human. The natives rejoined, "It may be well for you to say so, because you are white people; but as for us Malagasy, when our sovereign frowns upon us we are as people soon dead!" The ascription of divine honours to King Agrippa in the shout, "It is the voice of a God, and not of a man," was paralleled (but, of course, with a far less degree of blame) by the former appellation of Malagasy sovereigns, who were called *Andria-*

mànitra hita-maso—"the god seen by the eye," the visible divinity.

When passing the chief entrance of the palace-yard, and noticing the crowd of people and officials sitting at the gateway, I have often been reminded of the Eastern custom of suitors for any favour or office "sitting at the king's gate" (2 Sam. xi. 9; Esth. ii. 19). This is not only seen at the royal gateway, but also at the entrance of the houses of the highest officers of state; people are there "watching daily at his gates, waiting at the posts of his doors" (Prov. viii. 34). And just as in the East, those who seek to have justice done to them in any law-suit, have to wait and waylay the great men, and by their very importunity force them to attend to their cause (see Luke xviii. 1–5), so have we known women who have sat for days together at the palace gate, for the purpose of pressing their case upon the attention of the high Government officers as they went in and out from the presence of the Queen.

There is also in Madagascar a custom that if, on any royal progress, a criminal can contrive to put himself in the way of the sovereign, so as to be seen and looked upon by her, he can claim pardon for his offence. (Malagasy offenders are not, as a rule, kept in prison, but have light fetters put upon them, so that they can walk about and get employment in various out-door work. When, therefore, the sovereign goes abroad, orders are issued that all convicts (*gàdra làva*) must keep out of the way.) This is strikingly like Eastern customs, for there are numerous passages which show that to "look upon," or to "regard," &c., are expressions equivalent to gaining favour and compassion (see Exod. ii. 25, iv. 31; 1 Sam. i. 11; 2 Sam. xvi. 12).

When a Malagasy sovereign goes on a journey to any distant portion of her dominions, she is always accompanied by an immense crowd of her subjects, including all the upper classes of the people, with their bearers and attendants. Like the Queen of Sheba, she goes "with a very great train," "a very great company, she and her servants" (1 Kings x. 2). On recent royal "progresses" the number of these followers has amounted to as many as from 20,000 to 30,000 people!

And in the preparations for these journeys we always have illustrations of many Scripture passages. As there are no roads, properly speaking, in Madagascar, the local authorities along the line of march are responsible for improving the paths, or, in many places, for making an altogether new road. The elevations are cut down, the hollows filled up, timber bridges are constructed, and the jungly grass and thickets are cleared out of the way. It is, in short, an exact illustration of the words, " Prepare ye the way of the Lord, make straight in the desert a highway. Every valley shall be exalted, and every mountain and hill shall be made low ; and the crooked shall be made straight, and the rough places plain " (Isa. xl. 3, 4). At every halting-place on the journey the camp is formed with most scrupulous care and order: the royal scarlet tent in the centre, and around it its court; opposite the entrance are the tents of the chief officers of state, and then in regular order on all four sides are those cf the different tribes and ranks of the people. The whole, when viewed from an elevation, bears a striking resemblance to the camp of the Israelites, as it must have appeared on their march through the desert.

Throughout the whole of the East it is indispensable, when seeking an interview with a person of authority or influence, that a present be brought to propitiate his favour ; for "a man's gift maketh room for him, and bringeth him before great men" (Prov. xviii. 16). It is exactly the same in Madagascar; nor can these presents be properly termed bribes, for as the majority of Government officials have no regular or fixed salary, such presents are one of the chief means they have of keeping up their position. So much is this the custom that, even when coming to see us, their missionaries, the people usually bring some little offering—a bunch of bananas, half a dozen oranges, or other fruit, or a young fowl ; and if they have nothing they make an elaborate apology for coming empty-handed. And I have often thought, when reading that story of Saul and his servant when seeking his father's asses, how like it is to Malagasy usages—their concern at finding they have nothing left to offer in approaching the great man, Samuel ("But, behold, if we go, what

x

shall we bring the man ? for the bread is spent, and there is
not a present to bring to the man of God : what have we ? "
1 Sam. ix. 7); the servant's finding a quarter-shekel; his
master's immediately appropriating it—all this is true to the
life to what continually happens in Madagascar.

As among the Jews and most Eastern nations, the staff is a
sign of office and authority, so also it is among the Malagasy
(see Numb. xvii.). When the elders of the people, chiefs of
villages and tribes, come in from the country to the capital,
they frequently carry with them this staff or rod of office as
a sign of their position.

Up to a very recent period, the punishments for political
and other crimes in Madagascar were very severe. The code
of laws in the time of sovereigns preceding the present one
commenced by denouncing death for a number of offences;
but beside this it provided also that the wife and children of
the culprit should " be lost," that is, reduced to slavery. And
so " the sins of the fathers were visited upon the children," a
thing which, although prohibited by the law of Moses (Deut.
xxiv. 16 ; Ezek. xviii. 20), was often practised by Jewish
rulers, as well as by neighbouring nations (see 2 Kings x.
6, 14, xi. 1 ; Dan. vi. 24).

In the case of popular risings against obnoxious counsellors
of the sovereign, as was the case in May 1863, when a number of the king's friends were accused and put to death, their
houses were in several instances set upon by the populace,
torn to pieces, and all the property destroyed in a very few
minutes, giving a striking and rather terrible illustration of
the passage, " Let his habitation be desolate, and let no man
dwell therein" (Ps. lxix. 25 ; Acts i. 20).

We are accustomed in this country to consider all Government officials as servants of the public; but in Madagascar,
as in the East generally, the reverse is usually the case. And
so, any little petty officer can command service and assistance by pronouncing the magic words, *Fanjakàn' Andriana*,
" Queen's business " (literally, " Kingdom of the sovereign").
" Dressed in a little brief authority " given by his connection
with the Crown, he can lord it over people much his superiors
in every way, and everywhere require obedience to his demands

by the use of words much the same as the text, "The king's business requireth haste."

The power of the Crown itself is theoretically unlimited over the property and personal service of the people, so that for all Government work, such as building a palace or fort or workshop, every one is liable for an uncertain amount of labour and expense until its completion, and without any payment. The description given by Samuel to the Israelites as to the demands that would be made upon them by their future king, with its somewhat sarcastic conclusion as to their ultimate chagrin on account of their folly, might have been applied very well to Malagasy sovereigns up to a recent period. But the present Queen, under the influence of Christian teaching, has shown a laudable desire to lighten the burdens of her subjects, and is known universally by the appellations, *mòra bé sy malémy fanàhy, i.e.*, "exceedingly kind and gentle-spirited."

Marriage and Family Life.—In few countries is more respect paid to age and to elders than in Madagascar, and very fully is the precept carried out, " Thou shalt rise up before the hoary head, and honour the face of the old man ". (Lev. xix. 32). And such sentiments as those expressed by Elihu, " I am young, and ye are very old; wherefore I was afraid, and durst not show you mine opinion " (Job xxxii. 6), might be paralleled by many a passage taken from the *kabàrys* or public speeches which have been noted down. And this respect for age is also carried out to a considerable extent for seniority. Thus, if two brothers are taking a journey and any burden is to be carried, the younger one always carries it, as a matter of course.

In customs connected with marriage, the betrothal is regarded as a much more formal and binding ceremony than it is in England, so that a betrothed girl is much more like a wife than with us, just as was also the case under the Jewish law; and this, notwithstanding the fact that marriage was held in far lower estimation in heathen times than it is now.

The Hebrew law, by which a man was, on the death of his elder brother, bound to marry his widow and so preserve his name and family possessions, finds a very close parallel in

Malagasy usages (Deut. xxv. 5, 6); and there are special
phrases to denote such marriages. This is closely connected
with the strong family and clannish feelings of the Malagasy,
in accordance with which people very seldom marry out of
their own tribe and family, so that property may be kept
together; just as by the Jewish law all land was to be
retained in the possession of the same tribe and family
originally holding it. (See Numb. xxxvi. 7, "The inheritance
of the children of Israel shall not remove from tribe to tribe;
for every one shall keep to himself the inheritance of the
tribe of his fathers.")

As, however, large families are very uncommon amongst
the Malagasy, and a considerable number of women are
childless, adoption is far more common among them than it
is with Western nations, and, therefore, many passages in
the Epistles, such as "the adoption of sons," "the spirit of
adoption," &c., have a greater force to the people of Madagascar than they have to us. And further, as there is much
less extreme poverty among the Malagasy than in our over-
crowded Western civilisation, children are most easily
supported, and are ardently longed for, often with the pas-
sionate earnestness shown by Hannah the mother of Samuel
(1 Sam. i. 10–16). (For further particulars on this subject,
see chapters on Curious Customs, and on Relationships.)

Benedictions, Curses, and Salutations.—From what has just
been stated, it naturally follows that to have children is
looked upon as one of the greatest of all blessings; and the
benediction upon a bride in the patriarchal times, "Be thou
the mother of thousands" (Gen. xxiv. 60), finds its parallel
in the Malagasy blessing, *Maròa fàra aman-dìmby*, "May thy
heirs and descendants be multiplied."

In Malagasy benedictions and salutations the Divine
Name is most frequently invoked, as it is indeed by all
Eastern peoples; but it would be an utter mistake to
suppose that this frequent use of sacred words is any
evidence of deep religious feeling. On the contrary, now
that our Christian people are beginning to appreciate the
obligations imposed by the Third Commandment, we always
consider that a man is rather more of a heathen than others

if he is profuse in the use of the name of God. Ignorance of this Eastern habit has led to some very edifying, but most mistaken, comments upon such passages as that in the Book of Ruth, where Boaz says to his reapers, " The Lord be with you ; and they answered him, The Lord bless thee " (ii. 4). And it has been sometimes inferred from these phrases that there was a delightful and earnest religiousness of character in those using such beautiful language. But the fact is, that these were, and are still, the ordinary Oriental salutations, common to all religions ; and a reference to other passages shows that people of very questionable character were equally profuse in similar pious language ; see what was said by the murderers of Ishbosheth (2 Sam. iv. 8), by Saul after disobedience to a plain command (1 Sam. xv. 14), by Laban, and by many others. And just in the same way, the *Tahin' Andriamànitra hianao* (" May you be blessed of God ") of the Malagasy is the most common expression of thanks and of farewell, and is used in the vast majority of cases without any more religious feeling than we are conscious of when we say " Good bye " (God be with you) or " Adieu."

The Malagasy are a very polite people, and look with contempt upon those who neglect the ordinary usages and salutations. In speaking with a friend of his house, or land, or other property, it is common for him to call it *antsika,* *i.e.,* " ours," an inclusive form of possessive pronoun signifying a thing to be common both to the speaker and the spoken to. But going beyond this, they will sometimes tell you that all they have is yours ; it is, however, only a complimentary figure of speech, no more meant to be taken literally than were Ephron's polite offers of his land to Abraham, when he told the patriarch, " The field give I thee, and the cave that is therein, I give thee ; in the presence of the sons of my people give I it thee ; " proceeding immediately to charge an uncommonly good price for the land. All this was thoroughly Malagasy, as was also his apparently generous indifference to money, " What is that betwixt me and thee ? " and not less so was the request of Abraham that others would act as mediators between himself and Ephron, who was there present, for in almost every business of importance a third party must be employed as a go-between (see Gen. xxiii. 8–16).

Turning from the blessings to the curses used by the Malagasy, many points of similarity might be noted between them and those found in Scripture; but one only need be mentioned here, namely, a close analogy between the peculiar Hebrew form of imprecation by the use of "If," as in the words, "So I sware in my wrath, *if* they shall enter into my rest" (see margin of Bible, Ps. xcv. 11), a specially solemn form from its vaguely indefinite terms. In like manner, there are certain Malagasy imprecations with the same conditional particle.

Amongst all the tribes of Madagascar the commands of a father or an ancestor are held as most sacredly binding upon his descendants; and so one frequently meets with tribes or families who are prohibited from passing a certain place (as the royal family are bound not to pass along a particular road in the capital), or from doing certain acts, or from eating some kinds of food. One of my bearers was bound by the injunction of an ancestor not to eat pork, and another not to eat onions. We have examples of this in Scripture in the commands of Jacob to his sons, and of Joseph concerning his bones (Gen. xlix. 1–25); and also in the injunctions of Rechab to his descendants not to drink wine, or plant or sow, or live in houses (Jer. xxxv. 6, 7); and something similar in the abstinence of the Jews from a certain sinew in the thigh (Gen. xxxii. 32).

Dress and Food.—The native dress of the Malagasy, like that of the inhabitants of all warm countries, is much more loose and flowing than the stiff and ungraceful fashions of Western peoples. But the specially national article of dress is the *lámba*, a piece of cloth about three yards long and two wide; this is folded round the body above the arms, and one end thrown over the shoulder, and as worn by the people, and falling in graceful folds, is most elegant and dignified in its effect, somewhat resembling the Roman *toga*. It is made of various materials,—silk, cotton, hemp, banana or *rofia* palm fibre, according to the rank and wealth of the owner; and is common to both sexes, although there are numerous slight differences in the way of wearing it. The làmba is the outdoor or walking dress, and the arms are not free, as they are enclosed in its ample folds. But when in preaching or other public addresses the speaker gets excited, the làmba is thrown off one shoulder, leaving the arm free; so that the Scripture expression of "making bare the arm" is a most familiar one to the Malagasy. And then when about to engage in any active work, the làmba is thrown entirely off the shoulders, and is bound tightly round the waist, here again being exactly the "girding the loins" so frequently mentioned in Scripture. Our native servants, like those mentioned in the Parables, gird themselves before serving us at meals (Luke xii. 37), and their Malagasy masters constantly make use of these girded-up làmbas as towels for wiping their hands before and after taking food (see John xiii. 4, 5). This làmba can, of course, like the garment of Bartimeus, be easily taken off and cast away (Mark x. 50), or left in the hand of a pursuer, the wearer escaping (see Gen. xxxix. 13; and Mark xiv. 51, 52,—the young man with a linen cloth cast about him); and in the case of the poor, it is also their covering for the night as well as for the day, as it was with poor Israelites; although there is no such merciful provision in the Malagasy law as in the law of Moses, forbidding that it be retained in pledge for a debt (see Exod. xxii. 26, 27; Deut. xxiv. 12, 13). The great majority of the people do not wear shoes, but when going on a journey, especially if the roads are rocky, or the grass prickly, they prepare a rough kind of sandal or *kàpa*, bound round the foot with thongs after the manner of Eastern peoples.

In taking food, the hands are largely used by the Malagasy (as in the East generally) in serving others and in feeding themselves. From this it becomes a necessity to wash before and after eating (see Matt. xv. 12), and for this purpose a servant comes round and pours water over the hands, just as did "Elisha, who poured water over the hands of Elijah" (2 Kings iii. 11). And when they invite friends to a feast, the host and hostess themselves serve at the table, considering it an honour to wait upon their guests, just as did Abraham when entertaining his three unknown, but heavenly, visitors at Mamre (Gen. xviii. 8). It is also the custom for the Malagasy to send a servant at the exact time the feast is ready to bid the guests come and partake (see Luke xiv. 17).

The Christianised Malagasy are scrupulous about not eating food until a blessing has been asked, but this takes a superstitious form, from being considered not so much as the thanksgiving of the partaker as a consecration of the food itself, which is then termed *vìta fìsaorana*, or "properly blessed;" much indeed as the people of Zuph (?) would not eat of the sacrifice until it had been blessed by Samuel (1 Sam. ix. 13). So they ask of any food, "Is it blessed?" and it is said that some graceless people, who wished to save themselves trouble, have been so economical of time as to ask a blessing over the whole store of provision in their rice-pit! considering that all future thanksgiving would thus be unnecessary.

In the more primitive state of society existing in the still heathen tribes of Madagascar, it is common to see menial offices, which are left to slaves in the more civilised capital of the country, performed by the female relatives of the chiefs. Thus at Ivòhitròsa, among the forest people, I remember being much surprised to see the daughters and wives of the King and his family pounding rice and fetching water, &c., while still arrayed in the ornaments proper to their rank. But it will be remembered that this is just what both Rebekah and Rachel did, although they were near relatives of a wealthy and prosperous man, doubtless a sheikh, or chief of the district where he resided (see Gen. xxiv. 15–20; xxix. 9, 10). There is, however, the same distinction among the Malagasy as among Easterns in the way of carrying the water pitcher; free women carry it *on the shoulder*, as did Rebekah (Gen. xxiv. 15), while slaves carry it on the head. Almost every Malagasy town and village presents the same scene now, morning and evening, as is described in 1 Sam. ix. 11: "Young maidens going out to draw water" for the daily use of each household; and in every house there are two or more waterpots placed, as there were at Cana in Galilee (John ii. 6).

Mention was made just now of the "rice-pit." These are dug in the hard red clay soil of Imérina, and are a bottle-shaped excavation for storing rice in the husk; a flat stone is placed over the mouth, and then the whole is covered with earth, so that it is not very easy for a stranger to discover the store of food. These rice-pits form a common place of concealment from an enemy, and many Christians have been hidden in them during the time of persecution, just as the cisterns of the East are often used as hiding-places (see 2 Sam. xvii. 15–21, describing the stratagem by which Jonathan and Ahimaaz were concealed in the cistern, and so escaped Absalom's servants).

Weapons.—Before the introduction of European arms and disciplined methods of warfare, the shield and spear were the chief weapons of the Malagasy. The former is a round or oval piece of hard wood, about twenty inches in diameter, covered on the outer convex side with untanned ox-hide, and having a handle cut out of the wood at the back. The spear is a light shaft of ebony or other hard wood, about six feet in length, and with a blade often eight or nine inches long. Like the Eastern spears, it is shod with iron, ending in a short spade-like point, by which it can be stuck into the ground. This blunted foot is, however, capable of inflicting a wound, just as Abner, in self-defence, was able, and indeed obliged, to kill Asahel who was pursuing him, by striking backward "with the hinder end of the spear" in his hand (2 Sam. ii. 23). The bow and arrow is not now used by the Malagasy generally; one or two only of the native tribes seem to be accustomed to it, and to the majority of the people it has for nearly a century past been superseded by the European musket.

Houses and Towns.—In the central provinces of Madagascar where a hard red clay abounds, most of the houses are made of that material. The clay is laid in courses, and makes a tolerably substantial and durable walling. But it is easily cut through with a spade or any sharp instrument, and accordingly, a Malagasy housebreaker almost always chooses this way of stealing. As in the East, "thieves *break through* and steal," and, "in the dark they dig through houses, which

they had marked for themselves in the daytime" (Job xxiv.
16).   Extraordinary stories are told of the ingenuity of some
of these people in taking away the bedding and clothes from
under persons who are sound asleep.

And then again, as in the East, the movable property of
the people largely consists of " changes of raiment," in other
words, of a store of handsome làmbas; so that our Lord's
words about "moth corrupting" them are hardly less appropriate
than they were to His Jewish hearers.   And like them also,
the money of the Malagasy is generally kept in the house,
buried in a hole in the ground, usually near one of the chief
posts supporting the roof; so that " hid treasure," so frequently mentioned in Scripture, is quite a familiar idea to the
Malagasy (see Josh. vii. 21 ; Job iii. 21 ; Isa. xvii. 4 ;
Prov. ii. 4 ; Col. ii. 3 ; &c.)

In the unsettled state of society which prevailed in the
central provinces up to the end of the last century, every
town and village was built on the summit of a hill, often of
considerable height; so that throughout Imérina and Bétsiléo,
as well as in other parts, all ancient towns are " cities set on
a hill, which cannot be hid."   The capital of the island is
built on the summit of a long rocky ridge, 400 to 500 feet
high, and is visible in some directions from a distance of
thirty to forty miles; and many villages in Bétsiléo are on
hills 700 feet high above the surrounding country.

Tombs and Burial.—Like most Easterns the Malagasy do
not use coffins for their dead, but wrap the body in a great
number of cloths, proportionate to the rank and wealth of the
deceased (see John xi. 44; Acts v. 6).   At the death of an
aged officer of the native army in 1875, a veteran said to be
about a hundred years old, the Queen ordered that he should
be wrapped in a hundred red làmbas, of which number she
herself sent about a third as a mark of respect.   The Malagasy spend large sums upon their tombs, and they consider
it as the greatest calamity not to be buried in their own
family vault.   So that those Hova officers who die at the
military posts in various parts of the island far away from
their native province, are always brought up to Imérina to be
buried with their ancestors; and so it is also with those who

die in war, their *bones* at least must be brought home and laid in their own tomb. It is much the same strong tribal and family feeling which led Joseph to give " commandment concerning his bones," and made Jacob say, " Bury me with my fathers, in the cave which Abraham bought for a possession of a burying-place," and recalling how he had there laid the remains of his nearest relatives (Gen. xlix. 29-31).

Roads and Paths.—The poetical books of Holy Scripture are full of figures taken from roads and paths, for we constantly meet with such expressions as "way," "goings," "leading," "guiding," "footsteps," "slipping," "sliding," "stumbling-block," and many others. And such language is by no means unfrequent even in the prose portions of the sacred writings; so that the figures have long ago passed over into our Western speech and become so naturalised that when we speak of taking a right or wrong path (as regards conduct), it hardly seems a figurative expression at all. But further, on account of the perfection attained by our modern civilisation, all these figures have become faint and weak to us compared with their force to those who live in the East. With our wonderful railway system covering the whole country, with our smooth roads and paved streets, travelling has been divested of almost all its discomfort and of a large proportion of its danger, and we must live in a country like Madagascar, which is *without roads*, to realise the vividness of such expressions as, " Teach me, O Lord, the way of Thy statutes," " Teach me Thy way, and lead me in a plain path," " He set my feet upon a rock and established my goings," &c. How often as I have picked my way up or down a rough rocky staircase rather than a road, or toiled painfully along a slippery clay slope, have I recalled the words, " Hold up my goings in Thy paths, that my footsteps slip not," " Ponder the path of thy feet, and let thy ways be established;" and at other times, either on foot, or borne on the shoulders of my stout bearers, or occasionally on horseback, when skirting the edge of a sheer precipice by a narrow path, have I realised the terrible force of some of the curses in the Bible, " Let their way be dark and slippery," " Their footsteps shall slide in due time;" or with more cheerful feelings have rejoiced in the words, "When my foot slipped, Thy mercy, O Lord, held me up."

And while the paths in Madagascar are difficult enough in the day, they become positively dangerous by night. As we stumble into a deep hole, or our feet come in sharp contact with a rough stone, we find new meaning in the words, "Make straight paths for your feet," "Take up the stumbling-block out of the way of My people," "Thou shalt walk, and thy foot shall not stumble." And should we chance to be overtaken by darkness after the brief tropical twilight, how we recall the prayer, "Lighten my darkness, O Lord," and welcome the approach of a friendly torch or lantern, and are reminded of the text, "Thy word is a lamp unto my feet, and a light unto my path."

In such circumstances as these a large class of words in the Bible have a freshness and reality which they never acquire in our own country.

Symbolic Acts and Figurative Language.—When reading the Bible we frequently meet with examples of the use of symbolic acts to impress some important truth upon the witnesses of such actions. The prophets of the Old Dispensation frequently received Divine commands to use such teaching; thus, Ezekiel taught by eating a roll (iii. 1–3), by the mimic siege of a tile upon which Jerusalem was portrayed (iv.), by the use of a chain (vii. 23), of a boiling pot (xxiv. 1–4), by the uniting of two sticks (xxxvii. 15–17), and by many other symbolic actions; and false prophets also did the like, one of them making horns of iron to give vain confidence to an ungodly king (see 1 Kings xxii. 11).

In Malagasy history there are some interesting examples of a similar employment of symbolic actions, especially before the general use of writing had made written letters common. Towards the close of the last century the King of Imérina, the central province of Madagascar, had reduced under his authority a great part of the interior of the island, and, confident in his own power, sent a messenger to the principal chief of the southern central province, Bétsiléo, telling him that he was "his son" (a common Malagasy expression, implying that one person is subordinate to another), and requiring him to come and acknowledge his father. The Bétsiléo chief, however, replied that he was no son of the Hova king, but that they were brothers, each possessing his own territory. The Hova returned for answer, "I have a large cloth (to cover me), but thou hast a small one; so that if you are far from me you are cold; for I am the island to which all the little ones resort, therefore come to me, thy father, for thou art my son." When the Bétsiléo chief received this message he measured a piece of wood between his extended arms (the *réfy* or standard measure of the Malagasy, between the tips of the fingers when the arms are stretched apart to the utmost), and sent it to the king, with the words, "This wood is my measure, bid Andrianampòina (the Hova king) equal it; if he can span it, then I am his son and not his brother." Upon Andrianampòina trying it he was unable to reach it, for the Bétsiléo chief was long in the arms. But the Hova king would not give up his point, and replied, "My measurement of the wood is of no consequence, for kingship does not consist in length of arms; thou art little, therefore my son, I am great, therefore thy father."

Still the southern chief was unwilling to submit, and sent a particular kind of native cloth ornamented with beads, with a request that an ox should be cut up upon it, as another sign whether he was to acknowledge the Hova king as his superior or not. This test also turned out to his own advantage; but at length Andrianampòina would have no further trifling. He sent back the cloth with a piece cut off one end of it, and a spear hole through the middle, as a significant warning of his intentions unless immediate submission was made. The lesson was not lost upon the weaker chief; he returned a humble answer, begging that he might not be killed, saying, "While it is to-day, all day let me eat of the tender (food) of the earth, for Andrianampòina is lord of the kingdom."

Something of a similar kind of symbolic act is related of Queen Ranavàlona I. When she came to the throne in 1828 there was a little boy not many months old at that time, of the true seed royal, and descended from the line of the ancient kings. The Queen then announced that she had made this boy her adopted son, and that he should be her successor; even if she should have children of her own, his right to the throne should remain good. Afterwards she had a son of her own, whom she named Rakòton-dRadàma; many thought that her own son would succeed her, but the declaration in favour of the other was never rescinded, and hence arose much animosity between the two princes. When the Queen became old and feeble, the subject of the succession came up, and she settled it in a singular way, substantially as follows :—She held a meeting of her officers, judges, and heads of the people with great solemnity within the palace, when she announced her intention of making a valuable present to each of the two princes. Two fine vases or covered vessels were placed on the table, and the two young men were called in; the elder was first directed to choose which he would have. He did so, and on opening the vase, it was found to contain some beautiful gems and valuable ornaments. The younger, her own son, then opened his vase, and found it contained only a handful of earth. The Queen then addressed the assembly, saying that the elder prince was to be advanced to high honour and riches in the land; but, as the land could not be divided, the younger prince, who had received from God the handful of earth, should be her successor.* (He eventually became king under the name of Radàma II., but only reigned about eighteen months.)

Turning from the symbolic *acts* to the figurative *language* used by all the tribes in Madagascar, many interesting parallels might be pointed out between what is common to Malagasy speech and the language used in Scripture. Reference was just now made to the iron horns which the false prophet Zedekiah made to encourage King Ahab; and it will be remembered how very frequently the horn is employed in the Bible as an emblem of power, strength, and confidence. It is used very much in the same way in Madagascar, for the long-horned and humped cattle are the largest and most formidable animals known in the island, and the horns of cattle are frequently seen as ornaments or symbols. Numbers

* Quoted from *R.collections of Missionary Life in Madagascar*, by James Cameron, Esq.

of them, together with the skulls, are fixed upon poles near graves; and in some places, enormous carved representations of horns surmount lofty mast-like poles in the same situation. Amongst the Bétsiléo iron horns are used as a cresting for the massive upright monoliths raised above tombs, and carved horns, either close imitations of the real thing or conventionalised representations of them, surmount the gables of houses in Imérina and other portions of Madagascar. (See also figurative use of the word in complimentary speeches; p. 159, and pp. 198, 231, 232.)

Agriculture.—Many illustrations of Scripture might be derived from Malagasy usages in the cultivation of rice, their staple food, but two or three only must suffice. As rice stands in water during all the stages of its growth, it is a common figure to describe things which are inseparable to " rice and water." One may frequently see the sower "casting his bread upon the waters;" and as the plots of land where the rice is sown are often narrow slips of ground along the margin of rivers and streams, one recalls the words, " Blessed are ye that sow beside all waters, and send forth the feet of the ox," if not also the ass; for the former animal is employed in many parts of Madagascar to trample over the ground which has been previously softened with water, and so render it fit for the reception of the young rice-plants taken from the small plots where they have grown from seed.

Malagasy threshing-floors are, like those of the Jews, formed on the sides of rising grounds, so as to get the benefit of any breeze, and so be rid of " the chaff, which the wind driveth away."

Slavery.—Malagasy slavery, like that to which frequent reference is made in the Bible, is a patriarchal and family institution. Slaves in Madagascar usually identify themselves with the interests of the family to which they belong, and often hold positions of great trust and confidence, like Abraham's servant Eliezer, or Joseph in the household of Potiphar. The system certainly presents outwardly few repulsive features, although its essential injustice is, of course, unaltered. And as it was in the time of our Lord, so now, people can be reduced to slavery for debt, and if that is insufficient to discharge their obligations, their wives and children can also be enslaved, just as in the Parable, where the lord of a certain "servant commanded him to be sold, and payment to be made" (Matt. xviii. 25). As to the marriage of a freeman with a slave girl, and the close similarity between what is enjoined by the Malagasy law and by the law of Moses, see p. 256.

This chapter may be appropriately concluded by a remark upon *time* as reckoned by the Malagasy. I have been repeatedly struck by the exact correspondence there is between their way of reckoning time, and that of the Jews, viz., in the *inclusive* way of counting days. For instance, from a Friday to a Sunday they would call three days, as it is reckoned in the Gospels, when speaking of the time our Lord lay in the tomb, and which is so puzzling to English readers. In like manner they call a week eight days, as we see in Luke ix. 28 ("about an eight days after these sayings;" cf. Matt. xvii. 1, Mark ix. 2). They also reckon the day to begin after sunset, just as in Genesis we read, "and the *evening* and the morning were the first day," &c.

It will be seen from the foregoing examples that in our intercourse with such a people as the Malagasy we are constantly reminded of Scripture customs and allusions. Very many others might no doubt be given, but these will be sufficient to show how wide a range of subject there is; and it is pleasant to think that in many cases the words and figures of the sacred writings have a familiarity to our people which must help to impress the most important truths upon their understandings, and eventually, we may hope, upon their hearts and lives.

CHAPTER XVII.

MALAGASY CHURCH LIFE, AS ILLUSTRATIVE OF THE HISTORY OF THE APOSTOLIC AND EARLY CHURCHES.

AS REGARDS MORALS—RISE OF SUPERSTITIOUS PRACTICES AND SACRAMENTA-LISM—CHURCH DIVISIONS—CUSTOMS CONNECTED WITH WORSHIP—CHURCH OFFICES AND GOVERNMENT—RELATIONS BETWEEN THE CHURCH AND THE STATE.

Morals.—In perusing portions of the New Testament, a thoughtful reader must frequently be struck by the some-what strange prohibitions which are found in the apostolic epistles, and addressed to the Churches of that early age; precepts which refer, not to matters of faith and doctrine, but to what we are accustomed to call mere worldly morality. We find, for instance, the admonitions, "Let him that stole steal no more," "Lie not one to another," "Let no evil communication proceed out of your mouth," together with many others of similar import; and it strikes us as somewhat extraordinary that the apostles should think it necessary to address such commands to those whom, in the very same epistles, they call "sons of God," and "called to be saints." There appears at first sight to be a strange inconsistency in such differing language being addressed to the same people. But we in this Christian England, where the gospel has been a power for so many centuries, raising the tone of morals and purifying the whole social system, forget that what the world now claims as *its* morality—mere honesty, and truthfulness, and purity—is really the offspring of Christian teaching, and that these things were not recognised as duties by the mass of society in the old Pagan world.

Those, however, who labour in heathen countries, or amongst peoples only lately emerged from heathenism, see at once the need of such admonitions as were addressed by the

Y

converts. And when we first engage in mission work, we often feel strangely shocked and pained by finding what a low moral sense exists among our professedly Christian people. We are surprised to find men and women who are capable at times of rising to a sublime elevation of self-denial for Christ's sake, sometimes descending to very low and unworthy actions; we occasionally detect them in lying, cheating, and falling back into sins of impurity, in a way that is intensely disappointing and perplexing to us. And therefore superficial observers, especially those who have little or no sympathy with any Christian work, are exceedingly quick to point out these inconsistencies, and from them to infer that the religion of such weak brethren is a piece of hypocrisy and deceit from beginning to end. But such a conclusion is as untrue as it is unfair and short-sighted. Such severe critics judge these newly Christianised converts by a standard only rightly applicable to people who have been long under the purifying influence of the gospel. They forget, and even we their missionaries are apt to forget, the heathen influences to which the Malagasy people have been exposed for long past ages, and which are still very strong all around them. In their heathen state there was no stigma attached to such sins as impurity, or deceit, or fraud; these latter indeed were rather admired as proofs of superior cunning, as things to be imitated, so far at least as they would not bring the offender within the penalties of the native laws. We forget that time is required to form a purified public opinion, an enlightened " Christian conscience," in a people; and while we strive, and not unsuccessfully, to raise the whole tone of feeling about morals, we can make allowances for those who occasionally sin flagrantly against our higher standard of right and wrong. And we come to perceive that although some of our people do at times fall into gross moral offences, they yet are not hypocrites and deceivers when they profess to love the Lord Jesus Christ; they do really believe in and serve Him, although not as yet fully " purged from their old sins." In this, as in numerous other instances, light is thrown upon the apostolic and early Church history by missionary experience in modern days.

There are, however, several other points in which missionary experiences in Madagascar (in common, no doubt, with many other heathen countries) illustrate and explain Church history in early times; and prominent among these is the *Rise of Superstitious Practices and Sacramentalism.*

The Malagasy mind, like that of most other semi-civilised peoples, is a fertile soil for the rapid growth of all sorts of superstitious notions. Malagasy idolatry is mainly a belief in *òdy* or charms—charms to prevent evil of various kinds, or to obtain certain benefits. So that unless great care is taken on the part of the teachers and guides of such people when they have only lately come out of heathenism, their superstitious ideas are almost inevitably transferred to the two great symbolic ordinances of the Christian religion; and Baptism and the Lord's Supper are immediately regarded as the Christian *òdy* or charms. So much is this the case that I have often seriously debated whether it would not be best to defer for a considerable time the introduction of both sacraments until the people's minds have been further enlightened, and some groundwork of knowledge laid down. Otherwise they are almost certain to regard these two symbolic observances as means of obtaining some vague benefit, quite irrespective of the moral condition of those receiving them.

It would be ludicrous, were it not also saddening, to see how baptism is regarded amongst the semi-heathen Malagasy. In some cases people have come up from the country districts saying they wished "to pray to the baptism;" in others they ask that they may "drink baptism," probably confounding the two sacraments together. Soon after the burning of the idols in the central provinces in 1869, when the Queen and Government gave in their adhesion to Christianity, there was a great rush to worship; and when they heard that their sovereign and the Prime Minister had been baptized, immediately eager crowds came forward to receive the ordinance while yet utterly ignorant of its meaning. And in very many places, especially in those away from the control of a missionary or an enlightened native pastor, great numbers of people, some-

do as their rulers had done was almost the sole motive of their action, while in others there was probably the vague expectation of gaining some unknown spiritual benefit. Even among our more intelligent Christian people it is curious to see what a superstitious notion often attaches to the symbol itself. Some few years ago one of my brother missionaries was preaching in a village congregation in his district, not far from the capital, and being the first Sunday in the month he had to preside at the Lord's Supper. But before that was partaken of he had also to baptize several people, and the water for that purpose was brought (as is frequently the case) in one of the cups used for the wine at the other sacrament. As soon as the baptism was over the cup was, of course, needed for its special purpose; but here a difficulty occurred to the good deacons, What was to be done with the water? A little consultation took place; they appeared to think it improper to throw away what had been used for a sacred purpose, and so at last, to solve the difficult problem, one of them took up the cup, and drank off its contents!

But the sacrament of the Lord's Supper is still more liable to abuse by ignorant and half-enlightened people. An incident which occurred in my own experience not very long ago suggested to me how very innocently, almost imperceptibly, high sacramental ideas of the ordinance grew up in the early Church. One day the pastor of one of the congregations under my care, himself a most intelligent and earnest Christian man, came to ask my opinion as to a request which had been made to him. He said that on the previous sacrament Sunday, several of the church members were unable to be present through sickness, and that they were grieved at being thus prevented from joining with their relatives and friends in the sacred feast. They had therefore sent to ask that the deacons might be allowed to take to their own houses a portion of the bread and a small quantity of the wine, so that although at home they might still partake of the sacrament. He appeared to think that this was a very reasonable and proper request, and so in fact, for a moment, it appeared to me. But immediately I saw how superstitious a notion would inevitably be attached to the symbols; that they would soon be regarded as a kind of charm, having some mysterious virtue in themselves; and I therefore pointed out to him the erroneous ideas which would be encouraged by compliance. But it is easy to see how, from such, at first, most innocent and very natural feelings, the doctrine of the "reserved sacrament" arose in the early Churches, accompanied by all kinds of superstitious notions growing around the simple ordinance of remembrance and spiritual communion.

Another superstitious notion regarding the Lord's Supper I also found growing up in the minds of several of my own people at Ambòhimànga, a notion, it will be observed, exactly like the Romish and Ritualist idea of what is proper before receiving that sacrament. We are asked whether we did not fast before communicating, as they always did themselves, believing that it would be improper to allow the sacred elements to be mixed with common food. There is also a strong feeling that no other time than the forenoon is proper for observing the supper; and to a vast majority of the people any proposal for celebrating it on any other Sunday than the first in the month would be regarded with great suspicion, and much more would they be astonished at partaking of it on any week-day.

By a considerable number of the communicants the Lord's Supper is certainly regarded as a kind of charm, for many come to no public service except that on the first Sunday morning of the month, when very large congregations assemble; and they evidently think that by thus once a month receiving the sacrament they have sanctified the rest of the time, and gained some spiritual advantage. Not a few do not even attend the preceding service of worship and preaching, but just come in for the communion service only; while now and then, some will even slip in towards the conclusion of the service, and ask the deacons to procure them some bread and wine, so that they may thus expend no time at all in hearing the Word of God, or in praise and prayer.

Truly and sadly we may say to such, " This is not to eat the Lord's Supper."

Of course the only effectual remedy for such errors is faithful scriptural teaching and an increasingly firm discipline, by which, in time, the crowds of people who a few years ago came into the churches before any efficient control could be exercised, shall be no longer children in knowledge, or shall go out from a communion which they see is only for the spiritually minded. Happily this is increasingly the case in all the better instructed congregations.

Occasionally this reverence for the sacrament has been manifested in a way that could hardly be blamed, although it might soon degenerate into something not greatly differing from the old worship of charms. Some five years ago a journey was taken by two of the most intelligent students in our Theological College to visit the congregations towards the north-west. At a village called Ambòdiamòntana, not more than sixty miles from the capital, they were much surprised to find the following ceremonies observed by the people :—Taking their own account of them and translating it literally, they say : " When about to pound rice [for making the bread for the sacrament] the people wash their clothes and bathe, and the pestle and rice mortar are thoroughly cleaned ; then they close the doors of the house while pounding and cooking the rice. And again, when the sacrament is concluded, if there is any bread left they take it into the Government House, and there pray before eating it. So we asked them, ' What is the reason of your doing these things ? What do you consider the bread to be ?' They replied, ' We act in this way because we don't want the unbelievers to know how it is made lest they should despise it, and therefore we thus honour it.' Upon this we hardly saw what to say to them, for we were both astonished and puzzled. However, we ventured upon a word of caution : ' Take good care,' we said, ' lest you pay a superstitious regard to these emblems, and so become forgetful of Jesus Christ. What you do is proper enough if intended as honouring Christ, and not the bread and wine ; but if these only you honour, and do not remember Christ, then you are altogether in the wrong.' "

Church Divisions.—On still another poi
the Lord's Supper has our missionary exp
gascar recalled some of the incidents in
history; in this case, however, the evil i
extreme to a superstitious reverence for the
rather a profane abuse of it, and a mak
division and strife between contending part
The following incident forcibly recalled to
quarrels and disputes in the Corinthian Chu
severely censured by the Apostle Paul in the
of his Second Epistle. At a village church
miles from the capital, there was a diffi
about the election of a pastor, who, some c
had been forced upon them by an undue ex
by the chief man of the village. The
become divided into two parties, whose fe
other had at last grown so strong, that
Sunday, when the Lord's Supper was abou
the pastor broke the bread, &c., at the
while the other party also brought bread
own, and called to their friends to come an
bread and wine; so that there were actuall
services going on at one time in the church
time, several meetings, and a great expend
and persuasion to reconcile the opposing p
them to shake hands with each other.
believe that several of the leaders were rea
and were sincerely anxious to uphold what
right. Their conduct really arose from the
independence of the Church had been wro
with. At another village, very near to
brother missionary had almost as painful a
of some position, who had been excluded for
was encouraged by those who sided with
bread by force, so that the table had to b
more literal sense than Presbyterians mea
this word in connection with the Lord's Su

Yet it would be a great mistake to take
exceptional cases, or to conclude that tl

more, blame in some of the churches founded by the apostles and instructed by men who had the miraculous gifts of the Holy Ghost. Such passages as 1 Cor. i. 10–13; iii. 3; v.; xi. 17–34, point to abuses in the Corinthian Church quite as scandalous as any of those which occasionally perplex us in the Malagasy churches. For while in matters calling for censure, the assemblies of Malagasy Christians sometimes furnish parallels to the apostolic churches, I have again and again thought how the order and quiet reverence seen in scores of our churches at the communion service recalled the description given by Justin Martyr of the celebration of the eucharistic feast by the churches of his age. The same simple forms and ceremonies are common to both: the thanksgiving prayer by the " president " (not the priest); the *sitting* at the reception of the elements by the communicants, the bread and wine being carried to them by the deacons (showing that the *kneeling* at the holy table is a later practice); the reading of the Scriptures and the singing of a hymn—all these are reproduced in our modern mission churches; and, as already mentioned, the taking of some of the bread and wine by the deacons to absent members would also be easily introduced were there not some one to caution the people against the use of superstitious practices.

In still another direction does missionary experience in Madagascar present some interesting analogies to the history of the early Churches, viz., in the *Customs connected with Worship*.

In our less intelligent country congregations, where many of the people still seem to need schooling like children in proper behaviour in public worship, the native deacons usually constitute themselves directors of the congregation. They stand up in various parts of the building during the prayers, keeping a vigilant eye on the people, lest any should look about or otherwise misbehave themselves. No sooner does the pastor or missionary say, " Let us pray," than the deacons shout out, *Mivàvaka!* (" Pray !") in stentorian tones, until

every head is bowed down. I have frequently thought that
here we have just the *Oremus* of the early church deacons, as
they called upon the congregation to join in the prayers about
to be offered. Then, again, as soon as the benediction is pronounced, our native officials are equally forward in calling to
the people, *Miràva!* ("Break up!" or "Disperse!"), which is
very much the Malagasy form of the words, *Ite, missa est,* of
the deacons in early times, when the morning prayer was
ended, and the catechumens were bidden to retire before the
celebration of the Holy Supper.

It may be also noted here that in Madagascar the Lord's
Supper is commonly called *ny Famakìa-mòfo,* an exact equivalent of the apostolic church phrase, "the breaking of
bread" (Acts ii. 42, 46; xxi. 7); and the man who presides,
ny Mpamàky mòfo ("the breaker of bread"); although the
sacrament is also as frequently called *ny Fandraisana* ("the
taking," *i.e.,* of bread and wine), and the communicants, *ny
Mpandray* ("the takers," or receivers, of the ordinance).
Further still, as *names* are always worthy of notice, it is a
significant fact that the Christian religion has, from a very
early period after its introduction into Madagascar, been known
all over the island as *Ny Fivavàhana, i.e.,* "the praying."

It is evident from the New Testament that from the
very earliest times there was something of a responsive
element in the public worship of the Church, an element
doubtless retained from the Jewish practice (see Neh. viii. 6;
v. 13); for the Apostle Paul reproved the praying in an unknown tongue, from the inability of the congregation to
intelligently respond to such prayers by saying the "Amen"
at the thanksgiving (1 Cor. xiv. 16). In our Malagasy congregational worship this audible response is also usual, although
much less general now than it was formerly, when a loud and
universal "Amen" used to show the assent of the worshippers
to the prayers offered.

Readers of ecclesiastical history will remember that in the
days of the "golden-mouthed" preacher and bishop, John
Chrysostom, his congregation showed their approval of his
eloquent periods by vociferous applause, a practice which he
frequently sternly reproved. Our Malagasy hearers are accus-

duced by the tongue; and when this is heard it is always a sure sign that something has been said which has touched their feelings or excited their admiration. Occasionally, this is also heard during the prayers; and when some of the more gifted natives preach, men who are born orators, repeated rounds of this clicking noise run through the building, having a very curious effect to one only accustomed to our very decorous and usually unmoved English congregations.

While speaking of preaching, it may be here mentioned that in the early history of the modern mission in Madagascar we had something like what is described as seen in the Church at Corinth in its earlier history, when " every one had a psalm, a doctrine, a revelation, an interpretation " (1 Cor. xiv. 26). Much in the same way also, the public services at that earlier period of our mission history (1862–1870) were very informal in character, almost every church member considering it his privilege to rise and give out a hymn, offer a prayer, and make an exhortation, as he felt disposed. For a considerable space of time our services were often very lengthy: from early morning until far on into the forenoon would the people remain together; sometimes *four* sermons (or what were meant for such) would be delivered; each with its accompanying hymn, prayer, and reading. These were often very meagre substitutes for sermons, in our idea of the word, but they were the best instruction that could be got for many of the congregations at that stage of the people's religious history. Very different is the preaching now heard in almost all our larger churches; and it is far more difficult to induce our Malagasy friends to preach than it used to be; for they are beginning to learn how little they really know, and they generally desire time for careful preparation before venturing to address a congregation.

In the early churches there seems to have been a practice of giving to their members going to distant parts "letters of commendation" to the congregations there, as a guarantee of their character and standing (see 2 Cor. iii. 1; 3 John 9).

Similar precautions have been found quite as necessary in Madagascar, for the preacher's office is so honoured that any one going to places distant from the capital can easily get much respect and advantage by getting up and preaching, although he may be of very indifferent character. Accordingly, for some time past, formal " epistles of commendation " have been prepared to be taken by preachers as evidence of their being held in confidence by the churches of Imérina, and the distant congregations have been warned that if any one brings not such certificates of character they should " receive them not, nor bid them God speed " (2 John 10).

Another illustration of early Church history, although not exactly connected with this part of the subject, may be here noted. Among the books which the Malagasy Christians most prized during the twenty-five years of persecution, was the "Pilgrim's Progress," of which a very idiomatic translation was made by the Rev. D. Johns. This was often bound up with a small edition of the New Testament, and thus acquired a position in their esteem second only to that of the inspired book itself. We see, therefore, how easily in early times, by the mere placing together of canonical and non-canonical books, some of these latter were for a time regarded in some places as Holy Scripture. And so the " Shepherd " of Hermas, and the Epistles of Barnabas and Clement and others, were included in some early lists of the canon. Some of the less-informed country people sometimes inquire of us if the magazines and works issued at our press were written by the Apostles; while they gaze with wonder at the English books on our shelves, and ask if they are all Bibles.

With regard to *Church Offices and Government,* our Malagasy experience offers many illustrations of early Church history in the development of ecclesiastical systems. For many years, indeed until the year 1870, the London Missionary Society's mission was concentrated at the capital city of Antanànarìvo; following apostolic precedent the great centre of intelligence and civilisation and government was first occupied; just as Antioch and Ephesus and Corinth and Rome early became seats of the most powerful churches. And accordingly, just as these, with other cities, came to have a great influence and authority over the less important churches, becoming the seats of patriarchates, so does the capital of Madagascar exercise a very powerful influence over the more ignorant country congregations. On the whole, this influence is most salutary and helpful to these *pagani*, but it might easily and almost insensibly develop into an arbitrary authority over the weaker brethren connected with each city congregation's *zàna-piangònana* or "offspring churches."

And then again, the way in which districts, containing congregations numbering from thirty to eighty, are bound together by rules as to discipline and instruction, illustrates the beginning of synods and presbyteries among the early churches. In the capital there are nine strong congregations who act as mother churches to as many districts radiating from the city. These having mostly an English missionary presiding over them form a kind of diocese, of which he is a virtual bishop or overseer. And when, as will doubtless eventually be the case, foreign superintendence shall have been withdrawn, it can hardly be doubted that the native *mpitandrina* or overseer of these larger churches will continue to exercise a very sensible influence over the congregations in his district, and will retain very much of the position of a bishop, at least *primus inter pares*, if not much more of a veritable *episkopos*.

But we may hope and trust that by giving the pastors and teachers of the present Malagasy congregations a thorough acquaintance with the history of the early Church, by pointing out the evils which the infusion of a worldly spirit effected in that Church, and, above all, by continuing to teach them that the Bible is the only authoritative rule as to faith and discipline also,—we may hope that Christianity in Madagascar will be preserved from those evils and corruptions which ecclesiasticism worked in post-apostolic and mediæval times. The Malagasy Christian people will doubtless eventually develop a Church system and discipline of their own, probably combining the features of more than one, or two, ecclesiastical organisations; but we may hope that their Independency will never degenerate into isolation and weakness, that their Episcopacy may never become a prelacy, a lordship over God's heritage, nor their Presbyterianism fulfil again the taunt of a by-gone age that "new presbyter is but old priest writ large."

On one other point only can a word be here said, and that is as to the analogies between modern Malagasy history and ancient Church history in the matter of the *Relations between the Church and the State.* This is, however, such a wide subject, and so difficult to be understood without full details, that it could not be treated satisfactorily at the end of a chapter; besides which, the time has not yet arrived for judging how far the experience of ancient times, in this respect, will be reproduced in modern times in Madagascar. From the very circumstances of the country, and the habits of the people, there are undeniable tendencies in the direction of a control of religion by the State. But it may with some confidence be hoped that by the constant inculcation of scriptural teaching as to the independence and spirituality of the Church, the Christian congregations may retain their freedom, especially as the Government have repeatedly and publicly expressed their adhesion to a policy of non-interference in religious matters.

Such are a few of the side-lights which are thrown by mission experiences in Madagascar upon the history and development of the apostolic and early churches. The subject is a wide one, and is doubtless capable of ample illustration from other mission fields. I trust that these slight contributions to it may meet the eye of some of my missionary brethren in other countries, and may induce them to note down and make known other facts, showing how history—ecclesiastical history—repeats itself, and the new is ever illustrating the old.

CHAPTER XVIII.

THE MADAGASCAR OF TO-DAY:—ITS PROGRESS AND PRESENT POSITION, SOCIALLY AND RELIGIOUSLY.

MADAGASCAR has for many years past been regarded with deep interest by the Christian people of England, especially by those connected with the Congregational Churches of this country. It is now (1879) a little more than sixty years ago since the first Protestant missionaries set foot upon its shores; and since that period its religious history has been one of remarkable changes, and often of startling and painful interest. The earliest efforts made by the London Missionary Society (in 1818) to evangelise the Malagasy people were soon interrupted by disease, and by the death of almost all who were engaged in the work, so that it was not until the year 1820 that the mission was resumed, and Christian teaching was commenced in the interior of the island, at the capital city of Antanànarìvo.

For sixteen years the small body of earnest men who laboured there were permitted to continue their efforts to benefit the people. And it was a noble work which they accomplished in that space of time: they reduced the language to writing, and gave the Malagasy their own tongue in a written form; they prepared a considerable literature, both educational and religious; they founded a school system, through which many thousands of the natives received the elements of a good education; they introduced many of the useful arts of civilised life; they translated and printed at their own press the whole Word of God; and they gathered several Christian congregations, of whom not a few had received the good seed in an honest and good heart. "Their works do follow them," and in Madagascar the names of

The sixteen years of planting the gospel in the interior of the island were, as is well known, followed by a quarter of a century of determined persecution of its adherents. The more prominent incidents of that terrible time have now become a part of Church history, and have given another confirmation to the old saying, that "the blood of the martyrs" was "the seed of the Church." Their blood was again, as Tertullian said, "the red rain that made the harvest grow." The fury of the persecuting Queen Rànavàlona I. only defeated its own purpose: it strengthened and deepened, and extended far and wide the influence of Christianity; about two hundred faithful men and women laid down their lives for their love to Christ; "those who were persecuted went everywhere preaching the word," and at length, when those twenty-five years were over, the number of professing Christians had increased twenty-fold!

And now, another period of sixteen years has passed away since the London Missionary Society's mission was re-established at the capital of the country; and we who have been labouring in Madagascar during this third stage of its Christian history can look back and see wonderful changes and advances during that period. For these sixteen years have been chequered in their experiences. For a few months during the reign of Radàma II., the sunshine of royal favour took the place of royal frowns. But the state of things during the short reign of the young King was thoroughly unsatisfactory, and had it continued longer, would probably have injured the prospects of real religion far more than the years of open persecution. Then came the reign of Queen Rasohérina, during which, for five years, the gospel made steady and solid progress. With a fair field and no favour from the Government, but with no opposition, Christianity was permeating and influencing all ranks of society in the capital city and its neighbourhood. The younger and more intelligent of every family of position were among its adherents, and it was gradually becoming an acknowledged power in the country, and making its influence felt even far away from the central province.

But with the death of Queen Rasohérina in April 1868, and the accession of her cousin Ramòma, came another great advance. The advisers of the sovereign had for some time seen very clearly the course events were taking. They perceived that Christianity was becoming an element in the country which could no longer be ignored. They therefore resolved to put themselves at the head of the new movement, and not allow such a mighty influence to be altogether independent of the State.

And so, at the coronation of the Queen (afterwards known as Rànavàlona II.), a kind of public acknowledgment of Christianity took place; for no idol was brought to sanctify the ceremony, but a Bible occupied a conspicuous place close to the Queen's right hand, while on the canopy over her head there were written in large characters words taken from the angelic hymn, "Glory to God," "Peace on earth," "Good will to men." It was evident that a new era had that day been inaugurated.

This open recognition of Christianity was soon followed by still more decisive measures in favour of the once proscribed religion. In February of the following year (1869), the Queen and the Prime Minister were both baptized in the presence of a large number of the chief people of the kingdom; public worship was commenced in one of the royal houses; the foundation of a chapel-royal was laid in the palace-yard; and in September of the same year, the insolent behaviour of the idol-keepers led to the burning of the royal idols, and, immediately afterwards, to a like destruction of those belonging to private individuals and separate tribes throughout the central provinces of the island.

With a people like the Malagasy, accustomed to move in crowds, and to follow implicitly anything which is favoured by their rulers, the effects of this Government patronage may be easily imagined. The immediate results were an enormous numerical increase in the attendance upon Christian services; every chapel was crowded to excess; new places of worship were hastily erected in every village; the people eagerly

came forward to be baptized and to becom
and every missionary was pressed with w
whelmed with the responsibility thrown
number of congregations in the central p
increased in two years more than tenfo
dants upon public worship in a somewhat
fact, almost the whole population of Iméri
selves to be Christians.

The news of this wonderful movement
great enthusiasm in England, and caused
and incorrect notions to be formed as to
real significance of the change which had co
society. A little consideration would hav
that a vast proportion of these new convert
tians because the Government favoured
would have probably become Roman (
Mohammedans with almost equal readiness
favoured those forms of religion. Beside
forgotten how large a country Madagascar
changes had only affected two or three out
ferent tribes; while the great majority of th
at least three-fourths of the whole popula
were hardly at all influenced by Christianity

There was, no doubt, great reason for th
fact, that in the central provinces all *exter*
the progress of the gospel had been remo
success had become its difficulty, and its
likely to prove its greatest embarrassment.
of Protestant missionaries resident in the ca
of 1869 (there were only ten of them) se
sufficient to guide and control the almost hea
filled the chapels and pressed into church c
to this very day, the presence of such nomi
the churches forms one of the greatest diffict
of perplexity with which the missionary has

But strenuous efforts were made to cope
press of work involved in the new state of th
the mission staff was largely increased, until,
years' time from the destruction of the ido

(including the members of the Friends' mission, always working in thorough harmony with that of the London Missionary Society), nearly forty missionaries, besides their wives. The churches of the capital sent out a considerable number of teachers and evangelists, and collected money for their support, and by grouping the vast number of country congregations into districts, and laying down many stringent rules with regard to discipline and the learning of elementary truths, a good deal was done to instruct and bring into some order the ignorant crowds of people who had pressed into the churches.

And now, it may be asked, what are the results of the last few years' labour? and to what extent does Christianity now influence society in the central provinces? In reply, it may be confidently affirmed that there are numerous undeniable facts which sufficiently testify that the gospel is a mighty power in Madagascar; facts, not only patent to the Christian missionary, but also to any honest and unprejudiced traveller, who knows what the country was a few years ago, and what is the state of things at the present day.

To begin with the matter of clothing, a subject always closely connected with morality. In their heathen state a dirty hemp or *rofia lámba* suffices for the great mass of the Malagasy, but as soon as a Christian congregation is gathered, a great change comes over the outward aspect of the people. Every woman must have her neat jacket and skirt of print or other stuff, and the men their shirts and pantaloons, as well as the flowing outer dress or *lámba* (common to both sexes) of European calico. Wherever Christianity comes, there immediately springs up a demand for foreign manufactured goods, and the trader follows in the wake of the missionary. It can be shown from consular returns, that so much has Christianity opened up trade in Polynesia, that every Protestant missionary is worth £10,000 per annum to European and American commerce. So much cannot yet be claimed for Christian missions in Madagascar, but perhaps it would not be too much to say that each missionary represents a value of from £2000 to £3000 per annum of foreign imports. In 1863 there was not one English commercial house at the great city of

Antanànarìvo, but now several firms carry on a profitable business, besides which a great amount of goods are brought up by the native traders. So true it always is that Christianity is the best civiliser, and the harbinger of all honest trade.

The erection of improved dwellings is also slowly leading to improved social habits. Instead of being all crowded together in a house of one room, a family has now in many cases two or three separate sleeping places; although in this respect there is still abundant room for improvement, as is also the case in the cottages of our English labourers and artisans. During the last few years the repeal of the ancient law forbidding the erection of any but wood or rush houses in the capital and other ancient towns has led to the almost entire rebuilding of Antanànarìvo; sun-dried brick is largely used for building houses and churches; the old wooden houses with their lofty high-pitched and thatched roofs have almost entirely disappeared, and have been replaced by scores of convenient two-storeyed and verandahed dwellings, many of them with tiled roofs. The erection of the Martyr Memorial Churches (1864–1874) gave a great impetus to the building art; it showed the people how to use their own stores of stone and clay, and timber and metal, and numbers of intelligent natives have become clever workmen.

But one of the most decided proofs of advance is the improved state of feeling with regard to polygamy and divorce, and the marriage relation generally. In their heathen state the Hovas were most immoral; chastity and purity were almost unknown, and a common proverb compared marriage to a knot which could be untied with the slightest touch; polygamy was general, and divorce a matter of everyday occurrence. But an enlightened public opinion, a Christian conscience, is growing up on all these subjects, and is strengthening year by year; so that now polygamy is at an end in Imérina, and divorce is vastly less frequent than it used to be. The sanctity of the marriage tie is more and more recognised by the people, so that infringement of its acknowledged obligations is increasingly condemned, while church censure makes itself felt as a very powerful restraint upon wrong-doers.

very favourab   with that of most English towns.   The
Government deserve praise for having, immediately upon
their adhesion to Christianity, stopped all public work on
that day, and closed all markets, thus giving a legal day of
rest; and a considerable proportion of the people of Imérina
attend public worship.   Not unfrequently the Government
has given a rebuke to the representatives of so-called Christian
powers, who wished to transact public business on the Lord's
Day.

The native authorities also merit the commendation of
every right-minded person for their persistent endeavours to
keep temptations to drinking out of the way of their people.
In almost every part of Madagascar, except Imérina, drunkenness is a fearful source of degradation to the people, threaten-
ing the very existence of some of the coast tribes; but,
owing to the very stringent laws against the manufacture or
importation of ardent spirits into the central province, a
drunken man is there very rarely seen in public, so that
Imérina is one of the most temperate countries in the world.
Most devoutly it is to be wished that the Government could
enforce similar laws on the eastern coast, where, to their
shame be it said, English and French traders yearly pour into
the country thousands of gallons of rum, to the ruin of the
weak and ignorant coast population.   To these poor people,
as yet unfortified against temptation by Christian teaching,
civilisation without religion means rum, and rifles, and the
vices of the Europeans, which often sweep them away, before
they have a chance of learning what true civilisation means.

The influence of Christianity upon public feeling in Madagascar has also been strikingly shown in the abolition or
disuse of the cruel punishments formerly inflicted for political
and other crimes.   Up to a recent period certain military
offences were punished by the frightful penalty of burning
alive, but in later cases this has been substituted by fine and
loss of rank.   During the writer's first stay in Madagascar
(1863–1867), he was frequently shocked and pained by the
utter disregard for human life and suffering shown by the

Malagasy, and more than once has he aided in rescuing persons who were on the point of being killed by the mob for trifling thefts. In former reigns many offences, political and otherwise, involved not only death to the offender, but also reduced his wife and family to slavery; but these cruel and unjust laws have now been abolished. It is not, of course, to be inferred that there is not yet immense room for improvement in all these matters; but still, the loving and merciful and kindly spirit of the gospel is exerting a great influence, and is making itself felt more and more powerfully every year. Hardly any capital punishments have been inflicted during the reign of the present sovereign, who is universally beloved for her kindness of heart and humane disposition.

But, perhaps, in nothing has the beneficent influence of Christianity been so evident as in the amelioration of war. In the early part of the present century, the Hovas, while making themselves masters of the interior and eastern portion of the island, carried on a series of cruel wars, in which great suffering was inflicted on the outlying tribes. Fire and sword were carried through the country; the men were mercilessly shot down or speared, and the women and children were brought up as slaves to Imérina, so that a deep feeling of hatred to the Hovas was left in the minds of the conquered people, a feeling still strong after the lapse of forty or fifty years. But in the last expedition against the Sàkalàvas (in 1873), one of the divisions of the army returned without firing a shot or taking a single life; the other had to attack the rebel stronghold, and in the conflict some few lives were lost; but, as far as is known, no other bloodshed took place. So that the Hova army returned to Imèrina, leaving a very different impression upon the minds of people to that made by former war expeditions. The people who at first fled from the Hova camp soon perceived that they had nothing to fear, and they found that its neighbourhood was the best possible market for the sale of their produce. More than that, on the Lord's Day divine service was held morning and evening in the camp, so that many of the ignorant heathen people heard for the first time the tidings of salvation. An

interesting native account relates that "as they repeatedly
heard the preaching, they said, 'What is this religion which
leads the Imérina people not to enslave us any more and
take us away by force ?' And they were answered, 'Because
Jesus Christ, the Son of God, the Redeemer of men, has
given the gospel to teach mankind to show mercy.'" So
many of our good pastors and preachers accompanied the
Hova forces as officers, that that military expedition really
became a missionary expedition, and led to Christ's name
being proclaimed in heathen portions of the country where it
had not been heard before. This was, no doubt, greatly due
to the excellent Christian character of many of the officers;
but it was also not less owing to the admonition of the
Prime Minister to the leaders of the army before their departure, when he said, " You are Christians now, and must
not use any cruelty to the people of the country you are
going to; you must not take any life, except there is armed
opposition to the Queen's authority." And so when that
Hova army was about to return, the heads of some of the
tribes came to the commander and said, "We thought that
when you Hovas had burned your gods you would be power-
less, but now we see that you are still able to fight although
you worship Jehovah ; and we perceive that this *filázantsàra*
(gospel) you preach is 'a showing of mercy.'" Surely this
was an honourable testimony to the real change which the
profession of Christianity had effected among the Hovas.

It will of course be understood that in all that has been here
said of progress made in morality, Sabbath observance, sobriety,
and humanity, it is not to be inferred that there is no room still
for immense advance and improvement. Ten years is a short
time, indeed, for a people to be purified from the evils and vices
and cruelties which are the growth of centuries. But there
is reason for hope and encouragement in the fact that great
changes have already taken place ; the gospel leaven is beginning to work in the so lately heathen masses of the people,
and by God's blessing will not cease to influence them until
in due time it shall have " leavened the whole lump."

It may, however, be asked by some, What is the vital and

spiritual influence which Christianity is now exerting upon the mass of the professedly religious people of Madagascar ?

Upon this point it is much more difficult to speak with certainty and confidence than on the matters already referred to. From what has been said as to the great advance in public morality it will be evident that the *indirect* results of the preaching of the gospel have been very real and unmistakable. But it is a more delicate task to gauge its influence upon the hearts of those who have professed to embrace it. And this, difficult everywhere and in any state of society, is specially so from the peculiar circumstances of Malagasy society during the last eight or nine years. It has, during all that time, involved no social discredit to make a profession of religion, it has rather been a disadvantage not to be a member of some church. To become baptized, and then, after a few months of probation, to join one of the churches, is looked upon as only a proper and becoming course of conduct, by which a man takes a creditable position in society. So that, in the language of the Bedford dreamer, " religion walks in his silver slippers, the sun shines, and the people applaud him." All this, it it evident, is unfavourable for the development of the more solid and enduring qualities of Christian character, and inevitably leads to a great deal that is only superficial. A very large proportion of the present adherents, especially in the more ignorant country districts, can only be regarded as Christians in name; and were there to be a change in the attitude of the authorities towards the form of religion now favoured by them, probably only a small remnant of these " pagani " would be found steadfast to their present profession. We could not expect it to be otherwise; nine or ten years' time, with most meagre instruction in many districts, is an utterly inadequate period in which to Christianise a nation. On more than one occasion, when unfounded reports had been circulated in the villages that the sovereign no longer favoured Christianity, a mere handful of people only have come together for several weeks afterwards, to represent a congregation of three or four hundred worshippers. In the capital city, and in many of the larger villages, where the congregations have had constances; and the experience of the time of persecution assures us that there is an element of persistence in the native character which would again brave suffering and death for Christ's sake.

It would have prevented much misapprehension as to the real character of the change which, nine or ten years ago, came over society in the central provinces, if it had been remembered that the vast majority of those who then pressed into the churches had never previously had any instruction whatever. They had just come out of absolute heathenism, and the great reason for their burning their idols and attending Christian worship was that their sovereign had burned *her* idols and had put herself under Christian instruction. There has been in Madagascar no parallel at all to that remarkable awakening which a few years ago passed over the native churches in the Sandwich Islands, and stirred up thousands to seek for forgiveness and salvation. Such a revival could not have been expected in Madagascar; the circumstances of the two countries were totally different: in the one, there had been many years of uninterrupted labour in a comparatively small field, and the Spirit of God came down to vivify seed which had long lain dormant in many hearts; but in the other, thousands of those who pressed into the hastily run-up mud chapels knew nothing whatever about even the elementary truths of religion.

It may also be added, that even among those who we cannot but think are sincere Christians there is remarkably little depth of feeling or emotion, as shown either in a feeling of guilt before God, sorrow for sin, earnestness in seeking salvation, or joy in a sense of pardon and believing in Christ. At any rate, it is rare to meet with any expression or manifestation of such feelings. No doubt this in part arises from the unemotional character of the whole Malayo-Polynesian race, to which family of people the Malagasy belong. But still, accepting the Divine criterion, "By their fruits ye shall know them," we have reason to believe that the gospel has come to not a few, not in word only, but in power. And when we see the graces of Christian character developing, and evil diminishing; when we see honesty and truthfulness, and liberality and purity, taking the place of the opposite characteristics; when we see larger sums devoted every year to religious objects, and men and women offering themselves for Christian service, we cannot doubt that the good Spirit of God is working, even if it be in ways somewhat different to what we had expected.

The native congregations in Madagascar are closely associated together in districts, which in some communions might be called "dioceses," in others "circuits," and in others "presbyteries." In fact, the government and order of the Malagasy churches may be considered as a combination of Episcopacy, Independency, and Presbyterianism, with an infusion of Methodism in its large use of lay agency or "local preachers." It is a system which has grown up rather from the necessities of the case than from any set purpose. Nine of these districts radiate from the capital, having their main strength at Antanànarìvo, as their common centre, in one of the old-established mother-churches of the city, and seven others are grouped round some of the most important towns in Imérina. Other mission stations are found in the Bétsiléo country, the southern province, having their headquarters at Fianàrantsoà, its chief town; while two have recently been formed in some of the outlying heathen tribes, one amongst the Sihànaka people, north-eastern central, and another at Mojangà, on the north-west coast, from which it is hoped that an entrance may be effected for the gospel among the wild Sàkalàva race. All these districts have an English missionary presiding over them; some of them include as few as thirty congregations, and others as many as eighty and upwards. These churches meet together by their representatives at regular intervals; they make rules as to discipline and instruction and school education, and exercise a very powerful and salutary influence over each congregation included in the district. With such a large field of work the position of the English missionary becomes that of an overseer of many churches, and not that of pastor of a single church; he endeavours to guide and elevate the native pastors and teachers ; he holds frequent classes at the chief villages, where, as from centres, the greater part of the congregations can be influenced through the more intelligent of the preachers ; and in this work the advanced knowledge and Christianity of the members of the city churches is a powerful auxiliary to the influence of the missionary.   Twice a year representatives from all the Imérina congregations meet together in the capital, in a kind of " Church Congress," or " Congregational Union," to discuss important subjects connected with the welfare and progress and discipline of the churches.   At these the debates are perfectly open and free to all who attend ; and the habit of thus freely discussing subjects often closely connected with social life, as well as with church life, is having a powerful effect in training the people to think and speak for themselves. It cannot fail eventually to influence political matters, and prepare the way for freer institutions than are practicable, or even desirable, at the present time.

A good deal has been done to raise up an instructed native ministry.   It has been felt from the first that upon this greatly depends the future of Malagasy Christianity ; and accordingly, for several years past, the most earnest and intelligent of the young men have been selected, and have received a good general and theological course of instruction at the Missionary College.   It may, therefore, be expected that in process of time a trained and well-taught pastor or evangelist may be placed in every village.   Of course native agency is largely made use of in the Malagasy churches ; without this nine-tenths of the congregations would be left without instruction, and a large body of " local preachers " is therefore attached to each mother-church.   These good men preach extensively according to a printed " plan " in the country district with which they are connected, and thus they give a large amount of help to their less advanced *zàna-piangònana* or " offspring of churches."

The object of the London Missionary Society has been from the first to draw out the self-help and liberality of its converts and churches ; not to keep them in leading-strings like children, or to do everything for them, but to encourage them to help themselves, to give for the erection of their own churches, and for the support of their own teachers and pastors, and to let all help from foreign sources be only supplementary and temporary, until they become self-supporting. This policy has led to a liberality which is yearly increasing on the part of the Imérina churches, so that during the past year no less a sum than $20,000 was contributed. This amount, though by no means so large in proportion as that given by some of the native churches in Polynesia, is yet one of the strongest possible proofs that Christianity has a growing power over the Malagasy.

During the last eight or ten years large sums have been expended in improved places of worship. Besides the four Memorial Churches and the Chapel Royal—which are handsome and solidly-built stone structures, with spires or towers, —erected under European superintendence—many very substantial and excellent churches have been built in Antanànarlvo and in the chief towns of Imérina, of sun-dried brick, a material which is also in extensive use for dwelling-houses, and makes, with proper precautions, very durable and substantial buildings. Indeed many of the village churches, with their neatly-plastered and whitewashed walls, glazed windows, matted floors, and appropriate fittings, may be considered as models of what such buildings should be. Their lofty tiled or thatched roofs now make quite a prominent feature in the landscape as they stand up above the villages all over Imérina.

And while the *buildings* for divine worship have been greatly improved during the last few years, the conduct and arrangements of religious services have greatly advanced during the same period. In all the more intelligent congregations, the Sunday services are conducted with much outward order and decorum. Some few of them have adopted the European fashion of standing during singing, but there has been little attempt—perhaps too little—to introduce in religious worship any of those becoming and seemly acts of outward reverence which are common to most European churches; and consequently the native habit of 'squatting lazily on the floor

During the last three or four years there has been what may be almost called a revival of congregational singing. A large number of good Malagasy hymns have been written, all in good rhythm, and many in rhyme, both by the missionaries and by natives. These have been set to lively tunes, many of those introduced by the American revivalists being now as popular in Madagascar as they were in England, and have spread rapidly all over the country; so that "Hold the Fort," "Ring the Bells of Heaven," "The Sweet By-and-by," and many others, are now as well known in their Malagasy dress as in their original English form. Besides these, many of the more classical English hymns have been naturalised in Malagasy, such, for instance, as "Rock of Ages," "Hail to the Lord's Anointed," and numerous others. In the capital and its neighbourhood these Christian hymns have quite supplanted the native songs, and are heard in every direction in the city and the villages at the close of the day, when the people are gathered together in family groups round their evening meal. The introduction of the Tonic-Sol-fa system has done very much to deepen and extend the national love of music and singing, and many hundreds of the younger people can now sing with ease from this notation.

In preaching also a great advance has been made. A few years ago almost any one would undertake to rise and address a congregation, for the Malagasy are naturally fluent and confident public speakers; but now, a general increase of intelligence on the part of the hearers has necessitated a much higher standard of ability on the part of the preachers; so that a constantly increasing body of intelligent men, well versed in the Scriptures and able to speak with power, is being raised up for the instruction of the native church. Some few of these men are orators of no mean order, and have great influence among the churches and in the country generally; and many of them can use their national legends and proverbs with very powerful effect.

In education and general enlightenment the central provinces of Madagascar stand in a somewhat advanced position

for a country so recently emerged fro
Almost every congregation has a school w
the simplest elements of knowledge is impa
training schools in the capitals of both Im
have already supplied the most important
with well-trained teachers, and it may be
ually every village will have one to ins
And although in the more ignorant distr
much suspicion among the people as to th
in obliging their children to attend schoo
has put strong pressure to enforce educatio
point wisely and rightly exercised its almost
Its action will certainly make the next gene
and enlightened one, and earn for it the gr
in Madagascar, as well as the respect of Eu

Higher education has been greatly pro
logical academy in Antanànarìvo, which
expanded into a general college. Here it
that by imparting a thorough training to
higher classes, they will be much better
fathers to become the future rulers of the c
the positions of governors, judges, and great

The spread of education has, of course,
class, and an extensive demand for popular
ture. For several years the presses conne
chief Protestant missions have been tasked
of elementary school books and lesson-sheet
pliances and first reading-books have been
thousands. But more advanced literature
a ready sale, and such books as Bible Dicti
and hermeneutical treatises, and science text
in great demand. It speaks something for
the young men of the capital that such a w
Geography should be one of the most po
rapidly pass into a second edition, while an
is also a very popular work! Besides this
month are sold of a cheap monthly magazine,
Words"); a quarterly, *Mpanòlo-tsaina* ("1
supplying articles of a higher class, and co

Honey"), a Malagasy edition of the "British Workman," and *Ny Sakaizan' ny Ankizy madinika* (" The Children's Friend "), a publication in which the Religious Tract Society's illustrations of " The Child's Companion " are used, have also a large sale. In several of these, articles by native writers, as well as by Europeans, frequently appear, and often display no small amount of ability and observation; while in all the mechanical processes of printing and book-binding, and in the combined mechanical and artistic skill required in lithography, native talent, under European guidance, produces books that may challenge comparison with those turned out of English workshops.

The energies of the native churches of the interior provinces of Madagascar are not entirely confined to their own part of the country, but are now being extended into some of the more distant and heathen portions of the island. As long ago as thirteen or fourteen years from now, the first native missionary was sent out by one of the Antananarivo churches to the Sihànaka province. There he did a good work, which is now being carried on in a much more complete way by an English missionary assisted by four native helpers. Since then other native evangelists have been sent out to others of the distant heathen tribes; in one instance, especially, a great work has been accomplished through the labour of one excellent man; and although some missions sent had to be withdrawn through the suspicions of the people, who feared a political meaning in them, the Imérina churches were not discouraged, but again sent out several evangelists last year (1878) to the south-east provinces. Five young men offered themselves at the missionary meetings in June, and money is also forthcoming for their support. The missionary spirit of the Malagasy churches has been fairly awakened, and a work has been begun which, we may hope, will not now stop until all the heathen tribes have been brought under the influence of the gospel.

From what has been already said it will be seen that the position of Madagascar at the present time is one of peculiar

over all the rest. The central province of Imérina, occupied by them, and especially its capital city of Antanànarìvo, has for several years past been a centre of intelligence, civilisation and Christianity, from whence these blessings are slowly spreading to distant portions of the great island. The capital and its neighbourhood have been largely Christianised, but even in the central province there is still (can we wonder at it ?) much darkness and superstition; and while in some of the other tribes Christian work has only just been commenced, many others are yet entirely untouched by the elevating influences of the gospel. But the history of the past gives hope and promise for the future, and the church in Madagascar is being aroused to a sense of its duty and responsibility to its heathen fellow-countrymen.

As already pointed out, the policy of the present Government has in many points been greatly in advance of that of all preceding ones. In their anxiety for education, in the repression of the traffic in intoxicating drink, in the upholding of the Sabbath, and in the amelioration of cruel customs and laws, and warlike usages, they deserve the praise of all; and in what they do to extend Christianity, although they do not always see the possible difficulties this may involve, the personal influence of the highest personages in the state has been exerted from the best motives, and from a deep and sincere interest in the extension of the gospel.

Civilised and Christianised, a great future lies before Madagascar; and as it has already become famous for the faith and devotion of many of its sons and daughters, so also from its commercial importance, its inexhaustible fertility, and the mental capabilities of its people, it will eventually take an important and honourable place among the nations of the world.

INDEX.

PRINTED BY BALLANTYNE, HANSON AND CO.
EDINBURGH AND LONDON